# GOD
## under fire

# Contributors

**Gerald L. Bray** (Litt. D., University of Paris-Sorbonne), Anglican professor of divinity at Beeson Divinity School at Samford University in Birmingham, Alabama.

**D. A. Carson** (Ph.D., Cambridge University), research professor of New Testament at Trinity Evangelical Divinity School in Deerfield, Illinois.

**William Lane Craig** (Ph.D., University of Birmingham, England; D.Theol., Lugwig Maximilens Universität—München, Germany), research professor of philosophy at Talbot department of philosophy, Biola University in La Mirada, California.

**R. Douglas Geivett** (Ph.D., University of Southern California), professor and department chair at Talbot Department of Philosophy, Biola University in La Mirada, California.

**Charles E. Gutenson** (Ph.D., Southern Methodist University), assistant professor of philosophical theology at Asbury Theological Seminary in Wilmore, Kentucky.

**Paul Helm** (M.A., University of Oxford), J. I. Packer chair of theology and philosophy at Regent College in Vancouver, British Columbia, Canada.

**Douglas S. Huffman** (Ph.D., Trinity Evangelical Divinity School), dean of admissions and records and associate professor of Bible at Northwestern College in St. Paul, Minnesota.

**Eric L. Johnson** (Ph.D., Michigan State University), associate professor of personality and pastoral theology at The Southern Baptist Theological Seminary in Louisville, Kentucky.

**Patrick Lee** (Ph.D., Marquette University), professor of philosophy at Franciscan University of Steubenville in Steubenville, Ohio.

**James S. Spiegel** (Ph.D., Michigan State University), associate professor of philosophy at Taylor University, Upland, Indiana.

**Mark R. Talbot** (Ph.D., University of Pennsylvania), associate professor of philosophy at Wheaton College in Wheaton, Illinois.

**Bruce A. Ware** (Ph.D., Fuller Theological Seminary), senior associate dean, school of theology and professor of Christian theology at The Southern Baptist Theological Seminary in Louisville, Kentucky.

Modern Scholarship Reinvents God

# GOD
## UNDER fire

*Douglas S. Huffman* ✦ *Eric L. Johnson*
General Editors

ZONDERVAN™

GRAND RAPIDS, MICHIGAN 49530 USA

*God Under Fire*
Copyright © 2002 by Douglas S. Huffman and Eric L. Johnson

Requests for information should be addressed to:
Zondervan, *Grand Rapids, Michigan 49530*

**Library of Congress Cataloging-in-Publication Data**

God under fire : modern scholarship reinvents God / Douglas S. Huffman and Eric L. Johnson,
    general editors.
       p.  cm.
    Includes bibliographical references.
    ISBN 0–310–23269–4
    1. God.   2. Apologetics.   I. Johnson, Eric L., 1956–.   II. Huffman, Douglas S., 1961–.
BT103.G63 2002
231 — dc21
                                       2002009297

This edition printed on acid-free paper.

*Interior production by Beth Shagene*

*Printed in the United States of America*

02 03 04 05 06 07 08 /❖ DC/ 10 9 8 7 6 5 4 3 2 1

*To those many individuals*
*—those currently living as well as those*
*who have lived in previous centuries—*
*who love God,*
*who want to know Him better,*
*and who, caring more for the Truth than for personal comfort,*
*have chosen to live their lives—and even give their lives—for His glory.*

*–DOUG*

✦

*To Laura and Iain,*
*Channels to me of God's love and delight,*
*May the living God of historic Christianity ever be your supreme joy.*

*–ERIC*

# Table of Contents

# PREFACE

We are grateful to the many people who have made this volume possible. First, we thank the people of Zondervan, specifically Stan Gundry for seeing merit to this project, and Jack Kuhatschek and Verlyn Verbrugge for seeing it to its realization.

Second, we are indebted to this volume's contributors. The modern professional disciplines of theology, biblical studies, and philosophy require not only skills in research and writing, but skills in a kind of juggling as well—the juggling of writing, speaking, and teaching commitments. Our contributors have made time for this project and have tolerated our suggestions and adjusted expectations. For their hard work, we are grateful.

Third, we thank the many who have lent a hand to us along the way. This includes our institutions—Northwestern College in St. Paul, Minnesota, and The Southern Baptist Theological Seminary in Louisville, Kentucky—and our colleagues and administrators there. We appreciate their encouragement and the leadership at these institutions. Several students helped with various research tasks, including Justine (Lund) Carlson, Ben Reese, and Carsten Christensen. We especially thank Keith Whitfield and Jonathan Leeman for compiling the indexes.

Finally, we thank our wives and children for their vicarious commitment to this project by their support of us in it.

# ABBREVIATIONS

| | |
|---|---|
| CSPR | Cornell Studies in the Philosophy of Religion |
| CWS | Classics of Western Spirituality |
| *JETS* | *Journal of the Evangelical Theological Society* |
| KJV | King James Version |
| LCC | Library of Christian Classics |
| NASB | New American Standard Bible |
| NIV | New International Version |
| *NPNF* | *Nicene and Post-Nicene Fathers* |
| NRSV | New Revised Standard Version |
| RSV | Revised Standard Version |
| *SJT* | *Scottish Journal of Theology* |
| *TrinJ* | *Trinity Journal* |
| *TynBul* | *Tyndale Bulletin* |
| WBC | Word Biblical Commentary |
| *WTJ* | *Westminster Theological Journal* |

Chapter 1

# Should the God
# of Historic Christianity
# Be Replaced?

*Eric L. Johnson and Douglas S. Huffman*

If God created us in his own image,
we have more than reciprocated.

VOLTAIRE

# 1. Introduction

For much of the twentieth century, the very notion of God was under fire. Belief in God was regarded by most Western intellectuals as a vestige of our premodern heritage, to be shed with all other superstition. The God of the Bible (and of the premodern era) was considered too powerful, too primitive, and too irritable for modern tastes and was let go.

But times have changed. Surveying developments of the past decade, one might think we are in the midst of a postmodern revival. *Time* and *Newsweek* are regularly carrying religious cover stories. For years *Touched by an Angel* has been touching millions in prime time, while by day Oprah was promoting a similar kind of warm and fuzzy spirituality. For more intellectual viewers, public television—long home to series like Carl Sagan's *Cosmos* (a universe devoid of God but populated with aliens[1]) or Leo Buscaglia's gospel of self-love—has been airing Bible studies on the book of Genesis. In the 1990s, best-selling books included *Conversations with God, God: A Biography*, and *The History of God*, and a singer famously asked, "What if God was one of us?" A number of movies of loving angels and a heaven for all good people currently compete in the video stores with less spiritual fare. We might not be as surprised that politicians, regardless of political persuasion or personal morality, make repeated reference to God. But when cultural leaders and pop icons throughout America call us to God after a national tragedy like 9/11, it is clear that God has been raised from the dead to which he was consigned in the 1960s. God is back and is being welcomed with open arms.

The careful observer will note, however, that God has come back from cultural exile quite different. This newer version is a kinder, gentler God—less threatening, more congenial, and more affirming.[2] No longer the almighty, all-glorious center of the universe, this God seems to be more centered on us, less interested in obedience, and more concerned with our happiness. This God is actually quite harmless, supportive of all religion, and on everyone's side. Since no one is alienated from this deity, no one needs salvation from sin; on the contrary, God seems to think quite a lot of us. Certain behaviors that used to bother God don't trouble this God anymore. Hell seems to have been largely done away with; if it exists at all, it is reserved only for the absolutely worst among us, a Hitler or Osama bin Laden.

---

[1]For a dated but marvelous exposure of this irony, see Walker Percy, *Lost in the Cosmos: The Last Self-Help Book* (New York: Farrar, Straus & Giroux, 1983).

[2]According to Placher, the seeds of domestication were planted centuries ago: William C. Placher, *The Domestication of Transcendence: How Modern Thinking About God Went Wrong* (Louisville: Westminster John Knox, 1996).

GOD UNDER FIRE

One wonders if this deity underwent psychotherapy while gone and came back more open and relaxed, having worked through whatever was bothering "him" back in those premodern days (that is another new feature: This God is gender-neutral, or possibly female, but is never to be referred to with the male pronoun). By most reckonings, God is much more acceptable than before being exiled. God seems to have learned some important lessons in how to relate to humans—and it worked. God is more popular than ever.

Not! Upon close inspection, it becomes obvious that this new, improved deity is not the same God as was vanquished earlier in the twentieth century. This God is an imposter. While he bears a superficial resemblance to the historic Judeo-Christian God in some important respects, other features are distorted, and still others are absent. In actual fact, the God of the Bible is no more popular than forty years ago; *that* God is still under fire and is not wanted back. The legitimacy of this covert substitution must be questioned. The purpose of this book is to draw attention to this changing of the divine guard in Western culture and to call instead for a reembracing of the transcendent and relational God of historic Christianity in this present, postmodern age, with the prayer that *that* God, the true and living God, will return in reviving power and love.[3]

## 2. Contemporary Alternative Christian Theologies

While one can describe in broad outline what this imposter-deity is like in popular culture, individual theologians and schools of theology have developed more sophisticated versions of this friendlier, anthropocentric God. One would expect alternative deities to arise from outside Christianity. (In fact, New Age and some Eastern thought appear to be quite compatible with this religious revival; consider the current popularity of the Dalai Lama.) However, many of those most critical of the historic Christian view of God claim allegiance, in varying degrees, to Christianity. This group of authors and thinkers has alleged that historic Christianity has misrepresented God, and so they have devised a number of similar, but distinct, alternative representations of God to revise Christianity's description of God in ways that are more compatible with contemporary sensibilities. These alternative Christian theologies can be broadly grouped into two different (but not necessarily mutually exclusive) camps, which we will call "Constructivist" and "Developmentalist" models. Let us examine each of them.

### 2.1 Constructivist Theologies: The God of Historic Christianity Should Be Rejected Because God Is in the Mind of the Beholder

Constructivism is a skeptical theological stance that questions the human ability to know much about God with any confidence. Rather than being primarily a

---

[3]We put it this way to acknowledge that the church in the West in the twentieth century has seemed to have experienced less of God's transforming power and love than has been evident sometimes in the previous eras of church history (e.g., in the early church and in periods/locations in the twelfth, thirteenth, sixteenth, seventeenth, and eighteenth centuries). So, we pray, come again, Lord Jesus.

theological position per se (concerned with God as an object of understanding), it is actually more an epistemological position (concerned with the human subject and its ability to know, an orientation that has significant implications for theology). Flowing fairly directly out of the Enlightenment skepticism of Immanuel Kant, Constructivism regards the theological enterprise as intrinsically compromised by humanity's inability to grasp things as they are in themselves, particularly things that lie beyond the empirical universe, which the natural sciences can describe.

As a result, much of modern theology since Kant has doubted whether it had much to say about God positively. Kant himself believed humans had no cognitive access to God; humans could "perceive" God solely through their moral awareness (or practical reason).[4] Schleiermacher, the father of modern theology, assumed a good deal of Kant's agenda but sought to locate the source of religion in neither belief nor morality, but in the religious experience of absolute dependence.[5] However, he remained thoroughly Kantian in his skeptical presupposition that particular cognitive-linguistic expressions of religious experience were necessarily fundamentally deficient in describing our experience of God.

Since Schleiermacher's time, Constructivism has maintained its emphasis on the human subject rather than the divine object and has become a major force in Western theology and philosophy. Perhaps the greatest Constructivist of the twentieth century was Paul Tillich.[6] Contemporary Constructivists include the so-called "revisionists" (David Tracy, Edward Farley, and Gordon Kaufman) as well as people like James Gustafson, Peter C. Hodgson, and Hans Küng.[7] Feminist theologians like Elizabeth A. Johnson, Johanna W. H. van Wijk-Bos, Sallie McFague, and Rosemary Radford Ruether have also developed Constructivist models, as have pluralists like John Hick and Paul F. Knitter.[8] Liberation and other ideologically

---

[4]David F. Ford, "Introduction," in *The Modern Theologians*, ed. David F. Ford, 2d ed. (London: Blackwell, 1997), 8.

[5]C. W. Christian, *Friedrich Schleiermacher* (Waco, Tex.: Word, 1979), 37; cf. F. D. E. Schleiermacher, *The Christian Faith* (Edinburgh: T. & T. Clark, 1928).

[6]Paul Tillich, *Systematic Theology* (Chicago: Univ. of Chicago Press, 1951).

[7]David Tracy, *Blessed Rage for Order* (Minneapolis: Seabury, 1975); idem, *The Analogical Imagination* (New York: Crossroad, 1981); Edward Farley, *Ecclesial Reflection: An Anatomy of Theological Method* (Philadelphia: Fortress, 1982); idem, *Divine Empathy: A Theology of God* (Minneapolis: Fortress, 1996); Gordon Kaufman, *Systematic Theology: An Historicist Perspective* (New York: Scribners, 1968); idem, *The Theological Imagination: Constructing the Concept of God* (Philadelphia: Westminster, 1981); idem, *In Face of Mystery: A Constructive Theology* (Cambridge, Mass.: Harvard Univ. Press, 1993); James Gustafson, *Ethics in a Theocentric Perspective*, 2 vols. (Chicago: Univ. of Chicago Press, 1981, 1984); Peter C. Hodgson, *Winds of the Spirit: A Constructive Christian Theology* (Louisville: Westminster John Knox, 1994); Hans Kung, *On Being a Christian* (New York: Doubleday, 1976); idem, *Eternal Life? An Enquiry* (London: Collins, 1984). Cf. James J. Buckley, "Revisionists and Liberals," in *The Modern Theologians*.

[8]Elizabeth A. Johnson, *She Who Is: The Mystery of God in Feminist Theological Discourse* (New York: Crossroad, 1992); Johanna W. H. van Wijk-Bos, *Reimagining God: The Case for Scriptural Diversity* (Louisville: Westminster John Knox, 1995); Sallie McFague, *Models of God: Theology for an Ecological, Nuclear Age* (Philadelphia: Westminster, 1987); Rosemary Radford Ruether,

based theologies are likewise expressive of the Constructivist approach in that they see the particular social context, not transcultural and normative revelation, as the basis by which to formulate theology.[9] (However, liberation theology is also a version of Developmental theology.

These authors and approaches have in common, to various degrees, a reticence to describe the nature of God with much confidence, and all of them believe that we are largely left to ourselves (currently, the *community* of human subjects) to come up with the best, most plausible understanding of God in light of the historical religions (like Christianity, but also others) and contemporary thought in philosophy and science. As a result of this orientation, the God of the Constructivists cannot be described infallibly; on the contrary, what truth claims they make about God are inevitably vague generalizations that seek to transcend the particularities of any historical religion, typically far removed from the personal God of Christian theism.[10] A number of them consider the task of theology to be one of "imaginative construction."[11] According to this approach, imagination is at least as important as rationality in theological activity; theology is believed to stand somewhere between poetry and philosophy.[12] Postmodernism has not radically altered Constructivism; it has just changed the locus of ultimate authority from the self and its reason to the community and its perspective. Neither modernists nor postmodernists, in undiluted form, believe they can make valid claims about God's nature with much confidence.

In contrast, historic Christianity has always maintained a realist theological epistemology. It has always assumed that because of God's revelation of himself in nature, humanity (particularly in Christ), and especially Scripture, humans can genuinely know God, including a good number of specifics about his nature. Historic Christianity has at the same time always maintained that God transcends our ability to know *everything* about him, but it has affirmed that we can certainly know enough to distinguish the true God from the false gods of non-Christian religions. This extra measure of confidence in revelation is inevitably ridiculed by

---

*Sexism and God-Talk: Toward a Feminist Theology* (Boston: Beacon, 1983); idem, *Gaia and God: An Ecofeminist Theology of Earth Healing* (San Francisco: HarperCollins, 1992).

John Hick, *God Has Many Names* (Louisville: Westminster John Knox, 1982); idem, *The Rainbow of Faiths: Critical Dialogues on Religious Pluralism* (London: SCM, 1995); Paul F. Knitter, *No Other Name? A Critical Survey of Christian Attitudes Toward the World Religions* (Maryknoll, N.Y.: Orbis, 1985).

[9]Gustavo Gutierrez, *A Theology of Liberation: History, Politics and Salvation* (Maryknoll, N.Y.: Orbis, 1973); Jose Miguel Bonino, *Doing Theology in a Revolutionary Situation* (Philadelphia: Fortress, 1975); Rosino Gibellini, ed., *Frontiers of Theology in Latin America* (Maryknoll, N.Y.: Orbis, 1975); Juan Luis Segundo, *The Liberation of Theology* (Maryknoll, N.Y.: Orbis, 1976); Leonardo Boff and Clodovis Boff, *Introducing Liberation Theology* (Maryknoll, N.Y.: Orbis, 1987).

[10]Sometimes the "God" of Constructivists is set forth as (merely) an impersonal reality, "the ground of being," as Tillich suggested. Cf., e.g., Kaufman, Farley, and Gustafson.

[11]Cf., e.g., the works of Kaufman, van Wijk-Bos, McFague, Tracy, and Hodgson.

[12]McFague, *Models of God*, 32.

Constructivists as being naïve, dogmatic, and hopelessly outmoded, a trusting in the "house of authority."[13] Constructivists must admit that theological realism has been the historic position of the Christian church but nonetheless believe it is paramount that humans construct a new Christian God more appropriate for contemporary culture.[14]

**2.1.1 A Representative Constructivist Theologian.** Gordon Kaufman is one of the most important, recent Constructivist theologians. He wishes to take seriously all human discourse (Christian, Buddhist, atheist, the natural and social sciences, poetry, etc.) but refuses to regard anything specifically Christian (such as the New Testament) as having a superior role in revealing the nature of God.[15] Kaufman understands our notions of "God" to be nothing more than a symbol, a "product of the human imagination,"[16] standing for something we really have no ability to comprehend. Yet, he argues that the "God symbol" can be a significant construct that helps us function in life and orients us to important values.

Kaufman powerfully (and perversely) argues that one of the most important functions of this symbol is to nullify and relativize all human attempts to assume any privileged epistemological position. "God" points beyond all our relative understandings and so calls us to humility and a recognition of our own inadequacy to establish what the truth "really is." Any attempt at such dogmatism, Kaufman argues, is simply idolatry, a worship of our understanding rather than "God." "To mistake our own imaginative constructs for that mystery is to fall into self-idolatry."[17] Amazingly, Kaufman claims that to say we can truly know God is the greatest of sins. Even biblical authority competes with "God's" authority over us, since the idea that God is a literal person who can speak to us exemplifies "some of the most anthropomorphic features of the tradition" and is "unthinkable."[18]

Kaufman's God is shrouded in such mystery that we can make out little beyond the idea that human thought is inadequate to grasp God and that God is "the eternal process" drawing us to that which is good.[19] In the end, Kaufman's "God" seems much closer to the "One" of Plotinus or the Brahman of Hinduism than it does to the God of Abraham, Moses, and Christ. Tragically, what Kaufman offers us, with an estranged brilliance, is a lonely universe where humans are essentially forced to be their own meaning-detectives, trying to make sense of their existence on their own and working toward the gradual improvement of human life, but where an impersonal "God" cannot act to genuinely guide us or relate

---

[13]Farley, *Ecclesial Reflection*.

[14]Constructivists all struggle with maintaining their Christian identity in the face of presuppositional allegiances lying outside historic Christianity, and well they should, for upon closer examination the residue of Christian content that remains bears little resemblance to the original.

[15]Kaufman, *In Face of Mystery*, xiii, 11, 42.

[16]Ibid., 39.

[17]Ibid., 352.

[18]Ibid.

[19]Ibid., 300.

GOD UNDER FIRE

with us. One is forced to conclude that Kaufman is extrapolating his theology from his own solitary experience, far removed from the relational God of historic Christian theism.[20]

**2.1.2 Religious Pluralism.** A common theological Constructivist model is that of religious pluralism. Some kinds of pluralism are desirable—for example, an appreciation for nonmoral cultural and ethnic differences and a genuine respect for all persons (regardless of their choices, lifestyles, or religious views, even where there is vigorous disagreement with those choices, etc.).[21] The kind of pluralism under consideration here, however, is a radicalization of this more benign respect. Modern and postmodern religious pluralism rightly values humility in making truth claims and rightly recognizes that humans and their knowledge are shaped by culture. But their religious pluralism goes much further than this by virtually denying objective truth altogether (at least in religion).[22]

The major thesis of religious pluralism can be summarized as follows: No individual religious system can claim absolute superiority over any other religious system. Different religions are expressions of the various cultures from which they originate, and they describe the human condition and transcendent experience in differing, but important, ways. This, of course, goes beyond the claim that all religious systems contain *some* truth or reflect *some* valid insights into reality. Many exclusive religions (those claiming to be the only true religion) will acknowledge that alternative religious systems have gotten some things right (we are, after all, all made in God's image and have the universe in common). But religious pluralism claims that all religious systems—in one way or another—have gotten *most* things right, that they all represent and express religious truth with virtually equal validity.[23] Stated negatively, religious pluralism declares necessarily false the claim

---

[20]Constructivist theologians such as Kaufman (and Gustafson) are critical of "anthropomorphizing God," that is, attributing agentic/personal characteristics to God, as is done in classical Christian theism. Cf. Kaufman, *In Face of Mystery*, 352; idem, "Models of God: Is Metaphor Enough?" in *Readings in Modern Theology*, ed. Robin Gill (London: SPCK, 1995), 80–81; Gustafson, *Ethics*, 1:61, 270. Their God is *so* transcendent as to be "beyond personality" and thus is incapable of relationship with other persons.

[21]D. A. Carson calls this sense of pluralism "empirical pluralism," noting others prefer "factual pluralism" or simply "plurality"; *The Gagging of God: Christianity Confronts Pluralism* (Grand Rapids: Zondervan, 1996), 13. Nevertheless, few people (Christian or non-Christian) take seriously the extreme pluralistic position that humans must respect *all* cultural differences, including moral differences such as wife-burning or genital mutilation.

[22]Carson (ibid., 19 n. 19) notes, with credit to Harold Netland, that *this* form of pluralism includes several modern philosophical positions that all deny the possibility of knowing objective truth: e.g., perspectivism (humans can only know reality from their individual perspectives and never as it really is), constructivism (what we call reality is merely a construct of our experiences), ontological nonrealism (there is no reality to be experienced or known), and various kinds of relativism (what is termed true or normative is only so within a particular context).

[23]See, e.g., John Hick and Paul F. Knitter, eds., *The Myth of Christian Uniqueness: Toward a Pluralistic Theology of Religions* (Faith Meets Faith Series; Maryknoll, N.Y.: Orbis, 1987), where the idea of "the unique definitiveness, absoluteness, normativeness, superiority of Christianity in comparison with other religions of the world" (p. vii) is challenged in several articles on the grounds of historical-cultural relativism, theological mystery, and the need for justice.

of one religion to be exclusively true or to be superior over all others. As a result, its "God," to the extent it is willing to describe it, is an open-minded, accepting deity towards which all religions are moving.

Clearly, then, religious pluralism must judge historic Christianity as seriously deficient, since it has traditionally claimed that the God of the Old and New Testaments is the true God and that he alone offers genuine salvation to humanity through faith in his Son Jesus Christ. As a result, Christians who hold to religious pluralism defend a Christianity that has softened such claims, making it more properly tolerant and accepting of the world's religions (and consequently more tolerable to others).

One of the best-known leaders in the pluralistic revision of historic Christianity is John Hick. He observes that all religious traditions have their own complex histories of development and their own unique mixtures of good and bad.

> In face of these complexities it seems impossible to make the global judgment that any one religious tradition has contributed more good or less evil, or a more favorable balance of good and evil, than the others.... We may well judge that in some respects, or in some periods or regions, the fruits of one tradition are better than, whereas in other respects or periods or regions inferior to, those of another. But as vast complex totalities, the world traditions seem to be more or less on a par with each other. None can be singled out as manifestly superior.[24]

Still embracing a form of Christianity, Hick claims that historic Christianity must be rejected for its exclusive and paradoxical faith in "a God of universal love who has ordained that only the Christian minority of the human race can be saved."[25] Rather, such a paradox demands that Christianity (as well as other exclusive religions) must be reconceptualized as merely one of many ways for humans to think about and experience God.[26]

According to Hick, the label "God" should be viewed as the Christian term used to refer to the ultimate, divine Reality, which is the same referent for other religions using other labels. This ultimate Reality is beyond human thought and speech and encompasses all representations of it, both personal and impersonal. Every religion is an "independently valid" means of experiencing Reality. "Salvation" happens when humans are transformed from self-centeredness to Reality-centeredness, and this transformation takes place in many ways in the various contexts of the world's diverse religious traditions.[27]

---

[24]John Hick, "The Non-Absoluteness of Christianity," in *The Myth of Christian Uniqueness*, 30; cf. idem, *A Christian Theology of Religions: The Rainbow of Faiths* (Louisville: Westminster John Knox, 1995), esp. pp. 11–30.

[25]John Hick, *Problems of Religious Pluralism* (New York: St. Martin's, 1985), 99.

[26]See Hick's reconceptualization of Jesus Christ in *The Metaphor of God Incarnate: Christology in a Pluralistic Age* (Louisville: Westminster John Knox, 1993); cf. idem, ed., *The Myth of God Incarnate* (London: SCM, 1977).

[27]Hick, ed., *The Myth of God Incarnate*, esp. 28–45; cf. John Hick, *An Interpretation of Religion: Human Responses to the Transcendent* (London: Macmillan, 1989), esp. 233–46; idem, *Disputed Questions in Theology and the Philosophy of Religion* (New Haven, Conn.: Yale Univ. Press, 1993), esp. 139–79.

GOD UNDER FIRE

The claims of religious pluralism only make sense from a Constructivist standpoint. The claim that different religions are all valid (albeit limited) human attempts to grasp that which is beyond our grasp makes sense only if one assumes that the true God cannot be infallibly known. How arrogant, then, of historic Christianity to set its own religious beliefs above others. But Constructivism, of course, has no way to *prove* that the God beyond our grasp has *not* infallibly revealed himself through a particular historical religion. Religious pluralism suffers from the malady that afflicts relativism in general. While it appears to be promoting the kind of general pluralism mentioned above, which respects nonmoral differences and all persons, it simultaneously attacks religious systems it perceives as intolerant, betraying its own intolerance. All forms of radical relativism fall victim to such self-refutation.[28]

## 2.2 Developmentalist Theologies: The God of Historic Christianity Should Be Rejected Because God's Being or Knowledge Is Changing

In contrast with Constructivists, Developmentalist theologians are more willing to make assertions about the nature of God and thus are generally less skeptical about our ability to know God. Nevertheless, Developmentalists also wish to jettison the historic Christian understanding of God because, contrary to historic Christianity, they believe that God is undergoing constant development as he interacts with humans and reacts to human actions, creativity, and cultural progress.

Descending from the thought of Hegel and bolstered by evolutionary theory, theological Developmentalists reject the historic understanding of God as absolutely independent of his creation and the bounds of time.[29] They see the historic Christian God as distant and remote from humans, and they prefer a fully temporal God who is more vulnerable and responsive to humans and universally committed to prospering human life and activity.

Hegel was the most historical of Western philosophers up to his time and perhaps the first to come up with a comprehensive philosophical system that took time and development seriously. At the core of his system was the historical unfolding of *Geist*, the Absolute Spirit or Mind, the source of the existence, order, and development of the universe. Hegel brought the human and the divine into a fundamentally interdependent relationship and identification, seeing the development of humanity in Western culture as the outworking of Absolute Spirit's own self-realization.[30]

---

[28]For critiques of religious pluralism, see Carson, *The Gagging of God*; Harold A. Netland, *Dissonant Voices: Religious Pluralism and the Question of Truth* (Grand Rapids: Eerdmans, 1991); Alvin Plantinga, "A Defense of Religious Exclusivism," in *The Analytic Theist: An Alvin Plantinga Reader*, ed. James F. Sennett (Grand Rapids: Eerdmans, 1998), 187–209.

[29]Cf. Eric C. Rust, *Evolutionary Philosophies and Contemporary Theology* (Philadelphia: Westminster, 1969).

[30]Cf. G. W. F. Hegel, *The Phenomenology of Mind*, trans. J. B. Baillie, rev. ed. (New York: Humanities, 1931).

Though Hegel's system was largely ignored during most of the twentieth century, his indirect influence through philosophers like Marx, Neitzsche, and Dewey (all of whom reacted against him) contributed to an increasingly historical, developmental approach to human existence throughout the century.

Even more influential than Hegel on modern developmental sensibilities was the contribution of the natural and human sciences.

- The theory of evolution is widely thought to have demonstrated that biological life, the most complex of natural phenomena, is not static but intrinsically fluid and changeable.
- Developmental psychology has shown how human life and thinking gradually change over one's life span.
- Einstein's theory of relativity in physics has shown that time is a fundamental dimension of the physical universe along with the three spatial dimensions of Newtonian physics. Modern physicists realized that humans cannot study any entity in the universe without taking temporality into account, since how a phenomenon looks depends on where the observer and object stand in spatial and temporal relation to each other.
- The fact of technological change has brought its own message. We live in a culture where technological progress occurs at dizzying speed (which has also made more large-scale cultural changes possible through mass media). Westerners have come to expect change and to see change as one of the highest of values.

Together, these influences have brought about a revolution in how people in the West conceive of reality. Thus, a general Developmentalist mind-set came to pervade Western thought in the twentieth century.[31]

---

[31]It must be pointed out that the charge that historic Christian theism was excessively influenced by classical Greek thought cuts both ways. Such critics betray a remarkable lack of self-awareness if they are suggesting they are freer from the non-Christian influences of our day than the early church was in its day. Developmental theologies such as process and open theism would have been inconceivable without the influences mentioned above. Nevertheless, this point is not made apathetically, as if Christianity is necessarily compromised by its intellectual and cultural context. On the contrary, Christianity sees itself as the product of revealed wisdom that is from above (James 3:17; Heb. 1:1–3; 1 Cor. 2), which enters into a world dominated by distorted and fundamentally false philosophies (Col. 2:8). Though never perfectly successful, the church in every age has recognized it is called to move, in its thought and life, away from the city of humanity, from which it was redeemed, towards the city of God, in reliance upon the Spirit of truth. Part of the rationale behind this book is the historic Christian assumption that the church is to resist the interpretive frameworks of communities outside the faith (the "world") or risk committing heresy. While we acknowledge their inevitable influence as well as their potential value (properly critiqued), we believe that the early church was largely successful in resisting and overcoming the corrosive effects of alien worldviews and substituting for them the biblical one (cf. ch. 4 in this volume by Gerald L. Bray). It is our conclusion that modern and postmodern alternative Christian theologies have been much less successful. Contrary to the majority stance of the early church, many modern/postmodern theologians actually glory in their conformity to non-Christian thought. Historic Christianity, in contrast, has always believed that the eternal truth of God is perennially relevant to every culture and that the church is to bring the truth from above to a humanity blinded by the god of this world (2 Cor. 4:4). This, Christians believe, is a divine "totalizing" and not a sectarian, human construction.

*a movement created by a*

**2.2.1 Process Theology.** Within this context, it was perhaps inevitable that some within Christian theology would eventually take a developmental approach to God. One thinker in particular pointed the way: Alfred North Whitehead.[32] A Unitarian and not a Christian, Whitehead developed a unique terminology for a metaphysical system that took temporality, change, and contingency as fundamental to both the universe and God. In Whitehead's scheme, God creates nothing *ex nihilo* but unites abstract potentiality with the concrete actuality of what exists in the universe. This God is both everlasting and unchanging (and "*actually* deficient and unconscious") as well as temporal and determined (and "fully actual, and conscious," particularly in relation to humanity).[33] God, then, becomes self-realizing through his relations with developing, increasingly complex societies of actual entities. Thus, "it is as true to say that God creates the World, as that the World creates God,"[34] and "God and the world are mutually necessary."[35] What all this means is that ultimately, the Whiteheadian God is dependent fully on the universe and cannot directly bring about emerging realities or effect changes without the cooperating activity of God's creation.

Whitehead's terminology was novel and complex and his system speculative, but he developed a way to think about God and human beings that has seemed extremely attractive to many modern/postmodern Christians. For one thing, Whitehead offered a temporal, developing, relational God, who persuades rather than coerces and therefore is better able, so he claimed, to relate to human beings than the alleged timeless, passionless, monarchical God of historic Christianity. In addition, this God, with no unilateral or final control over events in the universe, plays no role in the occurrence of sin and evil. This was believed to go a long way towards solving what many have felt is the Achilles' heel of historic Christianity, the problem of evil (i.e., how could an all-powerful, all-knowing, all-good God not prevent evil?). At the same time, it must be admitted that Whitehead's model makes the created order to be extremely important, even necessary, to God. Doubtless this provides one of the chief attractions of process thought for those accommodating themselves to a culture so taken with itself as is the West.[36]

---

[32]Pierre Teilhard de Chardin might be mentioned as a Christian theologian (Roman Catholic) who sought to develop a synthesis of evolutionary theory, Hegelian sensibilities, and Christian theology; see his *Christianity and Evolution*, trans. Rene Hague (New York: Harcourt, Brace, Jovanovich, 1971). However, his distinctive model has been much less influential than Whitehead's over the past thirty years.

[33]Alfred North Whitehead, *Process and Reality* (London: Cambridge Univ. Press, 1929), 489.

[34]Ibid., 528.

[35]Rust, *Evolutionary Philosophies and Contemporary Theology*, 113.

[36]Process thought "believes that because God can receive some benefit from our existence, there is an advantage in our existence. We decide something in God; namely, some aspect of the content of his knowledge. We perpetually create content not only in ourselves but also in God. And this gives significance to our presence in this world"; Santiago Sia, *God in Process Thought* (Dordrecht: Martinus Nijhoff, 1985), 87 (written in reference to Charles Hartshorne). Indeed, human significance approaches divine significance. Classical theism, however, sees humans as much smaller and God as much larger.

A few philosophers found this system attractive and accepted the main tenets of Whitehead's system, modifying it modestly—the most important of whom was Charles Hartshorne.[37] In addition, a number of Christian theologians, displeased with the God of historic Christianity, were likewise attracted to this model and have attempted to reformulate Christian thought in accord with it, including Schubert Ogden, John B. Cobb Jr., David R. Griffin, Norman Pittenger, and, more recently, Marcus Borg, creating a movement known as "process theology."[38]

In certain respects, process theology stands between pantheism and historic Christian theism. Pantheism claims that God and the world are somehow identical, whereas historic Christianity claims that God is independent of the world, even while creating it, overseeing its existence, and working to accomplish his purposes in it. Process theology sees these models of the relation between God and the creation as errant extremes. On the one hand, process theology rejects the historic Christian idea that God is the unchanging ruler over all creation.[39] On the other hand, in contrast to pantheism, process theology claims that God and the world are not identical, but God is nonetheless fundamentally determined by the world. God and the world are interdependent, much like one's mind and body are related.[40] This model of God's relation to the world is often called "panentheism."

The chief claims of process theology over against classical theism can be summarized as follows.[41]

---

[37]Charles Hartshorne, *The Divine Relativity* (New Haven, Conn.: Yale Univ. Press, 1948); idem, *Man's Vision of God and the Logic of Theism* (Chicago: Willett, Clark & Co., 1941). More recently, there has been an increasing interest in process thought among philosophers, esp. those interested in science; cf. Nicholas Rescher, *Process Metaphysics: An Introduction to Process Philosophy* (Albany, N.Y.: SUNY Press, 1996); Ian Barbour, *Religion in an Age of Science: The Gifford Lectures, 1989–1991*, vol. 1 (San Francisco: Harper & Row, 1990); Philip Clayton, *God and Contemporary Science* (Grand Rapids: Eerdmans, 1997).

[38]Schubert Ogden, *The Reality of God* (New York: Harper & Row, 1966); John B. Cobb Jr., *A Christian Natural Theology* (Philadelphia: Westminster, 1965); David R. Griffin, *God, Power, and Evil: A Process Theodicy* (Philadelphia: Westminster, 1976); idem, *God and Religion in the Postmodern World* (Albany, N.Y.: SUNY Press, 1989); Norman Pittenger, *Picturing God* (London: SCM, 1982); Marcus J. Borg, *The God We Never Knew: Beyond Dogmatic Religion to a More Authentic Contemporary Faith* (San Francisco: HarperSanFrancisco, 1997). Borg's work comes across as an evangelistic tract encouraging Christians to move from classical Christian theism (Borg's term is "supernatural theism") to process theism.

[39]John B. Cobb Jr. and David Ray Griffin, in *Process Theology: An Introductory Exposition* (Philadelphia: Westminster, 1976), 8–10, summarize five common views of God that process theology rejects: (1) God as Cosmic Moralist, (2) God as the Unchanging and Passionless Absolute, (3) God as Controlling Power, (4) God as Sanctioner of the Status Quo, and (5) God as Male. As will be discussed in this book, some of these items represent misunderstandings—not actual claims—of the classic Christian description of God.

[40]Ronald H. Nash, *The Concept of God: An Exploration of Contemporary Difficulties with the Attributes of God* (Grand Rapids: Zondervan, 1983), 23.

[41]Nash, ibid., 24–30, outlines eleven theses of process theology that we have augmented, summarized, and condensed here to seven. Process theology is not a monolithic movement, and consequently some of these points may be disputed by some process thinkers. David R. Griffin, "Process Theology and the Christian Good News: A Response to Classical Free Will

- Since every actual thing is an occasion of experience in the process of becoming, God also is in the process of becoming something he is not yet. As the Bible pictures God, panentheists note, he is changing, responsive, and personable, not a static, unmoved mover.
- God is not the independent Creator of the universe but an interdependent cooperator with it. God needs the world in order for his life to be complete and have meaning, and the world needs God in order to have a goal and permanence.
- God is not independent of time but experiences change in the process of time.
- Like classical Christian theists, process theologians say that God is "perfect," but they allow for God to continue to grow in perfection and so to surpass himself.
- God gains more and more knowledge as he becomes aware of experiences in the universe around him. God is "omniscient," but for process theology this means that God knows the past and the present perfectly but not the future, for the future is unknowable even for God.
- God is not so much the initial cause of the universe but rather the alluring goal of the universe. God tries to persuade the world to grow to fulfillment. "Process theology sees God's fundamental aim to be the promotion of the creatures' own enjoyment."[42]
- Process theology claims that God cannot guarantee future victory over evil. Because God is a persuader and not a controller, he risks being unsuccessful.

Thus, rather than being absolutely transcendent and above creation, according to process theology God is radically immanent and present with creation. In fact, for process theology, God is developing along with the creation, realizing God's own fulfillment even as God lures humans into greater love and fulfillment.

The process concern with love is undeniably of Christian origin and the chief reason that process theologians are able to make as much of a case for their position using Scripture as they do. The God they point to, however, is so much smaller than the God of the Bible, since the process deity is essentially limited by

Theism," in *Searching for an Adequate God: A Dialogue Between Process and Free Will Theists*, ed. John B. Cobb Jr. and Clark H. Pinnock (Grand Rapids: Eerdmans, 2000), 2–7, sets out more philosophically what he calls "core doctrines" of process theology, including hard-core commonsense notions, panexperientialism with organizational duality, the nonsensationist doctrine of perception, perpetual oscillation between subjectivity and objectivity, internal relatedness, naturalistic theism, and dipolar theism. For a readable historical introduction to process theology, see John B. Cobb Jr., "Process Theology and the Present Church Struggle," in *Introduction to Christian Theology: Contemporary North American Perspectives*, ed. Roger A. Badham (Louisville: Westminster John Knox, 1998), 154–65. See also Ronald H. Nash, ed., *Process Theology* (Grand Rapids: Baker, 1987), in which various Christian scholars address philosophical, theological, and practical issues regarding process thinking. For a helpful, brief critique of process theology, see Millard J. Erickson, *God the Father Almighty: A Contemporary Exploration of the Divine Attributes* (Grand Rapids: Baker, 1998), 49–66.
[42]Cobb and Griffin, *Process Theology*, 56.

the creation. While process theology seems to imply a God with specific, loving intentions toward humans, unfortunately, because the process deity is so dependent on the creation, God is unable to act assertively on our behalf, resulting in a rather passive personhood.[43] Just as a child loses respect for an overly doting parent who seems to lack an independent identity, so it is hard to worship a God whose existence is bound up in a kind of "codependent relationship" with humanity. On some level this may explain why process theologians are much less concerned about God's greatness and glory than those within historic Christianity; in a deep sense, their deity is less worthy of respect.

Earlier we saw that some Constructivists stress God's greatness (or "otherness") to the point that God is basically unknowable and impersonal and that historic Christianity stands against this by proclaiming a God who is transcendent but *personal*. Here, over against the passive deity of process theism, we must assert God's vigorous, *transcendent* personhood. The God of historic Christian theism interacts with humans individually, as an agent among agents, yet simultaneously achieves his foreknown purposes through the activity of his creation, which he providentially guides to its appointed ends. Historic Christian theism stands out starkly between the hyper-transcendence of (some) Constructivists and the hyper-immanence of the major Developmentalists.

**2.2.2 Open Theism.** Another, less radical Developmentalist model of God is that of "open theism," a relatively new approach to God, obviously influenced by process theism but defended by self-identified evangelicals.[44] Strongly sympa-

---

[43]Arthur Holmes, "Why God Cannot Act," in Nash, ed., *Process Theology*, 179–96; Richard Rice, "Process Theism and the Open View of God," in Cobb and Pinnock, eds., *Searching for an Adequate God*, 187.

[44]Several terms have been used to describe this school of thought (or parts of it) including *free-will theism*, *relational theology*, and *presentism*. We use the term *open theism* for several reasons: (1) The school of thought under discussion clearly distinguishes itself from classic Christian theism but the terms and concepts of "free will" and "relational" are many times used by those within classical theism. (2) While "presentism" describes an important aspect of this alternative theology (its view of God's relationship to time and his knowledge), this school of thought involves other issues as well. (3) "Open theism" seems to be the most encompassing term, a term commonly used by their proponents.

The volume systematically introducing open theism is the jointly authored book by Clark H. Pinnock, Richard Rice, John Sanders, William Hasker, and David Basinger, *The Openness of God: A Biblical Challenge to the Traditional Understanding of God* (Downers Grove, Ill.: InterVarsity Press, 1994). Several volumes individually authored by these men are important resources: Richard Rice, *God's Foreknowledge and Man's Free Will* (Minneapolis: Bethany, 1985) [original edition entitled *The Openness of God*]; John Sanders, *The God Who Risks* (Downers Grove, Ill.: InterVarsity Press, 1998); William Hasker, *God, Time, and Knowledge* (CSPR; Ithaca, N.Y.: Cornell Univ. Press, 1989); David Basinger, *The Case for Free Will Theism: A Philosophical Assessment* (Downers Grove, Ill.: InterVarsity Press, 1996); and Clark H. Pinnock, *Most Moved Mover: A Theology of God's Openness* (Grand Rapids: Baker, 2001). Gregory A. Boyd has contributed to the discussion with *Letters from a Skeptic* (Wheaton: Victor, 1994) (with Edward K. Boyd); *God at War: The Bible & Spiritual Conflict* (Downers Grove, Ill.: InterVarsity Press, 1997); *God of the Possible* (Grand Rapids: Baker, 2000); and *Satan and the Problem of Evil* (Downers Grove, Ill.: InterVarsity Press, 2001). See also Cobb and Pinnock,eds., *Searching for an Adequate God*.

thetic to process critics of the God of historic Christianity, these theologians and philosophers object to a God whom they perceive as distant and uninvolved in human life, unable to interact genuinely and lovingly with humanity nor to respond, for example, to prayer.[45] They point to a gap they see between historic Christian theologizing and practical Christian devotion. Christians pray as if they can genuinely impact God and cry out to him in their distress. But if all of history, including everything future, is foreknown, prayer is meaningless, and the God of historic Christianity can only feign interest in creaturely struggles and sufferings he has known about from before the foundation of the world.

While there are variations within the movement, open theists are united by a distinct blend of beliefs brought together from historic Christian theism and process theism.[46] With historic Christianity, open theists believe God is the self-existent, personal, all-powerful Creator of the universe, who can and does act in the world and who has given humans the power of free choice. In contrast to process theism, open theists have a high view of Scripture and believe God freely created *ex nihilo* and has the power to override human decisions if he wishes.[47]

But with process theists, open theists claim that God does not have exhaustive, infallible knowledge of the future, God changes his mind, and God does not exercise providential control over most events.[48] In particular, open theism is troubled by classic Christianity's commitment to God's exhaustive knowledge of all future creaturely choices in light of the implications it perceives of this doctrine for human freedom and its own theological and philosophical proposals for dealing with the problem of evil.[49]

---

[45]Note the statement of Rice, "Process Theism and the Open View of God," 183: "For the most part, proponents of the open view of God accept process philosophy's critique of classical theism. They, too, oppose the concept of an absolute Being, utterly unaffected by the world, whose ultimate goal is his own glory." Unfortunately, Rice's rhetoric maintains the same stereotype of the classical view of God as is found in process critiques.

[46]David Basinger (*The Case for Freewill Theism*, 37) notes several areas of difference between open theists: why God created the world as he did, the extent to which God can unilaterally intervene in the world, the type and effect of knowledge God possesses, the need for an afterlife and its nature, and God's decision-making ethic.

[47]Cf. Cobb and Pinnock, eds., *Searching for an Adequate God*, esp. William Hasker's article in that volume, "An Adequate God," 215–45.

[48]David Basinger, "Practical Implications," in *The Openness of God*, 156: "God . . . does not normally override such [human libertarian] freedom, even if he sees that it is producing undesirable results. . . . God does not possess exhaustive knowledge of exactly how we will utilize our freedom, although he may well at times be able to predict with great accuracy the choices we will freely make."

[49]For centuries orthodox Christians have debated the question of the balance between God's sovereignty and human freedom, with the two ends of the continuum oftentimes labeled Augustinianism versus Semi-Pelagianism, or (in Protestant circles) Calvinism versus Arminianism. But open theism pushes beyond the Semi-Pelagian/Arminian understanding of the balance. See Boyd's argument as to the ways in which Arminianism "has not removed itself far enough from classical-philosophical assumptions about God" in *God At War*, 48–51. For an open theist's approach to the problem of evil, see Boyd, *God at War*; idem, *Satan and the Problem of Evil*; and idem, *God of the Possible*. However, as Paul K. Helseth points out in "On Divine

The central tenets of open theism can be summarized as follows.[50]

- Love is God's central attribute. God cares for the well-being of others and is sensitive and responsive to them.

- Though God created the universe *ex nihilo*, he nonetheless has a dynamic relationship of genuine interaction with the world. Thus, not only does he influence the world, but the world influences him.

- God willingly created humans with a kind of freedom over which he does not have complete control (all open theists maintain that humans have incompatibilist or libertarian freedom).

- Similarly, while he has plans for the future, God does not meticulously control every event so that he can determine the future.

- Furthermore, God does not know exhaustively what the future will be like. In particular, God cannot know any future, free, creaturely choice or action in advance of its occurrence. Rather, God is a temporal being, and he learns as things happen. Therefore, God is genuinely surprised (and can be disappointed) when things happen that he did not expect.[51]

- Evil in the world is not part of God's plan but the results of free choices made by others. While God can intervene in earthly happenings, he so values the freedom he has given humanity that he normally does not override it.

- Nevertheless, God is flexible and endlessly resourceful in accomplishing his ultimate purposes for humanity.

---

Ambivalence: Open Theism and the Problem of Particular Evils," *JETS* 44 (2001): 493–511, the open theist distinctive over against process theism that God *can* intervene, but nevertheless doesn't most of the time, does nothing to help defend God against the problem of evil. At least the God of classical Christian theism uses evil for a higher good. The God of open theism allows all kinds of evil to happen that he sees are very likely going to occur (he knew of the plans of the terrorists who destroyed the World Trade Center months before they did it), yet the vast majority of the time he does not prevent them.

[50]Pinnock et al., *The Openness of God*, esp. Richard Rice, "Biblical Support for a New Perspective," 15–16, and David Basinger, "Practical Implications," 155–56. For a brief evaluation of open theism, see Erickson, *God the Father Almighty*, 67–92; for more thorough critiques of open theism, see Bruce A. Ware, *God's Lesser Glory: The Diminished God of Open Theism* (Wheaton, Ill.: Crossway, 2000), and John M. Frame, *No Other God: A Response to Open Theism* (Phillipsburg, N.J.: Presbyterian & Reformed, 2001).

[51]Most open theists would see the issue of God's knowledge as open theism's primary distinction from classic Christianity. The most common view of open theists is that God is "omniscient" in the sense that he knows all of the past and all of the present (and the natural consequences of those things), but none of the future acts of free agents. That is because these future acts cannot be known ahead of time, so God is not deficient for not knowing them. The future is yet to be created in part by the unknowable future choices of freewill agents (humans, angels, and demons). God, like humans, can only guess at the future. Of course, since God knows all of the past and present, he can make better estimates of what the future will hold, but he has determined to allow the unknown choices of others to have an impact.

Even though open theist David Basinger holds to this understanding of God's knowledge, he believes an open theist may hold to simple foreknowledge (i.e., that God knows all of the future but is unable to make use of that knowledge to change anything) or even some kind of

On the basis of these beliefs, open theism should be reckoned as a "tempered" Developmentalist theology. The God of open theism is a strictly temporal being who grows in his knowledge of reality as it unfolds in time; he develops in his memory (which, analogous to the development of human memory, is constantly increasing) and in the quality of his relationships with others as he comes to know them better through their actions. Of course, open theists do not see their acceptance of this developmental feature of God as syncretism. Nevertheless, the idea of God developing in these ways would be inconceivable for virtually anyone within the Christian (and Jewish!) tradition from its birth until the nineteenth and twentieth centuries (with the notable exception in the seventeenth century of the openness precursor, Sozzini, and his followers[52]).

Contrary to the assertions of open and process theists, historic Christianity has always strongly affirmed God's relationality and his genuine, concerned love of his creation, image-bearers, and children (including his empathic, suffering love, though this has been typically discussed in reference to Christ's human nature). The difficulty has always been how to square those aspects of God with his transcendence and glory, but relationality has always been central to historic Christianity. Nevertheless, the current Developmentalist critique provides a fresh opportunity for historic Christian theists to reflect more deeply on Scripture and appropriately reexamine its tradition, in order to know and love God better.[53] We hope this book fosters such reflection.

One more point should be made before moving on. Many open theists (though not all) have also indicated a preference for a modified pluralism, a view known as inclusivism. For example, several have suggested that devout practitioners of other religions will, in fact, find themselves in fellowship with the Christian God in the life hereafter. With historic Christian theism, open theists say that Jesus is the only

---

middle knowledge (e.g., that God knows all hypothetical possibilities but is unable to know in great detail all the possibilities that will come to be); *The Case for Freewill Theism*, 39–55. Basinger believes, however, that open theism is most distinguished from classic Christian theism by its view of God's power: "But what differentiates freewill theists from other standard theists is primarily their perspective on the nature of God's power, especially as it relates to the question, To what extent, if any, can God unilaterally control earthly affairs?"; *The Case for Freewill Theism*, 21–22. Open theists who see God's knowledge as the key point of difference are nevertheless not far from agreement with Basinger. Broadly speaking, open theism is distinct in its view of how God interacts with the world and we presume that what God knows largely determines how he acts. God's level of knowledge would make a distinctive impact on his effective power.

[52]Sozzini was the founder of a movement called "Socinianism" in English, widely regarded as heresy by orthodox theologians from that time until now. He denied the deity of Christ, the need for a substitutionary atonement, and God's foreknowledge of future events. Cf. Robert Strimple, "What Does God Know?" in *The Coming Evangelical Crisis: Current Challenges to the Authority of Scripture and the Gospel*, ed. John H. Armstrong (Chicago: Moody Press, 1996), 140–41; I. Breward, "Socinus and Socinianism," in *New Dictionary of Theology*, ed. S. B. Ferguson, D. F. Wright, and J. I. Packer (Downers Grove, Ill.: InterVarsity Press, 1988), 649.

[53]For example, Ronald Nash has already called for such reflection without resorting to a Developmentalist model; cf. Nash, *The Concept of God*, 113–15.

way of salvation (contrary to religious pluralists), but they add that Jesus will, nevertheless, eternally save some who do not believe on him in this life.[54]

Admittedly, of the positions examined in this book, open theism is the closest to historic Christianity, and historic Christian theists should be grateful for whatever beliefs open theists share with us. The differences between a Gordon Kaufman and a Clark Pinnock are considerable, and the discerning historic Christian theist will take them seriously. Nevertheless, the contributors spend a good deal of time in this book interacting with open theism. This is largely because most of us are evangelicals and therefore lay claim to the same heritage as do the open theists. Thus, it is only natural that we will want to interact with and respond to them.[55] In addition, open theism offers a recently developed, novel view of God, critical of the God of historic Christianity, which requires thoughtful cross-examination. Lastly, as James Spiegel suggests in his chapter in this volume, if the model of God of open theism can be shown to be inadequate, the other models of the alternate Christian theologies all likewise perish. Consequently, as the contributors to this volume have wrestled with contemporary ways in which the God of historic Christian theism is currently under fire, our attention has been repeatedly drawn to open theism.

### 3. The Living Tradition Of Historic Christian Theism

As suggested in the foregoing overview, those laying claim to some form of Christianity today are extremely diverse. Yet transcending the divisions of contemporary Christian ecclesiastical and theological diversity is a group to which we have been referring throughout: those who vigorously subscribe to the core beliefs of historic Christianity. These Christians sense a significant continuity

[54]Cf. Clark H. Pinnock, "An Inclusivist View," in *More Than One Way? Four Views on Salvation in a Pluralistic World*, ed. Dennis L. Okholm and Timothy R. Phillips (Grand Rapids: Zondervan, 1995), 93–148; idem, *A Wideness in God's Mercy: The Finality of Jesus Christ in a World of Religions* (Grand Rapids: Zondervan, 1992); John Sanders, "Inclusivism," in *What About Those Who Have Never Heard? Three Views on the Destiny of the Unevangelized*, ed. John Sanders (Downers Grove, Ill.: InterVarsity Press, 1995), 21–55; idem, *No Other Name: An Investigation into the Destiny of the Unevangelized* (Grand Rapids: Eerdmans, 1992). Here, it should be mentioned that a few classical Christians have also been drawn in this direction, including Origen, perhaps Gregory of Nyssa, and more recently, C. S. Lewis, Karl Barth, and a number of Catholics before and after Vatican II. Even so, a fair and honest reading of Scripture leads to the conclusion drawn by the vast majority of classical Christians over the centuries that, with the exception of some special circumstances (like mental incompetence or those who die in infancy), "people are not saved apart from explicit faith in Jesus Christ, which presupposes that they have heard about his salvific work on their behalf"; R. Douglas Geivett and W. Gary Phillips, "A Particularist View: An Evidentialist Approach," in *More Than One Way?* 214.

[55]On this score, the 2001 Annual Meeting of the Evangelical Theological Society, with the theme "Defining Evangelicalism's Boundaries," discussed at some length the question of open theism being considered evangelical. A vote affirmed, "We believe the Bible clearly teaches that God has complete, accurate, and infallible knowledge of all events past, present, and future, including all future decisions and actions of free moral agents." This vote was listed by *Christianity Today* (Jan. 7, 2002), 16, as one of its top ten religious stories of 2001.

between their understanding of God (and the main features of divine salvation) and that affirmed throughout Christian history. The core beliefs of this long tradition have been expressed in the Apostles', Nicene, and Chalcedonian creeds and in the writings of Christians like Tertullian, Athanasius, Augustine, Maximus, Bernard of Clairvaux, Anselm, Aquinas, Gregory Palamas, Julian of Norwich, Luther, Calvin, Cranmer, Teresa of Avila, Owen, Charnock, Pascal, Edwards, Wesley, Newman, Kierkegaard, Hodge, Machen, Barth, Chesterton, Lewis, von Balthasar, Henry, and Plantinga, to name quite a few. Today, believers united in their adherence to historic, creedal, supernatural Christianity can be found within the Catholic and Orthodox churches as well as Protestant, including both evangelical and mainline churches.[56]

Different terms have been used to refer to the body of beliefs that distinguish this system: catholic Christianity,[57] evangelical catholicism,[58] the Tradition,[59] the Great Tradition,[60] paleo-orthodoxy,[61] Christian theism,[62] traditional theology (usually used by critics),[63] and classical theism.[64] For the most part, we have settled on the *classical* or *historic Christianity* in this book to refer to the particular model of God that has been adhered to throughout the history of the church but that which has been under attack throughout the past one hundred years.

[56]Many have written in favor of such a broad understanding of historic Christianity, including Thomas C. Oden, *Systematic Theology*, vol. 1: *The Living God* (San Francisco: HarperSanFrancisco, 1987); idem., *Requiem: A Lament in Three Movements* (Nashville: Abingdon, 1995); Ellen Charry, *By the Renewing of Your Minds: The Pastoral Function of Christian Doctrine* (New York: Oxford Univ. Press, 1997); J. I. Packer, "On from Orr: Cultural Crisis, Rational Realism and Incarnational Ontology," in *Reclaiming the Great Tradition: Evangelicals, Catholics and Orthodox in Dialogue*, ed. James S. Cutsinger (Downers Grove, Ill.: InterVarsity Press, 1997), 155–75; Peter Kreeft, "Ecumenical Jihad," in the same book, 13–37; Kalistos Ware, "The Trinity: Heart of Our Life," in the same book, 125–45; Alister E. McGrath, *Evangelicalism and the Future of Christianity* (Downers Grove, Ill.: InterVarsity Press, 1995); T. F. Torrance, *Theology As Reconciliation: Essays Towards Evangelical and Catholic Unity in East and West* (Grand Rapids: Eerdmans, 1976); Carl E. Braaten and Robert W. Jenson, eds., *The Catholicity of the Reformation* (Grand Rapids: Eerdmans, 1996); Avery Dulles, *The Catholicity of the Church* (Oxford: Clarendon, 1985); Chuck W. Colson and Richard John Neuhaus, eds., *Evangelicals and Catholics Together: Toward a Common Mission* (Dallas: Word, 1995); D. H. Williams, *Retrieving the Tradition and Renewing Evangelicalism: A Primer for Suspicious Protestants* (Grand Rapids: Eerdmans, 1999).

[57]E.g., Braaten and Jenson, *Catholicity*; and Dulles, *Catholicity*.

[58]E.g., Carl E. Braaten, *Mother Church: Ecclesiology and Ecumenism* (Minneapolis: Fortress, 1998).

[59]E.g., Williams, *Retrieving the Tradition*.

[60]E.g., Cutsinger, ed., *Reclaiming the Great Tradition*.

[61]E.g., Oden, *Requiem*.

[62]E.g., H. P. Owen, *Christian Theism: A Study in its Basic Principles* (Edinburgh: T. & T. Clark, 1984); Alvin Plantinga, *Warranted Christian Belief* (New York: Oxford Univ. Press, 2000).

[63]E.g., Hartshorne, *Man's Vision of God*, 121.

[64]E.g., Ronald H. Nash, "Process Theology and Classical Theism," in *Process Theology*, ed. Nash, 3–29; Ogden, *The Reality of God*; Norman Pittenger, *Picturing God* (London: SCM, 1982). See also a positive use of the term "classical Christian belief" in Plantinga, *Warranted Christian Belief*, vii.

However, we should be clear that our agenda is ultimately not to defend a model per se. That would be essentially a modern/postmodern agenda. Rather, along with the other major figures of historic Christianity, we believe its model of God is the best representation of the God of the universe (the best *ektype* of the *archetype*), so our agenda is to commend *him* (and a deep, personal relationship with him), through the articulation of him that most corresponds to his nature, that of biblical and historical Christianity.

We are aware that there are some who will agree in large measure with the view of God defended in this book but will be uncomfortable with some of the terms listed above to designate this approach. Most controversial, perhaps, is the term *classical theism*, since it has been used to label specifically the theism of the early church or of Thomas Aquinas, both of which have been alleged to have been overly influenced by Greek thought (though see Bray's treatment of this allegation).[65] We recognize too that certain features of the God of classical theism have been questioned by contemporary members of the historic Christian tradition (e.g., his immutability and simplicity; see below, fn. 95). Nonetheless, the authors of this book maintain that there is far more overall continuity among those who adhere to historic Christian views of God, including those who subscribe wholly to the theology, say, of Thomas, than discontinuity, so that questions about such things as simplicity can legitimately be seen as "in-house."

Indeed, a purpose of this book is to underscore our overall continuity with the theologians of the early church and medieval periods regarding the doctrine of God. In particular, we believe that the emphasis on God's transcendence that was the hallmark of the patristic, medieval, and Reformation periods is largely warranted by Scripture. This does not mean that there can be no modifications or better articulations of this emphasis; it simply means that the understanding of God's transcendence (*and* relationality) as expressed by people such as Augustine and Aquinas was largely accurate. As a result, we embrace those who hold to "classical theism" and feel free to use the term to designate the broader movement of historic Christian theism, without necessarily subscribing to the precise understanding of all of God's attributes espoused by the church fathers or Aquinas.[66]

---

[65]E.g., Nash, "Process Theology and Classical Theism." Cf. also Hartshorne, *Man's Vision of God*, and Ogden, *The Reality of God*. See, however, Gerald L. Bray's treatment of this allegation in ch. 4, below ("Has the Christian Doctrine of God Been Corrupted by Greek Philosophy?").

[66]In the music of high culture in the West, the terms *classic/classical* have had two legitimate meanings. A distinction is made in symphonic and chamber music between the Classical period and classical music in general. Similarly, we may distinguish between the Classical *period* of Christian theism (beginning with the close of the canon to the dissolution of Roman culture and the beginning of the Middle Ages, also known as the patristic period) and the larger tradition of classical Christian theism (which, of course, includes the Classical period but embraces the medieval and Reformation/post-Reformation periods and more recent developments— Protestant, Catholic, and Orthodox—insofar as they are genuinely compatible with the classical tradition). Likewise, it is unnecessary to agree with every assertion of every early church father, scholastic, or Reformer in order to affirm the overall tradition within which they and we are a part.

GOD UNDER fire

So it is that the historic Christian tradition is a *living* tradition. By "living" we mean that it has been, is, and will continue to be characterized by intense, vigorous, intratradition dialogue.[67] According to MacIntyre, the vigor of an intellectual tradition is manifested in conflict.[68] Obviously, there cannot be conflict about *everything*, for to have a tradition, there must be some shared convictions that give the tradition its identity and coherence. Thus, a living tradition will engage in constructive dialogue about all sorts of secondary issues while it works simultaneously at shoring up its constituting assumptions, without which the tradition ceases to be. We believe that in spite of serious disagreements about many secondary matters (as will be evidenced in the diversity of this book!), throughout the last two thousand years there has existed substantial agreement within historic Christianity about its basic convictions—especially its understanding of God's nature, arguably its most foundational set of understandings. A summary of the essential teachings of historic Christianity regarding God's nature will be presented below.

Given the central importance of the doctrine of God to Christianity's self-understanding, we believe it is especially ominous when those particular constituting assumptions are under fire. Sadly, there are those today who want to continue to identify themselves in some sense with historic Christianity, yet who reject its core understandings of God. We question whether that can be done without implicitly moving away from that tradition. Unquestionably, considerations of the boundaries of a tradition require virtues such as patience, wisdom, humility, and charity.[69] To remain alive, a tradition must resist a petrified traditional*ism* that insists on an absolute conformity of *all* the beliefs of its members. For historic Christianity, this means that even God's nature as revealed in the Scripture must be a continual source of faithful questioning and loving examination.[70]

---

[67]Alasdair MacIntyre has described such tradition-activity, particularly in reference to the classical philosophical tradition during the Middle Ages; cf. his *After Virtue: A Study in Moral Theory*, 2d ed. (Notre Dame, Ind.: Univ. of Notre Dame Press, 1984), ch. 15; idem. *Three Rival Versions of Moral Inquiry: Encyclopaedia, Genealogy, and Tradition* (Notre Dame, Ind.: Univ. of Notre Dame Press, 1990), chs. 5, 6.

[68]MacIntyre, *After Virtue*, 222. "Traditions, when vital, embody continuities of conflict."

[69]Some members of a tradition pose problems for the tradition as a whole by departing significantly from it. Origen, for example, believed in the preexistence of souls and universal redemption, views which led to his condemnation at the Fifth Ecumenical Council in Constantinople in 513. Nevertheless, he is today reckoned as a member of the Great Tradition because of his significant theological contributions in matters judged orthodox, so that, in the judgment of the historic Church, on balance, his few explicitly unorthodox views were outweighed by his overall adherence to orthodox Christian belief. A dynamic tradition must make such boundary assessments, and, as the tradition continues to reflect on itself, these judgments may later be adjusted. It is also necessary to keep in mind that those in the early church did not have the benefit of subsequent centuries of reflection.

[70]Therefore, the editors are sympathetic to Grenz's call to focus on the center of the Christian faith rather than its boundaries (Stanley J. Grenz, *Renewing the Center* [Grand Rapids: Baker, 2000]). The present book raises questions about the orthodoxy of the alternative Christian theologies not for adiaphora, but because they are, in fact, rejecting central, defining features of the Christian tradition, core aspects of its historically agreed-upon doctrine of God.

Nevertheless, a living tradition must also pay attention to its tradition-defining assumptions (a set that itself must be open to examination[71]). At a certain point, a divergence from those assumptions constitutes a departure from the tradition and the formation of an alien tradition (albeit influenced by its origins). The unifying premise of this book is one of continuity: the triune God of the Bible is essentially the same as that described by the faithful in the early church, in the medieval church, and in the Bible-believing churches of the Reformation and post-Reformation eras, who is to be the object of our faith, worship, and love, today and forever.

### 3.1 What Is The Historic Christian Understanding Of God?

Over the centuries, Christian theologians have tried various ways of describing and categorizing God's characteristics or attributes. Some have distinguished God's "negative" (*via negativa*) attributes to deny imperfections of God on the one hand (e.g., "infinity"—not finite) and "positive" (*via positiva*) attributes to ascribe perfections to him on the other (e.g., "holiness").[72] Some have observed that God cannot share or "communicate" to creatures some of his characteristics (e.g., independence, eternality, immutability), labeling them God's "incommunicable" attributes. Characteristics that God does share (to some degree) with his image-bearers (e.g., knowledge, truth, love, etc.) are then called his "communicable" attributes.[73] Others have organized the attributes into similar two-category schemes such as immanent and transitive (i.e., what God is, in himself and in relation to the world), moral and nonmoral (or natural), and God's nature and character.[74]

---

[71]Of course, there is the rub. But a living tradition requires the inner composure to engage in such foundational dialogue without steering into either the shoals of unreflective dogmatism or an indistinct pluralism that would dissolve the tradition.

[72]See John Theodore Mueller, *Christian Dogmatics: A Handbook of Doctrinal Theology for Pastors, Teachers, and Laymen* (St. Louis: Concordia, 1955), 160–75; cf. Herman Bavinck, *The Doctrine of God*, trans. and ed. William Hendriksen (Grand Rapids: Eerdmans, 1951), 133–36; Stephen Charnock, *Discourses upon the Existence and Attributes of God*, 2 vols. in 1 (New York: Robert Carter & Brothers, 1873), 1:181–82; Oden, *The Living God*, 44–49.

[73]Bavinck, *The Doctrine of God*, 136–42; Louis Berkhof, *Systematic Theology*, 4th ed. (Grand Rapids: Eerdmans, 1941), 55–81; Wayne Grudem, *Systematic Theology: An Introduction to Biblical Doctrine* (Grand Rapids: Zondervan, 1994), 156–57; cf. Francis Turretin, *Institutes of Elenctic Theology*, 2 vols., ed. James T. Dennison, trans. George Musgrave Giger (Phillipsburg, N.J.: Presbyterian & Reformed, 1992) 1:191, 204, 206.

[74]William G. T. Shedd, *Dogmatic Theology*, 3 vols., reprint ed. (Grand Rapids: Zondervan, 1888–1894), 1:334–37; Bavinck, *The Doctrine of God*, 136–37; Berkhof, *Systematic Theology*, 55–56; Oden, *The Living God*, 52; and Robert L. Dabney, *Lectures in Systematic Theology*, reprint (Grand Rapids: Zondervan, 1972), 150–51. Millard J. Erickson modifies the moral and nonmoral by speaking of God's attributes of goodness and attributes of greatness; *Christian Theology*, 3 vols. in 1 (Grand Rapids: Baker, 1983, 1984, 1985), 267.

Oden (*The Living God*, 31, 50–52) distinguishes "a deepening sequence of four levels or layers or dimensions" of God's qualities. The first two layers describe God's *nature: essential* attributes focusing on the transcendent nature of God that he possessed logically prior to creation (53–66) and *relational* attributes focusing on the majesty of God that he exhibits in relation to his creation (66–82). The second two layers describe God's *character: interpersonal* attributes

GOD UNDER FIRE

Perhaps the most important distinction among God's attributes for our day is that between his transcendence and immanence. The God of historic Christianity has always been seen to have unlimited grandeur, radically distinct from the creation and beyond our ability to fully grasp, while simultaneously being present and immediately active throughout the universe, interacting with humanity in love, goodness, and righteousness (cf. Acts 17:24–28). Erickson distinguishes between attributes that refer to his *greatness* and those that describe his *goodness*.[75] God's goodness refers to his having moral purity, integrity, relationality, and love. God's greatness refers to his infinitude or unlimitedness (independence, eternality, freedom, omnipotence, omniscience, and omnipresence) and his unsurpassable consistency of being (spirituality, personhood, trinitarian unity, immutability, and sovereignty).

Regarding consistency, God is an unseen and immaterial *spirit* who is life itself (cf. John 4:24).[76] The Judeo-Christian God is not an impersonal force. The Bible portrays God as a *person* who has exhaustive self-consciousness, has created and sustains all things (including human persons), and freely chooses to interact with his human creatures (cf. Gen. 1–2; Ex. 20:1–17; Neh. 9:6; Isa. 48:13). Thus, God enters into friendship with human persons (e.g., with Abraham, James 2:23 and 2 Chr. 20:7; with Moses, Num. 12:8 and Deut. 34:10).[77] The Bible also presents God as one being (e.g., Deut. 6:4; 1 Tim. 2:5–6) and yet, particularly in the New Testament, as an individual plurality of three eternal and divine persons: Father, Son, and Holy Spirit (cf. Matt. 28:19; John 14:26; 15:26; 2 Cor. 13:14; 1 Peter 1:2). God is a threefold *unity*, labeled a "Trinity" by classical Christian theology.[78]

focusing on the freedom, personality, and will of God of which humans have limited analogous characteristics (83–97) and *moral* attributes focusing on the moral character of God (97–130). Oden sees his taxonomy as the "most satisfactory classification" of God's attributes since it encompasses many of the other ways of organizing them (52). Oden keenly senses his continuity with the early church fathers, scholastics, and Reformation theologians.

[75]Erickson, *Christian Theology*, 267. Of course we must not polarize these contrasts. God's greatness is good and his goodness is great.

[76]John Calvin, *Institutes of the Christian Religion*, 2 vols., ed. John T. McNeill, trans. Ford Lewis Battles (LCC; Philadelphia: Westminster, 1960), 1.13.1; Charnock, *Discourses*, 1:182–88; Bavinck, *The Doctrine of God*, 175–80; Charles Hodge, *Systematic Theology*, 3 vols. (Grand Rapids: Eerdmans, 1965), 1:376–80; Erickson, *Christian Theology*, 267–68; Oden, *The Living God*, 88–89; Grudem, *Systematic Theology*, 187–88.

[77]Carl F. H. Henry, *God, Revelation and Authority*, vol. 5: *God Who Stands and Stays: Part One*, reprint ed. (Wheaton, Ill.: Crossway, 1999), 141–56; Erickson, *Christian Theology*, 268–71; Oden, *The Living God*, 84–87; Robert Jenson, *Systematic Theology*, vol. 1: *The Triune God* (New York: Oxford Univ. Press, 1997), ch. 3, 116–24; Hans Urs von Balthasar, *Theo-Drama*, vol. 2: *The Dramatis Personae: Man in God* (San Francisco: Ignatius, 1990), 53–89.

[78]Augustine, "On the Trinity," in *Basic Writings of Saint Augustine*, ed. Whitney J. Oates, 2 vols. (New York: Random House, 1948), 2:667–878; Aquinas, *Summa Theologiae*, 1.Q11; Calvin, *Institutes*, 1.13.3, 6, 20; Bavinck, *The Doctrine of God*, 164–68; Mueller, *Christian Dogmatics*, 163; Oden, *The Living God*, 56–58; Grudem, *Systematic Theology*, 177–80; Thomas F. Torrance, *The Christian Doctrine of God: One Being Three Persons* (Edinburgh: T. & T. Clark, 1996); Eberhard Jungel, *God's Being Is in Becoming* (Grand Rapids: Eerdmans, 2001). The Council of Chalcedon in A.D. 451 settled on the language of describing God as one *substance* but three *persons*. See Millard J. Erickson, *Making Sense of the Trinity: Three Crucial Questions* (Grand Rapids: Baker, 2000).

God's greatness is such that he is *immutable* or unchanging in his existence, character, knowledge, morality, and purposes (Ps. 102:25–27; Heb. 6:13–20).[79] Furthermore, God is *sovereign* in his oversight of all things. He has a plan and works in and through all things to see that plan accomplished (Isa. 14:24–27; Eph. 1:11).[80]

The idea of God's sovereignty leads naturally to attributes that reveal his infinite or unlimited greatness. God is *independent* of all else and utterly free, unlimited in any way by things outside of himself (traditionally termed his *aseity*). He needs nothing outside himself for his existence or blessedness, for his being is self-sufficient, infinite fullness (Ps. 145:1–5; John 5:26; Rom. 11:33–36; Eph. 1:3–11).[81] God is also *eternal*, not subject to the limitations of time and death the way humans are, with the all-important exception of the incarnation of the Son of God (Deut. 32:40; Ps. 90:2–4; 93:2).[82]

God is free and has unlimited power and is able to do anything consistent with his nature. Thus, God is described as *omnipotent* (Isa. 45:7; Luke 18:27).[83] He is *all-wise* and *omniscient*. He knows what is best and has a true and exhaustive knowledge of all that is potential and actual, and of all reality past, present, and future. As such it is impossible for God to believe anything that is false or to have a mistaken understanding about anything past, present, or future (Ps. 145:3; Isa. 46:9–10; Heb.

[79]Augustine, *City of God*, in *Basic Writings*, 2:198; Aquinas, *Summa Theologiae*, 1.Q9; Charnock, *Discourses*, 1:318; Turretin, *Institutes*, 1:204–6; Karl Barth, *Church Dogmatics*, ed. G. W. Bromiley and T. F. Torrance, 4 vols. in 13 parts (Edinburgh: T. & T. Clark, 1957), 2/1:490–502; Mueller, *Christian Dogmatics*, 164; Erickson, *Christian Theology*, 278–79; Frame, *No Other God*, 161–78.

[80]Augustine, *City of God*, 2:68–70; Bonaventure, *Breviloquium* (St. Louis: Herder, 1947), 37–48; Aquinas, *Summa Contra Gentiles*, in *Basic Writings of Saint Thomas Aquinas*, ed. Anton C. Pegis, 2 vols. (New York: Random House, 1945), 2:113–45; Martin Luther, "Bondage of the Will," in *Martin Luther: Selections from His Writings* (Garden City, N.Y.: Doubleday, 1961), 180–87; Calvin, *Institutes*, 1.5.8; Turretin, *Institutes*, 1:250–53; Hodge, *Systematic Theology*, 1:440–41; Oden, *The Living God*, 270–89; D. A. Carson, *Divine Responsibility and Human Responsibility: Biblical Themes in Tension* (Grand Rapids: Baker, 1994).

[81]Bavinck, *The Doctrine of God*, 142–45; Barth, *Church Dogmatics*, 2/1:302ff.; A.W. Tozer, *The Knowledge of the Holy* (San Francisco: Harper, 1961), chs. 5, 6; Oden, *The Living God*, 54–56; Grudem, *Systematic Theology*, 160–63.

[82]Aquinas, *Summa Theologiae*, 1.Q10; Stephen Charnock, *The Existence and Attributes of God*, reprint ed. (Minneapolis: Klock & Klock, 1977), 69–97; Turretin, *Institutes*, 1:202–4; Bavinck, *The Doctrine of God*, 154–57; Barth, *Church Dogmatics*, 2/1:608–40; Mueller, *Christian Dogmatics*, 165; Erickson, *Christian Theology*, 274–75; Oden, *The Living God*, 61–64; John S. Feinberg, *No One Like Him: The Doctrine of God* (Wheaton, Ill.: Crossway, 2001), 375–436; Frame, *No Other God*, 143–60; William Lane Craig, *Time and Eternity: Exploring God's Relationship to Time* (Wheaton, Ill.: Crossway, 2001). Some classical writers prefer to think of God as "timeless," others that he is everlasting, and still others that he is simultaneously in every time ("omnitemporal"). Paul Helm presents the majority view, "divine timelessness," in ch. 5 of this volume: "Is God Bound by Time?" but other understandings are represented in this book.

[83]Aquinas, *Summa Theologiae*, 1.Q25; Charnock, *Existence*, 357–445; Turretin, *Institutes*, 1:244–50; Bavinck, *The Doctrine of God*, 241–45; Barth, *Church Dogmatics*, 2/1:522–607; Mueller, *Christian Dogmatics*, 173–74; Oden, *The Living God*, 75–81; Grudem, *Systematic Theology*, 216–18.

GOD UNDER FiRE

4:13).[84] God is also unlimited by the constraints of location and space. Thus, he is *omnipresent*; that is, God is fully conscious everywhere in the universe or, we might say, all things (and times!) are present to him simultaneously (1 Kings 8:27; Jer. 23:23–24).[85]

In the view of historic Christian theists, this God of unlimited greatness is also a God of absolute *goodness*. God is the maximal measure of all good things, including moral purity, integrity, and love. As for his *moral purity*, God is free of all evil. God's *holiness* is his utter uniqueness and transcendent untaintedness (Ex. 15:11). God's *righteousness* is the pure and right expression of his holy nature in word, thought, and deed, including his blameless and just treatment of others (Gen. 18:25) based on what they actually deserve (Ps. 58).[86]

God's *integrity* includes his *genuineness*, *veracity*, and *faithfulness*. He is genuine in that he is always true to himself and not duplicitous (though he and his ways are of necessity mysterious, so we must trust his integrity even when we may not see it in a given case). He has veracity in that he always tells the truth and neither knowingly nor unwittingly tells an untruth (Heb. 6:18; though this does not mean he is obliged to reveal everything). He is faithful in that he always proves true, always keeping his promises (Num. 23:19).[87]

God is also *love* (1 John 4:10, 16), a concept central to the ancient Trinitarian understanding of God. God exists in eternal, personal, loving communion in the Trinity, and the second person took on human nature, for love of the Father and humanity. In addition, the Scriptures make clear the transcendent, good God is deeply concerned with the affairs of human beings—their joys, suffering, and destiny—and engages with them for their good, challenging them, assisting them, thwarting them when he deems necessary, and responding to their prayers. These interpersonal interactions form the core of the drama of redemptive-history, the saga of God-human relations, of which God is the playwright and director, but in which he has also always been the main actor, even assuming a human role in the central Act in the person of Jesus Christ, for the sake of his glory and the salvation of the world.[88] God's unselfish concern for others shows itself in grace, mercy,

---

[84]Aquinas, *Summa Theologiae*, 1.Q14; Charnock, *Existence*, 181–260; Turretin, *Institutes*, 1:206–18; Bavinck, *The Doctrine of God*, 183–95; Barth, *Church Dogmatics*, 2/1:543–67; Mueller, *Christian Dogmatics*, 168–70; Erickson, *Christian Theology*, 275–76; Oden, *The Living God*, 69–74; see also ch. 6 below, "What Does God Know?" by William Lane Craig.

[85]Augustine, *The Confessions of Saint Augustine*, Books 1–10, trans. F. J. Sheed (New York: Sheed & Ward, 1942), Book 1; Aquinas, *Summa Theologiae*, 1.Q8; Charnock, *Existence*, 144–80; Turretin, *Institutes*, 1:196–201; Bavinck, *The Doctrine of God*, 157–64; Hodge, *Systematic Theology*, 1:380–85; Mueller, *Christian Dogmatics*, 165–67; Oden, *The Living God*, 67–69; Grudem, *Systematic Theology*, 173–77.

[86]Charnock, *Existence*, 446–657; Bavinck, *The Doctrine of God*, 209–23; Berkhof, *Systematic Theology*, 73–76; Barth, *Church Dogmatics*, 2/1:358–68, 375–406; Mueller, *Christian Dogmatics*, 172–73; Oden, *The Living God*, 97–110; Erickson, *Christian Theology*, 284–89.

[87]Aquinas, *Summa Theologiae*, 1.Q16; Dabney, *Lectures in Systematic Theology*, 171–72; Bavinck, *The Doctrine of God*, 199–202; Mueller, *Christian Dogmatics*, 173; Oden, *The Living God*, 114–16; Erickson, *Christian Theology*, 289–91.

[88]A study of classical Christian sermons down through the ages from Chrysostom to Spurgeon shows the universal assumption that the almighty God is thoroughly relational.

and patience (cf. Ps. 145:8–9).[89] God's grace is his love toward the undeserving, his mercy is his love toward those in distress, and his patience is his love shown in waiting for humans to repent (cf. Eph. 2:8–9; Tit. 3:3–5; 2 Peter 3:9).[90]

We might summarize the fullness of God's greatness and goodness as his *glory*. God's glory stems from and includes his perfection, blessedness, and supreme beauty.[91] His perfection consists in possessing all excellent qualities and lacking nothing good (Matt. 5:48).[92] God is blessed in that he is fully happy in himself and in all that reflects both his greatness and his goodness (1 Tim. 6:15).[93] "God's beauty is that attribute of God whereby he is the sum of all desirable qualities"[94] (cf. Ps. 27:4). God's glory consists of his perfect exemplification and enjoyment of goodness and in the undiminishable fullness of his greatness. This, then, is a necessarily brief (and thereby inadequate) summary of the good, great, glorious God of the Bible and of historic Christian theism.

## 3.2 Dynamic Dialogue About God's Nature

As should be obvious, there are many ways of thinking about God's attributes that are equally orthodox, so that any discussion of them is open to improvement. In fact, all human understanding of God is intrinsically incomplete and analogical, given our finitude and God's transcendence. As it is, we can only know God

---

Classical theologians could probably have historically done a better job describing God's immanence and relationality and their relation to transcendence. But in the main, historic Christian theism has always been marked by a striving for the biblical balance. Cf. recent treatments of these issues in Frame, *No Other God*, 49–56, 179–90; D. A. Carson: *How Long, O Lord? Reflections on Suffering and Evil* (Grand Rapids: Baker, 1990); idem, *The Difficult Doctrine of the Love of God* (Wheaton, Ill.: Crossway, 2000); Michael S. Horton, *Covenant and Eschatology: The Divine Drama* (Louisville: Westminster John Knox, 2002).

[89]Aquinas, *Summa Theologiae*, 1.Q20–21; Turretin, *Institutes*, 1:234–44; Bavinck, *The Doctrine of God*, 203–9; Oden, *The Living God*, 110–27.

[90]Erickson, *Christian Theology*, 294–97; cf. Hodge, *Systematic Theology*, 1:427–29; Barth, *Church Dogmatics*, 2/1:351–439; Mueller, *Christian Dogmatics*, 174–75. All three terms are used in 1 Tim. 1:13–16.

[91]Grudem (*Systematic Theology*, 218–21) lists perfection, blessedness, beauty, and glory as "summary" attributes and gives the caveat that God's glory is not really an attribute but is descriptive of the brilliance that surrounds God as an appropriate expression of his excellence (220–21). On God's glory, see Jonathan Edwards, "Dissertation on the End for Which God Created the World," in *The Works of Jonathan Edwards*, 2 vols. (Edinburgh: Banner of Truth, 1974), 1:94–121; Bavinck, *The Doctrine of God*, 248–51; Barth, *Church Dogmatics*, 2/1:640–77. Surely the most expansive and learned treatment of this subject was written by Hans Urs von Balthasar, *The Glory of the Lord: A Theological Aesthetics*, 7 vols., ed. Joseph Fessio and John Riches, trans. Erasmo Leiva-Merikakis (Edinburgh: T. & T. Clark, 1982).

[92]Grudem, *Systematic Theology*, 218; cf. Aquinas, *Summa Theologiae*, 1.Q4; Dabney, *Lectures in Systematic Theology*, 45; Bavinck, *The Doctrine of God*, 246–47; Berkhof, *Systematic Theology*, 60.

[93]Grudem, *Systematic Theology*, 218; cf. Aquinas, *Summa Theologiae*, 1.Q26; Bavinck, *The Doctrine of God*, 247–48; Oden, *The Living God*, 127–29.

[94]Grudem, *Systematic Theology*, 219; Augustine's works are filled with references to divine beauty. Cf. also Aquinas on the beatific vision, *Summa Theologiae*, 1.Q26; Jonathan Edwards, *On the Nature of True Virtue* (Ann Arbor: Univ. of Michigan Press, 1960); and esp. von Balthasar, *The Glory of the Lord: A Theological Aesthetics*.

GOD UNDER FIRE

to the extent that he has revealed himself to us (Matt. 11:27; see ch. 2 in this book), and he likely has features unknown to us (though necessarily consistent with what has been revealed).[95] In light of such considerations, classical theologians have spoken of God's incomprehensibility: God can be known truly, but he cannot be known exhaustively or comprehensively. This leads us to assume that some differences in our understandings of God will inevitably arise. As Bray comments in his discussion of John of Damascus's outline of divine attributes:

> If we want to rearrange the categories here and there, find other words to express what is meant, or conflate two or more words into a single umbrella idea, there is no real problem, since all we are doing is looking at the *form* in which the classical teaching was expressed. Tidying things up in this way is an age-old practice, and in fact it is what John himself thought he was doing. It is only when our thoughts turn to matters of *substance* that real problems arise.[96]

So what we know of God can always be improved upon. Thus, there has often been serious dialogue in the Christian community regarding God's attributes. A few examples will illustrate. Historic Christian theism has always held that God knows the future exhaustively, but within the tradition there has been debate about *how* God knows the future (e.g., simple foreknowledge, foreknowledge from fore-ordination, or "middle knowledge"). Aquinas and his followers taught that God is fundamentally a "simple" being—that is, God has absolutely no parts—and have seen this to be a fundamental attribute; others in historic Christianity, especially in recent years, have questioned the legitimacy of ascribing simplicity to God at all.[97] Similarly, some have seriously questioned the notion of God's immutability, particularly God's emotional unchangeableness or his impassability (lit., "inability to suffer").[98]

As mentioned above, MacIntyre suggested that a living tradition is characterized by a vigorous dialogue about a subset of issues conducted within a paradigm about which there is essential agreement. Historic Christian theists are united in their *overall* understanding of the divine attributes as broadly sketched above. However, there remains much disagreement at a secondary level about the

---

[95]Erickson, *Christian Theology*, 266; Oden, *The Living God*, 52; Henry, *God, Revelation and Authority*, 5:139–40.

[96]Gerald L. Bray, *Doctrine of God* (Contours of Christian Theology; Downers Grove, Ill.: InterVarsity Press, 1993), 102.

[97]Eleonore Stump, "Simplicity," in *A Companion to Philosophy of Religion*, ed. P. L. Quinn and C. Taliaferro (London: Blackwell, 1997), 250. Though taught by Aquinas (*Summa Theologiae*, 1.Q3), divine simplicity was not embraced by the early Reformers and has been questioned by those inside and outside of historic Christian theism in the twentieth century. Cf. Alvin Plantinga, *Does God Have a Nature?* (Milwaukee: Marquette Univ. Press, 1980); Nicholas Wolterstorff, "Divine Simplicity," in *Our Knowledge of God*, ed. Kelly J. Clark (Dordrecht: Kluwer, 1992), 133–49; Nash, *The Concept of God*, 85–97.

[98]Nash, *The Concept of God*; Frame, *No Other God*, 161–78; Bruce A. Ware, "An Evangelical Reformulation of the Doctrine of the Immutability of God," *JETS* 29 (1986): 431–46; idem, *God's Lesser Glory*.

proper understanding and implications of some of God's attributes. This should be welcomed.

This volume contributes to the dialogue by including chapters on several attributes that are currently being debated within (as well as outside) historic Christian theism (e.g., Helm on God's eternality, ch. 5; Craig on divine fore-knowledge, ch. 6; Spiegel on God's sovereignty, ch. 8; Lee on divine impassability, ch. 9; and Gutenson on immutability, ch. 10). These chapters defend specific views that would not be shared by all historic Christian theists.

Nevertheless, we intentionally include this diversity for several reasons. (1) The positions presented are genuinely representative of subtraditions within the historic Christian tradition. (2) They show how different orthodox Christian theists are responding to contemporary challenges to the historical Christian understanding of God. (3) While disputing with those who are outside the Tradition (or are moving away from it), it helps to underscore that the Tradition has never been so monolithic that there was not room for ongoing discussion on secondary matters. Classical theism would be sterile and destitute if it could not benefit from self-criticism (and from listening to its external critics). But as we suggested above, the *central* features of a tradition cannot be subjected to radical criticism without overthrowing the tradition itself. All of this has led to our conclusion that the very essence of Christianity is at stake in the contemporary attacks on the God of historic Christian theism outlined above.

## 3.3 A Diagram of Christian Theologies

We have distinguished three major, contemporary theological paradigms that all claim to be Christian. These paradigms, however, are not mutually exclusive. There is a certain amount of conceptual overlap with these categories of thought. Just as there are continuums of belief within each of the theological paradigms, there are continuums between the paradigms as well, as is illustrated in the diagram below.

The authors of this book believe that historic Christian theism is essentially synonymous with Trinitarian theism, the historic Christian view that sees God as the triune Creator and Redeemer, transcendent and absolutely self-sufficient, yet immanent and relational. As we have seen, Constructivism and Developmental theism offer the major theological options to classical Christian theism in the West today. The diagram attempts to portray how these general orientations regarding God can influence each other.

The variance of a pure Constructivist or Developmentalist theology from historic Christianity is fairly obvious. Far more problematic are the subtle syntheses of these paradigms coming out of certain Christian church bodies, colleges, seminaries, agencies, publishing houses, and journals. While claiming various degrees of allegiance to historic Christianity, the actual commitment of particular individuals (and institutions) to genuine Trinitarian theism is evidenced, we think, by the extent to which they are accommodating Christian truth to its primary religious competitors in our day. As contemporary orthodox Christians strive to avoid

## Relationships Between Various Christian Views

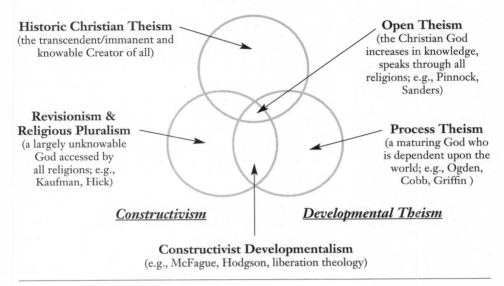

### *Trinitarian Theism*

**Historic Christian Theism**
(the transcendent/immanent and
knowable Creator of all)

**Open Theism**
(the Christian God
increases in knowledge,
speaks through all
religions; e.g., Pinnock,
Sanders)

**Revisionism &
Religious Pluralism**
(a largely unknowable
God accessed by
all religions; e.g.,
Kaufman, Hick )

**Process Theism**
(a maturing God who
is dependent upon the
world; e.g., Ogden,
Cobb, Griffin )

*Constructivism*           *Developmental Theism*

**Constructivist Developmentalism**
(e.g., McFague, Hodgson, liberation theology)

the anti-intellectualism, moral rigidity, arrogance, and cultural irrelevance of twentieth-century fundamentalism, we must not forget the lessons of the past 150 years and fall into the opposite, but very real, danger of a potentially heretical syncretism.

## 4. What Does This Book Hope to Do?

As suggested in the opening paragraphs, American culture is undergoing some sort of religious revival in our day. While at first Christians might have been encouraged by this new openness to the supernatural, it is becoming clear that a different deity has been brought in as a replacement for the God of historic Christianity. At the same time, the church must make every effort to capitalize on this period of reexamination of religion and testify concerning the nature of its God, the true Lord of the universe.

There is every reason to hope that God may be preparing America for a genuine revival of supernatural Christianity. This book sets out to provide a corrective to the major alternative Christian versions of God being offered in our day and to present, as best we can, the God of the Bible and of historic Christianity: at once the most beautiful and attractive Being in the universe, yet also the most awesome, even terrifying; a God who is supremely relational and supremely sovereign, the absolutely transcendent lover of our souls.

As should be obvious by now, the book will not be defending the views of any particular group within historic Christian theism but is advocating for "the salvation we share . . . the faith that was once for all entrusted to the saints" (Jude 3). So the book includes a diverse group of authors from a variety of ecclesiastical communities within the Great Tradition of classic Christianity, including Anglican, Baptist, Evangelical Free, Methodist, Missionary Church, Presbyterian, and Roman Catholic. As the reader will quickly see, the authors unavoidably argue from within their particular subtraditions. One result is that the book itself shows the curiosity, vibrancy, and health of historic Christianity in the present. Most noticeable are the significant differences among some of the contributors regarding just precisely how to make sense of God's interactive relationship with his human creatures. Nevertheless, this diverse group of authors shares a common allegiance to the classic understanding of the loving and transcendent God of historic Christianity.

The first section of the book deals with foundational issues: the role of Scripture and human reason in knowing God and the historical origins of classical Christianity. Mark R. Talbot begins the volume with "Does God Reveal Who He Actually Is?" by grounding human discourse about God in the Hebrew and Christian Scriptures and arguing for their adequacy as a sufficiently clear revelation of his nature, making possible confidence in the singular validity of the historic Christian understanding of God (as well as our ability to accurately interpret scriptural texts).

Eric L. Johnson responds to the question, "Can God Be Grasped by Our Reason?" Johnson affirms the realism of orthodox Christianity and the necessity of logic for knowing anything about God, but he maintains that the finite capacities of human reason cannot be allowed to determine what we think God's nature is or to legitimate the reinterpretation of some Scripture that appears to contradict other "preferred" Scripture.

In the following chapter, "Has the Christian Doctrine of God Been Corrupted by Greek Philosophy?" Anglican theologian Gerald L. Bray delves into the historical origins of classical Christianity to show that the early church cannot be accurately characterized as simply synthesizing Greek and Roman thought with biblical teaching, as some critics of classical Christianity have argued. Rather, though undoubtedly influenced by their intellectual climate, the early church leaders decisively challenged the fundamental assumptions and thinking of pagan thought and profoundly reoriented Western intellectual life toward the revelation of God.

The bulk of the book focuses on specific attributes of the God of historic Christianity that are under attack in our day. In chapter 5, "Is God Bound by Time?" Reformed philosopher Paul Helm offers a fresh articulation of the majority view within the classical tradition of God's relation to temporality, the view that God transcends time and exists outside it.

William Lane Craig next deals with God's knowledge of the future in "What Does God Know?" Many Developmentalist theologians have suggested that human freedom is impossible if God knows the future. While approaching God's relation to time from within a Molinist framework, Craig shows that, by any approach, when divine foreknowledge is understood as merely knowledge about true future events (rather than a "looking ahead" model), it is perfectly compatible with future free actions.

In Chapter 7, "How Do We Reconcile the Existence of God and Suffering?" R. Douglas Geivett deals with what is alleged to be the greatest threat to classic Christian theism and one of the main reasons that some Christians have resorted to alternative theologies: the problem of evil and God's relation to it. Against the approaches of liberation theology, process theology, and open theism, Geivett argues that we can logically know that God can have morally sufficient reasons for allowing evil without our knowing exactly what those reasons may be.

Examining the problem of evil from another angle, Reformed philosopher James Spiegel addresses more directly God's role in human activity in "Does God Take Risks?" Defending a "strong view" of divine providence, Spiegel exposes some of the exegetical, theological, and philosophical mistakes inherent in the view of God as being a "risk-taker."

Next, Roman Catholic philosopher Patrick Lee discusses the nature of God's passions in chapter 9, "Does God Have Emotions?" Affirming (with Augustine and Aquinas) that God's eternal bliss cannot be undermined by anything in his creation, Lee nevertheless offers two ways one can rationally affirm that God is emotionally affected by human actions and yet deny that he is fundamentally changed or perfected by anything in his creation.

From a Wesleyan perspective, Chuck Gutenson answers a related question in "Does God Change?" Gutenson argues that the early church fathers maintained a complex, nuanced view of God's nature as unchanging *and* relational, and he goes on to show how one can hold to God's immutable will, knowledge, and character in a way that takes seriously God's relationality and responsiveness to his image-bearers.

In chapter 11, "How Shall We Think About the Trinity?" Baptist theologian Bruce A. Ware defends the classical understanding of God as Trinity against the significant modifications being attempted by inclusivists and feminists. He also contributes to the contemporary dialogue on the Trinity by arguing for the ontological priority of the immanent Trinity and for a special kind of hierarchy within a Trinity of fully equal persons.

D. A. Carson finishes off the book by answering the question, "How Can We Reconcile the Love and the Transcendent Sovereignty of God?" From Scripture Carson shows that God is loving in five different but related ways, and, using open theism as his foil, he proceeds to make clear the deep, underlying compatibility of this truth with the revelation that God is the eternal, immutable, future-knowing, sovereign Lord of the universe.

We hope this book helps you to understand, worship, and love this God better, that is, the God of the Bible and of historic Christianity.

Chapter 2

# Does God Reveal Who He Actually Is?

*Mark R. Talbot*

# 1. Introduction

Christians have always acknowledged that God cannot be seen (John 1:18) and that he dwells in unapproachable light (1 Tim. 6:16). Yet they have also insisted that he has revealed himself to us in several ways—by means of creation and conscience (Acts 14:15–17; Rom. 1:18–20; 2:1–16), in Hebrew history and prophecy (Gen. 12:1–3 with Acts 7:2–3; Ex. 3:1–6 with Acts 7:30–32; Joel 1:1), and supremely through the life, death, and resurrection of his Son, Jesus Christ (Heb. 1:1–2; John 1:18; 14:5–10). These revelations are corroborated by and preserved for us in the Hebrew/Christian Scriptures.

Classical Christian theism finds its proper grounding in careful reflection on God's revelation of himself in Scripture. Often, our acceptance of historic Christian theism depends on our acceptance of Christianity's historic view of the Scriptures. Christians have traditionally taken the Bible as the supreme and final authority for all of their thinking, evaluating, and acting because they have recognized that it presents itself as God's written Word, where each and every word is to be acknowledged to be a word from God and where all of those words together make up a corpus of texts that are to be wholly believed, welcomed, and obeyed.

Ultimately, then, doubts about the God of classical Christian theism are often doubts about this view of the Scriptures. In some cases, these doubts are expressed openly (e.g., self-described "Christian" theological Constructivists such as Gordon Kaufman and Sallie McFague condemn the historic view as "fundamentalism"[1]). But at other times, doubts relating to the historic reliability of the Scriptures are less direct and most subtle. As the subtitle of *The Openness of God* indicates ("A Biblical Challenge to the Traditional Understanding of God"), some writers accuse classical Christian theism of departing from the Scriptures. But, as I will try to show, many if not all open theists are actually moving away from the historic Christian view of Scripture in clearly identifiable ways.

I aim, then, to defend the historic Christian view of the Scriptures against theological Constructivism's doubts about Scripture's credibility and authority as well as against what I will show to be open theism's doubts about Scripture's perfect errorlessness and fundamental self-consistency. In the process, I hope to make it clear that these sorts of doubts about the Bible's truthfulness and disagreements

---

[1]For McFague's view, see below. Kaufman's view is expressed in Gordon D. Kaufman, *In Face of Mystery: A Constructive Theology* (Cambridge, Mass.: Harvard Univ. Press, 1993), 55, 131, etc.

GOD UNDER FIRE

about how it should be interpreted are the primary reason historic Christian theism is being abandoned today. Addressing these doubts and disagreements is, then, crucial to the task of defending classical Christian theism.

## 2. From Human Speculation and General Revelation to Special Revelation

Suppose you want to answer some specific question. How will you proceed? That depends on *what* you want to know and *how* it can be known. For instance, "Where is Kenya?" can be answered by consulting an encyclopedia, looking at a globe, or asking someone who knows. Answering "Did I leave the bedroom light on?" usually requires going to the room to see or asking someone else to go. Consulting an encyclopedia or looking at a globe won't help.

"What is 12 x 12?" can be answered from memory (if you learned your multiplication tables) or by looking at a multiplication table, working out the answer on paper, using a calculator, counting out twelve rows of twelve sticks and then counting through them all, or (again) by asking someone who knows. It cannot be answered by looking at a globe. We ask "What are you thinking?" only of persons—and only the person who is being asked can answer it. We may guess, but we won't know for certain unless we are told. Consulting encyclopedias, looking at globes, going to another room, or trying to work out the answer on paper aren't good ways to answer this question.

Our primary question is, What is God like? That is *what* we want to know. Let us assume for the moment that it is possible to know some significant things about God. Yet still we must ask, *How* can we know them? Our answer to this question depends on the *kind* of being we think God is. Christians believe God is *transcendent*, existing outside our world of space and time (1 Kings 8:27; Ps. 90:2). As *spirit*, he doesn't exist in any particular location (John 4:20–24). He is not much like a country or a bedroom light. So we can't answer questions about him by just going somewhere or looking at a globe.

Such a God is clearly beyond the reach of our external senses; under normal circumstances, he can't be seen, heard, tasted, touched, or smelled. But is he completely beyond the reach of our minds? Answering some questions about him may not be entirely unlike answering "What is 12 x 12?" Perhaps we can discover that God possesses certain attributes—say, omnipotence and omniscience—just by thinking hard about what any transcendent spirit that ought to be called "God" would have to be like.[2]

Yet if God is also *personal*, then he has an "inner" life of thoughts, feelings, desires, and plans of his own. This means that not every question we can have about him—or even some of the most important ones for us, such as "What has God planned for human beings?"—can be answered by just thinking hard about what the answer must be (Isa. 55:6–9; Rom. 11:33–34). We can only know for sure what God is thinking or feeling or desiring or planning if he tells us. *He* must be willing to bridge what is *for us* an unbridgeable gap (1 Cor. 2:9–12).

---

[2]See, e.g., J. N. Findlay, "Can God's Existence be Disproved?" *Mind* 57 (1948): 176–83.

Almost any question can be answered by someone just telling us what the answer is. This is often the quickest and surest way to get an answer, even if we could discover it for ourselves. If God is transcendent personal spirit, then even if we can discover on our own that he possesses certain attributes, there is nothing to preclude his revealing to us that he possesses those attributes. And some of our questions about him won't get answered unless he tells us what the answers are.

*Revelation* involves the unveiling or disclosure of something "so that it may be seen or known for what it is."[3] The Bible characterizes God as one who "reveals his thoughts to man" (Amos 4:13). In Christianity, one form of revelation involves God simply telling us what we should know (2 Tim. 3:16; Heb. 1:1; 2 Peter 1:21). If this is true, then it is the quickest and surest way for us to answer some of our questions about God and his purposes for human beings. So it is only natural that we start by asking: "Does God reveal who he actually is?"

## 2.1 Conflicting Claims of Revelation

Many cultures have hoped for revelation,[4] and claims to revelation ground many religions. Muslims revere the Qur'an, in its original Arabic, as God's very words; and most Hindus recognize *sabda* ("transcendental testimony, i.e., revelation") as a source of knowledge.[5]

---

[3]"The Eng. word 'reveal', from Lat. *revelo*, is the regular rendering of the Heb. *gâlâ* and the Gk. *apokalyptô*... which corresponds to *gâlâ* in the LXX and NT. *gâlâ*, *apokalyptô* and *revelo* all express the same idea—that of unveiling something hidden, so that it may be seen and known for what it is" (J. I. Packer, "Revelation," in *New Bible Dictionary*, ed. I. Howard Marshall, A. R. Millard, J. I. Packer, and D. J. Wiseman, 3d ed. [Downers Grove, Ill.: InterVarsity Press, 1996], 1014).

Nicholas Wolterstorff has argued that Scripture is more adequately understood as *discourse* than as *revelation*, since God does more in Scripture than just reveal truths. To say that God *speaks* through Scripture is to acknowledge that God may do things such as *make promises* or *issue commands* in it. He may also aim to *affect us emotionally* through Scripture's words. The fundamental category for understanding Scripture is, then, *speech-act theory* rather than revelation. I think Wolterstorff is right, since this takes nothing away from the claim that God reveals truths in Scripture, but it acknowledges that God does more in Scripture than just that. See Nicholas Wolterstorff, *Divine Discourse: Philosophical Reflections on the Claim That God Speaks* (New York: Cambridge Univ. Press, 1995).

[4]For instance, Plato (*Phaedo*, 85c-d, in Edith Hamilton and Huntington Cairns, eds., *The Collected Dialogues of Plato, Including the Letters* [Princeton, N.J.: Princeton Univ. Press, 1961], 68), in relating a discussion about personal immortality that supposedly took place on the day Socrates was executed, has Simmias say:

I think, just as you do, Socrates, that although it is very difficult if not impossible in this life to achieve certainty about these questions, at the same time it is utterly feeble not to use every effort in testing the available theories, or to leave off before we have considered them in every way, and come to the end of our resources. It is our duty to do one of two things, either to ascertain the facts, whether by seeking instruction or by personal discovery, or, if this is impossible, to select the best and most dependable theory which human intelligence can supply, and use it as a raft to ride the seas of life—that is, assuming that we cannot make our journey with greater confidence and security by the surer means of a divine revelation.

[5]Ninian Smart, "Hinduism," in *A Companion to Philosophy of Religion*, ed. Philip L. Quinn and Charles Taliaferro (Cambridge, Mass.: Blackwell, 1997), 12.

Yet some claims to revelation conflict. The personal Yahweh of the Hebrew Scriptures is very different from the impersonal Brahman of classic Hindu Upanishadic thought. The unending cycles of existence in Theravada Buddhism contrast sharply with the Islamic Day of Judgment, which marks the end of the earth's history and the assignation of each of Allah's creatures either to paradise or hell. In other words, while having someone answer our questions is a quick way to get answers, it is also an easy way to get wrong ones. Usually, if two people give us conflicting answers to the same question, we assume that at least one of those answers is false. So conflicting claims to revelation can cause us to wonder if any of those claims is true.

Some religious skeptics take this conflict as good reason to reject all of the claims. They assume that if we ask the same question of several different people and they all disagree about what the answer is, then there is no reason to believe any of them. Sometimes they add that if God exists and we are obliged to worship and obey him, then he ought to make his existence and his requirements utterly plain. Conflicting claims are then taken as reason to doubt God's existence or goodness.

But the mere fact that we have several different answers to the same question does not imply that one of those answers isn't true, even if it accentuates the issues of how we might know which answer is true and why everyone's answer isn't the same. Yet raising these issues is not equivalent to showing that there are no satisfactory resolutions to them. How historic Christians resolve them will become clear as we proceed.

Radical religious pluralists take a different tack. They start from the conviction that religions express the cultures from which they come. Consequently, different cultures will express religious matters differently. Yet we have no reason to think any culture is significantly better than the rest; indeed, we are morally obliged to value each more or less equally. So we must take each culture's religion equally seriously, recognizing that "no religion can advance any legitimate claim to superiority over any other."[6]

Every religion makes truth-claims. So must we accept the truth-claims of all religions? But how can we do that, if they conflict? Here, as our editors note in their introduction, radical religious pluralism shows itself to be a species of theological Constructivism. Theological Constructivists doubt that we can have much real knowledge of God. Most of our religious claims are just shots in the dark. We can't get at the supersensible reality to which they supposedly refer, and so we can't corroborate their truth or their falsity. Yet religion still does things. Its "God" symbol, as an imaginative construct, transmits important social values and, if properly disciplined, can humanize us.[7] And practicing religion

---

[6]D. A. Carson, *The Gagging of God: Christianity Confronts Pluralism* (Grand Rapids: Zondervan, 1996), 26. This is not Carson's own position.

[7]This is Gordon Kaufman's view in his *In Face of Mystery*.

"de-centers" us—it saves us from our natural self-centeredness by moving us towards reality-centeredness.[8] In other words, religion has *social* and *salvific* value, even if it lacks ultimate truth value. Its value lies more in what it *does* to shape the "reality" in which we live than in what it *claims* about reality.[9]

But this kind of pluralism is an abstraction that flies in the face of the world's actual, historical religions. Those religions invariably make exclusivistic truth-claims.[10] Not all of them distinguish between their adherents and others in a way that places the latter outside the hope of salvation. The Indus Valley religions, for example, are generally slow to condemn doctrinal and cultic diversity. Yet even they differ from each other precisely because, for instance, Hindus and Buddhists have different beliefs and practices. Most of the world's actual, historical religions probably could not survive an attempt to mute their exclusivistic claims. Indeed, don't these pluralists contradict themselves by encouraging us to accept each religion more or less as it is, even as they urge each of them to surrender its conviction that it is uniquely correct?[11]

Moreover, the social and salvific power of a religion in a person's life seems to be closely linked to how sure that person is of its truth. If I am unsure whether "there is no God but Allah, and Muhammad is his Prophet," then I am not likely to obey what the Qur'an says about the necessity of giving alms to relieve the poor, slaves, debtors, defenders of Islam, and travelers. My giving may also be affected by whether I really believe that giving alms not only benefits others but purifies what remains for me and increases God's gen-

---

[8]This is John Hick's claim. See his *An Interpretation of Religion: Human Responses to the Transcendent* (New Haven, Conn.: Yale Univ. Press, 1989), 300: "The function of post-axial religion is to create contexts within which the transformation of human existence from self-centredness to Reality-centredness can take place." Post-axial religion, as Hick characterizes it, is primarily concerned with the quest for salvation or liberation. So it is *salvifically* oriented. In this book, Hick is careful to say that *not* all religions are of equal value and that their value must be measured soteriologically: "Religious traditions and their various components—beliefs, modes of experience, scriptures, rituals, disciplines, ethics and lifestyles, social rules and organisations—have greater or less value according as they promote or hinder the salvific transformation" (p. 300).

[9]See Hick, *An Interpretation of Religion*, chap. 20.

[10]Most religious pluralists concede this. For instance, Hick (*An Interpretation of Religion*, 2) says:

each tradition . . . has come over the centuries to regard itself as uniquely superior to the others, seeing them either as lying outside the sphere of salvation, or as earlier stages in an evolution of which it is the culmination, or as less full and authentic versions of itself.

[11]Hick raises this objection to his own project in the article on "Religious Pluralism" in *A Companion to Philosophy of Religion*, 613:

One of the main critical questions about this [kind of religious pluralism] is whether, in reducing the distinctive belief-systems of the different religions from absolute truths to reports of one human perception amongst others of the divine reality, it does not contradict the cherished self-understanding of each. Is it not inherently revisionary rather than purely descriptive?

god under fire

erosity to me because he considers it like a loan to himself that he will doubly repay.[12]

In fact, no one, not even the most diehard theological Constructivist, rides as loose on his or her own religious commitments as radical religious pluralism requires. Radical religious pluralists *sound* skeptical about religious knowledge until their own convictions are challenged. For example, they find the belief that "God has created vast numbers of people whom God knows will forfeit salvation" abominable, and so they vociferously oppose it.[13] In other words, they are so sure that this belief is false that their skepticism falters. Radical religious pluralists *seem* universally tolerant until their standard of universal tolerance is challenged. They then become implacably intolerant of intolerance—even as they are almost always vocally intolerant of the patriarchalism, imperialism, and triumphalism that they claim to find in most of the world's historic religions. Radical religious pluralism is unlivable.

These difficulties with religious skepticism and radical religious pluralism mean that we do not need to respond skeptically or pluralistically to conflicting claims to revelation. We can still maintain that, where religions differ, one of them may be right and the others wrong.

## 2.2 The Supremacy of Christian Revelation

This book naturally focuses on Christian claims to revelation. But must we not first address one more absolutely crucial question, namely, Why take Christianity, of all the world's religions, to be the true one? Are there good reasons to trust Christianity's claims to revelation over similar claims in other religions? Christians have often claimed that the miracles Scripture reports as having accompanied the gospel's first proclamation are sure signs of its truth (Mark 16:20; Acts 2:22; 14:3; Heb. 2:1–4). Yet other religions cite their own miracle claims in support of their own revelational claims. David Hume turned this clash of claims into an argument for distrusting all of them,[14] and many of our contemporaries accept his argument. Thus, the claim that Christianity ought to be trusted because God has miraculously corroborated its truth needs more defense. Yet attempting that defense here would take us far afield from our main task.[15]

---

[12]See Frederick M. Denny, "*Zakât*," in *Abingdon Dictionary of Living Religions*, ed. Keith Crim, Roger A. Bullard, and Larry D. Shinn (Nashville: Abingdon, 1981), 820. *Zakât*—or the giving of alms—is one of the five "Pillars of Islam"—that is, one of the fundamental ritual requirements that are its acts of service or worship.

[13]See Hick, "Religious Pluralism," 610.

[14]See David Hume, *An Enquiry Concerning Human Understanding*, sec. X.

[15]For such a defense, see R. Douglas Geivett and Gary R. Habermas, eds., *In Defense of Miracles: A Comprehensive Case for God's Action in History* (Downers Grove, Ill.: InterVarsity Press, 1997). Biblical Christianity has always recognized that miracles alone are inadequate to convince everyone of its truth (see Luke 16:30–31) and, indeed, that some demands for miraculous confirmation of the Christian message are signs of unbelief (see Matt. 12:38–39; 1 Cor. 1:22–23).

Some religions claim that any careful examination of their teachings will establish their truth. For example, Islam claims that "the absolute truth it espouses can theoretically be recognized and embraced by any perceptive human being."[16] Mahayana Buddhism goes even further, claiming in its *Lotus Sutra* that anyone who has heard the Buddha's teachings and either worshiped an image of him or made a *stupa* (a commemorative monument and reliquary) will become enlightened.[17]

Does Christianity make similar claims? Can we hope, as we proceed, that if historic Christian theism is true, then its truth will become apparent to everyone? No, for while Christianity claims that the truths that Christians believe by revelation constitute a kind of *knowledge* (John 6:69; Tit. 1:1; 1 John 5:18–20), it also maintains that this kind of knowledge, along with the heartfelt repentance that always accompanies it, must be granted to us by God's grace (Acts 11:18; Phil. 1:29; 2 Tim. 2:25).

This does not mean that there are no good reasons to trust Christianity's claims to revelation over similar claims. But it implies that these reasons may not affect everyone as they should. Part of the subtlety of the Christian revelation is that it explains why this is.

So what do Christians believe about the Christian revelation? Revelation unveils or discloses something "so that it may be seen or known for what it is." Some revelations are *verbal*, either spoken or written. But we may reveal things in other ways. For instance, I may *manifest* my anger without saying a word.

The Bible represents God as having revealed something of himself and his purposes to human beings in each of these ways. Sometimes God has *spoken* to us, either directly (Gen. 2:16–17; Ex. 20:1; Matt. 3:17) or through angelic or human intermediaries (Deut. 18:18; Luke 1:26–38; 2 Cor. 2:17). Sometimes he has communicated through *writing*, usually by prompting others to record his thoughts (Ex. 24:4; Jer. 30:1–2; 1 Cor. 14:36–38; 2 Tim. 3:16). And sometimes he simply *manifests* himself nonverbally (Acts 14:15–17; Rom. 1:18–20).

God *manifests* his existence, his glory as the world's Creator (Ps. 19:1–4; Rom. 1:18–20), his providential kindness (Acts 14:16–18; cf. Ps. 145:9, 17 [RSV]), and his moral requirements (Ps. 97:6; Rom. 1:32; 2:12–15) through *general revelation*. Paul declares that God "has made it plain" to everyone, everywhere, that he exists and that he ought to be glorified, thanked, and obeyed (Rom. 1:19). Ever since he created the world, God's "invisible qualities"—his "eternal power and divine nature"—have been "clearly seen" through what he has made (Rom. 1:20).

By manifesting certain truths about God, general revelation gives us some real although limited knowledge of him. Some knowledge of who God actually is—notably, that he "is powerful and that he possesses those properties normally associated with deity"[18]—is not merely available to everyone; it is pressed upon us all by God himself. God never leaves himself without a witness (Acts 14:17).

---

[16]Bruce B. Lawrence, "Islam," in *Abingdon Dictionary of Living Religions*, 346.
[17]See Kenneth K. S. Ch'en, "Buddhism," in *Abingdon Dictionary of Living Religions*, 129.
[18]Douglas J. Moo, *The Epistle to the Romans* (Grand Rapids: Eerdmans, 1996), 104. Moo is glossing the phrase "eternal power and divine nature" found at Rom. 1:20.

Consequently, we sin—indeed, we stand before God "without excuse" (Rom. 1:20)—when we do not adequately glorify, thank, and obey him.[19]

But God also *verbally communicates* more of himself and his purposes to particular people at specific times and places through *special revelation* (Heb. 1:1–2; 1 Peter 1:10–12; cf. Acts 2:14–36). Just as I may tell my children and friends things that I tell to no one else, so God shares some things only with those whom he chooses to be his "children" and "friends."[20] Christian faith is grounded in the belief that God specially revealed himself and his saving purposes to the biblical patriarch Abraham (Gen. 12:1–25:11; Luke 1:68–75; Rom. 4). A whole series of special revelations to the Old Testament prophets followed (Deut. 18:18–19; Jer. 1:9; Heb. 1:1), culminating in God's disclosure to his New Testament apostles of the *mystērion*—or "secret"—of what he has done, is doing, and will yet do through the work of his Son, Jesus Christ (Mark 4:11–12; Col. 1:25–27; 1 Tim. 3:16).[21] These apostles have then proclaimed this Good News to other human beings. And it is only by believing this proclamation that we can be saved from our sin (Rom. 10:13–15, 17).

This special verbal revelation is "the word of God in its fullness" (Col. 1:25). We are born again into a living hope and an imperishable inheritance through believing it (2 Thess. 2:13; 1 Peter 1:3–5). As it is now written in the New Testament (2 Peter 3:14–18), this word is able to "make [us] wise for salvation through faith in Christ Jesus" (2 Tim. 3:15). So Scripture, as the written record of God's past communications, remains the primary vehicle for his present communication (2 Peter 1:19). As Carl F. H. Henry neatly put it, through Scripture "God heralds his unchanging truth to [human beings] once for all and ongoingly."[22]

---

[19]See Thomas C. Oden, "Without Excuse: Classic Christian Exegesis of General Revelation," *JETS* 41 (1998): 55–68.

[20]See Ex. 33:11; John 1:12–13; 15:13–16; Rom. 8:15–16; James 2:23; 1 John 3:1–2. In *The Difficult Doctrine of the Love of God* (Wheaton, Ill.: Crossway, 2000), D. A. Carson shows that for us to become God's "friends" does not mean that we have entered into some give-and-take relationship with him. It means that God has revealed to us some of his plans and purposes (see pp. 41–43). Carson's book makes many relevant points for those who wish to make a biblically informed choice between classical Christian theism and its competitors.

[21]Good summaries of Scripture's use of the word "mystery" are found in G. W. Barker, "Mystery," in *The International Standard Bible Encyclopedia*, ed. Geoffrey W. Bromiley et al., rev. ed., 4 vols. (Grand Rapids: Eerdmans, 1986), 3:451–54; P. T. O'Brien, "Mystery," in *Dictionary of Paul and His Letters*, ed. Gerald F. Hawthorne and Ralph P. Martin (Downers Grove, Ill.: InterVarsity Press, 1993), 621–23.

As Barker says, the Greek word *mystērion* "is by no means an exact equivalent of the English word 'mystery'" (p. 451). Today "a mystery" is something unexplained. So once the explanation is found, the mystery disappears. "The Greek term, however, refers to a mystery of divine nature that remains hidden from human beings because their normal powers of comprehension are insufficient. Nonetheless, these mysteries are intended for human beings and when known prove profitable to them" (pp. 451–52). In its fullest New Testament sense, *mystērion* "refers to the secret thoughts, plans, and dispensations of God, which, though hidden from human reason, are being disclosed by God's revealing act to those for whom such knowledge is intended."

[22]Carl F. H. Henry, *God, Revelation and Authority*, 6 vols. (1976–1983; reprint, Wheaton, Ill.: Crossway, 1999), 2:7.

## 2.3 The Limitations of General Revelation

God, then, according to Christianity, has revealed himself to human beings. More particularly, he has manifested himself to everyone through general revelation. So why are there atheists? Scripture says that it is because God's general revelation is inevitably suppressed by sin (Rom. 1:18). Although we all know at some level that God exists and ought to be glorified, thanked, and obeyed, none of us has done as we know we ought (Rom. 3:9–20, 23). Indeed, since Adam and Eve's fall in the garden (Gen. 3; Rom. 5:12, 16–19; 1 Cor. 15:22), we have been alienated from God (Col. 1:21), our thinking has been futile (Rom. 1:21; Eph. 4:17), our minds and consciences are corrupt (Tit. 1:15), and our hearts are darkened (Rom. 1:21; cf. Gen. 8:21; Jer. 17:9; Eph. 4:18).

As strange as it initially seems, Scripture declares that no one has thought it worthwhile to retain his or her knowledge of God (Rom. 1:28). We have all deliberately (although usually somewhat subconsciously) turned away from him, rebelling against his truth and righteousness and applauding others who do the same (Rom. 3:10–12 with 1:32). As long as we remain untouched by God's saving grace, we are by nature prone to all kinds of idolatry and wickedness (Rom. 1:21–2:1; Eph. 2:1–3). So while God's general revelation is *objectively sufficient* to lead each of us to know that he is the world's all-powerful Creator and Sustainer, our sin renders it *subjectively insufficient* to produce all of the knowledge it should. Just as their defective retinas make those who are color-blind unable to see colors that are actually there to be seen, so sin makes us all *epistemically blind* to various aspects of God's general revelation.[23]

## 2.4 The Value of General Revelation

God's revelation of certain truths about himself through general revelation still gives us at least some vague awareness of him and his purposes for human beings (Acts 14:15–17; 17:16–31). Perhaps we can discover that God possesses certain attributes by careful reasoning. In any case, we usually know some of these truths by general revelation. Our awareness of them can help to warrant our acceptance of the gospel proclamation (see the Acts passages just cited, along with Rom. 3:9–21 and 2 Cor. 4:1–2),[24] even as it ensures that none of us can claim not to know whom we should be worshiping.

Yet *certainty* about God's nature and purposes comes primarily from special revelation. We can only know by special revelation that Jesus can save us from

---

[23]Somewhat roughly, a person, S, is *epistemically blind* regarding some truth, *p*, in the case where S does not know that *p* is true but should. For more on the concept, see my "On Christian Philosophy," *Reformed Journal* 34.9 (1984): 18–22; and my "Is It Natural to Believe in God?" *Faith and Philosophy* 6 (1989): 155–71.

[24]This is why Paul spends over two chapters of Romans establishing that everyone is a sinner (see Rom. 1:18–3:20) after having declared that he is not ashamed of the gospel (1:16–17). He is not ashamed of God's good news because the bad news of God's wrath against all human godlessness and unrighteousness is being constantly and universally revealed (1:18–32; cf. 2 Cor. 4:1–6; 5:11–21). Proclaiming the gospel brings Paul no shame because it is by that means that God's merciful provision for forgiving our unrighteousness is unveiled.

our sins. But our sinful blindness means that we also need it to confirm general revelation. In fact, only the repetition of general revelation's truths in Scripture has anchored human insistence that there is just one God, a transcendent person who both created and rules the universe and who is omnipotent, omniscient, and perfectly good.[25]

Non-Christians are blind to a wide variety of truths (Matt. 23:16–26; 2 Cor. 4:1–4). They only begin to apprehend these truths if God grants them faith (John 6:44; Phil. 1:29). Faith "comes from what is heard, and what is heard comes by the preaching of Christ" (Rom. 10:17 [RSV])—it depends on our coming into contact with God's verbal revelation and then being moved by his Holy Spirit (John 3:1–8; 1 Cor. 2:12, 14; Tit. 3:3–7) to believe it (2 Kings 23:1–3; John 5:24–25; Acts 8:26–38). God's Spirit then indwells us (Rom. 8:9–11; 1 Cor. 3:16; Eph. 1:13–14), and he, the very Spirit of truth (John 14:17), enables and encourages us to take the Bible for what it is, God's truth (2 Tim. 3:15–16; 2 Peter 1:19–21).

We can then start to see some of our blindness. We begin to realize that the Bible is right, that once we suppressed even the most elementary truths about God (Rom. 1:18) and exchanged God's truth for a lie (Rom. 1:25). We then begin to apprehend how our aversion to God has corrupted our minds, darkened our hearts, and made our perception of his general revelation unreliable (Rom. 1:21–22, 25; Eph. 4:17–19; Col. 1:21; Tit. 1:15). Contact with the Scriptures thus becomes crucial to assure us that we are thinking rightly about God; without the Bible we might well despair of achieving any certainty about him. In this way, our commitment to the truths of special revelation helps to hold our assurance of the truths of general revelation in place.

## 2.5 The Relation of the Bible to Classical Christian Theism

Christians, then, naturally turn to the Bible as they seek to know who God is. But at this point we find that classical Christian theism is being challenged from opposite sides. On the one hand, theological Constructivists like Gordon Kaufman, Edward Farley and Sallie McFague claim to be working from a Christian perspective even as they argue that we should no longer accept the Bible as our faith's supreme authority.[26] They claim that because classical Christian

---

[25]This notion that God's special revelation includes the restatement or "republication" of truths knowable through general revelation is found in Joseph Butler, *The Works of Joseph Butler*, ed. W. E. Gladstone, 2 vols. (Oxford: Clarendon, 1896), 2:277–80. Thomas Aquinas makes similar claims. See his *Summa Theologiae* (in *Basic Writings of Saint Thomas Aquinas*, ed. Anton C. Pegis, 2 vols. (New York: Random House, 1945), 1.Q1.A1. Étienne Gilson has made this point particularly convincingly by showing that philosophers unacquainted with special revelation have not discovered monotheism quickly or surely on their own. See his *Spirit of Medieval Philosophy* (1936; reprint, Notre Dame, Ind.: Univ. of Notre Dame Press, 1991) and esp. his *God and Philosophy* (New Haven, Conn.: Yale Univ. Press, 1941).

[26]See Kaufman, *In Face of Mystery*, ch. 2; and Sallie McFague, *Models of God: Theology for an Ecological, Nuclear Age* (Philadelphia: Fortress, 1987), 40–45. McFague's rejection of Scripture is not as radical as Kaufman's.

theism's source is historic Christianity's "house of authority" with its "Scripture principle," it is not generally credible today.[27]

On the other hand, open theists claim that classical Christian theism slights Scripture's authority. Its first proponents, they charge, were seduced by ancient Greek philosophy; and a truly biblical theism still awaits development.[28] More careful Bible reading, Gregory Boyd claims, has been the primary reason why he and most other open theists have come to abandon the classical view.[29]

Some classical Christian theists hold their position without much explicit reference to Scripture. Some of them have at times distorted the Christian doctrine of God with terms and categories borrowed from ancient Greek philosophy. But most classical Christian theists have based their beliefs about God on what they have found in the Scriptures. Some of us reject open theism's charge that we are preferring a God of human speculation *over* the God of Scripture precisely because we believe we find the God of classical Christian theism *in* Scripture. The real issue between us and these open theists is simply whether our God or their God corresponds to Scripture's God.

With theological Constructivists, the issue is more basic. It is whether a theological position that deliberately rejects historic Christianity's formal norm for Christian doctrine should still be called "Christian." These challenges require us to think carefully about biblical authority and interpretation.

## 3. Biblical Authority and Theological Constructivism

Christian theologians have always viewed Scripture as the authoritative repository of true Christian faith.[30] This was natural, given Christianity's Jewish roots, with its own strong tradition of scriptural authority (John 5:39; 10:35; Acts 17:2, 11). Judaism's view was modified by the distinctively Christian insights that these theologians believed were bequeathed to the apostolic writers by the Holy Spirit as they wrote the New Testament (John 16:13; Col. 1:25–27; 1 Peter 1:10–12; 2 Peter 1:19–21). This led almost all of them to view Scripture as "not only

---

[27]See Edward Farley, *Ecclesial Reflection: An Anatomy of Theological Method* (Philadelphia: Fortress, 1982).

[28]See especially Clark H. Pinnock, Richard Rice, John Sanders, William Hasker, and David Basinger, *The Openness of God: A Biblical Challenge to the Traditional Understanding of God* (Downers Grove, Ill.: InterVarsity Press, 1994), ch. 2.

[29]See Gregory A. Boyd, *God of the Possible: A Biblical Introduction to the Open View of God* (Grand Rapids: Baker, 2000), 12–13.

[30]J. N. D. Kelly, in his well-received *Early Christian Doctrines*, rev. ed. (San Francisco: Harper & Row, 1978), 29–30, says:

> Christianity came into the world as a religion of revelation, and as such claimed a supernatural origin for its message.... God Himself, all the early theologians acknowledged, was the ultimate author of the revelation; but He had committed it to prophets and inspired lawgivers, above all to the apostles who were eye-witnesses of the incarnate Word, and they had passed it on to the Church. Hence, when asked where the authentic faith was to be found, their answer was clear and unequivocal: in a general way it was contained in the Church's continuous tradition of teaching, and more concretely in the Holy Scriptures.

exempt from error but [as containing] nothing that was superfluous,"[31] as "sufficient, and more than sufficient, for all purposes," and as "consonant in all its parts, and [such] that its meaning should be clear if it is read as a whole." Indeed, Scripture was taken as the formal norm of Christian faith so that anyone deviating from it "could not count as a Christian."

These early affirmations of the doctrines of the Bible's *inerrancy, necessity, sufficiency*, and *clarity* represent the historic Christian position because Christians have historically accepted this view of Scripture as the one that Scripture, as God's written revelation, has of itself.[32] The Bible's supreme and final authority in Christian thought and life follows from this.

Scripture affirms its own authority by presenting itself as being *entirely* God's words. This is as apparent in its *assumptions* as in its outright *assertions*. Scripture often declares that "This is what the LORD says" (Isa. 37:6; Mal. 1:4; Rom. 9:14–15; Rev. 1:8) or that someone in Scripture is speaking in God's name (1 Kings 14:18; Zech. 7:4–12). It also asserts that God has inspired all of itself (2 Tim. 3:16; 2 Peter 1:20–21). More significantly, our Lord and other New Testament writers assume that each biblical word is a word from God. At Matthew 19:5, our Lord places the words of Genesis 2:24, which are not spoken by God in Genesis, in God's mouth (cf. Mark 7:9–13). In Acts, Peter identifies the words of two psalms as what "the Holy Spirit spoke long ago through the mouth of David concerning Judas" (Acts 1:15–16, 20 with Ps. 69:25 and 109:8; cf. Neh. 9:30; Acts 4:24–26; Heb. 3:7). He inserts a present-tense "God says" into a prophecy originally made by Joel (Acts 2:17). And Paul refers to the gospel that God "promised beforehand through his prophets in the Holy Scriptures" (Rom. 1:2; cf. Matt. 1:22; Luke 1:70; Acts 3:18, 21).[33]

---

[31]Ibid., 61. The following quotations are found on pages 43, 40, and 45, respectively.

[32]See, e.g., Wayne Grudem, *Systematic Theology: An Introduction to Biblical Doctrine* (Grand Rapids: Zondervan, 1994), 47–138: Part I—"The Doctrine of the Word of God."

[33]Some New Testament passages actually obliterate the distinction between God and Scripture. Romans 9:17 finds Paul saying that "the Scripture"—*not* God through Moses, as found in the original context (see Ex. 9:13–16)—"says to Pharaoh: 'I raised you up for this very purpose, that I might display my power in you and that my name might be proclaimed in all the earth.'" Here, as John Stott notes, "God says" and "the Scripture says" are functioning as virtual synonyms; see his *Romans: God's Good News for the World* (The Bible Speaks Today; Downers Grove, Ill.: InterVarsity Press, 1994), 269. At Galatians 3:8, Paul writes, "The Scripture foresaw that God would justify the Gentiles by faith, and announced the gospel in advance to Abraham: 'All nations will be blessed through you'" (see Gen. 12:2–3). Scripture here foresees what God will do, although foreseeing is a species of knowing, which is only properly ascribed to persons. Scripture elsewhere affirms that God alone has unerring foresight (see Isa. 42:8–9; 46:3–11; Rom. 16:25–27); and so Paul's attributing foresight to Scripture probably shows that he regards it as "an extension of the divine personality" (F. F. Bruce, *Commentary on Galatians: A Commentary on the Greek Text* [Grand Rapids: Eerdmans, 1982], 156). As Warfield observed, acts like *saying* and *foreseeing* "could be attributed to 'Scripture' only as the result of such a habitual identification, in the mind of the writer, of the text of Scripture with God as speaking, that it became natural to use the term 'Scripture says,' when what was really intended was 'God, as recorded in Scripture, said'" (Benjamin Breckenridge Warfield, *The Inspiration and Authority of the Bible* [Phillipsburg, N.J.: Presbyterian & Reformed, 1948], 299–300).

Our Lord and his apostles assume that we must believe *everything* in Scripture (Luke 24:25–27, 44; Acts 24:14; 28:23–28). Paul tells Timothy to continue in what he has learned and become convinced of, because he has known "the sacred writings" from infancy and these sacred writings—meaning primarily the Old Testament—"are able to instruct you for salvation through faith in Christ Jesus" (2 Tim. 3:15 [RSV]). He then declares that *all* of Scripture is "God-breathed" and thus "useful for teaching, rebuking, correcting and training in righteousness, so that the godly person may be thoroughly equipped for every good work" (2 Tim. 3:16, my translation).[34]

Elsewhere it is assumed that Christian faith is to be based *entirely* in the Scriptures.[35] Paul defends himself before King Agrippa by claiming that he is saying nothing more than what Moses and the prophets had said (Acts 26:22). Luke commends the Bereans for receiving Paul's message eagerly and then examining the Scriptures to be sure of its truth (Acts 17:11; cf. Isa. 8:20). Some Old Testament passages prohibit God's people from adding to or subtracting from its words (Deut. 4:1–2; 12:32; Prov. 30:5–6), and some New Testament passages suggest that the same holds for it (Rev. 22:18–19; cf. Gal. 3:15–22).

Additionally, each of the New Testament's fifty or so instances of the Greek word *graphē*—translated as "Scripture" or "Scriptures" at places such as Acts 17:11; Romans 9:17; Galatians 3:8; 2 Timothy 3:16; and 2 Peter 3:16—refers to some Old Testament passage. But two of these instances also refer to words or writings that were to become part of God's New Testament.[36] This suggests that the New Testament's writers were constantly aware of the boundaries of what could be called "Scripture" as well as of the fact that some of their own writings would receive the same status.[37]

Does Scripture reveal particular doctrinal truths? Can we expect it to help us to resolve the current controversy over who God actually is? This issue is somewhat confused by the fact that in four places the NIV renders the Greek as "spiritual truths" or "truths of the faith" or "the elementary truths of God's word" (1 Cor. 2:13; 1 Tim. 3:9; 4:6; Heb. 5:12) even though no Greek word for "truth" is found in those places. Moreover, many scholars have taken the Hebrew concept of truth to refer primarily to a person's *faithfulness* and *reliability*, not to the intellectual quality of *conformity with reality* that underlies our supposedly "Western"

---

[34]Other endorsements of the entire Old Testament are found at Matt. 5:17; Luke 16:17; John 10:35; and Rom. 15:4.

[35]This pertains at least to the doctrinal and moral bases of our faith. It is known formally as the doctrine of the *sufficiency of Scripture*. For a good short summary of what the doctrine comes to, see Grudem, *Systematic Theology*, ch. 8.

[36]The two instances are 2 Peter 3:16, where Peter ranks Paul's letters with "the other Scriptures," and 1 Tim. 5:18, where Paul quotes what was to become known to us as Luke 10:7 as part of what "Scripture says."

[37]See especially Sinclair B. Ferguson, "How Does the Bible Look at Itself?" in *Inerrancy and Hermeneutic: A Tradition, A Challenge, A Debate*, ed. Harvie M. Conn (Grand Rapids: Baker, 1988). See also Wayne A. Grudem, "Scripture's Self-Attestation and the Problem of Formulating a Doctrine of Scripture," in *Scripture and Truth*, ed. D. A. Carson and John D. Woodbridge (Grand Rapids: Baker, 1992), 19–59.

　　　　　　　　　　　　　　GOD UNDER FIRE

way of thinking about truth.[38] They then claim that the Hebrew concept carries over into the New Testament and thus dismiss orthodox Christianity's concern for doctrinal truth as foreign to the biblical writers' mind-set.

Yet sometimes Hebrew words for truth do indicate conformity with reality (Deut. 17:2–5; 1 Kings 10:6). And sometimes the Greek word bears the same meaning, as when Jesus tells the Samaritan woman the truth about her marital status (John 4:18) or when the emphasis is on a witness speaking truthfully (John 19:35; Rev. 22:6). In these last two passages, these truths are essential to specific doctrines of the Christian faith. Thus, the gospel has a specific factual content (1 Cor. 15:1–8; 1 John 1:1–3; 4:2) with particular doctrinal implications (Rom. 3:21–26; 5:6–11; Gal. 3:1–12). The NIV's renderings of the Greek phrases *to mystērion tēs pisteōs* (lit., "the mystery of the faith") as "the deep truths of the faith" (1 Tim. 3:9) and *ta stoicheia tēs archēs tōn logiōn tou theou* (lit., "the first principles of the word of God") as "the elementary truths of God's word" (Heb. 5:12) are then acceptable. For New Testament faith has a definite content, and "the first principles of God's word" can be articulated in a set of claims.

Scripture, then, presents itself as being, in whole and in each of its parts, God's own words. This authorizes it to set the bounds of Christian faith. In fact, its divine status implies that disbelieving or disliking or disobeying any of it is equivalent to disbelieving or disliking or disobeying God himself.[39] We who have been born again of God's Holy Spirit through hearing or reading God's special revelation are moved by him to take Scripture for what it is—God's own words, including God's own claims—and its complete truthfulness and rightfulness should become increasingly apparent to us as we hear and read it (Ps. 19:7–11; 119:160; John 17:17). Indeed, its truthfulness and rightfulness should become axiomatic for us,[40] including its assumptions and assertions about God's nature and attributes.

## 3.1 Theological Constructivism and the Bible

Sallie McFague condemns the foregoing view of Scripture as "fundamentalism."[41] Fundamentalism, she tells us, identifies God's word with human words,

---

[38]For an overview of the biblical evidence along with an evaluation of it, see Roger Nicole, "The Biblical Concept of Truth," in *Scripture and Truth*, 287–98.

[39]Scripture itself corroborates this: (1) regarding disbelief of God's Word, see Luke 1:18–20; (2) regarding disobedience of God's Word, see 1 Sam. 15:1–23; 1 Kings 20:35–36; (3) regarding being disaffected with God's Word, see Isa. 30:8–14; Jer. 6:10–11.

[40]Douglas Blount goes even further in his essay on "The Authority of Scripture," in *Reason for the Hope Within*, ed. Michael J. Murray (Grand Rapids: Eerdmans, 1999), 405: "Since I intend these remarks for Christians, I don't intend to include in them a defense of Scripture's claim to have been divinely revealed. That Scripture is a divine revelation seems to me to be an *axiom* of the Christian faith." Most Christians, from the beginning of the Christian era, would agree. For instance, in addition to Kelly, *Early Christian Doctrines*, see G. L. Prestige, *Fathers and Heretics: Six Studies in Dogmatic Faith with Prologue and Epilogue* (London: SPCK, 1940), ch. 1.

[41]There is no doubt, however, that this is the historic Christian position, as the distinguished liberal New Testament scholar Kirsopp Lake insisted early last century. Defining "Fundamentalism" as involving belief in "the Infallible Inspiration of Scripture, the Deity of

"notably those human words in the canonical Scriptures."[42] But this assertion "of univocity between human language about God and God or 'God's Word'" runs contrary to what she takes to be "the most basic characteristic of religious and theological language," namely, its "iconoclastic" or "destabilizing" character.

In typical theological Constructivist language, McFague asserts that we are now conscious "of the constructive character of all human activities, especially of those within which we live and therefore of which we are least aware: our world views, including our religions." Human existence is always creative and interpretive. We never experience reality "raw" or uninterpreted; our experience is always partly our construction, less imitative of reality than productive of it—and this includes our experience of God, who "is and remains a mystery."

We have become increasingly aware, McFague says, of "the power of language as the most distinctive attribute of human existence" as well as of "the ways in which we construct the worlds we inhabit through it." We do this primarily by using metaphors. *Metaphors* are words or phrases that properly belong to one context but are being used in another. For instance, calling God "Mother" takes "mother" out of its original context in order to see if it can help us to experience God more fruitfully. A metaphor's inappropriateness accounts for its constructive or interpretive power, for it is this that helps us to experience something new. Jesus' likening himself to a mother hen who wants to gather her chicks under her wings helps us to experience anew his loving care.

Religious and theological language becomes properly iconoclastic and destabilizing when we acknowledge that *all* God-talk is metaphorical. *All* of it "is human construction and as such perforce 'misses the mark'" of informing us, once and for all, of who God is. But Fundamentalism doesn't appreciate this, insisting, instead, "that only one construction (which is not admitted to be a construction) is true, right, and good."

---

Jesus Christ, the efficacy of the Blood Atonement, and the Second Coming of the Lord," he goes on to say (in *The Religion of Yesterday and To-morrow* [London: Christophers, 1925], 61):

> it is a mistake, often made by educated persons who happen to have but little knowledge of historical theology, to suppose that Fundamentalism is a new and strange form of thought. It is nothing of the kind: it is the partial and uneducated survival of a theology which was once universally held by all Christians. How many were there, for instance, in Christian churches in the eighteenth century who doubted the infallible inspiration of all Scripture? A few, perhaps, but very few. No, the Fundamentalist may be wrong; I think that he is. But it is we who have departed from the tradition, not he, and I am sorry for the fate of anyone who tries to argue with a Fundamentalist on the basis of authority. The Bible and the *corpus theologicum* of the Church is on the Fundamentalist side.

As Lake goes on to observe, Fundamentalism, as a cultural movement in early twentieth-century America, "is not the complete or the intelligent survival of the old theology." For instance, "the keen metaphysics of the doctrine concerning God and the insight into human nature of the doctrines of sin and of grace" that were part of classical Christian theism were lost (p. 62). I am making no brief for Fundamentalism where it is understood to include more than the four particular doctrines that Lake mentioned in defining it.

[42]McFague, *Models of God*, 22. All of the remaining quotations in this section are from the preface or the first two chapters of this book.

Yet as the elaboration of key metaphors, "theology is *mostly* fiction." Nietzsche said language deceives us "into believing it is fixed and definite, referring to something outside ourselves, when in fact it is nothing but the play of metaphors." McFague believes that language is a bit more than just the play of metaphors—our words refer to something beyond language that makes our metaphors more or less inappropriate, more or less inadequate. But no metaphor is always appropriate.

McFague concedes that Christianity is a historical faith, "one that claims in some sense an illumination, revelation, or rendering explicit of divine reality in history, specifically, in the paradigmatic figure of Jesus of Nazareth and the subsequent witness to that event in Scripture." Consequently, it "must always deal with the constant of its tradition." Yet it must not make its tradition finally authoritative or objectively true.

McFague admits that the church wanted to make Scripture an authoritative text of true claims that would be the formal norm for all subsequent theology. But Scripture, like all other texts, is just a "sedimentation" of interpreted experience. Its language about God is "principally adverbial, having to do with how we relate to God rather than defining [God's] nature." Consequently, its metaphors must not be "reified, petrified, or expanded so as to exclude all others." We must not let the Bible seduce us into taking its images and concepts as fixed and definite, referring to something outside ourselves. We must recognize that we live in "a post-Christian world," where "we cannot accept currency from former times as our truth." We must constantly remind ourselves that "our primary datum is not a Christian message [that is true] for all time . . . rather, it is experiences of women and men witnessing to the transforming love of God interpreted in a myriad of ways."

Scripture can serve only as "a model of how theology should be done, rather than as the authority dictating the terms in which it is done." It is "a case study, classic, or prototype" that encompasses a "plurality of interpretive perspectives." Taking this plurality seriously means having "to do the same risky, adventuresome thing that [Scripture itself] does: interpret the salvific love of God in ways that can address our crises most persuasively and powerfully." This "will not, cannot, mean using the terminology of two thousand years ago," and so we must reject "the language of dying and rising gods, personal guilt and sacrificial atonement, eternal life and so forth," as well as any references to God's omnipotence, omniscience, and omnipresence.[43]

---

[43]"The relationship between God and the world—in other words, between God's power and ours—has in the past been 'dualistic' and 'asymmetrical' and now needs to become 'unified' and 'interdependent.'" God must no longer be "viewed as a being externally related to the world" and "as the power that totally controls it" (ibid., 17). Indeed, predicates "such as omniscience, infinity, omnipotence, and omnipresence do not properly apply to God . . . for the meaning of all such language—knowledge, finitude, power, presence—applies properly only to our existence, not God's" (p. 39). These terms are "at most metaphorical forays attempting to express experiences of relating to God," for "how language, any language, applies to God we do not know" (ibid.).

For McFague, Scripture is not really a divine revelation. Consequently, she believes "that what we can say with any assurance about the character of Christian faith is very little and even that will be highly contested." She ventures that "Christian faith is ... most basically a claim that the universe is neither indifferent nor malevolent but that there is a power (and a personal power at that) which is on the side of life and its fulfillment." Christians also believe that "we have some clues for fleshing out this claim in the life, death, and appearances of Jesus of Nazareth." Yet she admits that you cannot get to her view of Christianity just by reading Scripture, for the Bible's texts are so distorted by oppressive ideologies that we must be suspicious of them.[44]

## 3.2 What Can We Learn From Theological Constructivism?

For all of its errors, McFague's approach to the Scriptures is right about this: Language is human life's most distinctive feature; without it, human life as we know it would not exist.

Scripture itself attests to this. The psalmist says, "I will instruct you and teach you in the way you should go; I will counsel you and watch over you. Do not be like the horse or the mule, which have no understanding but must be controlled by bit and bridle or they will not come to you" (Ps. 32:8–9). Instructing, teaching, and counseling is done primarily through language, which gives us the understanding we need so that we can make the sorts of thoughtful decisions that are part and parcel of our humanity.[45] Words are thus the vehicles by which we are made free (Ps. 119:45). Scripture stresses their importance again and again, so that by receiving them we can come to live good and godly lives (Prov. 2:1–22), and by using them we can do things, like confess (Rom. 10:8–13) and request mercy and forgiveness (Hos. 14:1–3; Matt. 7:7–12). In fact, words are so crucial that we will have to render account for each careless one on the Judgment Day; by our words we will be justified or condemned (Matt. 12:36–37).

We are, by nature, *verbivores*—word-eaters—whose lives take on the character of the words we digest. Jesus said this in rejecting Satan's challenge to turn stones into bread: "Man shall not live on bread alone, but on every word that comes from the mouth of God" (Matt. 4:4, quoting Deut. 8:3). Scripture everywhere assumes that life—real life, eternal life—depends on hearing or reading God's words (Deut. 11:18; Jer. 15:16; John 6:68; 1 Cor. 2:11–13; Phil. 2:16). This is not just a helpful metaphor; it is literally true. We *cannot* make sense of life without "digesting" some particular set of words—without being told *stories* that enable us to understand who we are as well as where we have come from and where we are going, without being given credible *evaluative categories* by which to judge what is true and false and good and bad, and without acquiring a cogent pattern of *metaphors* and *explanations* that helps us construe our lives in meaningful ways.[46]

---

[44]See ibid., 197 n. 26.

[45]For more on this, see my "Starting from Scripture," in *Limning the Psyche: Explorations in Christian Psychology*, ed. Robert C. Roberts and Mark R. Talbot (Grand Rapids: Eerdmans, 1997), 102–22.

[46]See ibid.; also see Roberts, "Parameters of a Christian Psychology," in *Limning the Psyche*, 81.

GOD UNDER FIRE

Life only begins to make sense for us within the framework of some particular and more or less consistent way of looking at the world and understanding ourselves that is conveyed to us through language. That is why the prospect of a word famine is so frightening. For without words we would indeed be condemned to "stagger from sea to sea and wander from north to east," searching for life's meaning without being able to find it (Amos 8:11–12).[47]

Theological Constructivism is right to insist that language is essential to distinctively human existence. Yet we must reject it when it evacuates Christian faith of its historic content by insisting that faith's historic language of Scripture has lost its credibility and therefore must be replaced. Christians have always held that Scripture—as God's special written revelation to us of what we must know to think and to live truthfully and righteously before him (2 Peter 1:2–3)—is the means by which we can acquire the particular stories (Deut. 6; Rom. 15:4; 1 Cor. 10:1–11), the specific evaluative categories (Ps. 19:7–11; Matt. 5; 1 Cor. 13; Gal. 5:19–23), and the appropriate metaphors (Ps. 23:1–4; Isa. 53:6; Matt. 18:1–4; Eph. 4:17–24; 6:10–17) and explanations for properly understanding and ordering our lives (Deut. 6:20–25; Rom. 5:12–21; 7:7–25; Heb. 9). Theological Constructivists deny this. Even more basically, they believe that the very idea of an authoritative divine revelation is inappropriate in our time.[48]

Well-versed, biblically faithful Christians will respond that skepticism about Scripture's credibility and authority is not new (1 Cor. 1:18–25). Scripture never is credible or authoritative for anyone until God's Spirit has worked in that person's heart (1 Cor. 2:6–16; Eph. 2:1–10). The Scriptures are indeed objectively sufficient to give each of us a proper knowledge of who God actually is, but their objective sufficiency is undercut by our sin. The fact that theological Constructivists do not find the language of Scripture credible or authoritative does not tell us anything about its actual credibility or authoritativeness; instead, it tells us something about them.[49] Thus, we should feel free, with Christians of other ages, to turn to the Scriptures to understand who God is.

---

[47]It is striking that those who become uncertain enough about their framework of meaning even lose their ability to orient themselves in physical space. See Heinz Kohut, *The Restoration of the Self* (New York: International Universities Press, 1977), 153–56.

[48]Here is the way that Kaufman puts it (*In Face of Mystery*, 48):

In a time when fundamental religious or theological claims are heavily questioned, when they seem dubious or unintelligible or even absurd, it is a serious mistake to invoke the *authority* of the major symbols of the tradition as the principal basis for theological work.... Theological work grounded principally on what is claimed to be authoritative "revelation" is simply not appropriate today. The concept of revelation is itself a part of the conceptual scheme which has become questionable.

[49]As Sinclair Ferguson has put it, those who possess God's Spirit "recognize the divine canonicity of the apostolic word. What Paul writes are the Lord's commands, *and a mark of a truly spiritual person is that he or she recognizes them as such* (1 Cor. 14:37)" ("How Does the Bible Look at Itself?" 51, my emphasis). Cf. J. I. Packer: "A professed Christian who is able to dig into the Bible but neglects to do so casts doubt on his own sincerity; for inattention to Scripture is right out of character for a child of God" (*God Has Spoken* [Grand Rapids: Baker, 1979], 14).

## 4. Biblical Interpretation and Open Theism

Historically, those who have been convinced that Scripture is God's special written revelation have taken that to ensure its complete truthfulness and consistency. Their reasoning went like this. Words mimic and betray a person's character (Matt. 15:18; Luke 6:43–45). So if God is Scripture's primary author and its every word is ultimately a word from him, then Scripture will be as truthful and consistent as God himself is. How truthful and consistent will it then be? Wholly truthful and completely consistent, for that is what God is and must be (1 Sam. 15:29; Ps. 119:160; Mal. 3:6; Heb. 6:16–19).[50] This prompted classical Christian theists to try to shape their conception of God to what the whole Bible, as God's one necessary and sufficient special revelation, reveals about him.

This kind of reasoning for the utter truthfulness and consistency of God's words is found in Scripture (Num. 23:19–20; Ps. 89:34; Tit. 1:2). Today, however, many open and process theists are questioning it. This, rather than some recognition of ancient Greek philosophy's undue influence on Christian theism, is probably the most basic cause of open theism's rejection of the God of classical Christian theism.

Open theists emphasize Scripture's authority. Clark Pinnock argues that Scripture must be Christianity's supreme and final authority if real Christian faith is to survive. He admits that "inspiration would mean very little if it could not guarantee a basic coherence in the Bible's teaching and a solid reliability in the Bible's narrative," for "broken would be the authority of a norm that could not rule."[51] Yet from these truths, he claims, "we cannot *deduce* what the Bible must be like in detail."

In particular, the case for Scripture's perfect errorlessness is not, Pinnock thinks, as good as it may seem. He concedes that "God cannot lie, but that," he declares, "is not the issue. God gave the Bible . . . by transmitting [it] through all manner of secondary authors," and so we "cannot determine ahead of time what kind of text God would give in this way."[52] We must approach Scripture *inductively* to ascertain its actual character. But we will then see that neither our Lord nor the New Testament unambiguously teaches its perfect errorlessness. At best, "one could say only that [total inerrancy] is implicit and could be drawn out by careful argument." Yet in the final analysis, inerrancy is "not well supported exegetically." Indeed, insisting that Scripture is unerringly true only serves to highlight the Bible's more perplexing features, which then overshadow the "wonderful certainties of salvation in Christ."

This rejection of Scripture's perfect errorlessness means that there is "a distance between the Word of God and the [Bible's] text."[53] There is "human weak-

---

[50]For a fuller account of this line of argument, including answers to some objections to it, see Grudem, *Systematic Theology*, 82–100.

[51]Clark Pinnock, *The Scripture Principle* (San Francisco: Harper & Row, 1984), 69. The final quotation in this paragraph is from p. 57.

[52]Ibid., 57. The remaining quotations in this paragraph are from pp. 58, 59.

[53]Ibid., 99. The next quotation is from the same page.

ness"—errors such as misidentifications and mangled references—"attaching to the sacred text." Yet Pinnock continues to affirm Scripture's fundamental self-consistency. We must, he says, "permit the biblical testimony to be what it is, namely, 'obviously fragmentary and unsystematic,'"[54] yet we are not thereby absolved of the obligation to try to make systematic sense of the entire text:

> Of course, passages must be studied first in their own right, but eventually they ought to be placed in the framework of [God's] whole revelation . . . [which] was the way of the older exegetical tradition, which operated out of a firm conviction about biblical inspiration.

Pinnock reminds us that historically "the unity of the Scriptures was assumed, and drawing out the systematic message of the Bible was the theologian's task." He takes this position to follow from "the fact of divine inspiration. . . . If Scripture is our inspired teacher, making us wise unto salvation, then we expect it not to confuse us or tell us lies but to communicate intelligibly with us."[55]

Yet some open theists do doubt Scripture's consistency. In his chapter in *The Openness of God*, Richard Rice asks, "What . . . is the biblical view of God?" and then responds:

> It is a challenge to ascertain the biblical view of almost anything, let alone the most important idea of all. The Bible contains an enormous range of material, and on almost any significant topic we can find diverse statements if not diverse perspectives as well. . . . This is why biblical scholars often object to expressions like "the biblical view of" or "according to the Bible." They insist that there are biblical *views*, but no one biblical view.[56]

This comes very close to denying that God is Scripture's primary author, as Rice almost admits:

> Different passages [of Scripture] often seem to support different points of view. To cite a familiar example, many people do not see how the same God

---

[54]Ibid., 60. The internal quotation is from I. Howard Marshall, *Biblical Inspiration* (Grand Rapids: Eerdmans, 1982), 30. The block quotation in the text is from Pinnock's *The Scripture Principle*, 68, and the final quotations in the paragraph are from p. 70.

[55]It is noteworthy that this conditional statement is clearly the first premise of an implicit deductive argument. So Pinnock's affirmation of Scripture's fundamental consistency comes at the cost of some personal inconsistency, since, as we have seen, he has denied the propriety of drawing deductive conclusions from Scripture's text.

[56]Richard Rice, "Biblical Support for a New Perspective," in Pinnock et al., *The Openness of God*, 16 and 177 n. 7. The next quotation is from the same footnote. This invocation of "biblical scholars" *en masse* is tendentious; some biblical scholars wrestle with Scripture's diversity precisely because they believe that Scripture is exactly what God intended it to be and so they believe that they must affirm both its diversity and its fundamental consistency. See, e.g., D. A. Carson's comments at the beginning of his *Difficult Doctrine of the Love of God* and John Piper's acknowledgment of "complex biblical tensions" that involve diversity but not contradiction in his "Are There Two Wills in God?" in *Still Sovereign: Contemporary Perspectives on Election, Foreknowledge, and Grace*, ed. Thomas R. Schreiner and Bruce A. Ware (Grand Rapids: Baker, 1995, 2000), 125.

could command Israel on occasion to utterly destroy its foes . . . and through Jesus instruct us to love our enemies.

If we accept this example, then we are well on our way to denying that the same God inspired both the Old and the New Testaments.

Other open theists deemphasize Scripture's unity. For example, in his *God Who Risks: A Theology of Providence,* John Sanders slights many crucial biblical texts. This may be because he, like McFague, considers all God-talk to be metaphorical. Scripture's assertions about God have "the peculiar quality of saying that something both 'is' and 'is not.'"[57] No biblical assertion about God is, then, literally true and thus such that it should govern our interpretation of the rest.[58]

Yet often particular biblical metaphors come to dominate our thinking, thereby becoming *key models* or *lenses* through which we view everything else. "Different key models," Sanders says, "embody different theologies," and many theological disputes "arise because we look at the [same] 'evidence' through different lenses." He looks at the Scriptures "through the lens of divine risk taking . . . in order to see what should be said concerning a risk-taking God." Yet since he is just developing "a particular theological model," he never mentions Philippians 2:12–13 nor does he attend to the full range of scholarly exegesis of passages like Romans 9, in spite of the fact that providence is necessarily concerned with how God's will and human wills relate.

In general, open theism's move away from affirming Scripture's perfect errorlessness and fundamental self-consistency does more to shape its conception of God than its affirmation of Scripture's supreme authority. For it allows open theists to evade the principles of biblical interpretation that tell against their readings of various texts.

Doubts about Scripture's utter truthfulness and consistency are natural for open theists because they have a view of human freedom that runs against Scripture's own witness to the unique kind of authorship that produced its texts. Open theists sometimes accuse holders of the historic view of Scripture's complete truthfulness and fundamental self-consistency with being committed to an outmoded theory of biblical inspiration, whereby God guaranteed Scripture's truthfulness and consistency by dictating its every word. Scripture's human writers were then no more than secretaries who just transcribed what God said. The historic position, recognizing that the assertion of God's primary authorship of Scripture means that he has ordained all of its details, is thus taken as implying that there is no real secondary human authorship of its texts.[59]

---

[57]John Sanders, *The God Who Risks: A Theology of Providence* (Downers Grove, Ill.: InterVarsity Press, 1998), 15. The remaining quotations from Sanders are from pp. 14–16.
[58]Here is McFague's way of putting this point (*Models of God,* 38–39):
Since no metaphor or model refers properly or directly to God, many are necessary. All are inappropriate, partial, and inadequate; the most that can be said is that some aspect or aspects of the God-world relationship are illuminated by this or that model in a fashion relevant to a particular time and place.
[59]See, e.g., Pinnock's comments in *The Scripture Principle,* 100–102.

GOD UNDER FIRE

But this accusation is false. Scripture does occasionally represent God or his angelic emissaries as dictating messages (Ex. 34:27; Jer. 30:1–4; Rev. 2:1, 8, etc.), but usually it implies that his influence over its human authors was quite different from that (1 Chron. 28:11–19; Luke 1:1–4; 2 Peter 3:15). God's authorship of Scripture can be overemphasized, where its status as God's Word cuts all motivation to attend to the humanity of its texts. But this violates the principle that because all of Scripture is "God-breathed," its *every* feature ought to be noticed, *including* those that stress its human authors' thoughts and purposes (Ps. 45:1, 17; Luke 1:3; John 20:31; 2 Cor. 2:3–4, 9; 13:10; Jude 3). Some Scriptures focus on what particular writers have written (Deut. 24:1–4 with Mark 10:2–9; Rom. 10:19–21), while others emphasize their style in writing it (2 Peter 3:16). So even when we bear in mind all that Scripture says about its divine aspects, we must acknowledge that it presents itself as both human and divine. Its individual books manifest their human authors' purposes and characteristics even as it overall reveals God's one wholly true and fundamentally self-consistent Word.

This implies that Scripture came about by a kind of dual authorship that process, and even open, theists cannot really accept. For them, we act freely only when we can choose to act otherwise than we actually do. If God ordains that I do something, then my doing it is not of my own free choosing. This is as true of writing as of any other act. In researching and writing his gospel, either Luke finally chose which words to use or God did.

Acknowledging the freedom of Scripture's human authors means conceding, then, as Pinnock puts it, that God has not "predestined and controlled every detail of the [Bible's] text." Divine inspiration cannot be "word for word," nor can the Scriptures be errorless. "Inerrancy thinking," as Pinnock says, "is deductive thinking rooted in the assumption of total divine control." Thus, Pinnock concludes, defending Scripture's verbal inspiration and inerrancy requires accepting a "Calvinistic cosmology."[60]

In creature-to-creature relations, something like the open view of freedom is often the case. Either I have written the words you are reading or someone else has. Moreover, in giving credit and assigning responsibility, we usually assume that only one agent or party of agents is finally responsible for a particular act.

---

[60]Ibid., 101, 104. For the identification of classical Christian theism and something close to Calvinism, see Pinnock et al., *The Openness of God*, 11.

Pinnock is an *incompatibilist* regarding human freedom. That means that he thinks that someone, S, is free with respect to a given action, X, at a given time, *t*, only if it is within S's power at *t* to perform X and also within S's power at *t* not to perform X. To say that action X is "within S's power" means that there is nothing about S or S's circumstances that makes it impossible for S to do X.

Calvinists, on the other hand, are typically *compatibilists* regarding human freedom. They believe that someone, S, is free with respect to a given action, X, at a given time, *t*, if S can at *t* perform X if S decides to do so and S can also not perform X if S decides not to do so. In other words, *compatibilists* hold that an action is free as long as it is done voluntarily.

*Compatibilism* is consistent with God ordaining that S decides to do X, so that S's doing X is inevitable and yet voluntary. *Incompatibilism* denies that S is free if God ordains that S decides to do X.

But Scripture portrays the relations between divine and human agency differently. Passages such as Acts 4:27–28, when the early church prayed,

> "Indeed Herod and Pontius Pilate met together with the Gentiles and the people of Israel in this city to conspire against your holy servant Jesus, whom you anointed. They did what your power and will had decided beforehand should happen . . ."

and Philippians 2:12–13,

> Therefore, my dear friends, as you have always obeyed . . . continue to work out your salvation with fear and trembling, for it is God who works in you to will and to act according to his good purpose,

suggest that the Creator's will relates to creatures' wills in a unique way, where God's choosing and a creature's choosing—God's *deciding* and human beings' *conspiring*, God's *working salvation in us* and our *working our salvation out*—are not mutually exclusive acts. In fact, Joseph's discrimination between his brothers' *selling* and God's *sending* him to Egypt assumes that when we are considering both divine and human agency, the same event can be explained as both God and human beings each carrying out their intentions without constraint. Joseph's descent into Egypt can be explained as God's having chosen to send him there in order to save many human lives, and it can *also* be explained as Joseph's brothers having chosen to sell him to those who were going there as a way to harm him (Gen. 45:4–8 and 50:20).[61]

Because Creator-creature relations are unique, it is hard to illustrate what these texts depict. Joseph's going to Egypt was not due *partly* to God's choice and *partly* to the choice of his brothers, as if God and they collaborated to produce one result. Rather, God freely chose to bring about his good purpose through ordaining that Joseph's brothers would freely choose to do their wicked act.

I cannot defend this view of human freedom now. Yet it is the view we arrive at when we consult the whole Bible and do not allow unscriptural intuitions about free will's conditions to override the overwhelming witness of Scripture's texts. It is process and open theists who are reading their own presuppositions into the text. And it is only those who hold this view of freedom who can unreservedly affirm, as Scripture demands, that God is the Bible's primary author and yet that there is also real secondary human authorship of its texts.

## 5. Principles of Biblical Interpretation

What principles of biblical interpretation should those committed to this kind of dual authorship embrace? Revelation involves not only God's unveiling or disclosing truths that are beyond the bounds of normal human cognition. Through Scripture's poetry, God intends to arouse our emotions. Through its

---

[61]See Gordon Wenham's comments on these passages in *Genesis 16–50* (WBC 2; Dallas: Word, 1994).

GOD UNDER FIRE

laws, he means to govern our conduct. The first principle of biblical interpretation, then, is this: *We must aim to allow the Scriptures, in whole and in each of their parts, to function as God intends.* We must not paste whatever meanings we would like onto its texts.

History is littered with wrong interpretations. The Scriptures have often been read *allegorically*, where someone believes that "above and beyond the literal meaning of a [biblical] text there stands a higher (or perhaps several higher) senses" that give it moral and spiritual meanings that any plain reading of it does not suggest.[62] Sometimes it has been maintained that *any* meaning that can be given to a passage is legitimate, so long as that meaning is found in some other biblical text. Augustine defends allegorical interpretation by appeal to God's primary authorship: "The Spirit of God who produced these texts ... foresaw without a shadow of doubt that [these interpretations] would occur to some reader or listener"— indeed, he planned for them and so they are part of the Bible's inexhaustible depth.[63] Consequently, he sometimes distorts the Bible's texts—for example, when Christ feeds the five thousand (John 6:1–5), the boy's five loaves signify the Pentateuch's five books; and their being barley, which is hard to crack, signifies how hard it is to reach the underlying spiritual message of the Old Testament through all its literal "chaff".[64]

Overemphasizing God's authorship of Scripture can thus pull readers away from a passage's central intent.[65] So Scripture's human authorship needs emphasis. Just as Joseph's going to Egypt can be explained in terms of God's choice *and* his brothers' choices, so all of Scripture except those parts that have been dictated can be explained both as God's having ordained them to be exactly as they are *and* as their human authors' having composed them from their own perspectives. For those committed to Scripture's fully dual authorship, both kinds of explanation must make sense: Scripture's human writers were inspired—indeed, "moved" [RSV] or "carried along" [NIV] by God's Holy Spirit (2 Peter 1:21)—to write as they did and yet in a way that did not violate their own agency.

The initial step in narrowing the acceptable interpretations of a biblical text is, then, to determine what its human author might have meant. Thus, the second principle of biblical interpretation is this: *The function or meaning of any individual biblical passage should first be sought by attempting to determine what its human author intended in writing it.* This involves investigating the passage's literary and historical contexts.

This means that passages a biblical author meant literally ought to be taken literally and passages meant metaphorically ought to be taken metaphorically.

---

[62]Gerald Bray, *Biblical Interpretation: Past and Present* (Downers Grove, Ill.: InterVarsity Press, 1996), 82.

[63]Augustine, *De Doctrina Christiana*, 3.38. I have quoted the new translation by Edmund Hill, *Teaching Christianity: De Doctrina Christiana* (Hyde Park, N.Y.: New City, 1996), 186.

[64]See Bray's summary of this, *Biblical Interpretation*, 110. For Augustine's own words, see Tractate 24 in his *Homilies on the Gospel of John*.

[65]However, it seems that not all allegorical interpretation is wrong as such. See Gal. 4:21–31.

Sometimes this line is clear: References to God as "the Rock of Israel" are obviously metaphorical, as their contexts show. For even when they call him a rock, the biblical writers do not cease to speak of God—and to him—as a person (2 Sam. 23:3; cf. Deut. 32:1–43; 2 Sam. 22:1–4, 47; Ps. 18:1–3; 19:14).

From this, some of classical Christian theism's claims fall out of the text quite quickly. Thus if we, unlike McFague, take Scripture as "the authority dictating the terms in which [theology] is done," then we will refer to God only as "he." For while the biblical authors sometimes liken God's care for us to a hen's concern for her chicks or to a woman in labor pains (Isa. 42:14; Matt. 23:37), they never call God "she."

This second principle requires us to place a writer in history so that we do not read him anachronistically. Since God's Old Testament revelation only foreshadows the Christian mystery (Col. 2:16–17; Heb. 10:1–18; 8:1–7), we must not construe an Old Testament writer's words so that they possess a definiteness of meaning that only those knowing God's New Testament revelation could intend (1 Peter 1:10–12). Special revelation's progressive nature means that Scripture's later writers, because they possess more revelation, may understand earlier revelations in new ways (cf., e.g., Acts 10:9–16 with Lev. 11). Thus, the Bible's unity is not simplistic. Its consistency is often not the kind we would anticipate. Thus, *pace* Rice, different eras in redemptive history may very well warrant the same God issuing seemingly contradictory commands.

Still, God is Scripture's primary author, and the same Spirit inspired both the Old and the New Testaments. Thus, the Scriptures will be fundamentally consistent. A third principle of biblical interpretation is then this: *Ultimately, our interpretation of any particular biblical passage must acknowledge and take into account the fundamental unity and consistency of God's whole written Word.* Our interpretation of a particular biblical passage must not ignore or dismiss any passages relevant to it.

We must try to make coherent sense of everything the Bible says about God because this is what it means to honor Scripture as God's Word and not just as human words about God. In other words, any Christian doctrine of God must grapple with everything the Bible says about him. Otherwise we will be prone to misinterpret specific Scriptures because we do not know everything God has said (Mark 12:18–27). This is why Jesus often opened his responses to questions and controversies with the words, "Haven't you read?" (Matt. 12:3, 5; 19:4; 21:16, 42).

Sometimes some of these passages may seem to conflict. Even within a particular redemptive-historical era, Scripture's consistency is not such that all of God's writers move in lockstep. Paul and James seem to disagree about faith and works, with James apparently denying exactly what Paul claims (cf. Rom. 3:21–30 and Gal. 3:1–5 with James 2:14–26). With that case, we have good reasons to think that the disagreement is more verbal than real,[66] but this is not always the case. Sometimes we will have to hold some Scriptures in tension because we cannot yet see how to reconcile them.

---

[66]See, e.g., Peter H. Davids, "James and Paul," in *Dictionary of Paul and His Letters*, 457–61.

god under fire

Historically, this third principle was referred to as the *analogia fidei* or "the analogy of faith." It reminds us that our first impressions of particular Scriptures must sometimes be nuanced to agree with the rest of the Scriptures.[67] Sometimes this means that a passage about God must be interpreted *anthropomorphically*, as giving us a view of God that Scripture itself makes clear ought not to be taken literally even though it helps us to relate meaningfully to him. In fact, this is the right way to handle the "divine 'repentance'" texts.[68]

## 6. The Fundamental Conviction of Classical Christian Theism

Biblically based classical Christian theists believe that consistent application of these principles—and especially of the *analogia fidei*—will establish that it is their God—and not, say, the God of open theism—who is revealed in Scripture. Defending this conviction in depth is others' task in this book. But one illustration of the application of my third interpretive principle may suggest how strong the case for classical Christian theism is.

Both process and open theists question why *omnipotence* should be taken as God's most fundamental attribute. Isn't "love rather than almighty power ... [the Christian God's] primary perfection"?[69] No, for omnipotence (or "almightiness") holds pride of place in both general and special revelation. Paul singles out God's "eternal power" when he is emphasizing what is manifested about God through general revelation. God's power as the Maker of "heaven and earth and sea and everything in them" also grounds his appeal to the people of Lystra to acknowledge God's bountiful kindness and thus turn to him from "vain [i.e., worthless and powerless] things" (Acts 14:15 RSV).

The NIV translates two Old Testament words as the divine title "Almighty" 433 times. This is far more often than any other title is applied to God. Throughout Scripture, God is described as "loving" and "kind" and "merciful," but these traits never become formal titles for him. Granted, in the New Testament God is only rarely called Almighty except in Revelation. Moreover, John does declare that "God is love" (1 John 4:8, 16). But do facts like these imply

---

[67]Those doubting the need for such nuancing should think about passages such as 2 Chron. 16:9, "For the eyes of the LORD range throughout the earth to strengthen those whose hearts are fully committed to him," or Ps. 33:13–14, "From heaven the LORD looks down and sees all mankind; from his dwelling place he watches all who live on earth." Virtually everyone agrees that consideration of the full range of Scripture's references to God leads us to take these verses as just vivid ways of stating that God knows everything that goes on in human life and that he is especially concerned to deliver those who rely on him. For a careful analysis of the concept of the analogy of faith, see Henri Blocher, "The 'Analogy of Faith' in the Study of Scripture," in *The Challenge of Evangelical Theology: Essays in Approach and Method*, ed. Nigel M. de S. Cameron (Edinburgh: Rutherford House, 1987), 17–38.

[68]For more on such anthropomorphism and its relationship to some of the claims of open theism, see Bruce A. Ware, *God's Lesser Glory: The Diminished God of Open Theism* (Wheaton, Ill.: Crossway, 2000), 86–90.

[69]Pinnock et al., *The Openness of God*, 114. The underlying premise here is, in Richard Rice's words, that "the statement *God is love* is as close as the Bible comes to giving us a definition of the divine reality" (p. 18).

that love rather than power is God's primary perfection? Applying the *analogia fidei* suggests not. For Scripture assumes that God's almightiness is the perfection through which perfections like his lordship over history and his love operate.[70]

So does God reveal who he actually is? Christians believe, on the basis of Scripture, that God has revealed himself to us in two different ways. His eternal power and divine nature are manifest to everyone. He has also specially proclaimed his saving mercy to specific people at specific times and places. Scripture preserves that special revelation, and through it God still speaks. Indeed, we should bow to whatever Scripture reveals about him.

We must, however, know how to approach the Scriptures. What does it mean to acknowledge their authority? How truthful and consistent should we take them to be? Historically, Christians have believed, on the basis of what Scripture itself assumes and asserts, that God is the Bible's primary author and thus it is wholly true, fundamentally self-consistent, and finally authoritative. This has compelled them to try to conform their conception of God to what the whole Bible, as God's one self-consistent special revelation, says about him. And that leads us to the adoption of specific principles of biblical interpretation that biblically based classical Christian theists are sure will continue to show that Scripture's God is indeed the God of classical Christian theism.

---

[70]Thus, God's *faithfulness* depends on his power (see 2 Sam. 7:8–16; Ps. 91:1–3; Isa. 31:4–5; Jer. 35:18–19; Hag. 2:23; Zech. 1:17; Rev. 19:11–16), as does the *trustworthiness* and *certainty* of his Word (see Jer. 7:3–7; 19:1–3, 15; 32:14–15; 38:17–23; Zech. 8:2–3; Rev. 19:11–16), his *power to save* (see Ps. 80:7; Isa. 47:4; 51:12–16; Jer. 11:20; 50:33–34; Mic. 4:1–4; Zech. 3:8–10; 12:5; Mal. 3:1; 4:1–3; Rev. 11:15–18; 19:1–8), and his *goodness* and *love* (see Isa. 25:6–8; Jer. 32:17–22; 2 Cor. 6:18; Rev. 1:5–8).

GOD UNDER fire

Chapter 3

# Can God Be Grasped by Our Reason?

*Eric L. Johnson*

✦

Humans do not know how what is
at variance agrees with itself.
It is an attunement of opposite tensions,
like that of the bow and the lyre.
zeno of elea*

✦

It is good to grasp the one
and not let go of the other;
The man who fears God
will avoid all extremes.
ecclesiastes 7:18

# 1. Introduction

A great battle is being waged in our day for the minds of God's people. It is a momentous intellectual battle because it concerns the most important of the objects of human thought: the nature of God. Many are arguing today for a radical reformulation of our understanding of God's nature and a rejection of the view of God of historic Christianity. The purpose of this article is to show how at least a part of this agenda is driven by an unvirtuous use of logic.

There are, in the main, two ways to go wrong regarding our understanding of God's nature. The first is to believe something false about God (such as, God is the same as the universe). The second is to rule out one belief about God simply because it does not comport easily with some other belief about God (such as, since God is love, God cannot send human beings to hell). False religions are characterized by the former, Christian heresy by the latter. When examined carefully, many of the objections that Constructivists and Developmental theists make to the historic Christian view of God are the result of an impatient favoring of one side of the truth at the expense of the other. Let's see how this happens.

We should begin by noting that controversies regarding God's nature are to be expected. It should come as no surprise that the greatest being in the universe is not easy to understand. Believers have always sensed this and have often expressed limitations in their understanding of God. Reflecting on God's omnipresence, David exclaimed, "Such knowledge is too wonderful for me, too lofty for me to attain" (Ps. 139:6). Much later, Zwingli famously suggested, "What God is, we have just as little knowledge of from ourselves as a beetle has of what man is."[1] Such limits in our understanding have led to profound differences in what people have affirmed about God, and such limits raise questions about the human mind's ability to comprehend God.

Some, from both East and West, question whether God can be known at all. Others, including people within the Christian tradition, have suggested that, at the very least, God's nature creates a scandal for the human intellect. Tertullian

The author wants to thank Doug Huffman, Merold Westphal, C. Stephen Evans, Ronald Nash, and Lyle Larson for their help in identifying weaknesses in earlier drafts. Special thanks are due to James Spiegel for extraordinary efforts to improve this piece. Its remaining problems are the fault of the author.

*Zeno of Elea, *Early Greek Philosophy*, ed. John Burnet (Cleveland: World, 1957), 136.

[1]Ulrich Zwingli, *On True and False Religion*, ed. Samuel M. Jackson and Clarence N. Helks (Durham, N.J.: Labyrinth, 1981), 61.

is alleged to have at least implied, "I believe because it is absurd."[2] Most Christians have been less cavalier, affirming that God can be genuinely understood by the human mind but also that the finite human mind can only grasp a "portion" of God's infinite being. The history of Christian reflection demonstrates these limits in its many intellectual conflicts involving the nature of God. During the last half of the twentieth century, this diversity has multiplied as the nature of God has been "reimagined" in many novel ways. The purpose of this chapter is to explore how the limitations of human reason may have contributed to such confusion and how best to understand the complexity of the God of the Bible.

## 2. Human Reason, Formal Logic, and Their Relation

The ability to use formal logic is clearly one of the human mind's most impressive capacities. But what exactly is "formal logic"? Logic as a discipline is the study of the methods and principles for distinguishing good from bad reasoning.[3] Good reasoning is reasoning that has adequate support, demonstrated with deductive and/or inductive arguments. Some arguments, however, are poorly arranged (e.g., a logical fallacy), while others have false premises. Both lead to unwarranted conclusions. Logic, then, consists of the rules and procedures that have been identified for formulating correct conclusions based on appropriate evidence.

"Human reason" refers to the human mind's ability to make use of the rules of formal logic. Reason is the set of mental abilities/structures that permit an individual to "work through" and understand an argument that corresponds to the rules and procedures of formal logic.[4] However, individual human reason is faced with certain limitations. To evaluate the soundness of an argument, human rationality must rely on working memory capacity (which has to maintain the evidence and previously taken logical steps during the evaluation), the activation of relevant long-term memory structures to provide the conceptual context for evaluation (including both logic rules and prior knowledge), and a host of mental skills that equip the individual reasoner to identify the potential problems being faced in a particular conceptual context. The capacities of all these increase throughout childhood and are more developed in some individuals than others.

Reason's ability to use formal logic is essential for human understanding and communication. Without assuming the rules of logic in our thought, nothing could be asserted as true or false, and so all statements would be essentially meaningless. Without logic, no progress could be made in understanding the underlying nature of the world. Science today is essentially the application of logic to our observations of the created order. Thus, the value of logic is inestimable.

---

[2]Tertullian never puts it quite that way. Cf. Etienne Gilson, *History of Christian Philosophy in the Middle Ages* (New York: Random House, 1955), 44–45.

[3]Irving M. Copi, *Introduction to Logic*, 7th ed. (New York: Macmillan, 1996), 3.

[4]This is what the psychologist Piaget termed "formal operations." Cf. Barbel Inhelder and Jean Piaget, *The Growth of Logical Thinking: From Childhood to Adolescence*, trans. A. Parsons and S. Milgram (New York: Basic Books, 1958).

## 3. The Law of Noncontradiction

The rule of logic of most interest for our present purposes is the *law of non-contradiction* (LONC), since many current disagreements about the nature of God relate to perceived violations of this law. The LONC states that no statement can be true and false at the same time and in the same respect.[5] Put another way, we cannot affirm that something is a certain way and at the same time affirm that in the same sense it is not that way.[6] For example, the two assertions "God is a person" and "God is an impersonal force" together violate the LONC. A genuine contradiction between beliefs demonstrates that at least one of those beliefs is false.

Logicians have identified classes of propositions or arguments that violate or appear to violate the LONC. The first two concern propositions. A *contrary* is made up of two statements that cannot both be true, though both could be false (e.g., "There are only two divine beings" and "There are twelve divine beings," for there could be another number, like one). A *contradictory* is made up of two statements such that if one is true, the other must be false, and vice versa (e.g., "God is all-good" and "God is not all-good").[7] All agree that at this level such violations prove that at least one of the statements is false.

However, other violations are more complex. A *paradox* is a set of arguments or statements all of which seem to be valid (or meaningful) but appear to lead to a contradiction or some clearly false conclusion or sense.[8] One example, a version of the "Liar's Paradox," consists simply of one sentence: "This statement is false." Logicians work at solving paradoxes, and some have been shown not to violate the LONC. For example, Quine distinguished between "veridical paradoxes," *apparent* contradictions that are composed of claims all of which can be shown to be true (e.g., a person can be twenty-three years old on his sixth birthday—if he was born on Feb. 29) and "falsidical paradoxes," which have been proven to be invalid in some way (e.g., Zeno's paradoxes).[9] Many paradoxes still remain to be resolved either way.

Paradoxes are valuable to logicians for they can illuminate mistakes in reasoning through the attempt to solve them.[10] However, labeling something a paradox is to recognize the *potential* violation of the LONC without assuming that the prob-

---

[5]Cf. Robert S. Tragesser, "Principle of Contradiction," in *A Companion to Epistemology* (London: Blackwell, 1992), 366; Morris R. Cohen and Ernest Nagel, *An Introduction to Logic* (New York: Harcourt, Brace & World, 1934), 181–82.

[6]F. H. Bradley, *The Principles of Logic* (Oxford: Oxford Univ. Press, 1883), 147.

[7]Wesley C. Salmon, *Logic* (Englewood Cliffs, N.J.: Prentice-Hall, 1963), 101–2; P. F. Strawson, *Introduction to Logical Theory* (Strand, England: Methuen, 1952), 16–19.

[8]John Etchemendy, "Paradox," *The Cambridge Dictionary of Philosophy* (Cambridge: Cambridge Univ. Press, 1995), 558–59.

[9]W. V. Quine, *The Ways of Paradox and Other Essays* (Cambridge, Mass.: Harvard Univ. Press, 1976), 3.

[10]John van Heijenoort, "Logical Paradoxes," *The Encyclopedia of Philosophy*, ed. Paul Edwards, 8 vols. (New York: Macmillan, 1967), 5:50–51. For a list of paradoxes and their attempted solutions, see Glenn W. Erickson and John A. Fossa, *Dictionary of Paradox* (Lanham, Md.: Univ. Press of America, 1998).

lem is necessarily a genuine contradiction. In contrast, the term *antinomy* is reserved for a falsidical paradox consisting of two arguments that individually seem valid but (like contradictories) are mutually exclusive and so *irresolvably* contradictory.[11] For example, one can construct an argument "proving" that the universe began with an uncaused cause as well as an argument "proving" that the world has always been in existence.[12] In such cases, there is no conceivable way that both arguments can be sound (since the universe cannot be both eternal and created).

At the farthest extreme lies an *absurdity*, which is a statement that is patently false or meaningless (e.g., "God is and is not").[13] Absurdities lack intelligibility, whereas both antinomies and paradoxes are at least intelligible. The difference between the latter two is that some paradoxes are *potentially* resolvable, while antinomies are not.

The LONC is necessary in our search for truth. First, it shows that contradictories, contraries, antinomies, and absurdities are false. Second, it serves a motivational purpose with paradoxes, since it leads thinkers to recognize the problem with a paradox and then sets them on the task of attempting to resolve it. As a result, philosophers consider paradoxes more intriguing and fruitful than the other challenges to the LONC. This point is important because some have assumed that to label something a paradox necessarily means it is a genuine contradiction. This just isn't true.[14]

---

[11]Robert S. Tragesser, "Antinomy," in *A Companion to Epistemology*, 17–18. Van Heijenoort describes an antinomy as the most extreme form of paradox in which two propositions are equivalent, yet one is the negation of the other; "Logical Paradoxes," *The Encyclopedia of Philosophy*, 5:45. Quine wrote that an antinomy is "a self-contradiction by accepted ways of reasoning" (*The Ways of Paradox*, 5).

[12]Immanuel Kant coined the term "antinomy" in his exploration of this and other logic problems; *Critique of Pure Reasons*, trans. N. K. Smith (New York: Macmillan: 1929).

[13]Cf. Robert S. Tragesser, "Absurdity," in *A Companion to Epistemology*, 8.

[14]Besides the above, more analytic, discussion regarding paradoxes, more programmatic works that approach paradox constructively from a Continental standpoint can be found in Howard P. Kainz, *Paradox, Dialectic, and System: A Contemporary Reconstruction of the Hegelian Problematic* (University Park, Pa.: Pennsylvania State Univ. Press, 1988); Howard A. Slaatte, *The Pertinence of the Paradox: The Dialectics of Reason-In-Existence* (New York: Humanities, 1968). Mention should probably be made of their Continental roots. Beginning at least with Kant's work on "antinomies," Continental philosophers have typically been more willing to confront the limitations of human reason than have Anglo-American philosophers. Kant demonstrated that formal logic can be used with different assumptions to derive exactly opposite conclusions. Radicalizing Kant's comparatively modest investigation, Hegel concluded that Mind (*Geist*) itself was composed of such rational tensions, and he argued that the development of Mind is best understood as a historical unfolding of dialectical themes into a higher synthesis or reconciliation of opposites; Georg W. Hegel, *The Phenomenology of Mind*, trans. J. B. Baillie (New York: Macmillan, 1931); idem, *Hegel's Science of Logic*, trans. W. H. Johnston and L. G. Struthers (London: George Allen & Unwin, 1929). While his overall system was a significant departure from classical Christianity, more than any previous thinker in the Western tradition, Hegel took seriously the logical tensions that exist in human thought.

Though there are few doctrinaire Hegelians today, in one way or another his insights into the often paradoxical nature of human thought was influential. Marx, Bradley, Nietzsche, Dewey, Husserl, Heidegger, Sartre, Ricoeur, Derrida, and Foucault all have made use of dialectical modes of thought and argument, for good and for ill.

Before moving on, let us add two more terms to our discussion: *concurrence* and *mystery*. Concurrence comes from the Latin "com" ("together" or "with") and "currere" ("to run"). To say two things are concurrent can mean they intersect, run parallel, operate at the same time, act in conjunction, or exercise jurisdiction over the same matter or area (by different authorities).[15] I will use the term *concurrence* in a novel way to refer to a set of propositions or arguments in which each member of the set expresses a truth that is extremely different from the others (they seem to run "parallel"), yet all members accurately refer to the same object or event (they intersect). Put another way, a concurrence is the conjunction of extremely different features in a single entity or event.

For example, let's examine these two sentences: "Human beings are naturally self-centered," and "Human beings are naturally altruistic." Both propositions are true statements about human beings (I would suggest); however, they make very different claims, worded in ways that appear to contradict but, properly understood, do not. So a concurrence is a veridical paradox (like, light is composed of waves and particles). This chapter proposes that some paradoxes regarding God are nothing more than concurrences as defined here.

The term *mystery* originated in the classical Christian tradition to refer to a true proposition about God (or set of propositions) that we have good reason to believe but nevertheless transcends human ability to grasp it in its entirety, either because aspects of the whole truth are not available to us or because it appears to outstrip the capacity of human reason to demonstrate its logical consistency. "God is love" is necessarily a mystery in the former way, since we cannot fully fathom the sentence; "God is triune" has been understood to be an example of the latter.

A concurrence is a mystery in this latter sense. Until a theological paradox is demonstrably solved, the Christian tradition has termed it a mystery in this sense, if there is sufficient, supporting evidence.[16] While the "mystery card" should not be pulled out too quickly, the label has long been used within the classic tradition to acknowledge the limits of human understanding while still rejecting irrationalism and relativism, and we should not fear its use. Looking to Proverbs 8 and John 1, believers have recognized that the rational order of the universe is derived from God's comprehensive understanding of all things. The Christian faith assumes that, though *our* minds can only go so far in knowledge and comprehension, God's intellectual perfection guarantees there are no absolute contradictions in his understanding or in the universe.[17]

---

[15] *Webster's New Collegiate Dictionary* (Springfield, Mass.: G. & C. Merriam, 1974).

[16] The theological usage of "mystery" has a long history in the classic tradition, but it differs from Paul's use of the term *mystērion*, which referred to a truth that had been concealed for ages but had come to be revealed in Christ through the gospel. Cf. P. T. O'Brien, "Mystery," in *Dictionary of Paul and His Letters*, ed. Gerald F. Hawthorne, Ralph P. Martin, and Daniel G. Reid (Downers Grove, Ill.: InterVarsity Press, 1993), 621–23.

[17] Etienne Gilson, *The Spirit of Medieval Philosophy* (New York: Charles Scribner's Sons, 1940), 238; Alvin Plantinga, "Divine Knowledge," in *Christian Perspectives on Religious Knowledge*, ed. C. Stephen Evans and Merold Westphal (Grand Rapids: Eerdmans, 1993), 56–57; Jonathan Edwards, "Notes on the Mind," in *Scientific and Philosophical Writings*, ed. Wallace Anderson

GOD UNDER FIRE

## 4. Scripture and Theology About God and the Limits of Human Reason

While Scripture does not address the use of logic directly, nevertheless, there is much we find there that is indirectly very relevant. Most of Job consists of a debate between two logically coherent perspectives. Job and his friends all seem to believe that Job's suffering requires a rational explanation. Job's friends conclude that since God is all-good and all human suffering is punishment from God for wrongdoing, Job must have done wrong. Job started out with those premises but had another: that he is innocent of wrongdoing. This led him to draw the inference that God may have slipped up. Each side was logically consistent, given its premises. God finally called into question both formal models and concludes the book by arguing that humans are unable to fully understand the ways of God.

That theme is found throughout Scripture. The author of Psalm 139 marvels at the infinite greatness of God. He is omnipresent and omniscient, his thoughts beyond number. Speaking through Isaiah, after calling sinners to repent and be restored, God declared: "For my thoughts are not your thoughts, neither are your ways my ways. . . . As the heavens are higher than the earth, so are my ways higher than your ways and my thoughts than your thoughts" (Isa. 55:8–9).[18] Back in Job, one of his detractors criticized Job's take on his suffering: "Can you fathom the mysteries of God? Can you probe the limits of the Almighty? They are higher than the heavens—what can you do? They are deeper than the depths of the grave—what can you know?" (Job 11:7–8). Later the young, but wise, Elihu said, "God's voice thunders in marvelous ways; he does great things beyond our understanding" (37:5). The earliest wisdom book in the Bible makes very clear that our understanding of God has limits.

Much later, in the book of Romans, after discussing God's mysterious dealings with the Jewish people, Paul exclaimed: "Oh, the depth of the riches of the wisdom and knowledge of God! How unsearchable [*anexeraunētos*] his judgments, and his paths beyond tracing out [*anexichniastos*]! 'Who has known the mind of the Lord? Or who has been His counselor?'" (Rom. 11:33–34). Elsewhere Paul prayed that "the peace of God, which transcends all understanding [*nous*]" might guard the hearts and minds of the Philippians (Phil. 4:7). And in Ephesians, Paul wrote of the unfathomable (*anexichniastos*) riches of

---

(New Haven, Conn.: Yale Univ. Press, 1980), 341–42; Cornelius Van Til, *The Defense of the Faith* (Philadelphia: Presbyterian & Reformed, 1955), 36–39.

[18]This saying doesn't mean that we must be logical but God can be illogical, as has sometimes been alleged. The cause of this exclamation in context is the "scandal" of God's offering forgiveness to *sinners* (who humans might suppose God would simply destroy). The argument moves from the particular to the general: God can forgive sinners (the particular) because (in general) his ways and thoughts are not equal or identical to ours. Thus, a useful principle is being stated: God's understanding transcends ours. We are being encouraged not to assume that just because something makes sense to us, we necessarily have the fullest understanding. His greater understanding brings in other considerations that may show our perspective to be deficient.

Christ (Eph. 3:8).[19] From Old to New Testaments, God and his understanding and salvation are perceived as "beyond our capacities," transcending humanity's ability to fully grasp them.

None of these passages refers to the LONC. Yet there is no reason to assume that these statements do not bear in some way on the logical tension we find in human thought about God. Rather, it seems likely they refer to the limits that our understanding experiences before an infinite God, including the paradoxes we find in God's revelation.[20]

## 4.1 Concurrences in Scripture and Theology

Scripture also contains many examples of concurrences. The most obvious may be Proverbs 26:4–5: "Do not answer a fool according to his folly, or you will be like him yourself. Answer a fool according to his folly, or he will be wise in his own eyes." Each verse is meaningful, but laid side by side they present contradictory admonitions. Of course, each verse gives a reason for its own exhortation that points toward a harmonization. But that does not remove the obstacle of apparently contradictory commands laid side by side. Why would the editor include both, and even put them next to each other? Perhaps because together they argue for the need of a higher understanding: the wisdom to know when to do what.

Jesus often used paradoxical language in his teaching. "For whoever wants to save his life will lose it, but whoever loses his life for me will save it" (Luke 9:24). "The greatest among you should be like the youngest, and the one who rules like the one who serves" (Luke 22:26). He used metaphors in contrary ways that created cognitive dissonance. One time he said, "Do not suppose that I have come

---

[19]Note, however, that Paul also prays that the Ephesians "may have power to *comprehend* with all the saints what is the breadth and length and height and depth, and to know the love of Christ which surpasses knowledge [*gnosis*], that you may be filled up with all the fullness of God" (Eph. 3:18–19, NASB). Paul prays that his readers might know that which is beyond knowledge. It seems we can move towards greater understanding of God even if a *full* understanding is not possible.

[20]There appear to be at least four ways that God's nature and relationship to the creation strain human understanding. (1) There are single truths that deal with infinity in some way and so outstrip our ability to fully grasp them. Such things would include the notion of an eternal being and an infinite being, and God's omnipresence and omniscience (including his knowledge of all numbers and all possibilities, all possible relationships, art works, speeches, etc., yea, all possible worlds). (2) Related to this is an appreciation of the immensity of his understanding and knowledge of everything about the creation, the physical laws of the universe, the functioning of the brain and every living cell, his knowledge of every subatomic particle in the universe and of every one of the billions of stars in the billions of galaxies in the universe, as well as the inner goings-on of every human heart, etc. (3) Genuine mystical experience of God provides a third awareness of God that transcends our mind's rational capacities (cf. 2 Cor. 12:4). (4) The final type is the focus of this article: the existence of *pairs* of truths that appear contradictory since they represent extremely different aspects of God or his relation with human beings. In each of these ways our understanding of God experiences limits.

to bring peace to the earth. I did not come to bring peace, but a sword" (Matt. 10:34); yet to Peter he said, "Put your sword back in its place . . . for all who draw the sword will die by the sword" (Matt. 26:52). After healing a blind man, he said, "For judgment I have come into this world, so that the blind will see and those who see will become blind" (John 9:39). He challenged his hearers to love their enemies (Matt. 5:44) and hate their parents and children (Luke 14:26). These sayings are not impossible to understand, but they show that the very *Logos* of God made use of paradoxical language in striking ways.[21]

Paul also taught with paradoxes. "For when I am weak, then I am strong" (2 Cor. 12:10b). "Continue to work out your salvation with fear and trembling, for it is God who works in you to will and to act according to his good purpose" (Phil. 2:12b–13). And some of his teachings are reminiscent of Jesus' paradox about living through dying, with a Christ-centered twist: "For you died, and your life is now hidden with Christ in God" (Col. 3:3); "I have been crucified with Christ and I no longer live, but Christ lives in me. The life I live . . ." (Gal. 2:20); "count yourselves dead to sin but alive to God in Christ Jesus" (Rom. 6:11). Concurrences pervaded Paul's understanding of the Christian life.[22]

Many scriptural paradoxes are only detected when we compare Scripture with Scripture. Systematic theology, as traditionally conceived, is the attempt to organize and harmonize the chief teachings of Scripture,[23] a task that can only be accomplished with the aid of formal logic. As a result, when systematization is attempted, concurrences leap out. Many, many other paradoxes have been identified in the creation itself.[24] If the universe created by God (a finite reality, infinitely lesser than God himself) is pervaded with paradox, it seems probable that we will find features of God's own nature and dealings with us that likewise challenge our capacity to understand them comprehensively.

## 4.2 Concurrences in God and His Relationship to the Creation

We turn now to consider some specific examples of concurrences regarding the nature of God and his relation to the creation. One of the greatest puzzles regarding God concerns his infinitude. How can a single being be infinite? Christians have long asserted that our knowledge of an infinite God can only be partial.[25] *Finitum non possit capere infinitum* ("the finite cannot grasp the infinite"). Since he is qualitatively of a different order, we have no suitable gauge by which to measure him so as to describe him. His being is "off the scale."

---

[21]Many other puzzles in Jesus' teaching are discussed by Ralph W. Sockman in *The Paradoxes of Jesus* (Nashville: Abingdon, 1936).

[22]See also Edmund B. Keller, *Some Paradoxes of Paul* (New York: Philosophical Library, 1974).

[23]Cf. Charles Hodge, *Systematic Theology*, 3 vols. (Grand Rapids: Eerdmans, 1995), 1:2; W. G. T. Shedd, *Dogmatic Theology*, 3 vols. (Grand Rapids: Zondervan, 1888, 1894), 1:19–20.

[24]See the appendix to this chapter on "Paradoxes Within Creation" for examples.

[25]Hodge, *Systematic Theology*, 1:337. Herman Bavinck, *The Doctrine of God* (Grand Rapids: Baker, 1977), ch. 1.

God's infinite being outstrips our finite capacities. This alone is not a paradox, but God's infinitude itself leads to concurrences in our understanding of him. For example, the consciousness of an omniscient, omnipresent being does not have a single, attentional focus (like humans) but is "spread out," as it were, over all of creation (and time), knowing all things at once. How is it that God can focus his "attention" on all things simultaneously? Similarly, through prayer believers interact with God as a singular person who acts in relation to them sequentially. Yet, God is interacting simultaneously with millions of people, like some kind of multiple person or set of persons. This is due to the one God's immensity, but for humans this paradox of God's personal but omnipresent relationality strains our comprehension.[26]

Another concurrence is also found at the very heart of the Christian revelation of God: God is triune, three-in-one. Yet this seems, on the face of it, like a simple contradiction. With regard to God, 3 = 1. Theologians have struggled with the doctrine of the Trinity since it was first developed, helped by the semantic distinction between person and being or essence: God is one being but three persons. But simple labels do not dissolve the complexity, and many have believed that the Trinity presents a logical problem that cannot be solved. Louis Berkhof, clearly no irrationalist, overstated what nonetheless has been a common intuition in historic Christianity that humans "cannot comprehend it and make it intelligible. It is intelligible in some of its relations and modes of manifestation, but unintelligible in its essential nature."[27] Some early Christian reflection on the biblical teaching showed signs of trying to reduce the logical tension in the direction of oneness (Arianism or modalism) or threeness (tritheism),[28] but the church resisted a simplistic logical solution and formulated the classic Trinity doctrine, a pluralistic monotheism. In response to the Trinity doctrine, Jews, Muslims, and Jehovah's Witnesses all believe the Christian religion is fundamentally irrational.

They may have also been thinking of the Incarnation, which Kierkegaard called the "Absolute Paradox." How could an omnipresent being be located somewhere in space, and how could an eternal being do something novel and

---

[26]Polytheism is at least partially related to finite humanity's (sinful) response to God's immensity.

[27]Louis Berkhof, *Systematic Theology* (Grand Rapids: Eerdmans, 1939), 89. See also Robert L. Dabney, *Systematic Theology*, 2d ed. (St. Louis: Presbyterian, 1878), 179: "I pray the student to bear in mind, that I am not here attempting to explain the Trinity, but just the contrary: I am endeavoring to convince him that it cannot be explained." More optimistic are contemporary Christian philosophers such as Stephen T. Davis, *Logic and the Nature of God* (Grand Rapids: Eerdmans, 1983), and Peter van Inwagen, *God, Knowledge, and Mystery* (Ithaca, N.Y.: Cornell Univ. Press, 1995), chs. 8–9, who have worked hard to elucidate the logical coherence of the Trinity doctrine.

[28]Thomas V. Morris, *Our Idea of God* (Downers Grove, Ill.: InterVarsity Press, 1991), 176; Berkhof, *Systematic Theology*, 82; Gerald L. Bray, "Tritheism," in *New Dictionary of Theology*, ed. Sinclair Ferguson, David F. Wright, and J. I. Packer (Downers Grove, Ill.: InterVarsity Press, 1988), 695.

enter time and history? How could the Creator become a creature? And how could the self-existent, living God die? The Incarnation creates problems for human reason because the terms *God* and *human* are, in all other uses, mutually exclusive.[29]

The Incarnation is in a class by itself, but there are many other concurrences in the relation between God and humanity. How could the eternal God create a temporal order? When did he begin to do this? God is beyond time and unchanging, and yet he also participates fully in history, interacting genuinely with humans.[30] How does God work through humans (so that their good works are really from him), and yet humans accomplish nothing without their own effort?[31] Scripture teaches that God permits evil, yet he is also wholly opposed to sin.[32] We are also told that God loves all people and wants none to perish, and yet God hates sinners who are called the children of wrath.[33]

With regard to salvation, Scripture teaches that God chooses those who come to life, and yet humans must themselves believe in Christ to be saved.[34] Similarly, God has foreordained all that happens, yet human prayer moves God to act in certain ways so that God and humans genuinely interact in time.[35] And while God knows and has planned the future, normal, adult humans are free agents who form their own plans, intentions, and actions, for which they are held responsible, without in any way being divinely constrained or coerced.[36] In all these cases, our understanding is faced with paradox.

God's nature, particularly his infinity, and his relation to the creation pose problems for the LONC. But do the problems presented above consist of contradictories or contraries and so are incoherent (or absurd)? Classic Christians have argued they are merely mysteries (i.e., veridical paradoxes), fundamentally rational and meaningful (since God understands, affirms, and reveals all the pieces of these puzzles). Admittedly, persons holding to different sides of these paradoxes

---

[29]For a discussion of the various charges of incoherence made against the doctrine of the Incarnation, see Thomas V. Morris, *The Logic of God Incarnate* (Ithaca, N.Y.: Cornell Univ. Press, 1986), ch. 1.

[30]Gen. 6:6; Ex. 3:14; 32:14; 1 Sam. 15:29; Job 2:3; Ps. 102:26–27; Isa. 40:28; 57:15; Mal. 3:6; Rom. 1:23, 25; 9:5; 2 Cor. 11:31; 1 Tim. 1:17; 6:16; Heb. 1:11–12. A true contradictory here would be "God is in every sense an eternal being beyond time" and "God is in no sense beyond time and is solely a temporal being."

[31]John 3:21, 27; 15:5; 1 Cor. 15:10; Eph. 2:10. A true contradiction would be "God is working through me" and "God is not working through me." Phil. 2:12–13 is the *locus classicus* text.

[32]Gen. 50:20; Job 1:12; 42:11; Isa. 45:7; James 1:13; 1 John 1:5. A true contradictory in this context would be "God hates sin" and "God loves sin."

[33]Compare John 3:16; Matt. 5:44–45; and 2 Peter 3:9 with Ps. 5:5 and Eph. 2:3. (The reader is encouraged to figure out the paradoxes in this and the following concurrences.)

[34]Compare Acts 13:48; 16:14; and Col. 3:12 with John 3:16; Acts 16:31; Rom. 10:9; and Rev. 3:20.

[35]Dan. 2:21; Ps. 33:10; Eph. 1:11; yet God delights in human prayer (Prov. 15:8) and responds to our requests (cf. his interaction with Abraham in Gen. 18:22–32; with Moses in Num. 14:11–20: "The LORD replied, 'I have forgiven them, as you asked'").

[36]Ps. 139:4, 16; Prov. 16:1, 4; 20:24; 21:1–2; Acts 2:23; 4:27–28.

have periodically "squared off," validating one side of the paradox at the cost of its "opposite." But the greatest teachers of the classic tradition have generally sought to preserve the unity of revealed truth.[37]

## 4.3 Historic Christianity and Concurrences

Over the centuries concurrences in Scripture and in theological reflection have pushed Christians to acknowledge the limitations of human reason and its inability to fully resolve such problems. For most of the classical and medieval periods, the paradoxical quality of many of these features of the Christian faith was appreciated but not highlighted as much as in the post-Reformation era. This may have been due originally to an apologetic concern. Greek and Roman culture so valued human reason (and logic) that church fathers like Augustine would have wisely emphasized instead the reasonableness of Christianity (against the skeptics). Later, Aquinas was much influenced by Aristotle (and the rules of logic he described). As a result neither of these worthies of the classic tradition underscored the paradoxical form of some truths the way some later Christians have.

In light of these influences, it is surprising that they both so fully accepted and worked on paradoxical doctrines such as the Trinity, the Incarnation, and the relation between human freedom and divine sovereignty. Their solution (and that of most classical Christians) was to refer to such topics as "mysteries," understandable to a point but ultimately transcending our ability to fully comprehend them.[38] Augustine presented Scripture on both sides of these paradoxes and insisted that the Christian was bound to both.[39] In some places, he went so far as to pit concurrences in God against each other in order to magnify the greatness of the God of the Bible.[40] In some cases, Aquinas presented the logical problems

---

[37]It should be mentioned somewhere that there are two cosmic contrasts that are fundamental to Christianity and cannot be reconciled in some "higher" harmony. (1) There is the Creator–creature distinction, which teaches that the creation is not to be identified with the Creator (as pantheism teaches and panentheism implies—the creation is "God's body"). (2) There is the absolute opposition between the holy God and sin: "God is light; in him is no darkness at all" (1 John 1:5). No Taoist "Yin/Yang" harmonization of God and sin is rational according to Christianity.

[38]Augustine refers to the Trinity as a mystery: *On the Trinity* 7.4.7 (*The Nicene and Post-Nicene Fathers*, series 1, ed. Philip Schaff, 1886–1889, 14 vols. [reprint, Grand Rapids: Eerdmans, 1971], 3:109); *Faith and the Creed* 9.16 (*NPNF*, 3:327); the Incarnation as mystery: *Enchiridion* 34, 108 (pp. 249, 272); *The City of God* 10.25 (*NPNF*, 2:195); and God's sovereign grace and human freedom as mystery: *On the Spirit and the Letter* 60 (*NPNF*, 5:110); *On Nature and Grace* 2 (*NPNF*, 5:122); *The Gift of Perseverance* 22 (*NPNF*, 5:533). Aquinas refers to the mystery of the Trinity in the *Summa Theologiae*, 1.Q32.A1 and 1.Q46.A2 (in *Basic Writings of Saint Thomas Aquinas* [New York: Random House, 1945], 1:317, 453); and the mystery of the Incarnation: 1.2.Q103.A2 and 2.2.Q1.A6 (in *Basic Writings*, 2:911, 1064).

[39]For example, "When you feel that you do not understand, put your faith in the meanwhile in the inspired word of God, and believe both that man's will is free, and that there is also God's grace, without whose help man's free will can neither be turned towards God, nor make any progress in God"; Augustine, *On Grace and Free Will, Two Letters Written From Augustine to Valentius*, Letter 1 (*NPNF*, 5:438).

GOD UNDER FIRE

in the Christian doctrine of God as logical objections to what he was teaching and then offered formal solutions, demonstrating that Christian truth is not opposed to reason.[41] In other cases, he simply stated that the whole truth in these matters was beyond reason.[42]

Bonaventure likewise affirmed both sides of the same paradoxical truths as Augustine and Aquinas.[43] Like Augustine, he also explored some of the paradoxes of the faith for the sake of advancing our wonder and admiration of God. For example, in one treatise he movingly points to paradoxes in the life of Christ, such as the contrast seen in the humility of God lying in a manger and in the majestic God being overwhelmed by suffering on the cross.[44]

Perhaps the first Christian to make concurrences in Christian theology a major theme in his writing was Nicholas of Cusa (1401–1464), who argued that God is a "coincidence of opposites." Being infinite, God transcends and contains within himself a set of intellectual concurrences or contrasts. He is both the greatest being (maximum) and yet is fully present at the smallest level (minimum). In him maximum and minimum are one. Since human reason must be governed by the LONC (and other rules), Nicholas asserted that human reason is confounded by this God. As a result, Nicholas believed we can have no more than an "approximate" (though genuine) knowledge of God.[45]

Luther also took concurrences in Christian thought seriously. Influenced by the nominalism of his day, Luther's reformational protest can be seen as a

---

[40]Cf. *The Confessions of Saint Augustine*, trans. F. J. Sheed (New York: Sheed & Ward, 1942), 4:

O Thou ... utterly hidden and utterly present, most beautiful and most strong, abiding yet mysterious, suffering no change and changing all things: never new, never old, making all things new, bringing age upon the proud and they know it not; ever in action, ever at rest, gathering all things to Thee and needing none ... ever seeking though lacking nothing. Thou lovest without subjection to passion, Thou art jealous but not with fear; Thou canst know repentance but not sorrow, be angry yet unperturbed by anger. Thou canst change works Thou hast made but Thy mind stands changeless. Thou dost find and receive back what Thou didst never lose; art never in need but dost rejoice in Thy gains, art not greedy but dost exact interest manifold.

[41]E.g., Aquinas's discussion of divine government, evil, and chance in the *Summa Theologiae*, 1.8.103, A7 and A8 (in *Basic Writings*, 1:959–61) and the relation of prayer and providence in *Summa Contra Gentiles*, 3.95–96 (in *Basic Writings*, 2:184–89).

[42]Aquinas believed that to attempt to prove the Trinity by natural reason detracted from the faith. (1) Since faith itself is concerned with things that exceed human reason, it is therefore belittling to it to have to prove such truths with the inferior faculty. (2) Proving with logic what belongs to faith will lead to the presentation of arguments that are invalid and result in ridicule by unbelievers who can see the fallacies. Let us be content, he says, that "what faith teaches is not impossible." Cf. *Summa Theologiae* 1.2.Q32.A1 (in *Basic Writings*, 2:317–18).

[43]See Bonaventure, *Breviloquium*, trans. Erwin E. Nemmers (St. Louis: Herder, 1946), Part 1, chs. 2–6 on the Trinity, ch. 8 on predestination, and ch. 9 on providence.

[44]"The Tree of Life," in *Bonaventure* (CWS; Mahwah, N.J.: Paulist, 1978), 117–76.

[45]Cf. Frederick Copleston, *A History of Philosophy*, 2 vols. (New York: Doubleday, 1963), vol. 2, ch. 15; Etienne Gilson, *History of Christian Philosophy in the Middle Ages* (New York: Random House, 1955), 534–40.

prioritizing of God's words over the philosophical speculations of the Middle Ages.[46] Consequently, he seemed to relish in making paradoxical statements that would scandalize human reason. Much of his theology consisted of a rich juxtaposition of concurrences—God as hidden and revealed, the believer as simultaneously sinner and saint, and the relations of the law and the gospel and the letter and the Spirit—such that critics have disparaged his work as containing logical contradictions.[47]

Luther's glorying in concurrence is seen most powerfully in his "theology of the cross," where he claimed God reveals himself in all his hiddenness: the majestic Son of God slain in weakness and humility, "omnipotent in impotence."[48] His language was sometimes guilty of overstatement. But Luther reveled in such apparent "contradiction" because he wished to magnify the wisdom of God above the mind of humans; he reckoned the Word of God a higher standard than the rules of logic, and faith in God's Word a higher human activity than reason.

Calvin wrote often of the limitations of human reason when considering God and his relation to humans. To cite one example, in his discussion of the relation of God's decree to human responsibility, sin, and personal faith, he noted that logical objections have often been made regarding God's predestination: It makes God a tyrant and the author of sin and would seem to excuse sinners; yet sinners are brought to judgment, so it seems unfair to judge sinners for actions that were foreordained.[49] Nonetheless, since the Bible teaches these truths, Calvin argued, we must submit to them regardless of the offense they seem to cause our reason. Closer to Augustine in how he treated such problems, Calvin did not so highlight the paradoxical nature of Christian doctrine like Luther, preferring to use the classical notion of mystery for such truths.[50] He simply argued that God's nature and judgments are beyond the reach of human reason. Paul "teaches how unworthy it is to reduce God's works to such a law that the moment we fail to understand their reason, we dare to condemn them." "Monstrous indeed is the madness of men, who desire thus to subject the immeasurable to the puny measure of their own reason."[51]

---

[46]Gerhard Ebeling, *Luther: An Introduction to His Thought* (Philadelphia: Fortress, 1970), 86.

[47]Ebeling sees such paradoxes as central to Luther's theology (*Luther*, 141–49). According to him, in Luther's thinking, each member of an apparent contrary "has its own limits. In fact one might be even more precise and say that one is not merely inevitably tolerated in conjunction with the other, but rather is accorded its own proper function as a result of this conjunction and distinction" (142).

[48]Ibid., 241.

[49]John Calvin, *Institutes of the Christian Religion*, ed. John T. McNeill, trans. Ford Lewis Battles, 2 vols. (Philadelphia: Westminster, 1960), 3.23.

[50]E.g., the *mystery* of the Trinity, Calvin, *Institutes*, 1.13.17; of Christ's two natures, 2.14.1; of faith, which is a gift, 3.2.33; and of salvation, 3.2.41.

[51]Calvin, *Institutes*, 3.23.4. Calvin's confidence in Scripture led him to embrace concurrent truths regardless of the problems they posed for reason.

Doctrines that are clear in themselves, but logically incompatible with one another, are placed side by side because Calvin finds them so in Scripture. He developed each

GOD UNDER FIRE

Also influenced by Augustine, the Christian thinker Blaisé Pascal was likewise disposed to respect reason's limits.[52] "The last proceeding of reason is to recognize that there is an infinity of things which are beyond it. It is but feeble if it does not see so far as to know this. But if natural things are beyond it, what will be said of supernatural?"[53] This great mathematician was keenly aware of the value of formal logic, but he recognized that the complexity of reality could not be grasped by a simplistic use of that logic. "The two contrary reasons. We must begin with that; without that we understand nothing, and all is heretical; and we must even add at the end of each truth that the opposite truth is to be remembered."[54]

More radical is the approach of Søren Kierkegaard. He was admittedly profoundly influenced by Hegel (though perhaps as much by reacting against Hegel's system as positively). But as a result, more so than perhaps any Christian in history, his work is pervaded by an unusual interest in paradox. In light of Hegel's efforts to take paradox seriously (and likely Luther's love of paradoxical thought), Kierkegaard brought it into the center of his understanding. That the eternal God could become a historical being struck Kierkegaard as absurd and incomprehensible to human reason and provided an intellectual scandal with only one way out: a leap of faith in the gospel.[55] A related paradox concerned how humans can stake their *eternal* well-being on a historical person such as Jesus and a historical event like his death. Kierkegaard believed paradox lurked nearby much of significant human understanding.

Kierkegaard's notion of paradox is, of course, controversial, and many philosophers have argued it is incoherent.[56] To say that the Incarnation involves

---

doctrine as he found it to its logical end, no matter how violently the conclusion might be controverted by some other theme similarly developed. In this pursuit Calvin was one of the most relentless of theologians and was sometimes called upon, to borrow words from Augustine or Bernard, to express his own wonderment before these antinomies [*sic*] of his thought that were to him none other than the mysteries of God's will. (Edward A. Dowey Jr., *The Knowledge of God in Calvin's Theology*, expanded ed. [Grand Rapids: Eerdmans, 1994], 37.)

Yet Calvin refused to accept that these truths were genuine contradictions. He was no irrationalist but valued human reason (within its limits), and he used it vigorously to solve logical problems where possible. "While Calvin as an exegete was a virtuoso at harmonizing surface inconsistencies in Scripture, he never conceived of his theological task as an effort to harmonize the deeper paradoxes of Scripture or to explain what he regarded as its central mysteries" (ibid., 40).

[52]Cf. Blaisé Pascal, *Pensées*, trans. W. F. Trotter (New York: Modern Library, 1941), ##229–31, 233, 268–84, 416–24.

[53]Ibid., #267.

[54]Ibid., #566.

[55]Søren A. Kierkegaard, *Concluding Unscientific Postscript*, trans. H. V. Hong and E. H. Hong (Princeton, N.J.: Princeton Univ. Press, 1992), 561.

[56]Alasdair MacIntyre, "Soren Aabye Kierkegaard," in *The Encyclopedia of Philosophy*, ed. Paul Edwards, 8 vols. (New York: Macmillan, 1967), 4:339; Robert Merrihew Adams, "Kierkegaard's Arguments Against Objective Reasoning in Religion," in *The Virtue of Faith and Other Essays in Philosophical Theology* (New York: Oxford Univ. Press, 1987), 25–41.

a genuine contradiction, an unresolvable paradox, an absurdity, would seem to suggest that Christianity is fundamentally irrational. As stated above, an absurdity is meaningless, nonsensical; yet clearly the notion of the Incarnation has meaning. Kierkegaard himself spent a great deal of time demonstrating (we might say, negatively) the "hidden rationale" of the Incarnation and the compelling sensibility of committing oneself to the historical person of Christ and his death. Thus, upon closer reflection, it would seem that Kierkegaard himself did not believe that the paradoxes of Christianity were genuine contradictions. Rather, he used the terms "paradox" and "absurdity" to highlight the scandal and challenge that Christian truth presents to human reason. Though Kierkegaard's use of the term "absurdity" was an unfortunate overstatement, it served to highlight the limitations of reason to resolve all the mysteries of the faith and the superlative value of a faith beyond and (in some ways) against human reason.[57]

A number of twentieth-century theologians built on Kierkegaard's appreciation of paradox, forming a movement known as neo-orthodoxy, which included the likes of Karl Barth, Emil Brunner, Dietrich Bonhoeffer, Otto Weber, and Reinhold Niebuhr, and influenced the Catholic Hans Urs von Balthasar, and in the present, T. F. Torrance and Eberhard Jungel.[58] The most important was Karl Barth. Reacting against the rationalism and historicism of liberalism, Barth pursued theological paradox with unusual (and notorious) thoroughness. Throughout his *Church Dogmatics*, Barth seemed to enjoy juxtaposing the complementary, yet concurrent truths of Christianity, including the nature of the Trinity, Jesus Christ the God-man, God as one yet consisting of many perfections, the relation between God's freedom and nature, God's eternality and temporality, the relation of grace and obedience, and the Scripture as the word of God and of human beings.[59]

---

[57]For a defense of this interpretation of Kierkegaard, see C. Stephen Evans, *Faith Beyond Reason* (Grand Rapids: Eerdmans, 1997); idem, *Passionate Reason: Making Sense of Kierkegaard's Philosophical Fragments* (Bloomington, Ind.: Indiana Univ. Press, 1992); cf. Cornelio Fabro, "Faith and Reason in Kierkegaard's Dialectic," in *A Kierkegaard Critique*, ed. Howard A. Johnson and Niels Thulstrup (New York: Harper & Brothers, 1962), 156–206.

[58]See Emil Brunner, *The Christian Doctrine of Creation and Redemption*, trans. Olive Wyon (Philadelphia: Westminster, 1952), 170–75; Reinhold Niebuhr, *The Nature and Destiny of Man*, vol. 2: *Human Destiny* (New York: Charles Scribner's Sons, 1943), 204; Otto Weber, *Foundations of Dogmatics*, trans. Darrell L. Guder, 2 vols. (Grand Rapids: Eerdmans, 1981), 1:379; T. F. Torrance, *Theological Science* (Oxford: Oxford Univ. Press, 1969), 139. Most important on this theme in the present is Eberhard Jungel's *God As the Mystery of the World*, trans. Darrell L. Guder (Grand Rapids: Eerdmans, 1983). Unfortunately, some neo-orthodox (e.g., Niebuhr, *Nature and Destiny*, 2:204) revealed a tendency towards irrationalism by sometimes seeming to speak of paradoxes as if they were genuine contradictions. This kind of careless approach among some has done much to discredit the value of paradox in Christian understanding among others in the twentieth century.

[59]See Karl Barth, *Church Dogmatics*, ed. G. W. Bromiley and T. F. Torrance, vol. 1, trans. G. T. Thomas and Harold Knight (Edinburgh: T. & T. Clark, 1956), ch. 2, §15, for a general discussion of the mystery of God's revelation; ch. 2, §§8–13 and 16, on the Trinity and the Incarnation (esp. §13); vol. 2, trans. T. H. L. Parker et al. (Edinburgh, T. & T. Clark, 1957), ch. 6, §29, on the divine perfections; ch. 6, §31, on divine freedom and necessity; ch. 8 §§36–39, on grace and obedience; and vol. 1, ch. 1, §4, on Scripture.

Barth clearly saw himself as an orthodox theologian, and liberals continue to reckon him as such (though those more orthodox have pointed out some significant aberrations). Like Kierkegaard, he was not as careful to defend the role of logic in theology as he should have been, and his views on the fall of humankind, the nature of Scripture, and the final state of unbelievers were suborthodox. However, charity would note he was moving away from liberalism toward Scripture throughout his life (a pattern analogous to Augustine's), and his painstaking use of logical argumentation throughout the *Church Dogmatics* make clear Barth was no irrationalist or relativist. For Barth, theology meant a "rational wrestling with mystery."[60]

Though strongly opposed to both Kierkegaard and neo-orthodoxy (but influenced by the continental theologians Bavinck and Kuyper), the conservative twentieth-century evangelical apologist Cornelius Van Til similarly made much of the apparent paradoxes of the faith. Van Til argued that some truths exist in a necessary, corollary interrelationship—for example, God's control over all human actions and human responsibility. These pairs of truths he called "limiting concepts," since each side of the intellectual tension was "limited" by the other, corollary truth; both were needed to obtain the fullest, most accurate understanding of reality. To hold solely to either side to the exclusion of its "opposite" was to end up in serious intellectual error.[61] He believed such paradoxes were inevitable for finite human reason and that their ontological grounding was found in God himself, who is three-in-one.

Two of Van Til's students, John Frame and Vern Poythress, have developed their own theological models ("perspectivalism" and "symphonic theology," respectively), which make the acceptance of concurrences fundamental to their theological method.[62] But many other evangelical theologians have argued for some appreciation of mystery and paradox in theology, including G. C. Berkouwer, Thomas Oden, Donald Bloesch, J. I. Packer, D. A. Carson, Millard Erickson, and Wayne Grudem.[63]

---

[60]Barth, *Church Dogmatics*, 1/1:368.

[61]See Cornelius Van Til, *Common Grace and the Gospel* (Philadelphia: Presbyterian & Reformed, 1974), 11, 38, 174; idem, *Defense of the Faith*, 3d ed. (Philadelphia: Presbyterian & Reformed, 1967), 44–46. Cf. John M. Frame, *Cornelius Van Til: An Analysis of His Thought* (Phillipsburg, N.J.: Presbyterian & Reformed, 1995), ch. 13. Van Til has been castigated by some logicians for being an irrationalist. A sympathetic reading of his work reveals that he was deeply committed to the fundamental rationality of the universe and of God. God himself, he wrote, was Absolute Rationality. One can as easily make the claim of this complex thinker that he was too much of a rationalist, as did Herman Dooyeweerd, "Cornelius Van Til and the Transcendental Critique of Theoretical Thought," in *Jerusalem and Athens*, ed. E. R. Geehan (Philadelphia: Presbyterian & Reformed, 1971), 81–89.

[62]John Frame, *The Doctrine of the Knowledge of God* (Phillipsburg, N.J.: Presbyterian & Reformed, 1987); Vern Poythress, *Symphonic Theology* (Grand Rapids: Zondervan, 1987).

[63]See G. C. Berkouwer, *Faith and Sanctification* (Grand Rapids: Eerdmans, 1952), 117; Thomas C. Oden, *Systematic Theology*, vol. 1, *The Living God* (New York: Harper & Row, 1987), 405–6; Donald G. Bloesch, *Essentials of Evangelical Theology*, 2 vols. (New York: Harper & Row,

This selective historical survey shows that many in the Christian tradition have recognized concurrences within Christian faith and thought, both Catholic and Protestant, ancient and contemporary.[64] Of course, specific positions lie on a continuum. Some (like Augustine and Aquinas) wrestled with concurrences without calling much attention to them, referring to them as "mysteries," while others (like Kierkegaard) so emphasized paradox that they have raised questions about the intelligibility of their position. Within these boundaries, however, lies a historic Christian orthodoxy that has insisted on the ultimate rationality of Christianity and the essential role of logic in understanding the faith, combined with a recognition of the limits of human reason—one of which is its typical inability to do full justice to the concurrences there are in God's nature and his relations to his creation.

## 5. Examples of How a Misuse of Formal Logic Has Distorted Models of God

Reason has been consistently highly esteemed in the Christian tradition as an essential tool of understanding, along with other sources, including sensory experience, intuition and personal experience, testimony, and Scripture. However, in the Enlightenment (combined with the scientific revolution) modern thinkers began to trust in reason (together with publicly verifiable, empirical research) as the primary adjudicator of truth, overturning all other criteria (at least until the advent of postmodernism and its precursors). The effects of this emphasis have been destructive for theology since this move has meant that modern understandings of God have been constrained by what can be comprehended by finite human reason. All too often, Enlightenment reason has formed premature conclusions about what is logical and what is contradictory, resulting in a rejection of

---

1978), 1:127; Millard J. Erickson, *Christian Theology*, 3 vols. in 1 (Grand Rapids: Baker, 1983–1985), 338–41, 733–34; Wayne Grudem, *Systematic Theology* (Grand Rapids: Zondervan; 1994), 34–35; J. I. Packer, *Evangelism and the Sovereignty of God* (Chicago: InterVarsity Press, 1967); D. A. Carson, *Divine Sovereignty and Human Responsibility: Biblical Perspectives in Tension* (Atlanta: John Knox, 1981).

It would be misleading, however, not to acknowledge that some twentieth-century evangelicals have argued against paradox. Carl F. H. Henry, for example, is deeply opposed to such language, feeling that to use it in reference to Christian truth compromises its essential intelligibility; see his *God, Revelation, and Authority*, 6 vols. (Waco, Tex.: Word, 1979), 3:232–36. Coming from a similar standpoint, Ronald H. Nash rejects the views of Kierkegaard, Bloesch, and Van Til as pious nonsense; see Nash's *The Word of God and the Mind of Man* (Grand Rapids: Zondervan, 1983), 91–112. Even the evangelicals cited above differ significantly in how they approach paradox, from Grudem, who is much closer to Henry and Nash in how he explains paradox, to Bloesch, who uses paradoxical language without proper qualification.

[64]There have, of course, been numerous defenders of paradox who are no friends of classical Christianity. Paul Tillich and Rudolf Bultmann, as well as many postmodern theologues, have defended dialectical/paradoxical and (in postmodernism) relativistic thinking, while departing significantly from Christian notions of God. The fact is that both orthodox and nonorthodox have appealed to paradox.

"contrary" evidence that seems to contradict other, preferred evidence. Examples abound in contemporary thinking about God.[65]

## 5.1 A Process God    $H\,6$

Since classical Christian theism became more self-reflective and began developing philosophical sophistication in the early church, it has asserted that God is absolutely independent of his creation. He is self-existent and self-sufficient and does not derive anything ultimately from the creation he made. Process theologians, however, have argued that this assumption is not logically compatible with God's involvement in and concern for the goings-on of his creatures, particularly humans. Schubert M. Ogden, for example, complains that there exists "an irreconcilable opposition between the premises of this supernaturalistic theism and the whole direction of our experience and reflection as secular men."[66] To begin with, secularists require "logical self-consistency as one of the necessary conditions for the truth of any assertion."[67]

Ogden then gives two examples of what he believes to be hopeless contradictions in classical theism. (1) This tradition has long maintained both that God freely created all things and yet that everything he does is a function of his simple, eternal, necessary being, which would seem to exclude all contingent events such as a novel creation. (2) Similarly, the classical God has created humans to serve and glorify him, and yet because this God exists in perfect bliss, he is completely unaffected by all that we do; our sin or suffering do not touch him, so that he must be wholly indifferent to our welfare. Ogden terms these "antinomies" and suggests they are incoherent because "they both deny and affirm that God's relation to the world is real and that he is relevant to its life because it is relevant to his."[68]

Ogden offers another vision of God, what he called in the 1960s "a secular faith," which cuts loose the self-sufficiency notions of God from the relational, offering God who is genuinely related to our life so that we and our actions make a difference in his actual being. To him, it is logically impossible to speak of the significance of human actions without this kind of God.[69] Notably, he accuses classical theism of one-sidedness. Since it focuses exclusively on God's transcendence, it is therefore required to deny that God is really related to our life at all. Ogden acknowledges that classical theists call God "Father" and refer to their relationship with him. But this can be nothing more than appearance, since God's relationality is logically incompatible with his aseity, something classical theists themselves prove

---

[65]Unfortunately, this section can provide no more than illustrations of how a one-sided favoritism is often paired with formal logic, with disastrous results in contemporary theology opposed to historic Christianity's view of God.

[66]Schubert M. Ogden, *The Reality of God and Other Essays* (New York: Harper & Row, 1966), 17.

[67]Ibid.

[68]Ibid., 18.

[69]Ibid., 47.

when they speak of the "anthropomorophic" qualities of God. "God is not *really* relational, he merely looks like he is"; thus, ultimately God is entirely untouched by us. Instead, Ogden argues for a "dipolar God," one who is both supremely relative to us (relational) and supremely absolute (a necessary being with some nonchanging features, e.g., God transcends the creation and God is love).

Admittedly, some classical theists have not always evenhandedly held on to both truths in some theological concurrences. Nevertheless, at its best the historic Christian tradition has always sought to hold the truths that God is genuinely interested in our lives, saddened by our suffering, delighted by our holiness, disappointed and angered by our sin; at the same time, he lives in transcendent, unalterable blessedness. More dangerously one-sided, Ogden eliminates the logical tension of historic Christianity by jettisoning one entire side of the paradox, so that the preferred, relational side is exalted at the expense of God's independence and transcendence. The absolute pole of the "dipolar God" is severely truncated, since this panentheistic God is unable to know, plan, or change the future apart from the independent actions of human creatures (though admittedly the process God is not quite as large a distortion as the God of pantheism). Ultimately, the construction of the process God was constrained by a rigid use of formal logic, resulting in a God bigger than us but tragically smaller than the God of the Bible.

## 5.2 A Feminist God

Feminists have had many difficulties with the God of historic Christian theism. Sallie McFague is one of a number who want to maintain an identification with the Christian tradition but critique it from the standpoint of secular feminist canons of justice.[70] In addition, a simplistic use of formal logic likewise distorts her conclusions regarding God's nature. Although she is loath to explicitly reject any model of God (given her thesis that such models are nothing more than *our* constructions of God), much of McFague's major book, *Models of God*, is an extended rejection of the God of historic Christianity since its model is patriarchical, monarchical, hierarchical, exclusive, and triumphalist. She opposes this model because it advances a view of God as distant from and uninvolved with the world and promotes attitudes of militarism and dominance on the one hand and passivity on the other, justifies escapism from responsibility, focuses on sin and obedience, undermines an appreciation for the nonhuman world/environment, and "condones control through violence and oppression."[71]

How can this litany of evils be laid at the door of historic Christian theism? Much of the force of her critique is derived from her contrasting the repudiated features of the historic Christian model with other, more favored aspects of God from within the Christian tradition and her allegation that these two sets of traits are logically incompatible. The favored set of traits includes God as nurturing, caring, and empathic, centering on God's identification with all of creation,

---

[70]Sallie McFague, *Models of God: Theology for an Ecological, Nuclear Age* (Philadelphia: Fortress, 1987).
[71]Ibid., 77.

including those who suffer. These traits promote a destabilizing but justice-promoting message of unqualified love that moves us to befriend the needy, the outcast, and the oppressed. She advocates a nonhierarchical model of God that sees God as acting "through persuasion and attraction," a coparticipant in human history with the cosmos as God's body.

According to McFague, these two sets of traits are fundamentally opposed. The former is a "direct assault" on the latter.[72] If we accept the historic interpretation, she says, "we not only accept a salvation we do not need but weaken if not destroy our ability to understand and accept the salvation we do need. The triumphalist mythology makes impossible the interpretation of the way to our salvation on several points."[73] She admits her portrayal of the historic Christian model could be a caricature but insists that her allegations "are the direct implications of its imagery."[74] "This is the logical implication of hierarchical dualism: God's action is on the world, not in it, and it is a kind of action that inhibits human growth and responsibility." It "implies the wrong kind of divine activity in relation to the world, a kind that encourages passivity on the part of human beings."[75] McFague's rigid use of logic drives a wedge between these two "models."

Most troubling is the panentheism of McFague's model, which results in a blurring of the Creator-creature distinction, a nonnegotiable postulate of orthodox Christianity. But her main problem for our purposes is her bias towards the God-traits of unqualified love, nurturance, and care. This favoritism presses her analysis into the caricature she senses but still affirms, because her inflexible use of the LONC makes it impossible for her to reconcile God's rule over humanity with his care for humanity, his supremacy with our well-being, and his holiness with his love. She understands these two sets of characteristics to be ultimately contradictory, mutually exclusive, and undermining of each other.

## 5.3 An Open God

Though there are sympathies between the foregoing models and the open view of God, the latter offers an understanding of God closer to historic Christianity since it posits definite personhood to God (contra McFague) and maintains a strong Creator-creature distinction (contra both McFague and Ogden). Nevertheless, open theism also departs from the historic Christian view of God. Here, we will limit ourselves to considering one open theist's treatment of the relation of God's sovereignty to human actions.

Christians within the historic tradition have wrestled with this topic for centuries. This is because, as noted above, Scripture teaches both that God foreknows all that happens, and yet God and humans can genuinely interact and humans are responsible for their actions, all of which provides a challenge for human reason. Open theism, however, departs from both the Augustinian/Calvinist and

---

[72]Ibid., 54.
[73]Ibid.
[74]Ibid., 65.
[75]Ibid., 68.

Semi-Pelagian/Arminian/Wesleyan resolutions of this paradox by asserting that God can neither determine nor know the future, free choices of humans.

Why do open theists hold this novel position? In the case of John Sanders, one reason is his rigid use of the LONC. Sanders points to the teachings in the Bible regarding God's being grieved, changing his mind, resorting to alternative plans, and being open and responsive to what humans do, and he maintains these teachings are logically incompatible with the view that God knows the future and especially with the Calvinist view that he has ordained it. "These sorts of things make no sense within the framework of specific sovereignty. If God always gets precisely what he desires in each and every situation, then it is incoherent to speak of God's being grieved about or responding to the human situation."[76] "My principle argument against exhaustive sovereignty is that it rules out certain experiences, decisions and actions that the Bible and many theists attribute to God."[77]

If God has determined the human actions that will come to pass (as Augustinians/Calvinists affirm), then it seems to follow logically that humans are puppets of God, and God cannot feel genuine sorrow over human sins and suffering or joy over their obedience. Logic, Sanders believes, forces us to opt for either a relational God or a God who determines the future. "One simply cannot have it both ways: either God controls everything and the divine-human relationship is impersonal, or God does not control everything and so it is possible for the divine-human relationship to be personal."[78]

---

[76]John Sanders, *The God Who Risks: A Theology of Providence* (Downers Grove, Ill.: InterVarsity Press, 1998), 213. He goes on:
> How can God be grieved if precisely what God wanted to happen did happen? If specific sovereignty is true, then it is *incorrect* to speak of God's getting upset with human sin because any sin is specifically what God wanted to come about. It is *inconsistent* to affirm exhaustive sovereignty and also claim that God wants to give us something but does not give it because we fail to ask him in prayer.... This does not *comport with* my reading of Scripture or my understanding of prayer. (italics mine)

[77]Ibid., 212.

[78]Ibid., 215. Sanders criticizes how Packer (and others) have used the notion of an "apparent" contradiction to refer to a problem that is intrinsically logically irresolvable *to us*. First, ignoring philosophical work on paradox, he says that something either is or is not contradictory; there is no in-between status. Second, Sanders believes that to say some truths are contradictory to us but not to God is irrational, because it is unknowable and no one can possibly confirm its truth value. Similarly, Sanders asks how we could possibly be sure that something that is contradictory to us is not also to God. But both these points suppose we are not within our epistemic rights to affirm something is true by faith. Lastly, Sanders argues that we cannot appeal to apparent contradiction since to affirm a contradiction to us defies the rules for intelligibility to which all humans must conform if we are to engage in meaningful discourse with one another. This too ignores contemporary work on paradox.

Sanders's dismissal of Packer's position as irrational and unintelligible is specious in the extreme. As we have seen, many problems in math, logic, physics, psychology, and sociology have been discovered that are "apparently contradictory" for at least a while (and some are still unresolved), and time must pass between the recognition of paradoxes and their resolution. In fact, their future resolution depends on the hope that one can be found. One need not be necessarily irrational to hold out for a resolution one day, whether in this age, or as Packer and others suggest, in the age to come. Perhaps the real problem for Sanders (among others) is

There is a logical tension here, and Christians have held a continuum of positions on this issue. Whereas open theists favor the relational passages of the Bible and distort the foreknowledge and sovereignty passages, hyper-Calvinists, at the other end, have distorted God's general love for all.[79] However, both sets of truths have a scriptural basis. When the open theist (or anyone) opts for one member of the pair as providing the true hermeneutic key, the other set of Scriptures ends up being either distorted or ignored.[80] Note, for example, that Sanders remarkably omits, in a book on providence, any reference to the book of Job. There God is revealed as expressly permitting (through the instrumentality of Satan; ch. 1–2) and even causing (see 42:11) the suffering of Job (which somehow included sin: the killing by the bandits).

As in the other alternative theologies we have examined, the understanding of God put forth by open theism is truncated by a rigid use of logic unable to do justice to evidence that appears to contradict its favored set of truths. In the face of the preponderance of scriptural evidence on both sides of such issues, the opponents of historic Christian theism must do more than assert that one line of evidence/argument contradicts another line of evidence/argument. Such an "argument" does nothing more than highlight the concurrence.

---

ethical: he is not patient enough. Perhaps the most virtuous response to two lines of substantial evidence/argument for now is a humble acceptance of both of them until they are constructively resolved in a way that preserves both truths.

Packer is following the majority of classical Christians who assume that God is fully rational and that the universe contains no genuine contradictions (square circles or colorless red cars) and concludes that there are therefore no genuine contradictions for God. So Sanders's accusation of unintelligibility simply amounts to a straw man. Packer's position would be unintelligible if he believed that genuine contradictions exist for God too, or that we could not assert anything meaningful about God. But why is it necessarily unintelligible to be agnostic about the reconciliation of two sets of arguments? Sanders is criticizing those who insist on submitting to Scripture, whatever it says, and so are unwilling to allow our present finite understanding to overturn clear lines of evidence/argument. This is no more irrational than the child who believes that Christ died on the cross for her sins even though she does not understand the logic behind the substitutionary atonement. Indeed, perhaps the Christian faith involves just the sort of submissive acceptance of transcendent truth that one finds in a child.

[79]Cf. John Gill, *Body of Divinity* (1839; reprint, Atlanta: Turner Lassetter, 1965), 472, where he argues that "the world" of John 3:16 does not refer to all individual humans (since Christ did not die for all of them) but to the world of Gentiles, so as to make clear the gospel's application to non-Jews. Gill is as logically consistent as the open theists. Both, however, have to distort or obscure passages that do not fit into their rigidly logical scheme.

[80]Another consequence of hyperlogicism is that the positions of opponents get misrepresented. Sanders, for example, repeatedly reads into his opponents conclusions they would reject; e.g., in *God Who Risks*, 212, he suggests that when a woman is raped and dismembered, those who hold to meticulous providence believe that God wanted that to happen, without qualification. Yet, as he surely knows, Reformed Christians have long sought to safeguard both God's holiness and his love for sinners with language like "the two wills of God" and "permission." Such language has problems, but Sanders is guilty of the grossest of distortions when he represents that the position of meticulous providence entails the belief that God wants women raped. But rather than accuse him of deliberate misrepresentation, we should understand his interpretation is justified, even required, given the lens of his simplistic system.

This is not to suggest that those within historic Christianity have never been guilty of emphasizing one member of a concurrent pair over the other. In fact, these alternative theologies may do the Christian tradition a service by pointing out when God's sovereignty or simplicity or impassability is so emphasized that the "opposite" truth is reinterpreted or ignored. Nevertheless, a study of the great sermons and writings of the church down through the centuries shows that its teachers have consistently affirmed a rich, complex view of God: a transcendent *and* relational God, who genuinely grieves, sorrows, and delights in his creatures while ruling over all their affairs.

## 6. The Development of Reason

We have seen that a simplistic use of formal logic can get in the way of understanding God in all his fullness, in spite of formal logic's indispensable role in understanding. How is it that the human use of logic can become a barrier to understanding? To help answer this question we must consider how the human use of formal logic develops.

### 6.1 Metasystemic Thought

Jean Piaget, the great Swiss cognitive-developmental psychologist, devoted his life to tracking the development of reason over the course of childhood and adolescence into its mature form in adults. As a result of his studies,[81] Piaget found that the ability to think logically develops over time in fairly discrete stages of increasing complexity,[82] with the ability to use formal logic beginning to develop in adolescence.[83] The first stage we could call "preformal" or "presystemic." (Piaget actually distinguished two childhood stages he called preoperational and concrete operational, but here we will treat them as one stage.)

Presystemic thought is the thinking of the child (and most adults too, when we don't need or want to think more complexly about a topic). School-age children have a limited ability to think logically. For example, they can draw inferences regarding material reality (the size and shape of objects) and relationships between objects (stick A > stick B, stick B > stick C, so stick A > stick C). However, preadolescents cannot think *abstractly*; they cannot think about their thoughts,

---

[81]Jean Piaget, *Judgment and Reasoning in the Child*, trans. M. Warden (Paterson, N.J.: Littlefield, Adams & Co., 1959); idem, *The Language and Thought of the Child*, trans. M. Gabain (London: Routledge & Kegan Paul, 1926); Barbel Indhelder and Jean Piaget, *The Growth of Logical Thinking*, trans. Anne Parsons and Stanley Milgram (New York: Basic Books, 1958).

[82]Some psychologists have raised questions about just how stagelike these differences really are, arguing that the same processes are evident at every stage or that domain-specific learning demonstrates nonuniversal mental structures. Nevertheless, many developmentalists accept the notion of stages of cognitive development since each stage is characterized by an identifiable level of complexity that appears to be qualitatively different from earlier ones. See Patricia H. Miller, *Theories of Developmental Psychology*, 3d ed. (New York: W. H. Freeman, 1993), ch. 1.

[83]However, subsequent researchers have found that not all humans end up being able to think using formal logic. Even by the college years, only about 50 percent of college students give consistent evidence of using formal logic (at least as understood and assessed by Piaget). See E. T. Pascarelli and P. T. Terenzini, *How College Affects Students* (San Francisco: Jossey-Bass, 1991).

they cannot relate thoughts to each other and assess their logical consistency, and they cannot organize their thoughts into a coherent system. Rather, their belief system contains internal contradictions, which they are unable to recognize, because they have not developed the cognitive ability to identify immaterial objects (like thoughts).

Piaget found that the ability to think abstractly or systemically—what he called the stage of "formal operations"—begins with adolescents. They can think about their thoughts (second-order mental operations), so they can organize and compare those thoughts and evaluate their logical consistency. As a result, they are able to develop a "system" of beliefs that do not contradict each other.

According to Piaget, the ability to use formal logic is the most complex form of thinking possible for humans. However, post-Piagetian researchers have noted significant differences in how formal logic is used by adults, distinguishing between "systemic" and "metasystemic" thinking. Systemic thinkers have a hard time grasping what happens when systems themselves change (e.g., historically) and when variables (and systems) interact with each other (as in the weather or in complex social interactions); they struggle in real-life problem-solving contexts where people don't have all the information necessary to solve the problem in a clear-cut way (e.g., should I change careers?); most importantly for the concerns of this chapter, rigidly systemic thinking seems unable to synthesize a number of single systems or perspectives into a larger picture, a "metasystem."[84]

As we have seen, some things in the universe have concurrences, features that seem very different and are hard to harmonize (e.g., light being composed of particles and waves). Faced with such concurrences, a systemic thinker typically applies the LONC *prematurely* and *unwisely* (crying "contradiction" *too soon*) and works out a one-sided solution that undermines the conceptual tensions, too quickly eliminating the contrast in order to provide superficially coherent, but simplistic, understanding. As a result, there is no motivational impetus to develop more complex thought structures that allow one to hold the truths in tension. The strict systemic thinker is "embedded" in the thought structures of a simple system.[85] This impatient formalizing agenda ends up obscuring the side of the concurrence not favored or valued.

---

[84]Michael L. Commons, Francis A. Richards, and Cheryl Armon, eds., *Beyond Formal Operations: Late Adolescent and Adult Cognitive Development* (New York: Praeger, 1984); John M. Rybash, William J. Hoyer, and Paul A. Roodin, *Adult Cognition and Aging: Developmental Changes in Processing, Knowing, and Thinking* (New York: Pergamon, 1986).

[85]Robert Kegan, *The Evolving Self: Problem and Process in Human Development* (Cambridge, Mass.: Harvard Univ. Press, 1982). Kegan describes cognitive development as the movement from being mentally embedded in a simpler subject-object balance to a higher-order (more complex) subject-object balance. For the systemic thinker the object is the propositions or beliefs that the subject analyzes from the standpoint of one's own system of logically consistent beliefs. He calls this kind of thinker, the institutional self. The move from the institutional self to the interindividual self involves a shift in subject-object understanding in which the object becomes the higher-order set of "systems" of propositions or beliefs, with the subject viewing them from the standpoint of the evolving metasystem. This explains why the strict systemic thinker cannot understand metasystemic relations. They simply transcend the thought structures of the early formal operational cognitive system.

To be fair, this *early* formal logical thinking is partly a result of the "egocentrism" that afflicts much adolescent and young-adult thinking, predisposing them to assume that how the world looks to them (now) must be the way the world is. This egocentrism, combined with their formal logical abilities, leads them to conclude prematurely that something is a genuine contradiction in spite of evidence for both lines of argument. Researchers in adult cognitive development have identified a later, more complex kind of reasoning transcending these limitations (without abandoning formal logic), which characterizes more mature thinkers. Some have termed this *metasystemic* thought.[86]

According to these researchers, metasystemic thinkers are able to think about their formal operations and so transform their understanding of systems (performing *third-order* operations), synthesizing the truths of multiple systems of thought that were initially perceived to be contradictory at the level of "single-system" thought. Rather than viewing these concurrences as genuinely contradictory, leading to an either-or affirmation of only one of the options, the metasystemic thinker sees such concurrences as a call to integrate the options into a fuller, richer understanding.[87] This happens as the genuine insights of the different systems are rationally understood and accepted, resulting in the forging of a new "synthesis" of ideas/systems that compose the "metasystem" (*without* regressing into preformal thought and affirming invalid, unsubstantiated, irrational conclusions).[88]

---

[86]Michael L. Commons, Francis A. Richards, and D. Kuhn, "Systematic, Metasystematic, and Cross Paradigmatic Reasoning: A Case for Stages of Reasoning Beyond Piaget's Stage of Formal Operations," *Childhood Development* 53 (1982): 1058–68; Francis A. Richards and Michael L. Commons, "Postformal Cognitive-Developmental Theory and Research: A Review of Its Current Status," in *Higher States of Human Development: Perspectives on Adult Growth*, ed. C. N. Alexander and E. J. Langer (New York: Oxford Univ. Press, 1990), 139–61; Michael Basseches, *Dialectical Thinking* (Norwood, N.J.: Ablex, 1984); Patricia M. King and Katherine S. Kitchener, *Developing Reflective Judgment: Understanding and Promoting Intellectual Growth and Critical Thinking in Adolescents and Adults* (San Francisco: Jossey-Bass, 1994); Dierdre A. Kramer, "Development of an Awareness of Contradiction Across the Life Span and the Question of Postformal Operations," in *Adult Development*, vol. 1: *Comparisons and Applications of Developmental Models*, ed. Michael L. Commons, Jan D. Sinnott, Francis A. Richards, and Cheryl Armon (New York: Praeger, 1989), 133–60.

[87]John M. Rybash, Paul A. Roodin, and William J. Hoyer, *Adult Development and Aging*, 3d ed. (Madison, Wisc.: Brown & Benchmark, 1995), 172. Metasystemic reasoning does not repudiate the laws of formal logic. They still operate within systems and continue to be used to evaluate evidence, relate specific propositions, and adjudicate truth. Metasystemic reasoning does nothing more than assume and build on formal logic, taking it into a higher "orbit."

[88]There is debate about whether postformal thought consists of a genuine, qualitative change in human thought (and so constituting a new stage) or simply an advanced application of formal operational abilities; cf. Dierdre A. Kramer, "Post-Formal Operations: A Need for Further Conceptualization," *Human Development* 26 (1983): 91–105; Rybash, Roodin, and Hoyer, *Adult Cognition and Aging*; Charles N. Alexander and Ellen J. Langer, eds., *Higher Stages of Human Development* (New York: Oxford Univ. Press, 1990), passim; Ronald R. Irwin and Ronald L. Sheese, "Problems in the Proposal for a 'Stage' of Dialectical Thinking," in *Adult Development*, vol. 1., 113–32. I personally think that metasystemic thought does constitute a higher organization of thinking, qualitatively different enough from systemic thought to

This stage requires more complex reasoning and metacognitive skills:[89] first, knowing when to temporarily "suspend" the demands of the LONC in order to fairly assess all the evidence, and second, if the evidence is sufficient, being able to affirm both sides of the concurrence as true, in the absence of an actual harmonization of them according to the LONC. At first, this requires living with a certain amount of disequilibrium, given that the two (or more) bodies of evidence appear to contradict each other. Yet each horn of the dilemma must be accepted as true for each to be taken seriously. Only then will one embrace both lines of evidence.

Gradually, the evidence leads the metasystemic mind to develop mental structures that permit the cognitive dissonance created by formal logic to give way to a metasystemic "resolution," in which both members of the concurrent pair are accepted and "given a place" within one's belief system. As each perspective is elaborated, a "region of discourse" or "local logic" may develop within which a coherent understanding is formed that conforms to its body of evidence, without necessarily resolving how these different "regions" logically relate to each other (at least for now). Both lines of evidence lead to the individual's being warranted to affirm the two sets of beliefs in the absence of a formal logical solution.

Of course, another constructive option is also available. Upon recognizing the paradox, one can pursue a formal logical solution to the apparent contradiction (as logicians and thinkers continue to do in many fields, e.g., physicists who try to harmonize the wave/particle dual nature of light or Christian philosophers who seek to demonstrate the logical consistency of the Trinity or the Incarnation using formal calculus). This book offers examples of such efforts, including Craig on God's foreknowledge, Lee on impassability, and Gutenson on immutability. We glorify God when we work towards such solutions, since this work assumes that a logical solution exists in the mind of God and seeks to make manifest that consistency.

However, Christians are also warranted in merely holding to both "sides" of the truth, in good metasystemic fashion, even when they cannot provide a logical solution to the paradox, if the evidence demands it (assuming all the rest of the conditions for knowledge are met[90]). If humans were not able to affirm beliefs the logical basis of which they could not establish for themselves, most normal adults would not legitimately hold most of the beliefs they do. Metasystemic

---

warrant the label of another stage (see Eric L. Johnson, "Growing in Wisdom in Christian Community: Toward Measures of Christian Postformal Development," *Journal of Psychology and Theology* 26 [1996]: 366). However, it is plausible to argue that metasystemic thought is simply formal logic applied to more complex objects of thought (systems).

[89]Metacognitive skills include mental skills that permit people to monitor their thinking and problem-solving, assess its success or failure, and apply strategies to assist their thinking and problem-solving. See Michael Ferrari and Robert J. Sternberg, "The Development of Mental Abilities and Styles," in *Handbook of Child Psychology*, vol. 2: *Cognition, Perception, and Language* (New York: John Wiley & Sons, 1998), 909–10.

[90]For a helpful description of such conditions, see Alvin Plantinga, *Warrant and Proper Function* (New York: Oxford Univ. Press, 1993); idem, *Warranted Christian Belief* (New York: Oxford Univ. Press, 2000).

reasoning provides a way for individuals to affirm concurrent truths, prior to their logical resolution, when they are warranted in doing so.[91]

## 6.2 Harmonizing the LONC and Metasystemic Thought Through Reason

Obviously, the initial metasystemic move is risky, for the LONC is essential for understanding. But in some very important cases, a hasty application of the LONC may automatically rule out certain sectors of evidence. Part of reasoning skill, then, involves being able to identify those intellectual contexts/topics that require metasystemic thought—when the evidence demands it, and so where reason decides on the basis of rational considerations that it is warranted. Therefore, a more mature reason uses both formal logic (including the LONC) and metasystemic reasoning.[92] This more mature reason, trained through learning about complex reality, comes to develop a metasystemic reasoning rule: *No line of reasoning/set of evidence can overturn any other reasoning/set of evidence if, after careful investigation and reflection, both appear independently plausible, even when they appear to be logically inconsistent* (unless *they constitute an antinomy or absurdity*).

Needless to say, the parenthetic qualification is important. Metasystemic thinking cannot justify genuine irrationality. Nonsense is nonsense, and antinomies and absurdities should be exposed and rejected. But in some important cases, sense can look like nonsense at first and can be prematurely rejected. As the noted logicians Cohen and Nagel recognized: "Great care must be exercised in making sure that what appear to be contrary instances are really so in fact."[93]

Let us return to an example from physics. There are two lines of experimental evidence regarding the nature of light that seem mutually exclusive, one of which shows light to be made up of particles and another to be composed of waves. These two sets of results appear to be contradictory. Perhaps eventually, through further research and reflection, physicists will be able to formulate a formally coherent, unified model of a "wavicle." Until then, they are warranted in affirming both bodies of reasoning/evidence without understanding how they cohere. Metasystemic reasoning makes it possible for us not to *foreclose* on truth simply because *at present* we cannot come up with a coherent solution.

Metasystemic thought is also *practically* important since few people have been endowed with a high enough intelligence to be able to resolve the logical para-

---

[91]Admittedly, no attempt is made to delineate the conditions for warranted metasystemic beliefs beyond the recognition of two plausible lines of evidence that appear to contradict. This deserves attention but is left for another time and probably to another person.

[92]Pascal recognized this kind of complexity. As we noted above, "the last proceeding of reason is to recognize that there is an infinity of things which are beyond it. It is but feeble if it does not see so far as to know this. But if natural things are beyond it, what will be said of supernatural?" Pascal, *Pensées*, #267. "Wisdom sends us to childhood" (#271). "There is nothing so conformable to reason as this disavowal of reason" (#272). The distinction between systemic and metasystemic reasoning, I think, helps us to make better sense of Pascal's insights.

[93]Cohen and Nagel, *Introduction to Logic*, 75.

GOD UNDER FIRE

doxes that face adult thinkers (and believers). Actually, most adults faced with such problems resort to presystemic (i.e., prelogical) thought, holding beliefs without rigorous logical reflection and so holding paradoxical beliefs without recognizing the contradiction (e.g., most Christians believe in the Trinity without really grasping the logical difficulty). However, some highly intelligent people (having extraordinary memory and logical abilities that permit them to comprehend complex concepts and long chains of reasoning) can work toward rigorous formal solutions to metasystemic problems. This is highly desirable when it can be done, but relatively few people have such abilities.

Moreover, some metasystemic problems have not yet had completely satisfactory logical solutions (e.g., God's sovereignty and human responsibility), and it may be the case that they will never be solved logically to our satisfaction. It may be that the chains of reasoning required for such problems, though within God's competence, are too great for any human mind. Metasystemic thought allows persons who recognize the problem of concurrences revealed by the LONC but who have not solved them logically to nonetheless submit to the authority of *all* the available evidence in the absence of a formal logical harmonization, at least for now.

Let us compare the cognitive dilemma of a paradox with the problem of coming upon a gorge during a backpacking trip (using the two opposing cliffs as an analogy for two concurrent truths). The gorge, unfortunately, is filled with a thick fog, so that the bottom cannot be seen from above. In hiking (and thinking), we have three (analogous) choices. (1) From the one cliff we can reject the hope of bridging the gap, of getting to the other side, since "they are not (logically) connected" and "it is (intellectually) dangerous." (This is the option taken by the rigid single-system thinker who rejects one or the other truth.)

(2) Since the cliffs are just barely within jumping distance, we can jump from one side to the other (concluding that the evidence for the other part of the concurrence is strong enough to warrant belief, even though we cannot see how it is connected to the "cliff" we started from). (This is something both presystemic and metasystemic thinkers can do, with the latter recognizing the logical difficulty of the jump.)

(3) However, a third option is possible for some: climbing down from the one cliff into the fog, crossing the stream at the bottom, and climbing up to the top of the other side. This is of course much harder than jumping, not everyone is able to do that kind of rigorous climbing (an elaborate string of formal argumentation), and there is the possibility that no (formal) passageway can be found (in this life). But everything we know suggests that it should be possible (since, if both members of the pair are true, God knows the formal solution), and there is every reason for capable Christian thinkers to work on these problems.

So how shall we answer the title of this chapter: Can God be grasped by our reason? The answer is, as you might suspect, both yes and no. Yes, God can be surely grasped by our reason, which is able to understand whatever Scripture teaches about God and to develop a coherent understanding of each "side" of biblical teaching. However, God cannot be *fully* grasped by our reason, which may be unable to trace out how both "sides" of biblical teaching about God are logically connected to each other.

Tragically, a simplistic use of formal logic may lead human reason to reject certain revealed features of God that seem contradictory to other revealed features. God can be better grasped by a wiser, metasystemic reason that uses the LONC with discernment, holding off on a premature conclusion that a concurrence is a genuine contradiction, if the evidence demands it, until such a time as the gifted among us provide a fuller, formal understanding of God that incorporates all the evidence available to us or until God increases our capacities considerably in the age to come. And yet, the wise lover of God is content to defer such conclusions indefinitely, if the evidence demands it, since she suspects that some of the mysteries of an infinite God must necessarily transcend the finite capacities of the created mind to grasp them.

## 7. A Rationale for Divine Concurrences

There are good reasons to work towards a formal solution of paradoxes regarding God's nature and his relation to us. However, there are also at least two good reasons for appreciating paradoxical truths as they are.

### 7.1 The Moral Good of Divine Concurrences

What if God has set up the universe, including our minds, in such a way as to promote our humility? What if he built an intellectual hurdle into the relation between the structure of reality and our own understanding in order to foster humility? He created the normal adult mind to be able to think formally. But a *created* mind must have finite attentional and memory capacity. Moreover, let's suppose God "set" the human mind's capacity at "average" intelligence (having a distribution from extremely mentally impaired to extremely gifted), but set in such a way that most would recognize these apparent contradictions in reality and in God's own nature, forcing us to "lay down our mental lives" and confess we cannot solve all of the world's intellectual problems. They are within our grasp to recognize but beyond our capacity to solve.

Concurrences (or offenses, to use Kierkegaard's term) are meant to reveal, to make clear to us our sinful tendency to put our selves (here, our intellectual selves) in place of the priority to be accorded to God and his revelation (particularly the Bible, which is *ipso facto* symbolic of his authority). The cognitive problem we are confronted with in metasystemic dilemmas, then, is not just the finitude of human understanding but also the problem of the sin of pride. If we could "figure God out" completely, we would be more inclined to exalt ourselves and our "divining" reasoning powers and less likely to submit to God and his challenging revelation. Concurrences lead us to seek the "foolish" wisdom of the Holy Spirit (1 Cor. 1– 2), manifested in an inner peace in the face of the disequilibrium that such concurrences create and an unwillingness to foreclose on truth. Concurrences, then, may help to lead us into virtue.

## 7.2 The Aesthetic Good of Divine Concurrences

The best reason to appreciate mysteries is aesthetic; such concurrences reveal a beauty to our minds. The beauty of God is a central theme of Jonathan Edwards. In one of his sermons, "The Excellency of Christ," he laid side by side some of the greatest paradoxes in the person and life of Christ in order to promote our worship of Him.[94] Beginning with Revelation 5:5–6, where Christ is said to be both a lion and a lamb, Edwards played with these contrary descriptions and extended the contrast into theological considerations. As God, Edwards wrote, Christ is infinitely great, yet as man he suffered shame and abuse. "Such a conjunction of infinite highness and low condescension, in the same person, is admirable."[95] Christ was of infinite majesty as well as transcendent meekness; he had the deepest reverence for God, yet he was equal with God. Utterly self-sufficient as God, he lived on earth in dependence on God and vulnerable to abuse by sinners. These contrasts, Edwards felt, reveal the supreme beauty of Christ. The greater the contrast of qualities in the same person, the greater that person's beauty and excellence.

Grasping such wondrous contrasts, because they challenge our reason, leads us to worship. In addition, there is a kind of cognitive depth and richness that occurs as each member of the concurrence is allowed to "play off" the other. Christ's majesty is especially beautiful when seen in relation to his humiliation, his majesty casts a glow on his humiliation that makes it that much more gorgeous, and so on. The more we simplistically eliminate theological paradoxes, the more we obscure God's revelation, water down the faith, and rob ourselves of reasons for worship and a deeper insight into God's infinitely great glory.

Many theologians in our day have insisted that they can scale the greatness of God with their own intellect. But in so doing they have had to reject the God of biblical revelation (or at least some "side" of that God). The primary error of certain "hyperlogicians" is to think, "God and reality cannot be any bigger or more complex than my formal reasoning can comprehend." Avoiding such hubris and using a chastened, wiser reason, may we submit our minds to *all* the revelation we have been given and so accept the mysteries that exist in God's nature and his relation to us, learning better how to give glory and praise to our infinitely excellent God.

---

[94]*The Works of Jonathan Edwards*, ed. E. Hickman, 2 vols. (Edinburgh: Banner of Truth Trust, 1974), 1:680–89.

[95]Ibid., 1:681.

## Appendix: Paradoxes Within Creation

In mathematics a number of paradoxes are related to infinity. In an infinite set of numbers, there are as many odd numbers as there are both odd and even numbers, and there are as many total integers as there are total fractions. Similarly, there are as many points between 0 and 1 inch as there are in the universe. In geometry, an infinitely large circle would have a circumference as large as its diameter. Such assertions seem counterintuitive since one member of the pair being compared seems self-evidently larger than the other; nevertheless, it can be proven mathematically that these pairs are equivalent (Bill Eppright, personal communication). Probably the most important paradox in modern mathematics was "the incompleteness theorem" presented by Gödel in 1931. He formally proved that it was not possible to develop a formal system of simple arithmetic without including at least one contradiction. As a result, Gödel demonstrated that number theory was necessarily incomplete and that elementary mathematics therefore cannot be completely formalized in one system (let alone, more complex mathematics).[96]

There are also many examples of paradoxes within logic, some of them going back to the early days of Greek philosophy. As suggested above, solutions have been developed for many of these paradoxes; however, this whole area continues to be an area of intense activity. Western philosophy has wrestled for centuries on such paradoxes as the One and the Many, the relation between being and change, beings and concepts, and essence and existence. Though thinkers often "take sides" on such issues, God comprehends the whole picture.

As was already mentioned, one of the great puzzles of modern physics is the nature of light. A set of experiments has been performed that demonstrates that light is composed of particles and another set that shows light to be a wave. Physics since Newton and into the twentieth century was divided into those, following Newton, who affirmed a particle theory of light and those who maintained that light was a wave. It was assumed, using formal logic, that light could be only one or the other. But physicists now affirm that light has both properties, defying what a simplistic application of the LONC had led researchers to expect.

Quantum mechanics research has revealed another sort of paradox. When attempting to measure the behavior of certain subatomic particles, researchers are unable to measure both speed and location (called Heisenberg's Indeterminacy Principle). If physicists set up their equipment in one way, they can measure its speed; if in another way, they can establish its location; but they can never do both simultaneously. There appears to be a fundamental limit to what humans are able to observe, a phenomenon that seems counterintuitive to reason.

Time also offers mysteries. Is time a sequence of discrete events or is it an ongoing, continuous, flowing process without parts? It is hard to say (Steven Ratliff, personal

---

[96]Quine gives this as a prime example of a veridical paradox in *The Ways of Paradox*, 16–18.

GOD UNDER FIRE

communication). Such paradoxes have provided constructive challenges for physicists. In the words of Niels Bohr, there is "no progress without paradox."[97]

Many features of human reality have paradoxical features. Humans have both immaterial and material qualities (mind and body), but it is hard to see how they relate. Clearly, humans are brain-dependent beings, yet some features of human life seem irreducible to brain events, e.g., the experience of color, emotion, and consciousness itself. In another vein, the human soul seems to be composed of a set of identifiable immaterial structures (reason, memory, emotional states, etc.), yet the soul is experienced as an ever-changing stream of consciousness and purposive activity, never fully defined by a finite set of thoughts and memories. Also, adult humans are to be treated as responsible individual beings, yet they also act as followers, members of the crowd, influenced by other humans. Some have argued that the best way to help disadvantaged minorities is to give them special privileges to help them overcome their poverty, while others argue that all humans need to take responsibility for themselves in order to better themselves. A similar quandary: Are minorities helped more by emphasizing our commonality or our diversity?

Other paradoxical problems: Human knowledge is forged within a subject–object dialectic. The object exists outside the subject, yet to know it, the subject must "internalize" features of the object. Scientists typically emphasize the need for objectivity and universally agreed-upon techniques for determining the object's nature, while literary critics typically focus on the subject's internal representations of reality. Each option seems rationally justified, though by itself, it is only a part of the truth. And can we ever *really* know another person? There seems to be a paradoxical tension between knowing *about* another and the sense that there is something indefinable about the other that is beyond our grasp. This is just a limited list of some of the paradoxes found in the creation.

---

[97]Alan Lightman, *Dance for Two* (New York: Pantheon Books, 1996), 32.

# Chapter 4

# Has the Christian Doctrine of God Been Corrupted by Greek Philosophy?

*Gerald L. Bray*

✦

# 1. Modern Challenges to the Doctrine of God

We are seeing a resurgence of interest among theologians in the doctrine of God, much of which has concentrated on rediscovering the importance of the Trinity for Christian theology. This has led to a recovery of many of the riches of the ancient orthodox tradition. At the same time, much time and energy have gone into rejecting something that modern writers have labeled *classical theism*, a philosophical term meant to express what Christians have traditionally assumed God to be and to be like.[1] To a point, *classical theism* can be equated with the orthodoxy of the creeds and councils of the early church, which have been universally accepted by all branches of Christendom, but their emphasis is slightly different. Where creedal theology is mainly concerned with the different persons of the Trinity, classical theism refers more to the nature and attributes of God that are common to all three divine persons.

In the patristic period the doctrine of the one God, which its modern detractors label *classical theism*, was assumed rather than articulated in a systematic way. Not until John of Damascus (c. 675–749) do we find a full and coherent exposition of it. Eventually this doctrine became a commonplace of medieval scholasticism, in which it was formally distinguished from trinitarian theology,[2] and in different guises it has remained part of Christian theology ever since.

In modern times, the main accusation leveled against such classical theism is that it is not biblical. According to its principal critics, it portrays a God who is *immutable*, a concept that is taken to mean that he never changes in any way. This immutability thus renders God unable to respond to human prayers, because any active response implies movement and, therefore, some form of change. Critics often correctly point out that such a doctrine is incompatible with the biblical concept of a living relationship between God and people, who live in a world of time and space, subject to constant change. The God of classical theism, their argument runs, cannot adjust to fit the dynamic theology of the Bible; thus, it must be abandoned.

Scripture portrays God as a person who relates to us, who hears our prayers, and who takes care of us as his people. Since we are constantly changing, God

---

[1]See, e.g., Clark H. Pinnock, Richard Rice, John Sanders, William Hasker, and David Basinger, *The Openness of God: A Biblical Challenge to the Traditional Understanding of God* (Downers Grove, Ill.: InterVarsity Press, 1994).

[2]It came under the heading *De Deo uno* ("On the one God") as opposed to the heading *De Deo trino* ("On the triune God"), which followed it.

cannot be said to stand still. He too must move and change in order to continue relating to us in meaningful ways. The divine immutability of classical theism is, therefore, a concept that is alien to Christian theology, and its presence for so many centuries has gravely distorted the biblical concept of God in the teaching of the church. A similar argument might be made for the rest of the classical package, though critics of classical theism tend to imply such a statement rather than argue it openly. But if divine immutability can be discredited, the rest hardly matters, since this in itself would be enough to send classical theism crashing to the ground.[3]

Those who argue this usually claim that fundamental to God's nature is *love*, the quality they say defines his essence in biblical terms. Love implies relationship, which in turn implies mutability, since all relationships grow and change over time. Therefore, if we are to maintain the biblical doctrine that "God is love" (1 John 4:16), we have little choice but to reject the static model of God offered by classical theism and to opt instead for a dynamic theology.

But if the Bible is as clear about this as the critics of classical theism say it is, how could the church have gone so wrong for such a long time? The answer the critics usually give to this is that Greek philosophy—by which they normally mean a form of Platonism—so dominated the thinking of the church fathers that ideas derived from it were accepted as the basic framework for doing Christian theology, and they have remained such ever since.[4]

The critics admit that this influence may have been challenged at certain times—notably in the sixteenth-century Reformation—but they insist that it was never fully removed. On the contrary, after an initial protest, the Reformers went back to the scholasticism they had theoretically rejected and did little more than produce an alternate version of it. It was therefore a Platonic theism—not biblical revelation—that dominated seventeenth-century Protestant orthodoxy, and it is to this theism that modern conservative Protestants mistakenly appeal, thinking that such orthodoxy is biblical when it is not.

---

[3]Another subject of great contemporary interest is the question of God's impassibility (inability to suffer), which is logically connected to his immutability. So many modern theologians have insisted that God can suffer that this is now virtually taken for granted in many circles. Recently, however, Dr. T. G. Weinandy of Oxford has produced an extensively documented rebuttal of this view, including a lengthy discussion of the patristic doctrine of God, see *Does God Suffer?* (Notre Dame, Ind.: Univ. of Notre Dame Press, 1999). See also chs. 8–10 in this volume: "Does God Take Risks?" by James Spiegel; "Does God Have Emotions?" by Patrick Lee; and "Does God Change?" by Chuck Gutenson.

[4]As a matter of historical fact, the Neoplatonism first expounded by Plotinus (c. 204–270) made the greatest impression on those who developed the ancient creeds of the church. But some early Christians (e.g., Tertullian) were more attracted to Stoicism and could be quite openly anti-Platonic at times. Then too, many theologians of the classical period were more influenced by Aristotle than they were by Plato, and Aristotelian concepts have dominated all expressions of "classical theism" since the time of Thomas Aquinas (1226–1274). The catch-all phrase "Greek philosophy" is therefore not helpful in elucidating the true nature of the philosophical currents that influenced Christian theologians in ancient and medieval times.

## 2. History, Philosophy, and Theological Terminology

The concept of classical theism and the main lines of the attack on it as outlined above originated in nineteenth-century Germany with men like Ferdinand Christian Baur (1792–1860) and August Neander (1789–1850). Later on, it was picked up by Albrecht Ritschl (1822–1889). But the most famous exposition of it was by Adolf von Harnack (1851–1930), expressed most clearly in a series of lectures delivered in Berlin in 1900 and published in English as *What Is Christianity?*[5] Harnack's thesis was developed further by Walter Bauer (1877–1960),[6] which has gained wide acceptance.

But the thinking of these German scholars has been refuted in considerable detail by such eminent scholars as J. N. D. Kelly (1909–1997)[7] and H. E. W. Turner (1907–1995).[8] They and others like them have demonstrated that the early church fathers confronted the philosophical theism of their time by fundamentally restructuring it. The fathers of the church were well aware that the Bible proclaimed a personal relationship with the living God, something of which Greek philosophy had no conception, and it was this awareness, given to them by the biblical revelation, that led them to develop Trinitarian theology.

At the same time, however, the church fathers also had to recognize that the Bible spoke of a Creator God who is essentially different from his creation and, in his nature, incompatible with it. This belief may have had some connection with different strands of Greek philosophy, but it was not dependent on any of them. On the contrary, such belief was rooted in the biblical insistence that any form of idolatry, that is, worship of the creature as a manifestation of the Creator, was a denial of the true God. It was the need to avoid idolatry—not any desire to imitate Plato or some other Greek philosopher—that led the early Christians to insist that God's being could only be described by what he was not.

For them, every concept of the human mind implied some form of definition and was therefore a limitation that could not adequately reflect the being of God. God's essence might perhaps be experienced by a mystical vision, but it remains unknowable and indescribable. Nevertheless, God can be known in and through the persons of the Trinity, one of whom became incarnate in Jesus Christ and another of whom now dwells in our hearts by faith. It is in this way that the hidden mystery of God relates to us, and it is by examining the relationship of the

---

[5]Adolf von Harnack, *What Is Christianity?* 2d ed. rev., trans. Thomas Bailey Saunders (New York: Putnam; London: Williams & Norgate, 1901). The German title was *Das Wesen des Christentums* (Leipzig: J. C. Hinrichs, 1901).

[6]Walter Bauer, *Orthodoxy and Heresy in Earliest Christianity*, 2d ed., appendices by Georg Strecker, trans. Philadelphia Seminar on Christian Origins, ed. Robert A. Kraft and Gerhard Krodel (Philadelphia: Fortress, 1971; reprint, Mifflintown, Penn.: Sigler, 1996). The book was originally published in German in 1934.

[7]See especially J. N. D. Kelly, *Early Christian Creeds*, 3d ed. (Harlow: Essex; New York: Longman, 1972).

[8]See H. E. W. Turner, *The Pattern of Christian Truth* (London: Mowbray, 1954).

persons of the Trinity to the unity of God that the objections raised by the opponents of classical theism must be answered.

A purely philosophical theology is not enough, because it has no doctrine of the Trinity—only biblical revelation can supply that. If *classical theism* is meant to be equated with traditional Christian orthodoxy, then it cannot be separated from the doctrine of the Trinity, which is the key to understanding it. Furthermore, whatever links there may be between classical theism and different types of Greek philosophy must be considered in the light of this. The ancient theological vocabulary of *substance* and *nature* may have been borrowed from philosophical sources, but these words have been given new meanings in Christian theology. To take them out of their trinitarian context is to ignore what H. E. W. Turner called the *pattern* of Christian truth, and the result can only be a fundamental misunderstanding of what the early Christians believed and the universal church has always taught.

Let us demonstrate what we mean by giving a few key examples. The fathers of the first council of Nicea (A.D. 325) had to contend with those who objected to the use of the word *homoousios* ("consubstantial") of the Son in relation to the Father because this word is not in the Bible. Centuries later, John Calvin lashed out in his *Institutes* (1.13) against those who refused to accept terms like *person* and *Trinity* on the same grounds. Calvin argued that if the realities these words are meant to describe are found in Scripture, then we can use such terms as a kind of intellectual shorthand, because we have a common understanding of what they are meant to convey. The pattern of Christian truth does not demand that we use only words found in the Bible, as long as it can be demonstrated that the words we do use reflect what the Bible teaches. Our vocabulary may be developed in response to challenges and objections that arise in the course of history as we seek to define our faith with respect to other religions and belief systems, but it may not go against the substance and content of what the Bible reveals about God.

We may therefore freely admit that many of the words we use in theology come from one pagan Greek philosophical source or another. A case in point is the term *theology* (meaning "God talk") itself. This term was probably invented by Plato, who used it in the *Republic* to mean what we would now call *mythology*. This is not surprising, because the gods about whom he was talking were understood in mythological terms. Plato did not believe that there was any direct connection between the Greek myths and the worship of the Supreme Being. What he seems to have thought is that mythology (or "theology," as he put it) was a popular explanation of reality intended for the consumption of the ignorant and uneducated. Those who progressed to the heights of philosophical reasoning, however, could separate the wheat from the chaff, which were mixed up together in the myths, and distill the pure truth of Reason. This Reason could then be applied to such things as the Homeric poems, which could be interpreted (or "deconstructed," as we might say today) so as to reveal their underlying rational basis. The process by which this was done is known now as *allegory*, and it quickly became a favorite means of reading ancient Greek literature in the philosophical schools of antiquity.

*Theology* is not a term found in the Greek New Testament, but there is no doubt that the Bible speaks about God; thus, it does contain a theology. But biblical theology is as different from mythology and allegory as the biblical God is from the many pagan deities that the word *theology* was invented to describe. As a purely generic term, *theology* can be used in both cases, but it is the thing being described that determines the content and meaning of a term, not the other way around. Christians used the term *theology* to describe the God of the Bible, which automatically gave it a radically different content from what had been customary before. In fact, it is because the Bible talks straightforwardly about God and the nature of his being that Christian theology appears much closer to Greek philosophy in this respect than to Greek religion/mythology and that the question of an interrelationship between them can be raised at all.

Of course there were many Platonists in early Christian times who understood this, and they were not at all happy with the way that Christians had apparently confused theology with philosophy when Plato himself regarded them as mutually exclusive. Men like Celsus (late second century) ridiculed Christianity as an irrational and barbaric superstition making absurd claims, and he argued that Christians could in no sense be dignified with philosophical or pseudo-philosophical terminology. But it is important to note that along with the ridicule went imitation. Little though they would admit it, the Neoplatonists of the third and fourth centuries A.D. absorbed more of Christianity than most people realize.

As far as the term *theology* is concerned, the climax of this borrowing was reached in the work of Proclus (c. 411–485). Even though he was a pagan philosopher, Proclus wrote a book called *The Elements of Theology*, in which he used the word in its Christian, not in its ancient Platonic, meaning. He wanted to show that it was possible to describe Plato's belief in a supreme Reason as a form of monotheism, but this was really a covert concession to the Christian worldview, since neither Plato nor Celsus would have used this word in that way.

What is true of the term *theology* is paradigmatic of the entire relationship between Christianity and the different forms of ancient Greek philosophy. The Greeks used words such as *ousia* ("being"), *physis* ("nature"), and *hypostasis* ("substance") in many different ways. In his book *Divine Substance*, Christopher Stead has demonstrated, by citing a wide range of examples, that these terms had no fixed meaning in Greek thought.[9] On the contrary, they were used in ways that were often vague and imprecise, causing problems for subsequent interpreters and allowing competing schools of disciples to claim that they were all following their chosen master(s). Precision in vocabulary did not come until Christians imposed it on themselves, because they had a definable God whom they needed to describe accurately. When Christians spoke of God as the "Supreme Being," they were not speculating about some abstract idea; they were trying to describe someone whom they already knew by personal experience.

---

[9]Christopher Stead, *Divine Substance* (Oxford: Clarendon, 1977).

GOD UNDER FIRE

The imprecision of existing Greek terminology was a hindrance to this, and the church had to sort it out in order to avoid misunderstandings. The word *ousia* had to be confined to the oneness of God's *being*, because to use it of the Father, Son, and Holy Spirit would imply that there were three gods. The word *hypostasis*, by contrast, came to be used of the persons of the Trinity, even though there were initially many people who thought of it as basically synonymous with *ousia*. This caused problems in the Latin world, because when *ousia* was translated as *essentia*, the Romans rejected it as a barbarous neologism.[10] Instead, they preferred to say *substantia*. As long as nobody saw any real need to distinguish between *ousia* and *hypostasis*, this was no problem, but Christian theology forced Roman believers to define their terms more precisely. Tertullian (c. 196–212) used *substantia* for *ousia*, but then he took a completely different word, which had never been used by any philosopher, and used it for expressing the threeness of God. This was the word *persona*, which we still use today.

Tertullian meant by *persona* what his Greek counterparts meant by *hypostasis*, but the Greeks did not understand or accept this for a long time. To them, the word *prosōpon* (*persona* in Latin) meant "mask" and was mainly used in the theater. Some Greeks imagined that Tertullian and his followers believed that the Father, Son, and Holy Spirit were merely masks worn by God in the drama of human history and that they did not represent genuinely distinct persons. This was the heresy known as "modalism,"[11] which they naturally rejected. It was not until Basil of Caesarea (c. 329–379) realized that the Latin terminology was different from the Greek—but that the underlying doctrine was the same—that the way toward a harmonization of the two traditions was opened up. Eventually, the Council of Chalcedon (A.D. 451) declared that *hypostasis* and *persona* were synonymous, and so they have remained ever since.[12]

The important point here is that no pagan philosopher could have spoken in these terms, even if the words the Christians were using would have been familiar to him. A pagan Greek would not have said that God (or anything else) was one *ousia* in three *hypostases* because he would not have understood what the distinction between these terms was supposed to be. He might have been able to accept it once it was explained (as many in fact did), but that explanation depended on the preaching of the Christian gospel, which made the distinction meaningful in the first place.

Moreover, a Roman would never have concluded that God was three *personae* in one *substantia* because, to his mind, the terms belonged to different worlds. The first one came from the theater and had been introduced into the law, whereas the second was primarily philosophical. It could be used in a legal context as well, but not in a way that had any relationship to the use of *persona*. In the

---

[10]This happened in the first century B.C. and had nothing to do with Christianity.

[11]Or "Sabellianism," after a certain Sabellius who was supposed to have preached it.

[12]For a discussion of modern attacks on the doctrine of the Trinity, see ch. 11 in this volume, "How Shall We Think About the Trinity?" by Bruce A. Ware.

law it normally meant a material thing, or property, as it does, for example, in the KJV rendering of Luke 15:13, where the prodigal son is described as "wasting his substance in riotous living." It would hardly have made sense to say that the persons of the Godhead might do the same with their "substance"! Without a prior acceptance of the Christian message, the terminology used in Christian theology would have been meaningless, even to those who were accustomed to using the same words—but in other ways.

Of course, there is no doubt that the early Christians were influenced by the philosophical currents surrounding them. They had to address their contemporaries in ways the latter would understand, just as modern theologians must do. It is no more surprising to find Origen or Augustine addressing the issue of the goodness of matter—a belief that was widely denied in ancient times—than it is to find their modern descendants grappling with the problem of suffering in a world that has experienced genocide on a previously unheard-of scale.

Furthermore, the early Christians had to find their way toward an authentic expression of Christian truth, and it is hardly surprising to discover that they did so by a lengthy process of trial and error. Tertullian was a materialist (believing that even spirits were refined forms of matter), and Origen apparently believed in a form of reincarnation. Gregory of Nyssa can be accused of universalism, and Augustine famously changed his mind on all sorts of things, not least his understanding of grace and free will.

The important thing to remember here is that these aberrations were sifted out over time, as it became apparent that they did not fit into the pattern of Christian truth. Sometimes (as in the case of Tertullian) they were just quietly ignored, but at other times they were explicitly condemned, perhaps several centuries later (as in the case of Origen). Even statements of undoubted orthodoxy, such as the affirmation that the Son of God was consubstantial (*homoousios*) with the Father, was subject to further debate and clarification until all the implications of the word were fully expounded.

Throughout this process, what we notice above all is that *the reality being described defines the parameters of meaning appropriate to the terminology used to describe it*. Of course, this does not mean that the words used in theology are totally unsuitable to begin with. For example, terms like *salt* or *jabberwocky* have nothing to commend them in advance as possible descriptions of God, and we would not think of using either of them. But given that we can find words that have the potential for saying something meaningful about God, the precise definition that will turn these words into technical theological terms is shaped to a considerable—and crucial—extent by the nature of the subject under discussion.

This is not obscurantism, as some might think, but the normal practice of every scientific discipline. The term *infinity*, for example, means one thing to a mathematician and something quite different to a theologian. In mathematics, infinity is really a finite term that implies no more than indefinite extension (e.g., "Between the numbers 1 and 2 there is an infinity of fractions."). No theologian would use the word like this, even if there is some overlap in meaning that makes the different usages comprehensible. There is nothing wrong with such linguistic flexibility as long as everyone agrees in advance what the framework of discussion is and how the words are being used in any given instance.

The term *being*, for example, will mean something different in relation to God from what it means when describing one of his creatures, because the nature of the divine being is different from theirs. As long as we know what we are talking about, there is no problem with this, and the term *being* can be adapted accordingly. But if we say that this term can only be used of a finite object, then it cannot be applied to God, and some other term must be found to describe him. This is basically what the critics of classical theism are saying, and some of them at least might be surprised to discover that the Christian theological tradition they have rejected agrees with them. There has always been a recognition that God is not a "being" in the sense that his creatures are, and the mystics even coined the term *nonbeing*, which they applied to God as a way of describing this contrast. Unfortunately, *nonbeing* confuses most ordinary people because they think it means that there is no God at all! So the term *being* remains in general use, though it can hardly be said that its meaning derives from any pagan philosophy.

All language used of God is necessarily analogical, expressing something that is true but which cannot be reduced to the dimensions of created nature. Far from being an unbiblical concept, analogy is one of the most common techniques used in Scripture to talk about God. There are times, for example, when he is compared with material objects such as fire or rock, or to natural phenomena such as the wind.

What does it mean, then, to say that "our 'God is a consuming fire'" (Heb. 12:29) or that he is our "Rock" (Ps. 28:1)? Some people have claimed that descriptions of this kind are survivals of primitive religious beliefs, antedating the more evolved religion of Moses. They say that there was a time when Israel, like other primitive peoples, worshiped fire and natural objects they believed contained a supernatural power. Perhaps that is true, but it does not explain why the Israelites continued to use such images after God revealed himself to the patriarchs as the Lord of heaven and earth and stated clearly that no graven image could be used to worship him. There must be something in those words that cannot be explained away as the survival of an earlier paganism, especially when they are readily used by the New Testament writers as well.

The answer, of course, is that these words are not meant to be taken literally or in every sense that they are capable of bearing. To say that God is a "consuming fire" means only that he destroys and purifies at the same time, an apparent paradox that is frequently attested in the Old Testament as the Lord's "visitation." This is always both a blessing and a curse, a combination that is readily pictured by fire. Similarly, God is not a physical rock but a spiritual presence that is solid and permanent, in the way that a rock appears to be. Here we not only see analogy at work; we also see what its limits are and how it must be understood.

Once again, then, *it is the nature of the object being described that determines what the parameters of analogy are*; characteristics of fire and rocks that do not fit God are simply excluded. For example, in Matthew 16:18 the apostle Peter is also called a rock, on which Jesus will build his church. Whatever that verse means, it cannot mean that Peter's bones were ground down to make cement for the foundation of the basilica in Rome that bears his name. One would have to have a singular lack of imagination to think something like that. Unfortunately, however, it sometimes seems that there are theologians who are too literalistic for their own good.

## 3. The Personhood of God

When we call God "Father," analogy takes on a human dimension, but the same principle governing analogy still applies. God's fatherhood is not simply a projection of human fatherhood, which is too broad a concept to fit God's fatherhood perfectly. There are many human fathers who are anything but good role models for their children, and we cannot say that God resembles them in any way. In such cases father-language about God can be unhelpful unless the deep-seated hostility some people have toward their human fathers is dealt with first. There is obviously no point in having such people transfer their anger onto God simply because the Bible describes him as our "Father." But this does not invalidate the analogy because, in this instance, the human circumstances that make it difficult to use are themselves abnormal. Properly handled, it may even be the case that some people can find comfort in a Father-God who compensates for what they did not receive from their human parent. If not, then the same truth about God can be expressed in other ways if necessary, as the Bible itself demonstrates.

From another perspective, human fatherhood involves creation and therefore a relationship of dependence, but the content of this will vary enormously from case to case. In some circumstances it may not mean much at all. But divine fatherhood implies a dependent relationship with God that is universal. To those who have the relationship right, it is eternal life; but to those who are rebellious, it is eternal damnation. Once again, the analogy is partial and selective, but it is possible to define its limits with a fair degree of accuracy. As always, it is the subject that determines the parameters of the analogy. We know God, and therefore we can say what about human fatherhood fits and what does not. Once we make that decision, the rest falls neatly into place, and there is no genuine problem.

The analogy of divine fatherhood is made possible by the fact that the God of the Bible is a personal being. This is so obvious that it hardly needs to be demonstrated, but exactly what that personhood involves is another matter. The ancient Greek gods were personal too, but they were very different from Yahweh. No Greek god, not even Zeus, was the Supreme Being; and when pagan philosophers began to talk of the latter, they did not think of it as personal. That is one of the major differences between any form of Platonism and Christianity, and it raises major questions about the nature and extent of the influence that the former is supposed to have had on the latter. However similar the two beliefs may have been in some respects, they differed radically at this point, and that essential difference had immense implications for the way in which their mutual relationship developed.

In fact, the question of divine personhood was one of the main areas where ancient Neoplatonists were convinced that Christians had muddied the waters of philosophical purity. The Christian notion that the Supreme Being was not merely personal but three distinct persons, one of whom had become a human being (thereby mixing the spiritual good with the material evil), was not just totally unacceptable—it was ludicrous.

That the masses of the population and even the state authorities should get caught up in a view of God as personal was absurd in their view, but these Neoplatonists comforted themselves in their knowledge that philosophical truth had always been the preserve of an elite. The diehards never were won over, and in 529, more than two centuries after the legalization of Christianity, the emperor Justinian closed the remaining philosophical schools at Athens because they would not accept the biblical revelation as true. The survivors emigrated to Persia, unwilling even at that point to come to terms with what to them was the latest insanity of an ignorant populace.

The inability of ancient philosophies to provide a framework for the construction of Christian theology is nowhere more evident than in their failure to produce a term that would adequately express the concept of God's personhood. It is, of course, true that the Israelites did not have a word for it either, although there were plenty of other ways in which they could (and did) express the same idea. In the Old Testament this was done primarily through the concept of the "name of God," which carried with it overtones of personal presence and authority that we find hard to imagine today. The Old Testament is full of examples where the name of God is appealed to as the basis for his merciful intervention in the affairs of Israel. Everything connected with God's holiness and power resided in his name, which was the basis of the covenant relationship that he established and maintained with his people.

Jews have never objected to the Christian assertion that God is personal, a fact that is even more significant when we remember that they have always rejected the doctrine of the Trinity. Divine personhood may not be called by that term in the Old Testament, but it is clearly there, and the Jews have always recognized it. It is those trained in ancient Greek philosophy, supposedly so influential in the construction of classical theism, who have had trouble with this idea, not Jews or orthodox Christians.

The early church fathers, for their part, never supposed that Platonism bore any real relationship to biblical faith, and they took a completely different approach to it. Even Justin Martyr (c. 100–156), who is frequently portrayed as a Christian writer who was more than usually sympathetic to the philosophers, thought of Plato as a blind man groping in the dark. Whatever truth Plato may have stumbled across was accidental, according to Justin, and his general worldview was simply false.

On the most fundamental point of all, where Plato believed that matter was evil, Christians insisted that matter is basically good because it was created by a God who is good (an insistence that made the sinless incarnation of a good God possible). The logical corollary of this was Christianity's equally strong belief in the resurrection of the flesh, a concept that became acceptable once it was asserted that matter is fundamentally good.

Platonists, by contrast, could never accept either of these basic Christian beliefs. Because they believed that matter was evil, they could not distinguish creation from the fall—the one implied the other. If they thought of "salvation" at all, they conceived of it as the liberation of the divine soul from the prison of its material body. Needless to say, this went completely against Christian teaching, and the church refused to give in to it, as virtually the whole of ancient orthodox Christology testifies.

These were the most important issues where the early Christians took a stand against the prevailing wisdom of their age, but we could point to dozens of others. In the end, they completely rejected the worldview of the ancient Greeks, and even those who spoke their language ceased to think of themselves as "Hellenes."[13] Rejection of the pagan past could hardly have gone any further than that.

The New Testament follows the same basic pattern, but with the addition that now God has spoken to us in his Son, the man Christ Jesus. In no way is this a call to worship another God; rather, Christians know the God of Israel in a new and deeper way. Perhaps the difference between the Old and New Testaments can best be expressed by using an analogy that finds some support in the Bible itself. In the Old Testament the Jews knew God on the "outside." He dwelt among them, but they could not enter his presence. Even to touch the ark of the covenant was to invite death. But in the New Testament, the veil in the temple has been torn in two, and we can go into God's presence to see him, as it were, on the "inside." When we do this, we discover that the one God of the Old Testament is in fact a Trinity of persons, each of whom exists in a relationship of perfect love toward the others.

This is stated in the New Testament mainly in the context of obedience—the love of the Son for the Father is demonstrated most fully in his obedience, even to the point of dying on the cross. This relationship of love is living and dynamic in every way that the critics of classical theism might wish for, but it is also perfect and unchanging. By the indwelling presence of the Holy Spirit, we have been admitted into that Trinitarian fellowship and can know God's love at work in our lives—never changing in its depth and commitment but, at the same time, new every morning in its blessings. There is no contradiction here between "static" and "dynamic" notions of God, since both pictures are present. Which is more appropriate in a given context depends on what one is talking about. We might even say, as the Bible does, that the daily newness of God's blessings is a feature of his unchanging character![14]

---

[13]This word meant "pagan" and was avoided by the Greeks themselves until the creation of a Greek state in the early nineteenth century. Before that time, they called themselves "Romans" or even just "Christians."

[14]See Lam. 3:22–23.

GOD UNDER FIRE

That this biblical understanding of God was neither lost nor obscured in the history of the church is amply clear from the *De trinitate* of Augustine (354–430). In this great work, Augustine demonstrated how the mutual relationship of the three divine persons perfectly matched the biblical assertion that "God is love" (1 John 4:16). For him, as for generations of Christians both before and since, God's love is known and understood in this Trinitarian context. That does not compromise the incomprehensibility of his being, which remains forever beyond our grasp, nor does it diminish his power in any way. In relating to us, the three persons of the Trinity remain just as immutable and impassible as they have always been. Yet within the structure of their mutual love, they can reach out to our needs and meet them fully and appropriately as they occur.

## 4. Conclusion

In conclusion we may say that it is a mistake to reduce classical theism to one side of God (his unknowable nature) and claim on that basis that such a God cannot relate to us. No orthodox Christian theologian has ever held such a position because, alongside the tenets of so-called classical theism, orthodoxy has always confessed a Trinity of loving persons, who are able and willing to gather us into their fellowship.

Furthermore, far from emphasizing the unknowable divine being over the Trinity, the classical Christian theological tradition has always done the opposite—putting the Trinity and our experience of the divine persons at the heart of our faith and worship. If this side of the matter has been obscured or downplayed by some people, then it is they who have gone astray, not the tradition. The whole story behind classical theism needs to be told—and remembered—before we jump to the conclusion that the church has taught a doctrine of God that is unbiblical and remote from daily life.

Perhaps some early Christians who were overly influenced by some aspects of Greek philosophy did that. But if so, the fathers of the church long ago tackled them and produced a doctrine of God that is both faithful to the Scriptures and confirmed by the daily experience of Christian believers. Their theology has proved its worth over time. It may not be perfect in every respect, but it has held up well, even in the face of modern challenges of the kind discussed above. Its modern detractors have not proved their case. Until they do, we may confidently assert that classical theism will continue to bear witness to the biblical faith for the foreseeable future.

Chapter 5

# Is God Bound by time?

*Paul Helm*

Before the mountains were born
or you brought forth the earth
and the world, from everlasting
to everlasting you are God.

psalm 90:2

## 1. Introduction

Jews, Muslims and Christians have confessed these sublime words for generations. They speak of the everlasting existence of God as compared to the existence of even the grandest and most impressive features of the earth. The mountains look pretty solid. But before them, from everlasting to everlasting, God was. Or rather, though the mountains were brought forth, God is.

There are other passages that speak similarly about God and his relation to time: God is the lofty one who inhabits eternity (Isa. 57:15); though his creation will grow old, he remains the same, his years never end (Heb. 1:10–12; see also 1 Cor. 2:7; 2 Tim. 1:9; and other verses that refer to God existing "before the foundation of the world").

All Christians recognize that God exists uncreated. He is self-sufficient. It makes no sense to ask where or when or how God originated. He is simply there, independent and sovereign. But the creation, the universe, and all that it contains derive from God. He has made it, and he sustains it. He was there before it. He has priority over it. The immediate picture we get from reading Psalm 90:2 is of God existing for ages, backwardly everlasting, and then at some moment decreeing to bring the universe into being—the earth, the mountains—out of nothing.

 Some Christians, particularly over the past fifty years, have concluded from such passages that God is in time. He is a temporal being like us and is situated in the present, able to look backward and forward as we do, though he has complete knowledge of the past and future. One consequence of this is that though God created space (i.e., a spatial universe), he cannot have created time. Time, then, would be a necessary feature of God's life; in fact, according to this view, God depends on time. God must wait for things to happen just as we do. This is very different from the way Christians have historically understood God.

Others have gone even further, departing from historic Christianity and concluding that God's location in time means God can only have knowledge of the past and present (that alone is what it means to say God is omniscient). He can have no knowledge of the future, at least of the future acts of his free creatures—human beings.

However, the majority of Western theists prior to the twentieth century—Jewish, Muslim, and Christian—have understood such verses to teach something more radical (and more sublime) than the thought that God existed in time before the universe was created. They saw in the repeated emphases of such texts, and particularly in the simple thought that God is (even before the mountains were brought forth), the idea that God exists apart from time or outside time. Thus,

GOD UNDER FIRE

even though at first glance such texts as Psalm 90:2 may seem to teach that God exists in time and then, at a certain moment, he created the universe, many have held that this text (and other similar passages of Scripture) teaches us not that God has always existed but that God does not exist in time at all. He is not time-bound, as his creation is time-bound. He is apart from his creation, transcendent over it, though immanent within it as he sustains his creation in its moment-by-moment existence.

In this classical view, there is a radical and sharp distinction between the Creator and his creation. One of the marks of the Creator is not simply that he is uncreated but that he is timeless and changeless, while his creation is in time and the changes of the creation are marked by time. Some suggest that God created the universe *with* time; if time is simply what you get when things change, this seems an attractive proposal. For after all, what is time? We use the word, sometimes, as if it is the name of a substance, like gold or chalk. We talk about having a lot of time, or a little; about time being precious, and weighing heavily. But many have argued that time is not a substance or a thing but a relation between things—or more exactly, a relation between changes in things. Time enters into our thought when there are things that change or that are liable to change, for time is simply the measure of such change. Time is not like a container in which the universe is placed, but it is simply the measure of the changes and the events that occur in the universe.

There is nothing to stop someone who thinks of God as being timelessly eternal (let us call such a person an "eternalist") from holding that there was time before the universe existed, but the more natural view, I think, is to hold that the universe was created *with* time.

What helps us form the thought that God is timeless (and spaceless) is the idea—surely a basic intuition of Christian theism—that God has fullness or self-sufficiency. Part of God's fullness is that he is changeless; he cannot change for the worse, and he does not need to change for the better. He exists as a complete unity, together. His existence is not spread out in time or in space, as we are, but his existence is all at once.

Consider, for a moment, some further implications of the alternative to this view. Suppose that God is in time, in a similar sort of way to the way in which you and I are in time. One of the striking facts about being in time, of having an existence that continues through time, is that each of us has a life that is stretched out in time, with some parts of our lives earlier than other parts. Whatever detailed philosophical story we tell about these parts, it is clear that there are parts of our lives that we cannot now affect—what we call *the past*—and other parts that we call *the present* and *the future* that we can affect by what we do and can be affected by what others do.

We may now make ourselves a cup of coffee, and we may have made ourselves a cup of coffee in the last week, but we cannot enjoy the last week's cup of coffee as we enjoy today's cup. We can remember our enjoyment of the coffee and so (in a sense) continue to enjoy it, but we cannot enjoy again as we did. We cannot go back in time to sip and savor last week's coffee as we savor today's. Even if we could go back in time, our experience of earlier phases of our lives that we would return to (even if such a return were intelligible) would have a different character from those phases when we lived them. A phase that we return to is obviously different in character from a phase when we first experience it.

In other words, a fundamental feature of time is that we, who exist in time, have lives that are stretched out through time. Our memories are of earlier phases and our hopes and expectations concern those later phases that we, or others, can affect.

Another feature of being in time is that we are bound by time in the sense that we cannot stop the process of change. We are the subjects of time, not its masters. We cannot stop the clock and allow some particular experience to linger and remain. In a sense, we are more the masters of space than we are of time, for we can choose to remain at the same place for a time, but we cannot choose to remain at some particular time. We can stop a movie film and examine one particular frame for as long as we like, but we cannot in a similar way stop the process of time and change itself. In this respect the hymn-writer Isaac Watts was correct when he compared time to an "ever-rolling stream" that "bears all its sons away."

Now suppose that God is in time in the sort of way that we are in time. It would follow that he has a life stretched out in time. Parts of his life are earlier than other parts, and the later parts of his life are untouchable in the sense of being unaffectable by him at a later time. Perhaps (making the reasonable supposition that he has always existed), God is backwardly everlasting. There never was a time when God was not. Nevertheless, it follows from the supposition that God is in time that there are segments of his life (namely, those segments that existed before the present moment) that together constitute a part of God's life he cannot affect. It is here that the eternalist will say that the idea of a life stretched out in time, some of the segments of which are now unaffectable, is incompatible with God's fullness and self-sufficiency.

Of course, if we suppose that God has moments of his life that are unaffectable, like us God may choose to "relive" these moments through the exercise of memory, but he cannot, literally, live them again. Nor would a divine analogue of time travel be of any more help, for the reasons we have already given. In a similar way, if God is in time, then he is not sovereign over time but is bound by it in precisely the same way as we are bound by it. The ever-rolling stream of time not only carries us along with it, it carries God along with it as well. This is surely a most unwelcome thought.

The same point applies when we think of God's relation to space. An elephant takes up more space than a flea. God is infinite. Does this mean that God occupies the infinite stretches of space, that part of him is here in England, another part in Outer Mongolia, another part in the region of the planet Mars? Surely this is an absurd idea. God does not fill space; rather, he is spaceless—outside of space and yet in full control of everything that occurs in space as well as in time.

So to many, the idea that God is in time is incompatible with divine sovereignty, with divine perfection, and with that fullness of being that is essential to

God. The temporalist view may be intelligible (there is nothing intrinsically incoherent about it), but it does not do justice to the nature of God's being.

But a Christian may say, "That is all very well, but is this intuition in accordance with the data of the Christian revelation, holy Scripture? For after all, all our thoughts, including our intuitions, ought to be made subject to the teaching of Scripture." In my view, God's timeless eternity *is* consistent with the teaching of Scripture, though the language of Scripture about God and time is not sufficiently precise so as to provide a definitive resolution of the issue.

Thus, it would be unwise for the eternalist to claim that divine timeless eternity is *entailed by* the language of Scripture. But this lack of entailment need not alarm us since such situations commonly arise in connection with the careful, reflective construction of Christian doctrines. For example, the doctrine of the Trinity as formulated by church fathers is not entailed by the very words of Scripture, but it is widely regarded as being a brilliant epitome of the biblical teaching on the Godhead. So the wise eternalist will claim that biblical passages such as Psalm 90:2 *strongly suggest* the doctrine of divine timeless eternity without insisting that such passages *entail* the doctrine.

But is not citing such biblical verses as I did a few paragraphs ago terribly one-sided? Granted that there are such data and that they may be interpreted in eternalist fashion, ought they not to be supplemented by the pervasive biblical language about God that cannot be interpreted in eternalist fashion but seems not only to suggest but actually to entail that God is in time? I am thinking about references to God's learning and forgetting or to his changing his mind. While there may be verses such as Psalm 90:2 that teach, or seem to teach, or at least allow for the idea that God is timelessly eternal, are there not plenty of other passages that teach us perfectly clearly that God changes?

How, for example, can we understand God's dealings with Moses and Israel in the desert, or the story of Jonah, or the death of Hezekiah (or, perhaps, the Incarnation itself) except on the reasonable supposition that God changes his mind? What is petitionary prayer but an attempt to persuade God to change? If in fact, God changes his mind, if he forgets, learns, and remembers, surely it follows that he is in time. This is an important question, and I will return to it later.

We need an approach to this issue that does not simply set one set of texts over against another set, allowing each of us the luxury of making our own choice, our own preferred "model" of God. For those who set store by the unity of Scripture, it is important to strive to think about God in ways that are consistent with the entire revelation, that not only take in texts that teach God's changelessness (and so seem to imply his timelessness) but also texts that appear to teach that God changes (and so seem to imply that God is in time). We need a way of thinking about God that does justice to the entirety of revelation, not simply a "model" of God based on certain select texts. In the rest of this chapter I will propose such a way of understanding the total revelation, with divine timelessness as its cornerstone.

Not only do eternalists believe their position is more consistent with the entire biblical data about God and time than is temporalism, but they hold that the idea of timelessness makes possible a clearer distinction between the Creator and the creature. This develops the fact that divine creation is a unique metaphysical action, the bringing into being of the whole temporal order and not the creation of the universe by one who is already subject to time. God creates every individual thing distinct from himself. What is in time is created.

Now that we have grasped the basic rationale behind the eternalist's claim, let us look at some representative statements from Christian theologians of God's eternality and at the way the connection is made between divine eternity and divine fullness. Augustine of Hippo (354–430) makes the linkage explicit:

> In you it is not one thing to be and another to live: the supreme degree of being and the supreme degree of life are one and the same thing. You are being in a supreme degree and are immutable. In you the present day has no ending, and yet in you it has its end: "all these things have their being in you" (Rom.11:36). They would have no way of passing away unless you set a limit to them. Because "your years do not fail" (Ps.101:28), your years are one Today.[1]

And Anselm (c. 1033–1109):

> On the other hand, if this Nature (i.e., the divine nature) were to exist as a whole distinctly and successively at different times (as a man exists as a whole yesterday, today and tomorrow), then this Nature would properly be said to have existed, to exist, and to be going to exist. Therefore, its lifetime—which is nothing other than its eternity—would not exist as a whole at once but would be extended by parts throughout the parts of time. Now, its eternity is nothing other than itself. Hence, the Supreme Being would be divided into parts according to the divisions of time.[2]

And, most famously perhaps, Boethius (c. 480–524):

> It is the common judgement, then, of all creatures that live by reason that God is eternal. So let us consider the nature of eternity, for this will make clear to us both the nature of God and his manner of knowing. Eternity, then, is the complete, simultaneous and perfect possession of everlasting life; this will be clear from a comparison with creatures that exist in time.[3]

These representative statements substantiate the previous discussion by suggesting that divine eternality has two main sources: the data of Scripture combined with a priori reflection on the ideas of the divine fullness and self-sufficiency and on the Creator-creature distinction.

---

[1]Augustine, *Confessions*, trans. Henry Chadwick (Oxford: World's Classics, 1992), 8.

[2]Anselm, *Monologion*, in *Anselm of Canterbury*, vol. 1, trans J. Hopkins and H. W. Richardson (London: SCM, 1974), 34.

[3]Boethius, *The Consolation of Philosophy*, trans. V. E. Watts (Harmondsworth, England: Penguin Books, 1969), 5.6.

## 2. Is Timeless Eternity Incoherent?

Some have argued that for all its distinguished pedigree in Christian theology, the eternalist view is straightforwardly incoherent. God's timeless existence makes it seem as if God exists simultaneously with all the events that occur in the universe. What else does the denial that God is in time mean but that everything is present at the same moment to God? But if God's timeless life is simultaneous both with, say, the time of the inauguration of President Wilson and the time of the inauguration of President Kennedy, then must not these events themselves have occurred at the same time? If two events occur at the same time, and a further event occurs at the same time as one of these, then that third certainly must occur at the same time as the other two. Whatever is simultaneous with event E is also simultaneous with whatever else is simultaneous with event E. Since it is absurd to suppose that the inauguration of President Wilson occurred at the same time as the inauguration of President Kennedy, the idea of divine timelessness is absurd. This would mean that every event takes place at the same time as every other event.

Thus, Sir Anthony Kenny claims that, on the eternalist view,

> my typing of this paper is simultaneous with the whole of eternity. Again, on this view, the great fire of Rome is simultaneous with the whole of eternity. Therefore, while I type these very words, Nero fiddles heartlessly on.[4]

Whatever else we may think we know about time and eternity, we know that if one event is later than another, then they cannot both occur at the same time. What can be said to this objection? First of all, it rests on a misunderstanding. The idea of divine timelessness is only incoherent in this sense if it is supposed that timeless eternity is a kind of time, having a kind of eternal duration, a duration that could be simultaneous with some event occurring in truly temporal time. *But there is no compelling reason to think that timeless eternity is a kind of time or that it has aspects of duration.* To say that everything is present to God is not to suppose that everything is *temporally* present to God, that God has an experience of everything happening at once.

However, we could interpret the words of Sir Anthony Kenny in a different way, not as providing a straightforward demonstration of the absurdity of divine timeless eternity but as issuing a kind of challenge to anyone who is tempted to uphold the idea of divine eternality. The challenge is to define clearly what we mean by divine timeless eternity. If it does not have elements of duration and so does not lend itself to the absurd consequences that Kenny suggests, then what exactly is divine timeless eternity? What is the life of the timelessly eternal God like? What is God's experience of the temporal universe like?

Here the eternalist needs to exercise a little caution, in my view, a caution that all Christians should exercise when invited to reflect on God himself. We need to

---

[4]Anthony Kenny, *The God of the Philosophers* (Oxford: Clarendon, 1979), 38–39.

retain a sense of restraint and of reserve in attempting to speak about the nature of God. We cannot hope to know God as he knows himself or to get anywhere near doing so. Is it not improper for us to try to imagine what the life of God is like? How could we, whose minds are designed to function in space and time, come to understand the nature of the one who exists outside space and time?

The fact that we ought to exercise reserve and caution in developing our ideas about God does not mean that we are then reduced to silence or allowed to talk any gibberish we like about God. We can with some confidence say what timeless eternity is not, as we have been doing thus far in this chapter. Moreover, we can gain some positive understanding, though not very much, by the use of analogies. For instance, it has been said that the relation between God and time is like that between the center of a circle and its circumference. The relation of the center of the circle to one point on its circumference is exactly similar to its relation to any other point on it.

Others use the analogy between God's eternal vision and someone at the summit of a hill taking in at a glance what is taking place beneath her. But the hilltop analogy (which Boethius first used) has been shown to be strictly speaking, unsatisfactory. For the person at the summit is herself in time. And the idea of God as the center of a circle with time being represented by the circumference is also defective because, of course, the temporal order is linear and not circular. So these analogies remain, as all analogies do, rather unsatisfactory.

Yet is it even necessary for a satisfactory articulation of the doctrine such as timeless eternality that one accurately describe what timelessness is like? Part of what it means to say that God is incomprehensible is to say that though we believe he is timeless, we do not and cannot have a straightforward understanding of what his timeless life is, of what it is like to be timeless.

Behind the difference between eternalists and temporalists lies an even deeper question. How legitimate is it to think of God in humanlike terms? Obviously, if we think that God is in time then he is much more humanlike than if we think that he is timelessly eternal. For he then shares with us a fundamental feature of existence. But if we think that God is timelessly eternal, then the distance between God and ourselves is much greater, with fewer points of analogy and a greater number of differences. In such circumstances we are in a better position, at least as regards God's relation to time, if we endeavor to say what timeless eternity *is not* rather than to attempt a comprehensive understanding of what it is.

Another objection to timeless divine eternity goes as follows. It may be thought that the ideas of God outside time and the universe as created with time are crude and prescientific. The modern physical view of the universe is that time and space are linked in fundamental ways. There is therefore no such thing as absolute time, and the debate as to whether God is in time or timeless is over, an outdated issue.

Let us suppose that this theory of the relationship between time and space is the correct view and that we are correctly interpreting it. Even so, this cannot be taken as a serious objection to the idea of divine eternality. For whatever the true scientific view of the relation between time and space is, such a view is but an account of some fundamental aspect of *created* reality. But the very point of asserting divine timeless eternity is to say a little of how it is that God transcends the creation. His timelessness is one eloquent way of expressing this transcendence. God transcends the entire space-time universe, however we are finally to understand this. We might then say that modern physical theory potentially presents more difficulties for the temporalist position than it does for divine eternalism!

## 3. Timelessness and Biblical Language

Earlier I said that the idea of divine eternality, if not clearly and explicitly taught in Scripture, is certainly consistent with the scriptural data. Nevertheless (as we also noted), any reader of Scripture is forcefully struck by the language of time and change as applied to God. In fact, there are at least two kinds of language in the Bible about God. First, there is language that asserts God's all encompassing knowledge, including knowledge of matters that are future to us and that encompass the free decisions of human agents. Such a view is implied by texts such as the following:

- Then Joseph said to them, "Do not interpretations belong to God? Tell me your dreams." (Gen. 40:8)
- "Will the citizens of Keilah surrender me to him? Will Saul come down, as your servant has heard? O LORD, God of Israel, tell your servant." And the LORD said, "He will." (1 Sam. 23:11)
- "... for the LORD searches every heart and understands every motive behind the thoughts." (1 Chron. 28:9)
- All the days ordained for me were written in your book before one of them came to be. (Ps. 139:16)
- "I will raise up Cyrus in my righteousness: I will make all his ways straight. He will rebuild my city and set my exiles free." (Isa. 45:13)
- "I make known the end from the beginning." (Isa. 46:10)
- "I foretold the former things long ago, my mouth announced them and I made them known.... Therefore I told you these things long ago; before they happened I announced them to you." (Isa. 48:3–5)
- "This is what the LORD God Almighty, the God of Israel, says: 'If you surrender to the officers of the king of Babylon, your life will be spared and this city will not be burned down; you and your family will live. But if you will not surrender....'" (Jer. 38:17–18)
- For Jesus had known from the beginning which of them did not believe and who would betray him. (John 6:64)
- "This man was handed over to you by God's set purpose and foreknowledge; and you, with the help of wicked men, put him to death." (Acts 2:23)
- Nothing in all creation is hidden from God's sight. (Heb. 4:13)

Then there is biblical language about God that implies that God learns, that he is surprised at what happens (because, apparently, he does not know what is going to happen before it does), and that he changes his mind. How, from an eternalist perspective, can we make sense of the biblical language of change, which implies that God is in time? Or the biblical idea that God repents?

If we look more closely at these two languages, we will see that the language that asserts or implies change in God invariably has to do with divine-human dialogue, to those situations in which God speaks to and acts on behalf of his people and his people speak and act in return.

Let's take the biblical story of Moses in Numbers 14 as an example. This chapter records the rebellion of the people of Israel and the Lord's change of mind. The Lord said to Moses: "How long will they refuse to believe in me, in spite of all the miraculous signs I have performed among them? I will strike them down with a plague and destroy them, but I will make you into a nation greater and stronger than they" (Num. 14:11–12). The Lord asserts that Israel is no longer to be his chosen people but they are to perish, and he will create a new people from Moses. So God has changed his mind about Israel. But once Moses expostulates with God, arguing against this (14:13), and the Lord responds acceding to Moses' prayer (14:20), so, it seems, he changes his mind once again.

Intrinsic to this incident is the fact that the Lord has a dialogue or conversation with Moses about his purposes for Israel and that (as it emerges) he wishes, by saying what he did, to put Moses to the test. The Lord and Moses encounter each other in a step-by-step way, and the outcome is the product of this dialogue. Intrinsic to this dialogue is the fact that the Lord first says one thing and then says another, different thing—thus appearing to change. If he really does change, then he is in time, and eternalism cannot be true.

But it is equally consistent with all the details of this passage—and, furthermore, consistent with what we know from other scriptural data about God's steadfastness and unchangeableness—to suppose that it was God's unchanging intention to remain faithful to Israel (despite their rebellion) but that he kept this back from Moses in order to test him and to elicit a response from him of the appropriate kind. We may also suppose that if God is truly to test Moses, he must not disclose to Moses (at this early stage) what his full and final intentions are. How could God put Moses to the test apart from testing him step by step and so appearing to change his mind in the course of doing so?

Thus, it appears from this story, and from other stories that we might examine, that it is a logically necessary condition of dialogue between persons that each of the partners in the dialogue should appear to act and react in time. If dialogue between God and humankind is to be real and not make-believe, then God cannot represent himself (in his role as dialogue partner) as wholly immutable, for then it would be impossible for him to elicit certain kinds of responses from his people. His purposes for his people, on whose behalf he intervenes in time, cannot be expressed in fully immutable fashion.

The fundamental point is that such language is not dispensable but necessary. If a timelessly eternal God is to communicate to embodied intelligent creatures who exist in space and time and to bring about his purposes through them—and particularly to gain certain kinds of responses from them—then as part of the process he must do so by representing himself to them in ways that are not literally true.

The language of change that God uses of himself is not the whole story about God, any more than the use of anthropomorphic language is. Nor is it there for rhetorical or ornamental effect, but its use takes us to the heart of biblical religion. So God accommodates himself to the human condition, and statements such as "God repented" are false, if taken literally, because God does not literally repent, and cannot do so.

But if such language is literally false, why does the Bible nevertheless assert that God repents? The answer is that some truth about God is nevertheless being conveyed by them. To make this clearer, let us consider some nontheological examples. Someone who upholds the principle of noncontradiction in logic nevertheless may, when asked if it is raining, say, "It is and it isn't." In uttering what is literally self-contradictory, he does not believe that he has actually flouted the principle of noncontradiction; moreover, he succeeds in conveying something intelligible using language that, strictly speaking, is incoherent. Similarly, someone who denies geocentrism as a theory about the heavenly bodies may nevertheless say, "It's warmer in the garden now that the sun has come out from behind the clouds."[5]

Each of these sentences, though literally false, may be taken to convey a truth. Sometimes looseness in speech signifies waffle and incoherence. But at other times language may be loose but economical, the very opposite of waffle. It is hard to believe that such language accommodation, when used of God, is invariably or typically misleading or wrong any more than it is misleading to say that it is and it isn't raining. It is language that records the appearance of things in an unpedantic and vivid way.

Does the use of such language involve God in insincerity, then? It is clear that the Lord's desire to test Moses and for Moses to pass the test is perfectly sincere. For this sincere intention to be carried out, it does not follow that each separate element in his dialogue with Moses, when isolated from all the other components, should take the form of a sincerely uttered truth; only that the entire testing should be sincerely intended.

## 4. Eternity and Creation

Earlier we touched on the idea of God as the Creator and claimed that reflection on this idea is one of the sources of divine eternalism. We must now examine the compatibility of divine timeless eternity and the fundamental Christian idea of creation out of nothing. According to this doctrine, the universe is the outcome of God's free decision. There is no necessity about God's creating. He did not have to, and perhaps he did not have to create any universe at all. Although God himself is in some sense necessary—necessary at least to the extent that he has his existence from himself and not from any other—the universe has its source

---

[5]For these examples, see Peter van Inwagen, *Material Beings* (Ithaca, N.Y.: Cornell Univ. Press, 1990), 101.

in God, and had God willed it, no universe, or some other universe than ours, would have occurred.

We normally think of decisions as involving deliberation as alternatives are considered. Deliberating takes time. But if God is timelessly eternal, then his "deliberation" whether to create some universe or other, and if so which, cannot take time. So the eternalist has to argue that God has a relation to the universe that he might not have had (since the universe might not have existed) and that nevertheless this relation is eternal. There never was a time when this relation did not exist.

But this is not incoherent. God's decree to create the universe is not the end product of a process that took time; yet there could have been a different decree from the one that he in fact made. God has a relation with the temporal universe that happens, as a result of his contingently decreeing it, to be as it is. Put differently, this means that this universe is not part of God's nature, as being wise is part of his nature. God would still have been God had there been no universe. But he would not have been God had he failed to be wise, since wisdom is part of the very nature of God.

Some modern views of God—those influenced to some degree or other by "process" thought—think of God as needing a creation in order to complete himself. But this is not the mainstream Christian view, which sees the created universe not as something God needs but as an expression of his overflowing goodness and generosity. Eternalism, with its strong intuitions about divine independence and self-sufficiency, strongly endorses this historic Christian position.

So an eternalist may consistently deny that God's being the eternal creator of a temporal universe is inconsistent, and one may also deny that if God is related to the temporal world in virtue of creating it, then God is temporal. Note these other representative scriptural statements about God and his relation to time. God is the lofty one who inhabits eternity (Isa. 57:15); though his creation will grow old, he remains the same, his years never end (Heb. 1:10–12; see also 2 Tim. 1:9; 1 Cor. 2:7; and other verses that refer to God existing "before the foundation of the world.")

For the eternalist, temporality is an essential feature of creatureliness. As we noted above, in its classic expression (e.g., in the thought of Augustine) the universe is created by God *with* time, *not in* time. It is created "all at once" only in the sense that the creation is the product of one divine timeless decree. We also noted modern views of space and time, including the fact that if they are true, they depict an aspect of created reality and therefore cannot address the question of whether or not God is timelessly eternal.

In the same way, for the eternalist God's creation of all that is ("the universe") is not a scientific event, like the exploding of a star or the splitting of an atom; nor is it a unique historical event, like the Battle of Hastings or the coronation of the Queen. God brings the universe into being from a standpoint outside it. For this reason the idea that God exists (timelessly) "before" the universe cannot mean that God exists temporally before it in the same way in which breakfast is before dinner, or Napoleon was before Hitler. God exists before the universe, I argue, in rather the way in which the Queen exists before the Prime Minister, age comes before beauty, or duty comes before pleasure. These "befores" are not temporal "befores," but "befores" of another kind of priority, signaling a constitutional or hierarchical or normative arrangement. There was no time when the Creator was not, any more than there was a time when the creation was not. Yet the Creator exists "before" the creation. It is in some such way as this that we may interpret the apostolic claim that Christ is before all things (Col. 1:17).

Thus, at the heart of the eternalist understanding of God and creation is the idea of a *scale of being*, with God existing eternally and necessarily and the universe existing contingently. God exists before the universe in a hierarchical sense; he does not exist temporally before it. Eternalists are unwilling to think of God in human terms, to "anthropomorphize" him. So God is before the creation not by virtue of existing at a time when the universe was not yet in existence, but by virtue of the fact that he exists necessarily, whereas creation is only contingent (for it might not have been). Everything created (except the temporal order itself) is necessarily in time, mutable, and (so) corruptible; anything that exists uncreatedly is necessarily eternal, immutable, and incorruptible.[6]

In talking about a timeless God causing or bringing about the universe, we are, of course, using "cause" in an unusual sense. Normally we think of causes as being before (in time) their effects, and we think of causes and effects as being events. One moving ball comes into contact with a stationary ball and causes the second ball to move. A state of one ball causes a change in the state of another. In the case of creation, God's action is causal but not temporal. Nor is his decree an event, since events occur in time. The creation of the universe from nothing does not bring about a change in the universe since there was nothing to undergo change before it came into existence. And in virtue of the divine power, the cause ensures that the effect will occur.

All these are significant departures from the usual ways in which we talk of one event causing another. Moreover, they are also departures from the ways in which philosophers usually talk about causes and effects. If someone wishes to define "cause" in temporal terms, he or she is free to do so. But then the eternalist will simply substitute another expression, such as "brings about," to characterize God's creative role. Whatever precise words we use, the eternalist maintains that the idea of eternal creation (or of eternal "bringing about") does not result in a sense of "cause" or "bringing about" that is so stretched that it conveys no clear meaning.

## 5. God's Action in the World

The idea of timeless creation leads naturally to a consideration of a timeless God's actions in the world. Creation is God's action in bringing the universe into being from nothing, and we have seen that this requires an understanding of

---

[6]Here I deliberately avoid the question of whether God may be thought to be the creator of necessary truths.

causation that is somewhat stretched by comparison with our ordinary usage. But given that God has timelessly created the universe, may he act within it and so produce changes in the universe that are much closer to the sorts of changes human or other temporal causal agencies can bring about?

#8 To many the very idea of an eternal God acting within his created universe has seemed incoherent. For them, God's timeless eternity has appeared to entail a form of deism, according to which such a God may timelessly create the entire temporal order and all that it contains but not be able to act within it. I will argue that this is a mistaken view. To start with, we have already noted that on the eternalist view, God is eternally active in upholding the universe moment by moment. He does not act like the God of the deists, according to whom God created the universe and then left it to continue under its own impetus.

Thus, God acts upon the universe by upholding it. But more than this, it is possible to see that not only may such a timelessly eternal God act within time, but he may also act in response to what happens in time. I will take these points in turn.

What is it to act, to perform an action? I suppose, somewhat crudely no doubt, that to act is to bring about something as the result of intending, desiring, or willing it and to have a purpose in doing so. It is, of course, fatal to the very idea of God's timeless eternity to imagine that in acting in the world, God acts as we do. We (typically, though not invariably, as we shall see) will in time to bring about some particular effect at a later time, though there may be little or no interval between the intention and the action. As I type this paper on my computer, I am intending to strike first one particular key of the computer and then another, and the effects of my intentions follow rapidly as the keys are struck. To suppose that God acts in anything like this way is to suppose that God exists at a time. But what alternative is there?

Let me answer this question by distinguishing between intending to do an action and then that action being done. This morning I intend to mow the lawn this afternoon, and I mow the lawn this afternoon. The intention is one thing, the carrying out of that intention is another. Why may we not suppose, in a parallel way, that just as it is possible to intend at one time to do something at a later time, it is also possible that a timelessly eternal God eternally intends to do something at some particular point in time?

There seems to be nothing incoherent about the idea that God eternally wills that some event—for example, the miraculous burning of the bush that attracted the attention of Moses (Ex. 3)—occur at some particular time. The most helpful way to think of God's eternally willing something in time is to think of one eternal act of will with numerous temporally scattered effects. One intention may have numerous effects occurring at different times.

As an analogy, we may think of a person's action in setting the timer on his central heating system. This (we may suppose) one action corresponds to God's eternal willing. But this one action, which has numerous temporally scattered effects, corresponds to the effects in time of God's one eternal act of willing. As a result of the one act of setting the timer, the central heating system fires at 7:00

A.M., goes off at 12 noon, fires again at 2:00 P.M., goes off again at 10.30 P.M., and it does so day after day (unless it is altered). The basic point is that one decision can bring about different effects at different times. This decision may be in time, as in our example, but there seems to be no reason why such a decision may not be timeless—as it would be in the case of the timelessly eternal divine decree. So God may timelessly decree that the bush burn at one time, that the walls of Jericho fall down at some other time, and so on.

The examples we have just used are instances of miracles, but it is not necessary that God's eternally willed actions in time are all miraculous. Far from it. As God sustains the universe, he does so by the occurrence of innumerable regular actions that are each the outcome of one eternal decree.

Aquinas put the essential point well:

> Note that to change your will is one matter, and to will a change in some thing is another. While remaining constant, a person can will this to happen now and the contrary to happen afterwards. His will, however, would change were he to begin to will what he had not willed before, or cease to will what he had willed before.[7]

Furthermore, it is consistent to suppose that not only can a timelessly eternal God will things in time without changing his will; he may also eternally will his own reactions in time to some human action. Suppose that God eternally knows that I will perform some particular action. Knowing this, he eternally decrees to bring about some action in the world as a response to my action. Thus, God may eternally will both the burning bush and his temporally subsequent utterances to Moses, eternally knowing that Moses' attention will be attracted by the burning bush. These are logically distinct elements, but not temporally distinct elements, of God's one eternal decree.

The Incarnation is, of course, a unique case of God, God the Son, acting in time. One cannot deny that the very idea of Incarnation carries with it some deep perplexities. But such perplexities are, for both the temporalist and the eternalist, caused by the very idea of God's being united to human nature. For example, on neither view can God the Son become entirely localized in Bethlehem and Nazareth as Christ's human nature was localized in these places. Although the eternalist may have different further difficulties over the Incarnation than the temporalist, neither position can smooth away these problems entirely.

Note that if God the Son is timelessly eternal and yet incarnate in Jesus Christ, there is no time in his existence when he was not incarnate—though since he became incarnate at a particular time in our history, there were times in that history before the Incarnation and times since. God eternally decrees to become incarnate at a particular time and place; he does not decree at that time and place to become incarnate.

---

[7]Thomas Aquinas, *Summa Theologiae*, 1a.19.7, in *Will and Providence*, trans. Thomas Gilby (London: Eyre & Spottiswoode, 1966), 33.

## 6. The Two Standpoints

As we have been developing the case for eternalism, we have seen that there are two standpoints, that of the eternal God and that of a creature, such as Moses, existing in time. One is tempted to confuse the standpoint of the Creator with that of the creature. From the Creator's standpoint, his creation is a timeless whole, including, as it does, the Incarnation. However, from the standpoint of an intelligent creature, the universe may be thought to be coeternal with God, for (if we suppose that the universe is created with time) there will be no time when the universe is not. For such a creature the universe unfolds as a temporal order.

We may elucidate this idea of the two standpoints, the divine and the human standpoints, a little further, by thinking of two physical standpoints. A building may be viewed from more than one standpoint: for example, from that of Jones standing in front of the building and that of Smith standing behind it. But while any building must be viewed from some standpoint or other, we can easily imagine the standpoints of Jones and Smith being switched.

In the case of two people occupying different temporal standpoints, there is considerably less flexibility, indeed perhaps no flexibility at all. I cannot now occupy the temporal standpoint I enjoyed twenty years ago. Someone living in 2002 cannot now take up Napoleon's temporal standpoint (though one can view the pyramids, say, from the same spatial standpoint as Napoleon did), and perhaps such a person could never have had Napoleon's standpoint. So in the case of temporal standpoints, there is no prospect of switching as there is in the case of physical standpoints.

The distinction between the eternal and the temporal standpoints, the respective standpoints of a timelessly eternal God and one of his creatures in time, is clearly not interchangeable at will. For anyone who occupies a temporal standpoint occupies some definite temporal standpoint or other willy-nilly. (This is part of what it means to be bound by time.) Similarly, the occupant of the eternal standpoint has no choice. If God is timelessly eternal, then he is necessarily so, and he cannot occupy any temporal standpoint; and no temporal creature can be timelessly eternal. For to be a temporal creature is to have the possibility of changing, while to be timelessly eternal, such change is impossible. God, if he is timelessly eternal, cannot translate his eternal standpoint into ours, nor can we, creatures of time, translate our various successive temporal standpoints into his.

This can be illustrated from the case that presents the greatest difficulty for the idea of two standpoints, the Incarnation. In the Incarnation God the Son enters into union with human nature. As the Son of God he has and retains the eternal standpoint, and he comes to be united to human nature, which necessarily has a temporal standpoint. He does not become man in any sense that implies that, by becoming man, he ceases to be God. If I take a pile of leaves and burn them, they become ash, and in doing so they cease to be leaves. But in becoming man God the Son does not cease to be God the Son; how could he, if God the Son is necessarily God the Son?

Thus, an eternalist will say that in the Incarnation, God the Son is united to what had a temporal standpoint without having that standpoint himself. The mystery and difficulty of the Incarnation is how it is that one person can have two standpoints, divine and human, and yet be one Mediator. But this is the general difficulty that besets orthodox Christology of whatever stripe; it is not a special difficulty that besets only eternalist understandings of God.

Given the untransferability of the eternal and the temporal standpoints, and assuming that any standpoint is either temporal or eternal, that we exist in time, and that God exists in timeless eternity, there cannot be a standpoint-less truth of the matter about events and actions in time, any more than there can be standpoint-less truth of the matter about timeless eternity. The temporal order that is the created universe must be understood either from a timeless standpoint, as a timeless God understands it, or from a temporal vantage point, as you and I understand it.

From our standpoint, God's creation is continuously unfolding; it is a *creatio continua*. The state of the universe at time *t1* does not logically necessitate the character nor even the existence of any phase of it at *t2* or later, even though there are discovered regularities between different past phases, and promised continuations of them, for as long as the created order persists. Thus, from our perspective the Creator may be said to be continuously creating the universe, in that there is more universe today than there was yesterday, for later phases of the universe build upon and are made intelligible by earlier phases. But from the divine standpoint, what is created is one temporally extended or ordered universe laid out before and eternally present to the mind of God.

#9 God's standpoint is not the view from nowhere or nowhen, but the view from his own unique "where" and "when," the "where" and "when" of timeless (and spaceless) eternity. For not only are we subjects, God is also a subject, with a unique epistemic and volitional standpoint, though he is not a subject of experience in quite the way we are. God as a subject stands outside space and time and views his creatures in a manner that is best expressed by us (though not fully comprehended by us) in ways that do not imply occupancy of time or space. God's view is not, of course, a literal viewing; nevertheless, God has a unique perspective on the world, a perspective necessarily free of temporal and spatial limitations.

From the divine standpoint, no single moment of the entire temporal series is privileged by being present; but as regards presentness, pastness, or futurity, all moments are in exactly the same position, even though some moments are earlier in relation to others in the series, some later. It is a temporal order every moment of which is also eternally present to God.

In contrast to those who wish to overturn the classical conception of God, the foregoing discussion offers some ways of making sense of God's relation to a temporal world while at the same time retaining God's absolute transcendence over time and over space. The eternal God of historic Christianity is not in any sense bound by the limits that arise from being located at a specific point in time, but everything is uncovered and laid bare before the eyes of him to whom we must give account.

Chapter 6

# What Does God Know?

*William Lane Craig*

# 1. Introduction

In a self-proclaimed postmodern age in which the reimagining of God by feminists, antirealists, and radical pluralists often takes bizarre and unconventional forms, the denial of divine omniscience on the part of otherwise very conservative theologians can seem a harmless and even welcome modification of the traditional concept of God. But it is the seeming innocence of this alteration that makes it dangerous, for whereas radical aberrations are easy to recognize and avoid, it is the subtle deviations from the truth that will more likely lead us astray.

The contemporary critique of divine omniscience focuses on God's foreknowledge of future contingents, specifically free human decisions. Some scholars today allege that God does not know which future contingent events will transpire and that therefore he is a "risk-taking" God. Moreover, they claim such a conception of God is faithful to biblical teaching.

# 2. The Biblical Doctrine of Divine Foreknowledge

The suggestion that the God described in the biblical tradition is ignorant of future contingents is on the face of it an extraordinary claim. For not only are the Scriptures replete with examples of precisely such knowledge on God's part, but they explicitly teach that God has foreknowledge of future events, even employing a specialist vocabulary to refer to such knowledge. The New Testament introduces a whole family of words associated with God's knowledge of the future, such as "foreknow" (*proginōskō*), "foreknowledge" (*prognōsis*), "foresee" (*prooraō*), "foreordain" (*proorizō*), and "foretell" (*promartyromai, prokatangellō*). Thus, the claim that the biblical concept of omniscience does not comprise knowledge of the future seems fatuous.

The affirmation of God's knowledge of the future is important in two respects. First, this aspect of divine omniscience underlies the biblical conception of history, which is not that of an unpredictably unfolding sequence of events; rather, God knows the future and directs the course of world history toward his foreseen ends:

> I am God, and there is none like me.
> I make known the end from the beginning,
>    from ancient times, what is still to come.
> I say: "My purpose will stand,
>    And I will do all that I please."
>
> (Isa. 46:9–10)

Biblical history is a salvation history, and Christ is the beginning, centerpiece, and culmination of that history. God's salvific plan was not an afterthought necessitated by an unforeseen circumstance. Paul speaks of "the administration of this mystery, which for ages past was kept hidden in God, who created all things" (Eph. 3:9), "his will . . . to be put into effect when the times will have reached their fulfillment" (1:9–10), according to "the eternal purpose which he accomplished in Christ Jesus our Lord" (3:11; cf. 2 Tim. 1:9–10). Similarly, Peter states that Christ "was chosen before the creation of the world, but was revealed in these last times for your sake" (1 Peter 1:20). God's knowledge of the course of world history and his control over it to achieve his purposes are fundamental to the biblical conception of history and are a source of comfort and assurance to the believer in times of distress.

Second, God's knowledge of the future—including the future free choices of humans—seems essential to the prophetic pattern that underlies the biblical scheme of history. The test of the true prophet was success in foretelling the future: "If what a prophet proclaims in the name of the LORD does not take place or come true, that is a message the LORD has not spoken" (Deut. 18:22). The history of Israel is punctuated with prophets who foretold events in both the immediate and distant future, and it is the conviction of the New Testament writers that the coming and work of Jesus had been prophesied.

The prophetic element, however, is not limited to the fulfillment of Old Testament predictions. Jesus himself is characterized as a prophet, and he predicted his own execution and resurrection (Luke 9:22), the destruction of Jerusalem, signs of the end of the world, and his own return as Lord of all nations (Matt. 24; Mark 13; Luke 21). In the early church, too, there were prophets who told of events to come (Acts 11:27–28; 21:10–11; see also 13:1; 15:32; 21:9; 1 Cor. 12:28–29; 14:29, 37; Eph. 4:11). The Revelation to John is a mighty vision of the end of human history: "The Lord, the God of the spirits of the prophets, sent his angel to show his servants the things that must soon take place" (Rev. 22:6). The prophetic pattern thus reveals an underlying unity not only between the two Testaments but also beneath the entire course of human history.

The biblical view of history and prophecy thus seems to necessitate a God who knows not only the present and past but also the future. Indeed, so essential is God's knowledge of the future that Isaiah makes knowledge of the future the decisive test in distinguishing the true God from false gods. The prophet flings this challenge in the teeth of all pretenders to deity:

"Present your case," says the LORD.
   "Set forth your arguments," says Jacob's King.
"Bring in your idols to tell us
   what is going to happen.
Tell us what the former things were,
   so that we may consider them
   and know their final outcome.
Or declare to us the things to come,
   tell us what the future holds,
   so we may know that you are gods.

Do something, whether good or bad,
  so that we will be dismayed and filled with fear.
But you are less than nothing
  and your works are utterly worthless;
  he who chooses you is detestable."
                    (ISA. 41:21–24)

Stephen Charnock, in his classic *Existence and Attributes of God*, comments on this passage:

Such a foreknowledge of things to come is here ascribed to God by God himself, as a distinction of him from all false gods. Such a knowledge that, if any could prove that they were possessors of, he would acknowledge them as gods as well as himself: "that we may know that you are gods." He puts his Deity to stand or fall upon this account, and this should be the point which should decide the controversy whether he or the heathen idols were the true God. The dispute is managed by this medium: he that knows things to come is God; I know things to come, *ergo* I am God: the idols know not things to come, therefore they are not gods. God submits the being of his Deity to this trial. If God knows things to come no more than the heathen idols, which were either devils or men, he would be, in his own account, no more a God than devils or men. . . . It cannot be understood of future things in their causes, when the effects necessarily arise from such causes, as light from the sun and heat from the fire. Many of these men know; more of them, angels and devils know; if God, therefore, had not a higher and farther knowledge than this, he would not by this be proved to be God, any more than angels and devils, who know necessary effects in their causes. The devils, indeed, did predict some things in the heathen oracles, but God is differenced from them here . . . in being able to predict things to come that they knew not, or things in their particularities, things that depended on the liberty of man's will, which the devils could lay no claim to a certain knowledge of. Were it only a conjectural knowledge that is here meant, the devils might answer they can conjecture, and so their deity were as good as God's. . . . God asserts his knowledge of things to come as a manifest evidence of his Godhead; those that deny, therefore, the argument that proves it, deny the conclusion, too; for this will necessarily follow, that if he be God because he knows future things, then he that doth not know future things is not God; and if God knows not future things but only by conjecture, then there is no God, because a certain knowledge, so as infallibly to predict things to come, is an inseparable perfection of the Deity.[1]

---

[1]Stephen Charnock, *Discourses upon the Existence and Attributes of God*, 2 vols. (1682; reprint, Grand Rapids: Baker, 1979), 1:431–32.

As Charnock notes, God's knowledge seems to encompass future contingencies. Just as God knows the thoughts humans have, so he foreknows the very thoughts they will have. The psalmist declares:

> O LORD, you have searched me
> and you know me.
> You know when I sit and when I rise;
> you perceive my thoughts from afar.
> You discern my going out and my lying down;
> you are familiar with all my ways.
> Before a word is on my tongue
> you know it completely, O LORD.
> You hem me in—behind and before;
> you have laid your hand upon me.
> Such knowledge is too wonderful for me,
> too lofty for me to attain.
>
> (Ps. 139:1–6)

The psalmist envisages himself as surrounded by God's knowledge. God knows everything about him, even his thoughts. "From afar" (*mērāḥôq*) may be taken to indicate temporal distance—God knows the psalmist's thoughts long before he thinks them. Similarly, even before he speaks a word, God knows what he will say. Little wonder that such knowledge is beyond the reach of the psalmist's understanding! But such is the knowledge of Israel's God in contradistinction to all the false gods of her neighbors. The God of Israel was conceived to possess foreknowledge of the future, a property distinguishing him from all false gods.

In light of the clear biblical affirmations of divine foreknowledge, it seems remarkable that some conservative theologians would deny that the Bible teaches God's foreknowledge of future events. They argue that God can only make intelligent conjectures about what free creatures are going to do. As a result, God is ignorant of virtually all of humanity's future since even a single free choice could turn history in a different direction than its present course, and subsequent events would, as time goes on, depart increasingly from history's present trajectory. At best God can be said to have a good idea of what will happen only in the very near future.

Such a view seems so obviously unbiblical that we might be surprised to hear that some persons think that it represents faithfully the doctrine of the Scriptures. Those who hold to this view, however, typically point to passages in the Scriptures that imply that God is ignorant of some facts (Jer. 26:3; 36:3). The problem with trying to base a doctrine of divine omniscience on such passages, however, is that it underestimates the degree to which the narratives of God's acts are anthropomorphic in character; that is, God is described in human terms, which are not intended to be taken literally. The Bible is not a treatise in theology, much less in philosophy of religion. It is primarily a collection of stories about God's dealings with his people. The storyteller's art is not to reflect philosophically on the narrative but to tell a vivid tale.

Thus, the Scriptures are filled with anthropomorphisms, many so subtle that they escape our notice. There are not only the obvious anthropomorphisms, such as references to God's eyes, hands, and nostrils, but almost unconscious ones, such as references to God's seeing the distress of his people, hearing their prayers, crushing his enemies, turning away from apostate Israel, and so forth. These are all *metaphors*, since God does not possess literal bodily parts by which to accomplish these actions. In the same way, given the explicit teaching of Scripture that God does foreknow the future, the passages that portray God as ignorant or inquiring are probably just anthropomorphisms characteristic of the genre of narrative.

Those who deny divine foreknowledge also appeal to passages in which God predicts that something will happen but then "repents," so that the predicted event does not come to pass (e.g., Isa. 38:1–5; Amos 7:1–6; Jonah 3). Obviously, since what God predicted did not in the end happen, the predictions were not foreknowledge of the future. The problem here is how to explain that while the authors of these passages were aware that God knew the future and could not lie (see Num. 23:19; 1 Sam. 15:29), yet they represent him as relenting on impending judgments he had commanded his prophets to proclaim.

The most plausible interpretation of such passages is that these prophecies were not simple glimpses of the future but pictures of what was going to happen *unless. . . .*[2] The prophecies contained the implicit condition of "all things remaining the same." Certain prophecies thus are forecasts or forewarnings of what is going to happen if all things remain as they are. Such events are sometimes referred to as conditional future contingents, and God's knowledge of such events is even more remarkable than simple foreknowledge, since it involves knowledge of what would happen were other circumstances to exist than those that will.

Not all of the prophecies in the Old and New Testaments are mere forewarnings, however. Prophecies of events that are brought about not by God but by human beings and that could not have been inferred from present causes cannot be interpreted as forewarnings but must be considered to express simple foreknowledge on God's part.

How do the detractors of divine foreknowledge explain Scripture passages that illustrate God's knowledge of the future? Typically, they attempt to dismiss each example of divine foreknowledge as being one of the following: (1) a declaration by God of what he himself intends to bring about, (2) an inference of what is going to happen based on present causes, or (3) a conditional prediction of what will happen *if* something else happens.

Such an account seems inadequate, however. As far as (3) is concerned, if conditional predictions do not reduce to (1) or (2), they must be expressions of divine middle knowledge, which is even more remarkable than divine foreknowledge

---

[2]Witherington calls these "conditional prophecies"; Ben Witherington III, *Jesus the Seer* (Peabody, Mass.: Hendrickson, 1999), 3.

and, indeed, may provide the basis for divine foreknowledge.[3] Hence, to try to explain away divine foreknowledge by means of (3) is counterproductive.

As for (2), while it might be claimed, say, that Jesus predicted Judas's betrayal or Peter's denial solely on the basis of their character and the surrounding circumstances, there can be no question that the Gospel writers themselves did not understand such predictions in this manner. To try to explain biblical prophecies as mere inferences from present states of affairs denudes them of any theological significance. The writers of Scripture clearly saw prophecy not as God's reasoned conjecture of what will happen but as a manifestation of his infinite knowledge, encompassing even things yet to come.

As for (1), it is true that many prophecies in Scripture are clearly based on God's irrevocable intention to bring about certain future events on his own. In such cases, prophecy serves to manifest not so much God's omniscience as his omnipotence, his ability to bring about whatever he intends. But the problem with (1) is that it simply cannot be stretched to cover all the cases that its proponents need it to cover. Divine foreknowledge of free human actions cannot be accounted for by (1), since it negates human freedom. Explanation (1) is useful only in accounting for God's knowledge of events that he himself will bring about directly. But Scripture provides many examples of divine foreknowledge of events that God does not directly cause, events that are the result of free human choices.

Finally, none of the three explanations comes to grips with the Scripture's doctrinal teaching concerning God's foreknowledge. These explanations try to account only for examples of prophecy in the Bible and say nothing about the passages that explicitly teach God's foreknowledge of the future. Thus, we have strong biblical warrant for the doctrine that God's omniscience encompasses all things, including knowledge of all future contingents.

## 3. Philosophical Grounds for Affirming Divine Foreknowledge

Not only are there *biblical* grounds for affirming God's foreknowledge of future contingents, but there are good *philosophical* reasons for thinking that God foreknows the future. As Anselm argued, the concept of God is the concept of a perfect being—what Anselm termed "the greatest conceivable being." (Just ask yourself whether any being that is less than perfect would be worthy of worship.) Now the greatest conceivable being, a perfect being, must be all-knowing or omniscient. For ignorance is an imperfection; all things being equal, it is greater or better to be knowing than ignorant. Therefore, if there are truths about future contingents, God, as an omniscient being, must know these truths. Since there are such truths about the future—that is to say, since statements about future

---

[3]Middle knowledge involves knowledge of subjunctive conditionals, such as *If Goldwater had been elected in 1964, he would have won the Viet Nam war*. See my article "The Middle-Knowledge View," in *Divine Foreknowledge: Four Views*, ed. James K. Beilby and Paul R. Eddy (Downer's Grove, Ill.: InterVarsity Press, 2001), 119–43.

contingents are either true or false, and they are not all false—God must therefore know all truths about the future. In other words, he knows what will happen.

One might try to escape the force of this reasoning by contending that future-tense statements are neither true nor false. Such a view cannot, however, be plausibly maintained. Here several points deserve mention.

First, there is no good reason to deny that future-tense statements are either true or false. Why should we accept the view that future-tense statements about free acts, statements that we use all the time in ordinary conversation, are in fact neither true nor false? What proof is there that such statements are neither true nor false?

About the only answer of any substance ever given to this question goes something like this: Future events, unlike present events, do not exist. Now, a statement is true if and only if it corresponds to what exists, and false if and only if it does not correspond to what exists. Since the future does not exist, there is nothing for future-tense statements to correspond with or to fail to correspond with. Hence, future-tense statements cannot be true or false.

Now, since I am inclined to accept the view of time that this proposed answer presupposes (namely, the unreality of the future), the issue is whether, given such a view, the definition of truth as correspondence requires us to deny that future-tense statements are either true or false. Those who think so seem to misunderstand the concept of truth as correspondence. A view of truth as correspondence holds merely that a statement is true if and only if what it states to be the case really is the case. For example, the statement "It is snowing" is true if and only if it is snowing.

Although this might seem too obvious to be worth stating, it is sometimes misunderstood. Truth as correspondence does *not* mean that the things or events that a true statement is about must exist. Indeed, it is only in the case of true present-tense statements that the things or events referred to must exist. For a past-tense statement to be true it is not required that what it describes exist, but only that it *has* existed. For a future-tense statement to be true it is not required that what it describes exist, but that it *will* exist. In order for a future-tense statement to be true, all that is required is that when the moment described arrives, the present-tense version of the statement will be true. The idea that the concept of truth as correspondence requires that the things or events described by the statement must exist at the time the statement is true is a complete misunderstanding.

To say that a future-tense statement is now true is not, of course, to say that we may now know whether it is true or to say that things are now so determined that it is true. It is only to say that when the time arrives, things will turn out as the statement predicts. A future-tense statement is true if matters turn out as the statement predicts, and false if matters fail to turn out as the statement predicts—this is all that the notion of truth as correspondence requires. Hence, there is no good reason to deny that future-tense statements are either true or false.

Second, there are several good reasons to maintain that future-tense statements are either true or false.

(1) The same facts that guarantee the truth or falsity of present- and past-tense statements also guarantee the truth or falsity of future-tense statements. Nicholas Rescher explains:

> Difficulties about divine foreknowledge quite apart, it is difficult to justify granting to
> 1. "It will rain tomorrow" (asserted on April 12)
>    a truth status different from that of
> 2. "It did rain yesterday" (asserted on April 14)
>    because both make (from temporally distinct perspectives) *precisely the same claim about the facts*, viz., rain on April 13.[4]

Think about it for a moment. If "It is raining today" is now true, how could "It will rain tomorrow" not have been true yesterday? The same facts guarantee that a future-tense statement asserted earlier, a present-tense statement asserted simultaneously, and a past-tense statement asserted later are all true.

(2) If future-tense statements are not true, then neither are past-tense statements. If future-tense statements cannot be true because the realities they describe do not yet exist, then by the same token past-tense statements cannot be true because the realities they describe no longer exist. But to maintain that past-tense statements cannot be true would be ridiculous. Since the two cases are parallel, one must either deny the truth or falsity of both past- and future-tense statements or affirm the truth or falsity of both.

(3) Tenseless statements are always true or false. It is possible to eliminate the tense of the verb in a statement by specifying the time at which the statement is supposed to be true. For example, the statement "The Allies invaded Normandy" can be made tenseless by specifying the time: "On June 6, 1944, the Allies *invade* Normandy," the italics indicating that the verb is tenseless. If the tensed version is true, then so is the tenseless version.[5] Thus, correlated with any true past- or present-tense statement is a true tenseless version of that statement.

Furthermore, a tenseless statement, if it is true at all, is *always* true. This is precisely because the statement is tenseless. If "On June 6, 1944, the Allies *invade* Normandy" is *ever* true, then it is *always* true. Therefore, this statement is true prior to June 6, 1944. But in that case, it is true prior to June 6, 1944, that the Allies on that date will invade Normandy, which is the same as saying that the future-tense version of the tenseless statement is true. Moreover, since God is omniscient, he must always know the truth of the tenseless statement, a fact that entails that he foreknows the future.

Third, the denial of the truth or falsity of future-tense statements has absurd consequences. For example, if future-tense statements are neither true nor false, the statement made in 1998 "George W. Bush either will or will not win the

---

[4]Nicholas Rescher, *Many-Valued Logic* (New York: McGraw-Hill, 1969), 2–3.

[5]Thomas Bradley Talbott, "Fatalism and the Timelessness of Truth" (Ph.D. diss., University of California at Santa Barbara, 1974), 153–54.

presidential election in 2000" would not be true. For this statement is a compound constructed from two simple future-tense sentences—"George W. Bush will win the presidential election in 2000" and "George W. Bush will not win the presidential election in 2000." If neither of these individual statements is true or false, the compound statement combining them is also neither true nor false. But how can this be? Either Bush will win or he will not—there is no other alternative. But the view that future-tense statements are neither true nor false would require us to say that this compound statement is neither true nor false, which seems absurd.

Worse still, if future-tense statements are neither true nor false, it would be impossible for us to say that a statement like "Bush will both win and not win the presidential election in 2000" is false. For this is a compound statement consisting of two simple future-tense statements, neither of which is supposed to be true or false. Therefore, the compound statement cannot be true or false either. But surely this statement is false, for it is a self-contradiction: Bush cannot both win and not win the election!

We must conclude that with no good reason in favor of it, persuasive reasons against it, and absurd consequences following from it, the view that future-tense statements about free decisions are neither true nor false is untenable.

The view that God's omniscience does not encompass foreknowledge is thereby seen to be untenable, since as an omniscient being, he must know all true statements, including all true future-tense statements (and tenseless statements about the future). Detractors of divine foreknowledge often therefore try to redefine the concept of omniscience in such a way that *being omniscient* does not entail *knowing all truths*. Thus, they must reject the usual definition of omniscience:

> O. For any agent $x$, $x$ is omniscient = def. For every statement $s$,
>    if $s$ is true, then $x$ knows that $s$ and does not believe not-$s$.

What (O) requires is that a person is omniscient if and only if he knows all truths and believes no falsehoods. This is the standard definition of omniscience. It entails that if there are future-tense truths, then an omniscient being must know them.

So as not to deny God's omniscience, opponents of divine foreknowledge have suggested revisionary definitions of omniscience in order to be able to affirm that God is omniscient even as they deny his knowledge of future contingents.[6] William Hasker's revisionist definition is typical:

> O'. God is omniscient = def. God knows all statements that are
>    such that God's knowing them is logically possible.

---

[6]For the following definition see William Hasker, "A Philosophical Perspective," in Clark Pinnock et al., *The Openness of God: A Biblical Challenge to the Traditional Understanding of God* (Downer's Grove, Ill.: InterVarsity Press, 1994), 136.

Revisionists then go on to claim that it is logically impossible to know statements about future contingents; thus, God may count as omniscient despite his ignorance of an infinite number of true statements.

As it stands, however, (O') is drastically flawed. For it does not exclude that God believes false statements as well as true ones. Worse, (O') actually requires God to know false statements, which is incoherent as well as theologically unacceptable. For (O') requires that if it is logically possible for God to know some statement *s*, then God knows *s*. But if *s* is a contingently false statement, say, *There are eight planets in the sun's solar system*, then there are possible worlds in which *s* is true and so known by God. Therefore, since it is logically possible for God to know *s*, he must according to (O') actually know *s*, which is absurd.

What the revisionist really wants to say is something like:

O". God is omniscient = def. God knows only and all true statements
that are such that it is logically possible for God to know them.

Unlike (O'), (O") limits God's knowledge to a certain subset of all true statements.

The fundamental problem with all such revisionary definitions of omniscience as (O") is that any adequate definition of a concept must accord with our intuitive understanding of the concept. We are not at liberty to "cook" the definition in some desired way without thereby making the definition unacceptably contrived. (O") is guilty of being "cooked" in this way. For intuitively, omniscience involves knowing all truths; yet according to (O") God could conceivably be ignorant of infinite realms of truths and yet still count as omniscient. The only reason why someone would prefer (O") to (O) is due to an ulterior motivation to salvage the attribute of omniscience for a cognitively limited deity rather than to deny outright that God is omniscient. (O") is therefore unacceptably contrived.

A second problem with (O") is that it construes omniscience in modal terms—speaking not of knowing all truth but of knowing all truth that is knowable. Some of the revisionists want to view God's omniscience in analogy to God's omnipotence. Just as we recognize that God is omnipotent even though he does not use all his power, so we should recognize God as omniscient even though he does not know all truths. But omniscience, unlike omnipotence, is not a modal notion. Roughly speaking, omnipotence is the capability of actualizing any logically possible state of affairs. But omniscience is not merely the *capability* of knowing only and all truths; it *is* knowing only and all truths. Nor does omniscience mean knowing only and all knowable truths, but knowing only and all truths, period. It is a categorical, not a modal, notion.

Third, the superiority of (O") over (O) depends on there being a difference between a truth and a truth that it is logically possible to know. If there is no difference, then (O") collapses back to (O), and the revisionist has gained nothing. But it is far from evident that there is any difference. For what is a sufficient condition for a statement to be logically knowable? So far as I can see, the only condition is that the statement be true. What more is needed? If the revisionist thinks that something more is needed, then we may ask him for an example of a statement that could be true but logically impossible to know. A statement such as *Nothing exists* or *All agents have ceased to exist* comes to mind; but on traditional theism these statements are not possibly true, since God is an agent whose nonexistence is impossible. Unless the revisionist can give us some reason to think that a statement can be true yet unknowable, we have no reason to adopt (O"). It seems that the only intrinsic property that a statement must possess in order to be logically knowable is truth.

The revisionist will claim at this point that future contingent statements are logically impossible for God to know, since if he knows them, then they are not contingent.[7] We will examine the revisionist's argument for this latter claim below; but here we may note that even if we concede that this argument is sound, it still does not follow that future contingent statements are logically impossible for God to know. The revisionist reasons that for any future-tense statement *s* it is impossible that God know *s* and *s* be contingent; therefore, if *s* is contingent, it is not possible that God knows *s*. But such reasoning is logically fallacious.

The fallacy in this thinking can be exposed as follows.

From
(1) Not-possibly (God knows *s*, and *s* is contingent)
        and
(2) *s* is contingent,
        it does not follow logically that
(3) Not-possibly (God knows *s*)
        but merely
(3') Not (God knows *s*).

In other words, what follows from (1) and (2) is merely that God does not know *s*, not that it is impossible that God knows *s*. Thus, even *granted* the revisionist's premise that it is impossible that God know *s* and *s* be contingent, it does not follow from the contingency of *s* that *s* is such that it is logically impossible for God to know *s*. Therefore, even on the defective definition (O") proposed by the revisionist, the revisionist's God turns out not to be omniscient, since *s* is a true statement that, so far as we can see, is logically possible for God to know, and yet God does not know *s*. Thus, the revisionist must deny divine omniscience and therefore reject God's perfection—a serious theological consequence indeed.[8]

---

[7]Ibid., 147–48.

[8]Notice, too, that the revisionist's position is ultimately logically incoherent. For by his own lights it is logically possible to know any true, present-tense statement. But if future-tense statements are true or false, then there will be present-tense statements like "Future-tense statement *s* is presently true" that must be known to God. It cannot reasonably be denied that God must know such present-tense statements. For God knows what properties presently inhere in existing things. But then he must know that "Truth presently inheres in future-tense statement *s*." Hence, the detractor of divine foreknowledge cannot coherently affirm that there are true future-tense statements and yet deny that God knows such statements—he must deny the truth or falsity of future-tense statements, a radical position.

## 4. Philosophical Objections to Divine Foreknowledge

Opponents of the biblical doctrine of divine foreknowledge usually raise two objections to that doctrine: (1) Divine foreknowledge is incompatible with future contingents, and (2) there is no basis on which God can know future contingents. We will explore each of these in turn.

### 4.1. The Compatibility of Divine Foreknowledge and Future Contingents

The first objection raises the issue of fatalism, the doctrine that everything we do, we do necessarily, and that therefore human freedom is an illusion. It is alleged that if God foreknows the future, then fatalism is true. Since fatalism is not true, it follows that God must not foreknow the future. *wrong*

What is the argument that allegedly demonstrates the connection between divine foreknowledge and fatalism? Letting "$x$" stand for any event, the basic form of the argument is as follows:

(1)  Necessarily, if God foreknows $x$, then $x$ will happen.
(2)  God foreknows $x$.
(3)  Therefore, $x$ will necessarily happen.
Since $x$ happens necessarily, it is not a contingent event. In virtue of God's foreknowledge everything is fated to occur.

The problem with the above form of the argument is that it is logically fallacious. What is validly implied by premises (1) and (2) is not (3) but:

(3')  Therefore, $x$ will happen.

The fatalist (and the revisionist who appeals to this fatalistic reasoning) gets things mixed up here. It is correct that in a valid, deductive argument the premises necessarily imply the conclusion. The conclusion follows necessarily from the premises; that is to say, it is impossible for the premises to be true and the conclusion to be false. But the conclusion itself need not be necessary. The fatalist illicitly transfers the necessity of the *inference* to the conclusion *itself*. What necessarily follows from (1) and (2) is just (3'). But the fatalist in his confusion thinks that the conclusion is itself necessarily true and so winds up with (3). In so doing he simply commits a common logical fallacy.

The correct conclusion (3') is in no way incompatible with human freedom. From God's knowledge that I shall do $x$, it does not follow that I must do $x$ but only that I shall do $x$. That is in no way incompatible with my doing $x$ freely.

Undoubtedly a major source of the fatalist's confusion is his conflating *certainty* with *necessity*. One frequently finds in the writings of contemporary theological fatalists statements that slide from affirming that something is *certainly* true to affirming that it is *necessarily* true. This is sheer confusion. Certainty is a property of persons and has nothing to do with truth, as is evident from the fact that we can be absolutely certain about something that turns out to be false. By contrast, necessity is a property of statements, indicating that a statement cannot possibly be false. We can be wholly uncertain about statements that are, unbeknownst to us, necessarily true (imagine some complex mathematical equation or theorem). Thus, when we say that some statement is "certainly true," this is but a manner of speaking indicating that we are certain that the statement is true. People are certain; statements are necessary.

By confusing certainty and necessity, the fatalist makes his logically fallacious argument deceptively appealing. For it is correct that from premises (1) and (2) we can be absolutely certain that $x$ will come to pass. But it is muddle-headed to think that because $x$ will certainly happen, $x$ will *necessarily* happen. We can be certain, given God's foreknowledge, that $x$ will not fail to happen, even though it is entirely possible that $x$ fail to happen. $X$ could fail to occur, but God knows that it will not. Therefore, we can be sure that it will happen—and happen contingently.

Contemporary theological fatalists recognize the fallaciousness of the above form of the argument and therefore try to remedy the defect by making premise (2) also necessarily true:

(1)  Necessarily, if God foreknows $x$, then $x$ will happen.
(2')  Necessarily, God foreknows $x$.
(3)  Therefore, $x$ will necessarily happen.

So formulated, the argument is no longer logically fallacious, and thus the question becomes whether the premises are true.

Premise (1) is clearly true. It is perhaps worth noting that this is the case, not because of God's essential omniscience or inerrancy but simply in virtue of the definition of "knowledge." Since knowledge entails true belief, anybody's knowing that $x$ will happen necessarily implies that $x$ will happen. Thus, we could replace (1) and (2') with

(1\*)  Necessarily, if Smith correctly believes that $x$ will happen, then $x$ will
     happen.
(2\*)  Necessarily, Smith correctly believes that $x$ will happen.

And (3) will follow as before. Therefore, if any person ever holds true beliefs about the future (and surely we do, as we smugly remind others when we say, "I told you so!"), then, given the truth of premise (2), fatalism follows from merely human beliefs, a curious conclusion!

Indeed, as ancient Greek fatalists realized, the presence of any agent at all is really superfluous to the argument. All one needs is a true, future-tense statement to get the argument going. Thus, we could replace (1) and (2') with:

(1\*\*)  Necessarily, if it is true that $x$ will happen, then $x$ will happen.
(2\*\*)  Necessarily, it is true that $x$ will happen.

And we will get (3) as our conclusion. Thus, philosopher Susan Haack rightly calls the argument for theological fatalism "a needlessly (and confusingly) elaborated version" of Greek fatalism; the addition of an omniscient God to the argument constitutes a "gratuitous detour" around the real issue, which is the truth or falsity of future-tense statements.[9]

In order to avoid the above generalization of their argument to all persons and to mere statements about the future, theological fatalists will deny that the second premise is true with respect to humans or mere statements, as it is for God. They will say that Smith's holding a true belief or some future-tense statement's being true are not necessary in the way that God's holding a belief is necessary.

That raises the question as to whether premise (2') is true. Now at face value, premise (2') is obviously false. Christian theology has always maintained that God's creation of the world is a free act, that God could have created a different world in which $x$ does not occur, or even no world at all. To say that God foreknows any event $x$ necessarily implies that this is the only world God could have created and thus denies divine freedom.

But theological fatalists have a different sort of necessity in mind when they say that God's foreknowledge is necessary. What they are talking about is *temporal necessity*, or the necessity of the past. Often this is expressed by saying that the past is unpreventable or unchangeable. If some event is in the past, then it is now too late to do anything to affect it. It is in that sense necessary. Since God's foreknowledge of future events is now part of the past, it is now fixed and unalterable. Therefore, given God's free creation of this particular world, it is said, premise (2') is true.

But if premise (2') is true in that sense, then why are not (2*) and (2**) true as well? The theological fatalist will respond that Smith's belief's being true or a future-tense statement's being true are not facts or events of the past, as is God's holding a belief about something.

But such an understanding of what constitutes a fact or event seems quite counter-intuitive. If Smith believed in 1997 that "Clinton will be impeached," was it not a fact that Smith's belief was true? If Smith still held that same belief today (viz., "Clinton will be impeached"), would it not be a fact that Smith's belief is no longer true (since Clinton's impeachment is past and no further attempt will be made to impeach him)? If Smith's belief thus changes from being true to being false, then surely it was a fact that it was then true and is a fact that it is now false. The same obviously goes for the mere statement "Clinton will be impeached." This statement once had the property of being true and now has the property of being false. In any reasonable sense of "fact," these are past and present facts.

Indeed, a statement's having a truth value is plausibly an event as well. This is most obvious with respect to statements like "Flight 4750 to Paris will depart in five minutes." That statement is false up until five minutes prior to departure, becomes true at five minutes till, and then becomes false again immediately thereafter. Other statements' being true may be more long-lasting events, like "Flight

---

[9]Susan Haack, "On a Theological Argument for Fatalism," *Philosophical Quarterly* 24 (1974): 158.

4750 to Paris will depart within the next hour." Such statements' being true are clearly events on any reasonable construal of what constitutes an event.

No theological fatalist that I have read has even begun to address the question of the nature of facts or events that would make it plausible that Smith's correctly believing a future-tense statement and a future-tense statement's being true do not count as past facts or events. But then we see that theological fatalism is not inherently theological at all. If the theological fatalist's reasoning is correct, it can be generalized to show that every time we hold a true belief about the future, or even every time a statement about the future is true, then the future is fated to occur—surely an incredible inference!

Moreover, we have the best of reasons for thinking that premise (2') is defective in some way, namely, that fatalism posits a constraint on human freedom that is unintelligible. For the fatalist admits that the events foreknown by God may be causally indeterminate; indeed, they could theoretically be completely uncaused, spontaneous events. Nevertheless, such events are said to be somehow constrained. But by what? Fate? What is that but a mere name? If my action is causally free, how can it be constrained by the mere fact of God's knowing about it?

Sometimes fatalists say that God's foreknowledge places a sort of logical constraint on my action. Even though I am causally free to refrain from my action, there is some sort of logical constraint upon me, rendering it impossible for me to refrain. But insofar as we can make sense of logical constraints, they are not analogous to the sort of necessitation imagined by the theological fatalist.

For example, given the fact that I have already played basketball at least once in my life, it is now impossible for me to play basketball for the first time. I am thus not free to go out and play basketball for the first time. But this sort of constraint is not at all analogous to theological fatalism. For in the case we are envisioning, it is within my power to play basketball or not. Whether I've played before or not, I can freely execute the actions of playing basketball. It's just that if I have played before, my actions will not *count* as playing for the first time. By contrast, the fatalist imagines that if God knows that I shall not play basketball, then even though I am causally free, my actions are mysteriously constrained so that I am literally unable to walk out onto the court, dribble, and shoot. But such noncausal determinism is utterly opaque and unintelligible.

The argument for fatalism, therefore, must be unsound. Since premise (1) is clearly true, the trouble must lie with premise (2'). And premise (2') is notoriously problematic, for the notion of temporal necessity appealed to by the fatalist is so obscure a concept that (2') becomes a veritable mare's nest of philosophical difficulties. For example, since the necessity of premise (1) is logical necessity and the necessity of premise (2') is temporal necessity, why think that such mixing of different kinds of modality is valid? If the fatalist answers that logical necessity entails temporal necessity, so that premise (1) can be construed merely in terms of temporal necessity, then how do we know that such necessity is passed on from the premises to the conclusion in the way that logical necessity is? Indeed, since $x$ is supposed to be a future event, how *could* it be temporally necessary? Since $x$ is neither present nor past but has yet to occur, it could not possibly be characterized by the temporal necessity that is supposed to inhere in events once they have occurred. Thus, we have every reason to think that temporal necessity is not transitive.

Even if this peculiar sort of necessity were transitive so that $x$ is temporally necessary, how do we know that this sort of necessity is incompatible with an action's being free? It is plausible that so long as a person's choice is causally undetermined, it is a free choice even if he is unable to choose the opposite of that choice.[10] Imagine a man with electrodes secretly implanted in his brain who is presented with the choice of doing either A or B. The electrodes are inactive so long as the man chooses A; but if he were to choose B, the electrodes would switch on and force him to choose A. If the electrodes fire, causing him to choose A, his choice of A is clearly not a free choice. But suppose that the man really wants to do A and chooses it of his own volition. In that case his choosing A is entirely free, even though the man is literally unable to choose B, since the electrodes do not function at all and so have no effect on his choice of A. What makes his choice free is the absence of any causally determining factors of his choosing A.

This conception of libertarian freedom has the advantage of explaining how it is that God's choosing to do good is free even though it is impossible for God to choose sin; that is, his choosing is undetermined by causal constraints. Thus, libertarian freedom of the will does not require the ability to choose other than as one chooses. So even if $x$ were temporally necessary, such that not-$x$ cannot occur, it is far from obvious that $x$ is not freely performed or chosen.

All of the above problems arise even if we concede (2') to be true. But why think that this premise is true? What is temporal necessity anyway, and why think that God's past beliefs are now temporally necessary? Theological fatalists have never provided an adequate account of this peculiar modality. I have yet to see an explanation of temporal necessity, according to which God's past beliefs are temporally necessary, which does not reduce to either the *unalterability* or the *causal closedness* of the past.

But interpreting the necessity of the past as its unalterability (or unchangeability or unpreventability) is clearly inadequate, since the future, by definition, is just as unalterable as the past. By definition the future is what will occur, and the past is what has occurred. To *change* the future would be to bring it about that an event that will occur will not occur, which is self-contradictory. It is purely a matter of definition that the past and future cannot be changed, and no fatalistic conclusion follows from this truth. We need not be able to *change* the future in order to *determine* the future. If our actions are freely performed, then it lies within our power to determine causally what the course of future events will be, even if we do not have the power to change the future.

---

[10]See Harry Frankfurt, "Alternative Possibilities and Moral Responsibility," *Journal of Philosophy* 66 (1969): 829–39; Thomas V. Morris, *The Logic of God Incarnate* (Ithaca, N.Y.: Cornell Univ. Press, 1986), 151–52. For an application to theological fatalism, see David P. Hunt, "On Augustine's Way Out," *Faith and Philosophy* 16 (1999): 3–26.

The fatalist will insist that the past is necessary in the sense that we do not have a similar ability to causally determine the past. The nonfatalist may happily concede the point: Backward causation is impossible. But the causal closedness of the past does not imply fatalism. For freedom to refrain from doing as God knows one will do does not involve backward causation.

One may happily admit that there is nothing I can now do to cause or bring about the past. Thus, I cannot cause God to have had in the past a certain belief about my future actions. But it may well lie within my power to freely perform some action A, and if A were to occur, then the past would have been different than it in fact is. Suppose, for example, that God has always believed that in the year 2000 I would accept an invitation to speak at the University of Regensburg. Let us suppose that up until the time arrives, I have the ability to accept or refuse the invitation. If I were to refuse the invitation, then God would have held a different belief than the one he in fact held. For if I were to refuse the invitation, then different future-tense statements would have been true, and God, being omniscient, would have known this. Thus, he would have had different foreknowledge than that which he in fact has. Neither the relation between my action and a corresponding future-tense statement about it nor the relation between a true future-tense statement and God's believing it is a causal relation. Thus, the causal closedness of the past is irrelevant. If temporal necessity is merely the causal closedness of the past, then it is insufficient to support fatalism.

No fatalist, as I say, has to my knowledge explicated a conception of temporal necessity that does not amount to either the unalterability or the causal closedness of the past. Typically, they just appeal gratuitously to some sort of "fixed past principle," to the effect that it is not within my power to act in such a way, that if I were to do so, then the past would have been different—which begs the question. On analyses of temporal necessity that are not reducible to either the unalterability or the causal closedness of the past, God's past beliefs always turn out *not* to be temporally necessary.[11] It is interesting that, as I have tried to show elsewhere, precisely parallel conclusions follow with respect to the temporal necessity of past events in cases of time travel, backward causation, precognition, and the special theory of relativity, which provide intriguing analogues to the theological scenario of God's holding beliefs about future contingents.[12]

Thus, the argument for theological fatalism is unsound. It provides no cogent basis on which to deny the biblical doctrine of divine foreknowledge.

## 4.2. The Basis of Divine Foreknowledge of Future Contingents

What, then, about that second question raised by divine prescience, the basis of God's knowledge of future contingents? Detractors of divine foreknowledge

---

[11]See, for example, Alfred J. Freddoso, "Accidental Necessity and Logical Determinism," *Journal of Philosophy* 80 (1983): 257–78.

[12]William Lane Craig, *The Only Wise God* (Grand Rapids: Baker, 1987).

sometimes claim that because future events do not exist, they cannot be known by God. The reasoning seems to go as follows:

(1)  Only events that actually exist can be known by God.

(2)  Future events do not exist.

(3)  Therefore, future events cannot be known by God.

Now premise (2) is not uncontroversial. A good many physicists and philosophers of time and space argue that future events do exist. They claim that the difference between past, present, and future is merely a subjective matter of human consciousness. For the people in the year 2015 the events of that year are just as real as the events of our present are for us, and for those people, it is we who have passed away and are unreal. On such a view God transcends the four-dimensional space-time continuum, and thus all events are eternally present to him.[13] It is easy on such a view to understand how God could therefore know events that to us are future.

Nevertheless, I do think that such a four-dimensional view of reality faces insuperable philosophical and theological objections, which I have discussed elsewhere.[14] Therefore, I am inclined to agree with premise (2) of the above argument. So the question becomes whether there is good reason to think that premise (1) is true.

In assessing the question of how God knows which events will transpire, it is helpful to distinguish two models of divine cognition: the *perceptualist* model and the *conceptualist* model. The perceptualist model construes divine knowledge on the analogy of sense perception. God "looks" and "sees" what is there. Such a model is implicitly assumed when people speak of God's "foreseeing" the future or having "foresight" of future events. The perceptualist model of divine cognition does run into real problems when it comes to God's knowledge of the future, for, since future events do not exist, there is nothing there to perceive.[15]

By contrast, on a conceptualist model of divine knowledge, God does not acquire his knowledge of the world by anything like perception. His knowledge of the future is not based on his "looking" ahead and "seeing" what lies in the future (a terribly anthropomorphic notion in any case). Rather, God's knowledge is self-contained; it is more like a mind's knowledge of innate ideas. As an omniscient being, God has essentially the property of knowing all truths; there are truths about future events; *ergo*, God knows all truths concerning future events.

---

[13]See ch. 5 in this volume, "Is God Bound by Time?" by Paul Helm, for a presentation of this perspective.

[14]See my companion volumes *The Tensed Theory of Time: A Critical Examination* and *The Tenseless Theory of Time: A Critical Examination* (Dordrecht: Kluwer, 2002).

[15]Notice, however, that if we think of statements as being in God's purview, then even on a perceptualist model, God can know the future. For he perceives which future-tense statements presently have the property of truth inhering in them. Thus, by means of his perception of presently existing realities he knows the truth about the future. Cf. note 8 above.

As long as we are not seduced into thinking of divine foreknowledge on the model of perception, it is no longer evident why knowledge of future events should be impossible. A conceptualist model furnishes a perspicuous basis for God's knowledge of future contingents.

## 5. Conclusion

In summary, we have seen that an objective assessment of the biblical data leads to the conclusion that God's knowledge encompasses knowledge of future contingents. Attempts to avoid this conclusion are rooted in a naïve hermeneutical approach to Scripture and cannot plausibly account for the many passages that either teach or illustrate God's knowledge of the future.

Philosophically, we saw that God, as the greatest conceivable being, must be omniscient and therefore know all truth. If, then, there are true future-tense statements, God must know them. Attempts to deny that future-tense statements are true (or false) face serious objections, and there are, on the contrary, good grounds for thinking that there are true future-tense statements. Although revisionists have sometimes maintained that God can still be omniscient despite ignorance of future-tense truths, we saw that their redefinitions of omniscience both are inadequate and fail to solve the problem. Finally, we saw that fatalistic arguments against divine foreknowledge are either invalid or unsound and that demands for a basis of God's knowledge of future contingent truths is illicitly predicated upon a perceptualist model of divine cognition, which we have no reason to accept.

In short, neither the problem of theological fatalism nor the question of the basis of divine foreknowledge provides adequate grounds for denying the testimony of both Scripture and reason to the truth of the doctrine of divine omniscience and, in particular, God's knowledge of future contingents.

Chapter 7

# How Do We Reconcile the Existence of God and Suffering?

*R. Douglas Geivett*

# 1. Introduction: Evil and Theological Practice

Due in part to the high readings registered on the Geiger counter of human travail during the twentieth century, contemporary theologians have been especially sensitive to the problem of suffering. In fact, this problem has inspired a deliberate and multidirectional movement away from classical theism. Nothing inspires novelty in theology like the problem of evil. This is because there is no greater impetus to the practice of theology than the experience of suffering. In theology we formulate questions about God and seek answers that have the merit of seeming to be true. And theology is most centrally occupied with questions about God's relationship to the world—our world. But our world manifests a staggering array of evils suffered by human and other sentient beings. Thus, in addition to the questions we have *about* God, there are questions we have *for* God. Such existentially pressing questions translate our otherwise abstract theological efforts into matters of genuine personal significance.

Topping the list of questions we have for God is the question: "Why, God, suffering, why guilt? Why have you ... taken no precautions against evil?"[1] This question, confesses Johann-Baptist Metz, governs the whole of his own theological work.[2] "The question of God in the face of suffering" lies near the epicenter of all theological rumblings. *It is very largely because of evil that theology matters.*

This is true not only for Christian theology, but for all serious religious reflection. In his book, *Problems of Suffering in Religions of the World,* John Bowker observes:

> It is because suffering, in one form or another, is a common experience that religions give to suffering a place of central importance or consideration— indeed, it is often said that suffering is an important *cause* of religion, since the promises held out by religion represent a way in which men can feel reassured in the face of catastrophe or death.... There are few better ways of coming to understand the religions of the world than by studying what response they make to the common experience of suffering.[3]

Bowker adds that "suffering occurs *differently* as a problem in each religion."[4]

---

[1]Johann-Baptist Metz, contribution to *How I Have Changed: Reflections on Thirty Years of Theology,* ed. Jürgen Moltmann, trans. John Bowden (Harrisburg, Penn.: Trinity Press International, 1997), 36.

[2]Ibid., 31–33.

[3]John Bowker, *Problems of Suffering in Religions of the World* (Cambridge: Cambridge Univ. Press, 1970), 1–2.

[4]Ibid., 2; see also idem, "Suffering as a Problem of Religions," in *The Meaning of Human Suffering,* ed. Flavian Dougherty (New York: Human Sciences Press, 1982).

Though there are different ways in which theologians have in recent years recommended a revision of classical theism, the three perspectives examined in this chapter all have in common an increased emphasis on divine relationality. They are theologies of liberation, process theology, and openness of God theology. Each of these approaches deserves closer inspection than I can offer in the space of a single chapter. But a brief investigation of each within the scope of a single chapter has the merit of illustrating the emergence of a theme within contemporary theology—namely, the relationality of God, as this is to be understood in light of the presence of suffering in the world.[5]

These three perspectives in theology have at least four things in common. First, they all affirm the value of and capacity for human self-determination. In the case of liberation theologies, this is seen in the conviction that conditions of social injustice are not inevitable. Oppressed individuals may become "agents of their own destiny."[6] In both process theology and openness of God theology, human freedom is characterized as freedom to do otherwise than what one actually does, so that nothing either external to oneself or internal to oneself determines that one does what one does. In philosophical anthropology, this is called "libertarian" freedom.[7]

Second, as already noted, each perspective emphasizes, in one way or another, the relationality of God. The sort of relationality envisioned is one of loving relationship between God and human persons, who have significant freedom of self-determination. God is social and dynamic in his relationship to the world of human persons and history. The clear emphasis is on God's responsiveness to the world. Process theology and openness of God theology both explicitly maintain that God is in some significant sense dynamic in his own being, and that this is a necessary condition for the sort of relationality that is required to address the problem of evil in a satisfactory way. A similar theme can be discerned in liberation theology, where God is regarded as "the God of the oppressed," a God who stands in unique solidarity with the most alienated sectors of human society.

Third, for each perspective, the need for a theological understanding of human suffering dominates its conception of the theological task and the nature of God. This is borne out in different ways for each perspective. For liberation theology, as its name suggests, liberation from oppressive conditions is the core idea and the chief goal of theology. A distinguishing feature of process theology—

---

[5]See Ronald Goetz, "The Rise of a New Orthodoxy," *Christian Century* 103.13 (April 16, 1986): 385–89.

[6]This phrase comes from Gustavo Gutiérrez.

[7]For those who savor more precise definitions, here is one that will do the trick for the concept of libertarian freedom: "Necessarily, for any human agent S, action A, and time t, if S performs A freely at t, then the history of the world prior to t, the laws of nature, and the actions of any other agent (including God) prior to and at t are jointly compatible with S's refraining from performing A freely"; Thomas P. Flint, "Two Accounts of Providence," in *Divine and Human Action: Essays in the Metaphysics of Theism*, ed. Thomas V. Morris (Ithaca, N.Y.: Cornell Univ. Press, 1988), 175. See also Thomas P. Flint, *Divine Providence: The Molinist Account* (CSPR; Ithaca, N.Y.: Cornell Univ. Press, 1998), 89.

namely, its recasting of the doctrine of divine omnipotence—is motivated by the notion that God, who can be counted on to desire the prevention or elimination of suffering, is simply unable to guarantee this result. Open theism denies that God has infallible knowledge of future free acts and thus presumes to explain more adequately the presence of certain types of evil in the world.

Fourth, each perspective explicitly acknowledges that it stands in contrast to classical theology in important respects. In fact, it is in explicit contrast to classical theology that proponents of these perspectives often define what is distinctive about their respective approaches. Recurring temblors of human suffering threaten to shake the contours of classical Christian theology. Again, it is largely because of evil that theology matters.

For all of these similarities, there are important differences. Some of these differences will emerge during the course of examination, considering first liberation theology, then process theology, and finally openness of God theology. By treating these three perspectives in this order, I hope to show important relations that exist among them. It is impossible to do justice to the rich variety of perspective within each general approach to theology considered here. I seek a balance between general treatment that is fair to these perspectives as they are endorsed by leading proponents and specific analysis afforded by the consideration of a single leading proponent of each perspective: Gustavo Gutiérrez on liberation theology, David Ray Griffin on process theology, and William Hasker on openness of God theology.

To appreciate what is at stake throughout this discussion, I begin with a brief characterization of the problem of evil to which theologians have often addressed themselves. I then turn to an examination of each perspective, noting how the concept of divine relationality is characterized in each case in response to the problem of human suffering. I conclude with a brief summary of why traditional theism need not resort to the theologies of liberation or process or divine openness in order to answer the question about evil and God's relationality.

## 2. What Is the Problem of Evil?

Classical Christian theism holds that God is all-powerful, omniscient, and perfectly morally good. The most significant obstacle to rational belief in such a God is the reality of evil in the world. Contemporary philosophers of religion distinguish two main ways in which evil may be thought to count as a challenge to rational belief in God. Arguments from evil against the existence of God, in other words, take two different forms.

One form of the argument from evil against classical theism is sometimes called the *logical argument* from evil. This argument seeks to establish that it is logically inconsistent to believe the following two propositions:

(1) God is omnipotent, omniscient, and perfectly morally good.
(2) Evil exists.

GOD UNDER FIRE

The clearest and most influential version of this argument was presented by J. L. Mackie in an article called "Evil and Omnipotence," published in 1955.[8] Mackie argues that classical theism is "positively irrational" in that "several parts of the essential theological doctrine are inconsistent with one another, so that the theologian can maintain his position as a whole only by [an] . . . extreme rejection of reason. . . . He . . . must be prepared to believe . . . what can be *disproved* from other beliefs that he also holds."[9]

Mackie believes he can demonstrate the irrationality of classical theism by focusing exclusively on the conviction that God is "all-powerful" (omnipotent) and "wholly good" (perfectly morally good).[10] Mackie explains:

> In its simplest form, the problem is this: God is omnipotent; God is wholly good; and yet evil exists. There seems to be some contradiction between these three propositions, so that if any two of them were true the third would be false. But at the same time all three are essential parts of most theological positions: the theologian, it seems, at once *must* adhere and *cannot consistently* adhere to all three.[11]

To simplify matters, let us say that, according to Mackie, the proposition (1) God exists and is omnipotent and perfectly morally good, and the proposition (2) Evil exists, are logically incompatible. To make explicit the incompatibility between propositions (1) and (2), Mackie states two additional principles that function as crucial auxiliary premises in his argument:

(1A) A perfectly morally good being always eliminates evil as far as it can.
(1B) There are no limits to what an omnipotent being can do.[12]

Mackie confidently asserts that the only way out of this problem is for the theist to abandon some aspect of traditional theism. "If you are prepared to say that God is not wholly good, or not quite omnipotent, or that evil does not exist, or that good is not opposed to the kind of evil that exists, or that there are limits to what an omnipotent being can do, then the problem of evil will not arise for you."[13] It is uncontroversial that propositions (1) and (2) are incompatible if we assume that premises (1A) and (1B) are true. Mackie's argument is valid. But classical theists have responded to Mackie by arguing against the truth of either (1A) or (1B), or both.[14]

---

[8]See J. L. Mackie, "Evil and Omnipotence," *Mind* 64.254 (1955): 200–212; all page references to this article by Mackie are from the reprint in *God and Evil: Readings on the Theological Problem of Evil*, ed. Nelson Pike (Englewood Cliffs, N.J.: Prentice-Hall, 1964), 46–60.
[9]Ibid., 46–47.
[10]Mackie ignores the implications of divine omniscience.
[11]Ibid., 47.
[12]See ibid.
[13]Ibid., 47–48.
[14]See the exposition of this in Marilyn McCord Adams, *Horrendous Evils and the Goodness of God* (CSPR; Ithaca, N.Y.: Cornell Univ. Press, 1999), 7–11.

Although the logical argument from evil was the dominant form of the argument against classical theism during most of the twentieth century, most philosophers of religion, many of whom are atheists or agnostics, now hold that this form of the argument is totally ineffectual. Those who accept this verdict and yet still believe that evil counts against the rationality of classical theism have resorted to an alternative formulation of the argument from evil. This formulation is widely known as the *evidential argument*. It allows that classical theism may not harbor a contradiction, as asserted by Mackie. Nevertheless, it maintains that evils of certain kinds make it *highly unlikely* that a God who is omnipotent and perfectly morally good exists. This argument reasons that if proposition (2) is true, then proposition (1) is *probably* false.

Some who favor this line of argument replace proposition (1) with the following proposition:

(3) God exists and is omnipotent, omniscient, and perfectly morally good.[15]

For them the evidential argument from evil is from proposition (2) to the improbability of proposition (3). It is customary for evidential arguments to reason from the existence of "plainly pointless evils"[16] to the irrationality of belief in the God of classical theism.

It turns out that the evidential argument is more precisely an argument from the existence of *apparently* gratuitous evils—evils that, at least from the human point of view, are pointless—such that there is no morally sufficient reason available to God that would justify his permission of just those evils. Such evils are said to be "inscrutable" in that whatever morally justifying reasons God could have for permitting them, if there are such, are completely beyond our ken.

This is a merely probabilistic argument from evil because it may be conceded that it is logically possible that God has morally justifying reasons for permitting inscrutable evils. But two factors are supposed to leave the force of the evidential argument from evil completely unaffected by this logical possibility. First, the conclusion of the argument is that belief in God is rendered irrational. That God actually exists and has a morally justifying reason for permitting all the evils there are is compatible with the irrationality of belief in God.[17] But if the question is not whether the nonexistence of God is demonstrable but whether belief in the existence of God is rational for us, given our perspective and the available evidence, then our inability to think of a morally justifying reason for God's permission of certain evils is reason enough to believe that God does not exist.

Second, this is especially true if the evils in question are not merely inscrutable but particularly horrendous. "Horrendous evils" are evils whose inscrutability is

---

[15]Notice that proposition (3) includes reference to omniscience as an attribute of God essential to traditional theism.

[16]This is the term used by Marilyn Adams in her exposition of the evidential argument (*Horrendous Evils*, 15).

[17]N.B.: Proponents of the so-called argument from divine hiddenness may disagree and hold that if God exists, his existence must be manifest.

compounded by their particularly horrendous quality, so that it can seem repugnant even to suppose in the abstract that there is some plausible explanation for God's permission of them. The very attempt at theodicy seems insensitive and misguided. Such evils are the worst imaginable, and they are dubbed "horrors" because of their "life-ruining potential."[18]

These, then, are the two primary ways in which nonbelievers in God have reasoned from the reality of evil against the rationality of belief in God. In philosophy of religion, the term "the problem of evil" is commonly used to refer to one or the other or both of these forms of the argument from evil against theistic belief. It will be helpful in this chapter to use the term "theodicy" in the highly general way characterized by Keith Yandell, who says "a theodicy is an account of why God allows, or even causes, evil—of the role evil plays in the great scheme of things, how it relates to divine providence, how God can bring good from evil, how God's love can triumph over evil, and the like."[19]

It is now commonly remarked that what Christian philosophers offer in response to the theoretical or philosophical problem of evil is pastorally inadequate. Indeed, it is so woefully inadequate that those confronted with the religious or pastoral problem of evil are strongly advised to resist the temptation to trot out standard philosophical replies to the theoretical problem of evil as if this will somehow speak to the existential need of the moment. This seems to me to be generally good advice that philosophers would do well to heed.[20] In my judgment, Christian philosophers who engage in abstract theoretical reflection on the philosophical problem of evil do a pretty good job conceding this point and following this counsel.[21]

---

[18]See Marilyn Adams, *Horrendous Evils*, 26–28.

[19]Keith Yandell, *Philosophy of Religion: A Contemporary Introduction* (London: Routledge, 1999), 124.

[20]On this aspect of the problem of pain, I encourage readers to consult John S. Feinberg, *Deceived by God? A Journey Through Suffering* (Wheaton, Ill.: Crossway, 1997); idem, "Why I Still Believe in Christ, in Spite of Evil and Suffering," in *Why I Am a Christian: Leading Thinkers Explain Why They Believe*, ed. Norman L. Geisler and Paul K. Hoffman (Grand Rapids: Baker, 2001), 249–54; Gary R. Habermas, *Forever Loved: A Personal Account of Grief and Resurrection* (Joplin, Mo.: College Press, 1997); C. S. Lewis, *A Grief Observed* (New York: Bantam Books, 1976); Gerald L. Sittser, *A Grace Disguised: How the Soul Grows Through Loss* (Grand Rapids: Zondervan, 1995); Brad Stetson, *Tender Fingerprints: A True Story of Loss and Resolution* (Grand Rapids: Zondervan, 1999); and Nicholas Wolterstorff, *Lament for a Son* (Grand Rapids: Eerdmans, 1987). Each is written by a leading Christian intellectual with refreshing and yet painful honesty about his own experience with suffering.

[21]See, for example, Marilyn Adams, *Horrendous Evils*, 181–84; Robert Merrihew Adams, *The Virtue of Faith, and Other Essays in Philosophical Theology* (New York: Oxford Univ. Press, 1987), 75; R. Douglas Geivett, *Evil and the Evidence for God* (Philadelphia: Temple Univ. Press, 1993), 3–4; William Hasker, "On Regretting the Evils of This World," *Southern Journal of Philosophy* 19 (1981): 425; Michael L. Peterson, *God and Evil: An Introduction to the Issues* (Boulder, Colo.: Westview, 1998), 111–27; Alvin Plantinga, *The Nature of Necessity* (Oxford: Clarendon, 1974), 195; idem, *Warranted Christian Belief* (New York: Oxford Univ. Press, 2000), 482–98; Richard Swinburne, "Knowledge from Experience, and the Problem of Evil," in *The Rationality of Religious Belief: Essays in Honor of Basil Mitchell*, ed. William J. Abraham and Steven W. Holtzer (Oxford: Clarendon, 1987), 167; Yandell, *Philosophy of Religion*, 124.

Some critics, however, are not satisfied to hear philosophers accept the restriction referred to above. They go further and maintain that theoretical responses to suffering are not only in bad taste but are an offense against moral rectitude. As we will see, this sentiment lies close to the heart of the perspective of liberation theology, to which we now turn.

## 3. Theologies of Liberation

In 1978, Robert McAfee Brown suggested "that we are at a time theologically when the established harmonies are not as 'established' as they once were, when it is not at all clear that the theological future will be 'more of the same.'" Contemplating the key into which "the theology of the future will be transposed," Brown predicted that it would be "a key in which those who have had *no* voice will for the first time be heard, in which those who have been silent can burst forth in new song, in which those whose selves have been denied can affirm themselves."[22] He was speaking of the theology of liberation.

### 3.1. What is Liberation Theology?

It would be desirable to explore questions about God and evil in relation to several varieties of liberation theology, including black, feminist, Asian, African, as well as Latin American. Because the questions pursued here have a narrow focus and because I seek to track these questions in relation to other traditions besides liberation theology, I confine my attention to Latin American liberation theology as developed by one of its most influential exponents.[23]

In 1971, just a few years prior to Brown's prognostication, Peruvian theologian Gustavo Gutiérrez published the Spanish edition of the work that was to become a kind of manifesto or charter for liberation theology: *Teología de la*

---

[22]Robert McAfee Brown, *Theology in a New Key: Responding to Liberation Themes* (Philadelphia: Westminster, 1978), 23–24.

[23]Feminist theologians reflecting on the problem of evil often focus especially on the Christian doctrines of sin and salvation. See Mary Potter Engel, "Evil, Sin, and Violation of the Vulnerable," in *Lift Every Voice: Constructing Christian Theologies from the Underside*, ed. Susan Brooks Thistlethwaite and Mary Potter Engel (San Francisco: HarperSanFrancisco, 1990), 152–64; Daphne Hampson, *Theology and Feminism* (Oxford: Basil Blackwell, 1990), 121–31; Rosemary Radford Ruether, *Sexism and God-Talk: Toward a Feminist Theology* (Boston: Beacon, 1983), 159–92; Lynn Japinga, *Feminism and Christianity: An Essential Guide* (Nashville: Abingdon, 1999), 84–92. But see Elizabeth A. Johnson, *She Who Is: The Mystery of God in Feminist Theological Discourse* (New York: Crossroad, 1992), 246–72, for a somewhat different emphasis. It should be noted as well that many feminist theologians wed their liberationist perspective to the metaphysics of process theism. Also, varieties of liberation theology are often brought into explicit relation to one another, as in the case of "black feminist consciousness"; see Katie Geneva Cannon, "The Emergence of Black Feminist Consciousness," in *Feminist Interpretation of the Bible*, ed. Letty M. Russell (Philadelphia: Westminster, 1985), 30–40. There are also liberation theologies of creation, which pay more attention to the problem of natural evil than is customary for liberation theologians generally; see Thistlethwaite and Engel, *Lift Every Voice*, 126.

*liberación, Perspectivas.*[24] In the opening chapter, Gutiérrez develops a new conception of theology as "critical reflection on praxis" and introduces the notion of "orthopraxis" as the complement to "orthodoxy." "Orthopraxis" stands for theology's effort to investigate with real seriousness "the importance of action in Christian life," for what it means to "do the truth." Characterized in positive terms, it seeks "to recognize the work and importance of concrete behavior, of deed, of action, of praxis in the Christian life."[25]

This emphasis on orthopraxis is not the retrieval of a lost or neglected component of traditional Christian theology, nor is it merely added to the classical tasks of Christian theology. Rather, it is a new paradigm in theology that is predicated on the explicit borrowing and adapting of a distinctively Marxist notion, which, says Gutiérrez, "[focuses] on praxis and [is] geared to the transformation of the world."[26] The specific inspiration for this is Karl Marx's well-worn aphorism, "The Philosophers have only interpreted the world in various ways; the point, however, is to *change* it."[27] Marx's notion of praxis, together with his dependence on the tools of social analysis for diagnosing the ills of humanity, is a major inspiration for Latin American liberation theology.[28]

As the touchstone for all theology, then, orthopraxis entails a reorientation of the classical tasks of theology. As Gutiérrez says in the introduction to his book, the goal of liberation theology is

> to give reason for our hope from within a commitment which seeks to become more radical, total, and efficacious. It is to reconsider the great

---

[24]Gustavo Gutiérrez, *Teología de la liberación, Perspectivas* (Lima, Peru: CEP, 1971). This text was published in 1973 under the English title, *A Theology of Liberation: History, Politics and Salvation*, trans. and ed. Caridad Inda and John Eagleson (Maryknoll, N.Y.: Orbis, 1973).

[25]Ibid. (Eng. ed.), 10; see all of ch. 1.

[26]Ibid., 9. See Rebecca S. Chopp, *The Praxis of Suffering: An Interpretation of Liberation and Political Theologies* (Maryknoll, N.Y.: Orbis, 1986), for a development of the claim that liberation theology is a new paradigm for doing theology.

[27]Karl Marx, "Theses on Feuerbach," in *On Religion*, by Karl Marx and Friedrich Engels (New York: Schocken, 1964), 72 (no. xi).

[28]Gutiérrez is explicit about the affinity between Marxism and liberation theology on this point:

> The Marxist influence began to be felt in the middle of the nineteenth century, but in recent times its cultural impact has become greater.... Contemporary theology does in fact find itself in direct and fruitful confrontation with Marxism, and it is to a large extent due to Marxism's influence that theological thought, searching for its own sources, has begun to reflect on the meaning of the transformation of this world and the action of man in history. (Gutiérrez, *A Theology of Liberation*, 9)

I do not deny that liberation theologians, while sympathetic with Marxist themes, adopt a critical posture toward Marxism. See the irenic and judicious treatment of this in Harvie M. Conn's two articles, "Theologies of Liberation: An Overview," and "Theologies of Liberation: Toward a Common View," in *Tensions in Contemporary Theology*, ed. Stanley N. Gundry and Alan F. Johnson, 2d ed. (Grand Rapids: Baker, 1983), 327–92, 395–434. By contrast, there is evidence of a sometimes desperate search for convergence between the biblical text and Marxist thought.

themes of the Christian life within this radically changed perspective and with regard to the new questions posed by this commitment.[29]

What new questions are posed by this commitment? I have already described the general way in which theology is sensitive to the reality of human suffering. In the liberation theology of Latin America, the singular incentive to practice theology is the concrete experience of those for whom "to live is to suffer" and "to be born is to become a victim."[30] If theology is at all motivated by problems raised by suffering and if orthopraxis takes as its point of departure the concrete situation of living persons, then, in the Third World context in which Latin American liberation theology is born, it is entirely natural that the suffering that gives this theology its peculiar character is the suffering of the poor and the oppressed. What could be more basic a form of suffering, what greater stimulus to a theology concerned primarily with "the praxis of suffering,"[31] than the suffering of the mass of humanity that is, as it were, "born to adversity"?[32]

How do liberation theologians themselves justify their exclusive focus on this manifestation of evil? Gutiérrez explains that liberation theologians "pay special attention . . . to the critical function of theology with respect to the presence and activity of man in history." This is what it means to place orthopraxis at the top of the agenda in theology. But, as he observes, "the most important instance of this presence in our times, especially in underdeveloped and oppressed countries, is the struggle to construct a just and fraternal society, where people can live in dignity and be the agents of their own destiny." The term *liberation*, says Gutiérrez, best expresses "these profound aspirations."[33] Henceforth, everything in theology is done from the point of view of this controlling concern.

We can now ask the questions that relate directly to the focus of this chapter: Does liberation theology acknowledge a problem of evil for Christian belief? If so, what form does this problem take from within a liberationist perspective? And how does the problem that arises from a liberationist perspective relate to the traditional problem of evil as defined in the previous section of this chapter? Answers to these questions will reveal how God's relationality is understood and emphasized within liberation theology.

## 3.2. Liberation and the Problem of Evil

Theology construed as reflection on praxis maintains that it is "through praxis that faith encounters the problems posed by human reason."[34] Strained through the filter of this conception of theology, how is the problem of evil to be understood?

---

[29]Gutiérrez, *A Theology of Liberation*, ix; see also pp. 13–14.
[30]Chopp, *The Praxis of Suffering*, 1.
[31]This is the title of Chopp's book.
[32]"It is the poor as 'nonpersons' to whom we must respond," writes Robert McAfee Brown (*Theology in a New Key*, 62–63).
[33]Gutiérrez, *A Theology of Liberation*, x.
[34]Ibid., 14.

In what way does the reality of suffering (especially the suffering of the oppressed) pose a problem for Christian theology? Clearly, the problem is fundamentally a practical problem with historical-social dimensions. Thus, the tools of human reason most needed to address this problem are those of the social sciences. Under current conditions, says Gutiérrez, "human reason has become political reason."[35]

This, too, is an important point of contact between liberation theology and Marxism. The explicit borrowing and adaptation can be appreciated by considering John Bowker's exposition of Karl Marx's approach to the problem of suffering:

> Marx concentrated, not on suffering as a theoretical problem, but on the actual facts and occurrences of suffering as he observed them. Suffering lies at the foundation of Marx's thought because he was first stirred to his vehement and passionate appeals for revolutionary action by his observations of the appalling conditions in which working people lived and died.[36]

Bowker continues with Marx's diagnosis of such suffering:

> The inevitability of class-struggle arises directly out of the conditions which have imposed suffering on the mass of the population. Those conditions can be summarized in a single word—a word that is the key to the Marxist understanding of suffering—"alienation." . . . Marx and Engels observed the realities of life around them in nineteenth-century Europe. . . . In their view the root cause of much human suffering lies in the conditions necessary for the perpetuation of capitalist societies—those societies, that is, in which the overriding motive and condition for survival is competitiveness. . . . In such societies, therefore, all the classic conditions for alienation are present, men alienated from each other in conflicting classes, and alienated in themselves because the conditions of a free and integrated life are not possible in a capitalist system.[37]

The parallels between the Marxian analysis and the perspective of liberation theology are unmistakable. Gutiérrez observes that the new liberationist approach to theology, using the tools of the social sciences, must pay "special attention to the root causes of the situation and [consider] them from a historical perspective."[38] What is revealed by this inquiry into root causes of underdevelopment in Third World countries? In Latin America, he reports:

> it has become ever clearer that underdevelopment is the end result of a process. Therefore, it must be studied from a historical perspective, that is, in relationship to the development and expansion of the great capitalist countries. The underdevelopment of the poor countries, as an overall social fact,

---

[35]Ibid., 47; see also p. 5, and Brown, *Theology in a New Key*, 64–67.
[36]Bowker, *Problems of Suffering*, 137.
[37]Ibid., 140–41.
[38]Gutiérrez, *A Theology of Liberation*, 81.

appears in its true light: as the historical by-product of the development of other countries. The dynamics of the capitalist economy lead to the establishment of a center and a periphery, simultaneously generating progress and growing wealth for the few and social imbalances, political tensions, and poverty for the many.[39]

Thus, suggests Gutiérrez:

only a class analysis will enable us to see what is really involved in the opposition between oppressed countries and dominant peoples. To take into account only the confrontation between nations misrepresents and in the last analysis waters down the real situation. Thus the theory of dependence will take the wrong path and lead to deception if the analysis is not put within the framework of the worldwide class struggle.[40]

When the concrete historical situation is the locus of the meeting of faith and reason, and when orthopraxis is the centerpiece of the theological enterprise, evil must be represented as a distinctively and intensely practical and systemic problem with a complex social history.[41]

Consistent with its emphasis on praxis, liberation theology envisions "a process of the emancipation of man in history."[42] It does not seek to explain the existence of evil in a way that is recognizably compatible with the existence of God. The only sort of explanation it seeks is a social-historical explanation of the causes of the conditions of oppression, for only this sort of explanation will contribute to the chief aim of a theology preoccupied with orthopraxis.

When the goal is to work toward the liberation of dispossessed peoples, it can be helpful to understand the causes of their dispossessed condition. Austere and abstract reflections on the possible purposes of God and his justice in permitting these conditions has no place within a theology consumed with praxis. Its construal of theology as "critical reflection on praxis," which gives pride of place to matters of social justice, renders liberation theology completely impervious to questions that might be raised about *divine* justice. The literature on liberation theology is vast, but scant attention has been paid to this puzzling and almost ironic neglect of traditional concerns about suffering by liberation theologians.[43]

---

[39]Ibid., 84.
[40]Ibid., 87.
[41]For an important recent analysis of Third World poverty as a systemic problem, by a prominent Hispanic economist, see Hernando DeSoto, *The Mystery of Capital: Why Capitalism Triumphs in the West and Fails Everywhere Else* (New York: Basic Books, 2000).
[42]Gutiérrez, *A Theology of Liberation*, 91.
[43]At least one prominent liberation theologian, Jon Sobrino, acknowledges that "this way of doing theology is exposed—more than other ways are—to the problems of theodicy"; Jon Sobrino, "Theology from Amidst the Victims," in *The Future of Theology: Essays in Honor of Jürgen Moltmann*, ed. Miroslav Volf, Carmen Krieg, and Thomas Kucharz (Grand Rapids: Eerdmans, 1996), 171. But this concession is seldom made by those who are most sympathetic with the concerns of liberation theology. See, for example, Brown, *Theology in a New Key*, and

GOD UNDER FIRE

Gutiérrez's writings are replete with expressions of confidence in the goodness of God. He speaks of "faith in a God who loves us and calls us to the gift of full communion with him and brotherhood among men."[44] God's love is the ground of his solidarity with the poor. Out of his goodness and love God exhibits a "preferential option for the poor."[45] Thus, God is regarded as lovingly engaged in the liberation of the oppressed.

Although the point is not developed in a systematic way, for Gutiérrez the love of God lies at the heart of the meaning of revealed theology.[46] From the biblical perspective, he claims, this aspect of God is foundational: "In the beginning was God's gratuitous love."[47] Orthopraxis is God's own priority in relation to the plight of the oppressed.[48] In his essay, "Understanding the God of Life," Gutiérrez endorses Pascal's differentiation between "the God of the Bible" and "the God of philosophy" and thus conveniently circumvents the need to explore the metaphysics of theism.[49] Instead, he emphasizes the mystery and ineffability of God. The only particular claim about God that he is bold to make is that "God is love that envelopes everything" and that this God "is someone who is revealed in history."[50]

Gutiérrez's vagueness about the nature of God and his unsystematic emphasis on the love of God is a consequence of his approach to religious knowledge. For Gutiérrez, our knowledge of God is historically and socially conditioned. "Human beings believe in God in the context of a particular historical situation; after all, all believers are part of a cultural and social fabric."[51] In a way, then,

---

Kenneth Surin, *Theology and the Problem of Evil* (Oxford: Basil Blackwell, 1986), both of whom see theodicy as a pernicious avoidance of praxis, which is tantamount to collusion with oppressors. See the excellent discussion of this point in Marilyn Adams, *Horrendous Evils*, 181–202.

[44]Gutiérrez, *A Theology of Liberation*, 10.

[45]See especially the essay "Preferential Option for the Poor," in Gustavo Gutiérrez, *Essential Writings*, ed. James B. Nickoloff (Maryknoll, N.Y.: Orbis, 1996), 143–46 (cf. Brown, *Theology in a New Key*, 73, 88–90). Black liberation theologian James H. Cone goes so far as to assert that "God is black," indicating a radical immanence and relationality about God and an almost parochial identification with a particular section of humanity confronted with injustice; see his *God of the Oppressed* (New York: Seabury, 1975). Cone's theology is centered on the question of "the meaning of God's presence in the world" within the context of "the black struggle for justice"; see James H. Cone, "Martin, Malcolm, and Black Theology," in *The Future of Theology*, 187. Like all liberation theologians, Cone conceives of theology as praxis, as poignantly reflected in his description of Martin Luther King Jr. as someone "who did theology with his life" (188). Cone has complained, as recently as 1996, that "even though black theologians were among the earliest exponents of liberation theology, we are often excluded when panels and conferences are held on the subject. One could hardly imagine a progressive divinity school without a significant interpreter of feminist and Latin American liberation theology. But the same is not true for black theology" (194).

[46]Gustavo Gutiérrez, "Theology, Spirituality, and Historical Praxis," in *The Future of Theology*, 180.

[47]Ibid., 181.

[48]Gutiérrez, *A Theology of Liberation*, 10 (cf. Brown, *Theology in a New Key*, 70–72).

[49]Gutiérrez, *Essential Writings*, 60–61.

[50]Ibid., 61.

[51]Ibid., 62.

human concepts of God are social artifacts. As social conditions change, so the way God is experienced and understood changes.

For a long time, for example, the consciousness of their own limitations and their realization of their dependence on the external world, both natural and social, led human beings to emphasize God's power and omnipotence. The consciousness of their finiteness sensitized them to the infinity of the Supreme Being. In our age, the assertion of the human person as subject of its own history, as well as our increasing ability to transform nature, has gradually led to a different approach to God. In the context of the phenomenon we call "secularization," there is a growing sensitivity to a God who is revealed in humility and suffering. Confronted with human beings who are conscious of their strength, theology speaks of a God who is "weak."[52]

"The lived experiences of God and the reflection on God that originates in the impoverished and marginalized sectors of the human race" yield a different perspective than the apparently anachronistic approach that emphasizes divine omnipotence. Gutiérrez believes the Bible bears the stamp of this new way of "feeling God," since it "is to a great extent the expression of the faith and hope of the poor," and "it reveals to us a God who loves perferentially those whom the world passes over."[53]

Since the Bible's authority on the question of God's nature is muted and subordinated to the subjectivizing effects of historically conditioned consciousness, it is not surprising that the doctrine of God in Gutiérrez's theology is undeveloped and lopsided. For our purposes, it is important to note the theodical implications of this.

On the one hand, with only God's loving preferential option for the poor to protect, it is not clear that there is enough left of the classical concept of God for the liberation theologian to defend against the argument from evil. So, in the words of J. L. Mackie, the logical problem of evil may not arise for the liberation theologian.

On the other hand, one wonders how, given the sad conditions of the poor and the marginalized, *faith in* God's loving perferential option for the poor can be sustained if such faith is conditioned by the dire circumstances of life. This is problematic in various ways. First, it might be thought that the plight of the poor, which often is felt as irreversible and self-perpetuating, would lead them to believe that they have been abandoned by God, if there happens to be a God. Second, if God is experienced as having a loving preferential option for the poor but does not have power commensurate with the aim of liberating the poor (or does not have power commensurate with preventing the condition of poverty in the first place), then *faith in God* may seem to be misplaced. Furthermore, how can we be expected to work to eradicate the great social evils of poverty and injustice if God himself is not directly involved in this effort? But what is the evidence that God is involved or has a promising plan to eradicate such evils eventually?

---

[52]Ibid.
[53]Ibid., 63.

Without a fuller conception of God along classical lines and without a secure foundation for such a conception, the *theology* of liberation is severely truncated. It may even be seen by some as a form of demagoguery, where vague and unsupported assurances of the love of God are used to tap into the religious psyche of a predominantly Catholic population and to inspire hope, without which liberation would not be possible—without which those mired in poverty would never be able to do *what they must do for themselves* if they are ever to be liberated. If, however, liberation theology is the sincere enterprise that I have every reason to believe it is rather than a ruse that ironically exploits the sincere faith of the oppressed, then its very emphasis on praxis should lead it to more serious reflection on the problems of theodicy.

## 4. Process Theology

In the previous section on liberation theology, we encountered the remark that "there is a growing sensitivity to a God who is revealed in humility and suffering. Confronted with human beings who are conscious of their strength, theology speaks of a God who is 'weak.'"[54] What is little more than a cautious intimation in the liberation theology of Gustavo Gutiérrez is the boldly announced hallmark of process theology. David Ray Griffin, who has been most systematic and exhaustive in the development of a process theodicy, says forthrightly and unabashedly, "My solution dissolves the problem of evil by denying the doctrine of omnipotence fundamental to it."[55]

The repudiation of the classical doctrine of divine omnipotence is no half-hearted measure designed to salvage whatever can be saved of the classical doctrine of God. On the contrary, it is a determined effort to completely supplant the classical doctrine in favor of a God in process—and the problem of suffering in the world is a major inspiration for this gambit.[56] Griffin envisions an easy wedding of liberationist themes with the metaphysics of theism first promulgated by philosopher Alfred North Whitehead.[57]

### 4.1. What Is Process Theodicy?

Whitehead, the fountainhead of process theism, observed that "all simplifications of religious dogma are shipwrecked upon the rock of the problem of evil."[58]

---

[54]Ibid., 62.

[55]David Ray Griffin, "Creation out of Chaos and the Problem of Evil," in *Encountering Evil: Live Options in Theodicy*, ed. Stephen Davis (Atlanta: John Knox, 1981), 105. For another exposition and defense of process theodicy, see Tyron L. Inbody, *The Transforming God: An Interpretation of Suffering and Evil* (Louisville: Westminster John Knox, 1997).

[56]See David Ray Griffin, *Evil Revisited: Responses and Reconsiderations* (Albany, N.Y.: SUNY Press, 1991), 3–4.

[57]See David Ray Griffin, "Values, Evil, and Liberation Theology," *Encounter* 40 (1979): 1–15; reprinted in *Process Philosophy and Social Thought*, ed. John B. Cobb Jr. and W. Widick Schroeder (Chicago: Chicago Center for the Scientific Study of Religion, 1981), 181–95.

[58]Alfred North Whitehead, *Religion in the Making* (London: Macmillan, 1926), 74; quoted in David Ray Griffin, *Reenchantment Without Supernaturalism: A Process Philosophy of Religion* (CSPR; Ithaca, N.Y.: Cornell Univ. Press, 2001), 218.

What did he mean by "simplifications of religious dogma"? Griffin suggests that Whitehead was speaking not of traditional theology in its inchoate state, but of traditional theology as systematically developed by professional theologians—and in particular of the traditional doctrine of God as all-powerful and wholly good.[59] Griffin's interpretation of Whitehead is plausible, since he, like all process thinkers, repudiated the traditional doctrine of God. Whitehead's comment indicates that the doctrine of God substituted by process theism for classical theism is very much a result of reflection on the problem of evil.[60]

Griffin's process theodicy is a response to "an expanded version" of Mackie's logical argument from evil.[61] Mackie's formulation of the argument is dubbed "the 'simple statement' of the problem of evil."[62] Griffin's expansion of this argument was originally presented in eight steps.[63] More recently, Griffin has recast the argument in seven steps, using slightly different language, as follows:

(4) To be God, a being must be omnipotent (with an "omnipotent being" defined as one whose power to bring about what it wills is essentially unlimited—except [perhaps] by logical impossibilities).

(5) An omnipotent being could unilaterally bring about a world devoid of genuine evil (with "genuine evil" defined as anything that makes the world worse than it could have otherwise been).

(6) To be God, a being must be morally perfect.

(7) A morally perfect being would want to bring about a world devoid of genuine evil.

(8) If there is a God, there would be no genuine evil in the world.

(9) But there is genuine evil in the world.

(10) Therefore there is no God.[64]

Griffin's given reason for expanding on the original Mackie-styled argument is that the original "simple statement" masks an ambiguity that clouds awareness of the real force of the logical argument. "The central ambiguity is that none of the premises indicate whether the evil to which they refer is *genuine* evil or merely *apparent* evil."[65] Thus, Griffin's preferred formulation of the argument makes

---

[59]See Griffin, *Reenchantment Without Supernaturalism*, 218.

[60]There are, of course, other contributing factors.

[61]The two primary sources for Griffin's approach to the problem of evil are David Ray Griffin, *God, Process, and Evil: A Process Theodicy* (Philadelphia: Westminster, 1976), and idem, *Evil Revisited* (1991). Two additional sources that are also helpful and important are Griffin, "Creation out of Chaos and the Problem of Evil" (1981), and idem, *Reenchantment Without Supernaturalism* (2001). Griffin's *Reenchantment Without Supernaturalism* (2001) is important in that his treatment of evil is considered in relation to a more fully developed exposition of the metaphysics of process theism, which he describes in the title as "reenchantment without super-naturalism."

[62]See Griffin, *God, Process, and Evil*, 18–19.

[63]Ibid., 19.

[64]Griffin, "Creation out of Chaos and the Problem of Evil," 103.

[65]Ibid., 103.

explicit that it is "genuine evil" that generates a problem for the traditional theist who desires to have logically consistent beliefs.

It is imperative, therefore, to understand what Griffin means by "genuine evil." It will by no means be enough to acknowledge the initial parenthetical gloss on this term in premise (5): "anything that makes the world worse than it could have otherwise been." A somewhat fuller explication of this concept of evil is provided in the remark that "those who claim that there is a logical inconsistency involved are thinking of 'evil' as 'genuine evil,' while those who see no logical inconsistency are thinking in terms of *prima facie* evil which is, or at least may be, only apparently evil."[66] In other words, what is "*prima facie* evil" is not real evil; it is only "apparent evil." Griffin implies here (and explicitly says elsewhere) that whereas Mackie and other exponents of the logical argument from evil assert the real existence of evil, traditional theists who "see no logical inconsistency" regard all evil as merely "apparent evil," which is tantamount to denying the reality of evil.

## 4.2. Towards Greater Precision

Unfortunately, Griffin equivocates in his use of the term "genuine evil," and he does so in the immediate context of these words of attempted explication. In the statement quoted above, "genuine evil" seems to mean "evil that really or actually exists rather than merely apparently exists." But in the clarifying remarks that follow, Griffin compares his terminology with the language used by other thinkers, who variously distinguish between (a) necessary and unnecessary (or superfluous) evil (e.g., H. J. McCloskey[67]), (b) evil that is justified and evil that is not justified (e.g., Alvin Plantinga[68]), (c) defeasible and indefeasible evil (e.g., Roderick Chisholm[69]), and (d) evil that is not pointless and evil that is pointless (e.g., Terence Penelhum[70]), where the second term in each pair of distinctions is regarded by Griffin as a synonym for his term "genuine evil."[71]

This is dangerously misleading, for if a traditional theist agrees to adopt Griffin's term "genuine evil" for evil that is pointless or gratuitous, and the traditional theist answers the logical argument from evil with the denial that there is pointless or gratuitous evil, then an unwary observer may conclude that the traditional theist concedes that the logical argument from evil can be answered only

[66]Griffin, *God, Process, and Evil*, 252.

[67]See H. J. McCloskey, "God and Evil," *The Philosophical Quarterly* 10.39 (1960): 97–114; reprinted in *God and Evil: Readings on the Theological Problem of Evil*, ed. Nelson Pike (Englewood Cliffs, N.J.: Prentice-Hall, 1964), 61–84.

[68]See Alvin Plantinga, *God and Other Minds: A Study of the Rational Justification of Belief in God* (Ithaca, N.Y.: Cornell Univ. Press, 1967), 129.

[69]Roderick Chisholm, "The Defeat of Good and Evil," *Proceedings of the American Philosophical Association* 42 (1968–1969): 21–38; reprinted in *The Problem of Evil*, ed. Marilyn McCord Adams and Robert Merrihew Adams (Oxford Readings in Philosophy; Oxford: Oxford Univ. Press, 1990), 53–68.

[70]Terence Penelhum, "Divine Goodness and the Problem of Evil," *Religious Studies* 2 (1966): 107.

[71]See Griffin, *God, Process, and Evil*, 252–53; see also idem, *Evil Revisited*, 3.

by denying the reality of evil, which would be fatal to traditional theism (and especially Christian theism, with its doctrines of the Fall, the Atonement, and hell).[72]

Griffin apparently holds that evil is "genuine" (real or actual) only on the condition that it is pointless or gratuitous. But this is a highly idiosyncratic and metaphysically suspect view. The term "genuine evil" seems to be more appropriately used for any evil that actually exists. It is not at all suitable as a label for "gratuitous" or "pointless" evils, for evils that are not gratuitous or pointless are no less genuine than those that are gratuitous or pointless. Still less is the term "genuine evil" suitable for labeling *apparently* gratuitous or pointless evils, for evils that are apparently gratuitous or pointless may not be actually gratuitous or pointless. It would be better for Griffin to use the more standard terminology of "gratuitous evil" (or "pointless suffering") instead of "genuine evil."[73] To reduce the possibility of confusion, then, it seems wise to replace premise (9) in Griffin's version of the argument with:

(9*) But there is gratuitous evil (or pointless suffering) in the world.

Griffin takes the logical argument from evil against traditional theism to be an argument from the existence of what he ill-advisedly calls "genuine evil," that is to say, evil that is actually gratuitous or pointless. This is the primary motivation for his expansion of Mackie's formulation of the argument. As he says, "the issue then becomes whether the reality of such evil should be affirmed.... Do events occur without which the universe would have been a better place, all things considered?"[74] In other words, should we affirm premise (9*)?

## 4.3. Evaluation of Griffin's Process Theodicy

Well, what evidence is there that (9*) is true? Here it is helpful to introduce the notion of "inscrutable evil." Let us say that an instance of evil (E) is inscrutable if (and only if) any reason that God may have for permitting (E), such that his permission of (E) would be justified, is completely beyond our ken. If there is a morally sufficient reason for God's permission of (E) (assuming that God exists), we have no idea what that reason is or could be. Let us say that any evil that is "apparently gratuitous" is "inscrutable"—really inscrutable. A really inscrutable evil is not necessarily really gratuitous, but it will seem so. And that it seems so is our evidence that it is so. The evidence for (9*) is the presence of (admittedly) inscrutable evil in the world.

Now we can ask: How does Griffin respond to this problem of evil? His solution hinges especially on his attitude toward premises (4) and (9*). As it happens, his verdict regarding these premises is also what distinguishes him from classical theists.

Consider, first, Griffin's attitude toward premise (9*). He is committed to the truth of (9*), though he acknowledges that it is "incapable of proof."[75] All it takes

---

[72]See Griffin, *Evil Revisited*, 21, for example (cf. p. 231).

[73]See Griffin's claim that, in one sense of the term, "process theists can deny the existence of gratuitous evil," in Griffin, *Evil Revisited*, 227.

[74]Griffin, *God, Process, and Evil*, 253.

[75]Ibid., 29; see Griffin, *Evil Revisited*, 80.

for premise (9*) to be true is for there to be "at least one thing [that] has happened without which the world would have been better."[76] Proof is not needed for belief of (9*) to be justified. Why? Because, he says, "it is one of those basic presumptions in terms of which we all live our lives, in spite of what we verbally affirm."[77] In another passage, Griffin writes of

> basic presuppositions which all persons inevitably hold in practice even if they deny them verbally, on the other. It is these basic presuppositions which must be used as the ultimate check upon the tenability of any proffered system of thought. For if we cannot help believing them, it simply does not make sense to doubt their truth.[78]

It is clear that Griffin includes belief of proposition (9*) among those which "all persons inevitably hold."[79]

Notice how incredibly weak Griffin's evidence for (9*) really is. His evidence is that everyone does actually believe that there is pointless suffering in the world. But such a generalization may be refuted by a single counterexample. To illustrate the ease with which this generalization, so important to Griffin's argument, may be refuted, I hereby declare that I, for one, do not believe that there is pointless suffering in the world. I doubt that there is a single practice from which Griffin could infallibly infer that I do in fact believe there to be pointless evils, despite my protests to the contrary. Furthermore, I accept the testimony of numerous other traditional theists, among whom I would include the authors of Scripture. It does not matter whether we who deny that there is pointless suffering are mistaken in our belief. The point is that we, mistaken or not, do actually deny proposition (9*). That in itself is enough to frustrate Griffin's effort to support (9*).

There is a second problem with Griffin's construal of the argument from evil, given the nature of his commitment to (9*). The evidence that he cites in support of (9*) is inherently experimental. Thus, (9*) is at best only *likely* to be true given the evidence used to support it. This means that the argument is not really a version of the logical argument at all. It is, rather, a version of the evidential argument from evil against traditional theism. To make this point explicit, it would be fitting to replace (9*) with:

(9') But probably there is gratuitous evil (or pointless suffering) in the world.

Of course, this also requires replacing the conclusion, proposition (10), with

(10') Therefore, probably there is no God.[80]

---

[76]Griffin, *God, Process, and Evil*, 28.

[77]Ibid., 29.

[78]Ibid., 125.

[79]See Griffin, *Evil Revisited*, 80.

[80]I find tacit agreement to this more precise characterization of Griffin's argument in his remark that "the task of philosophical theology is to find positions that are not merely free from logical contradiction, but that are also believable and livable" (Griffin, *Evil Revisited*, 80).

The balance of our assessment of Griffin's endorsement of (9') (or of [9*], for that matter) will be postponed until we have considered his attitude toward premise (4) of the argument.

What about premise (4)? Griffin says, "because I also consider the perfect goodness of God and the importance of self-consistency to be nonnegotiable, the only possible way to solve the problem of evil is to modify the traditional doctrine of divine power. That modification lies at the heart of a process theodicy."[81] Griffin denies the doctrine of *creatio ex nihilo* and with it its associated doctrine of divine power, namely, omnipotence. In other words, Griffin accepts Mackie's verdict that the only adequate solution to the logical argument from evil is one that abandons some aspect of traditional (classical) theism, and the aspect he chooses to abandon is commitment to divine omnipotence. He says:

> the problem of evil is uniquely a problem for those theistic positions that hold the doctrine of omnipotence implied by the doctrine of creation out of nothing. For the problem of evil can be stated as a syllogism validly entailing the non-existence of deity only if deity is defined as omnipotent in the sense of having no essential limitations upon the exercise of its will. And it is precisely omnipotence in this sense that the speculative hypothesis of *creatio ex nihilo* is designed to support.[82]

Why is Griffin prepared to accept (9*) (or [9']) and deny (4), rather than affirm (4) and deny (9*) (and [9'])? A major part of the answer has to do with his skepticism about standard sources of belief in the omnipotence of God. Some traditional theists have reasoned that "there are arguments independent of the problem of evil by which God's existence can be proved."[83] Griffin objects to this procedure on the grounds that the best arguments "at most suggest the probability of divine reality."[84] Other traditional theists rest their conviction that God is omnipotent entirely on the authority of biblical revelation. But "[Griffin's] position, by contrast, assumes that we have no infallible revelation." Indeed, "[his] understanding of the God-world relation does not allow any such revelation to occur."[85] The bottom line, then, is that "the reality of genuine [i.e., gratuitous] evil is overwhelmingly more evident to most people than the reality of anything nameable as 'God.'"[86] Of the two propositions, (9*) (or [9']) and (4), proposition (4) is the more evidentially vulnerable.

Griffin's ability to affirm premise (9*) (or [9']) is aided by his willingness to deny premise (4). In fact, I would say that his tenacity in affirming (9*) (or [9']) is

---

[81]Griffin, *Evil Revisited*, 3. Griffin opts for what he calls a "nonsupernaturalist understanding of divine power" (p. 4).

[82]Griffin, "Creation out of Chaos and the Problem of Evil," 104.

[83]Griffin, *God, Process, and Evil*, 255. This is approximately what I do in my own book, *Evil and the Evidence for God*.

[84]Griffin, *God, Process, and Evil*, 255.

[85]See Griffin, *Evil Revisited*, 50–52; the passages quoted appear on p. 52.

[86]Griffin, *God, Process, and Evil*, 256.

more a consequence of his easy willingness to deny (4). If premise (4) did not seem to Griffin to be so comfortably dispensable, then perhaps his relatively weak support for (9*) (or [9']) would not seem so convincing to him. Yet, Griffin's unwavering conviction that (9*) (or [9']) is true is often used to explain his willingness to abandon proposition (4). This is perhaps the Achilles' heel of Griffin's theodicy proposal: His confidence about the truth of premise (9*) (or [9']) is exaggerated, given the evidence of experience on which he relies. Yet he needs strong support for (9*) (or [9']) as a basis for denying (4).

It is logically possible that God has morally sufficient reasons for permitting all the evils there are, including inscrutable evils. If God does have morally sufficient reasons for permitting all the evils there are, including inscrutable evils, then (9*) is false. But (9*) could be false while (9') is true, since (9') refers to our epistemic perspective. In other words, even if it is *logically possible* that God has morally sufficient reasons for permitting all the evils there are (indeed, even if God *actually has* morally sufficient reasons for permitting all the evils there are), it appears from our own point of view that God does *not* have morally sufficient reasons for permitting all the evils there are.

But we must be clear about two possibilities. Does it appear that God does not have morally sufficient reasons for permitting some of the evils there are? Or does it appear, rather, that if God has morally sufficient reasons for permitting all of the evils there are, those reasons are beyond our ken? I hold that it is the latter for which we have evidence, not the former.

Proposition (9'), like proposition (9*), is generally supported by appeals to the existence of inscrutable evil. But inscrutable evil is not evidence for (9') (or [9*]) unless it is reasonable to assume:

(11) If God exists, there would not be inscrutable evils.

Now the plausibility of (11) does not seem to depend so much on the status of proposition (4). Divine omnipotence does not seem to imply (11). If anything, it implies that there are resources and means at God's disposal that we could not hope to fathom, resources and means that would ensure that there is no pointless suffering in the world.

Support for (11) must have a different source. One possibility is that we are so clever that we are entitled to believe that, for any evil for which God had a morally justifying reason, we would be able, with our inherent ingenuity, to discern that reason. I can think of no reason to believe this. An alternative possibility is that a morally perfect being would not permit inscrutable evils. But why think a thing like that? Perhaps the evil of the existence of inscrutable evils is an evil for which God has a morally sufficient reason that just happens to be beyond our ken. Or perhaps we can think of at least one sort of good that would justify God's permission of inscrutable evils. Perhaps his permission of such evils is valuable for the contribution they make to our filial relationship with God. Perhaps they provide an especially meaningful context for nurturing trust in God, whose ways are past finding out.

Another reason for Griffin's repudiation of divine omnipotence (and his denial of proposition [4]) is his concern that it leads to special theodical problems. In particular, if God is all-powerful, he would surely be able to intervene, even miraculously if need be, to prevent the most horrendous instances of suffering.[87] Since God is perfectly good, such intervention is to be expected of an omnipotent deity. But here again Griffin's concern turns on the plausibility of (9'). For if God has a morally sufficient reason for permitting horrendous instances of suffering, then that is a reason why God does not miraculously intervene to prevent such evils. And if the evidence that such evils are actually gratuitous is that they are inscrutable, then we are back to where we were before regarding inscrutable evils as evidence for (9').

Unfortunately, Griffin does not take seriously these limitations in his response to the argument from evil. The main alternative to which he seems most open, an alternative that has attracted the support of a growing number of traditional theists, holds that God is *self-limiting*. More precisely, God voluntarily limits the scope or exercise of his attributes—particularly his omniscience—when he creates persons with libertarian freedom. This outlook is reflected in the perspective of "open theism." As one prominent proponent of open theism remarks, the open view of God "is very much on a par with process theism in its treatment of the problem of evil."[88] Thus, we turn to consider a third position on God and evil that emphasizes the relationality of God.

## 5. Open Theism[89]

### 5.1. What is Open Theism?

According to William Hasker, open theism (or "free-will theism," as he sometimes prefers to call it[90]) is fundamentally a theory of divine providence. The label *open theism* derives from the suggestion that much (though not all) of the future remains epistemically "open" for God. Despite his omniscience, God does not know counterfactuals of creaturely freedom. This is the linchpin of the openness perspective. God does not have infallible foreknowledge of future free acts.

Consequently, as Hasker says, "God is open to us and to the future."[91] He explains: "God knows an immense amount about each one of us ... but he does not, because he cannot, plan his actions toward us on the basis of a prior knowl-

---

[87]See Griffin, *Evil Revisited*, 20.

[88]William Hasker, "The Problem of Evil in Process Theism and Classical Free Will Theism," *Process Studies* 29.2 (2000): 194.

[89]This section is a modified version of a paper to be published spring 2002 in *Philosophia Christi*, the journal of the Evangelical Philosophical Society.

[90]It is, more precisely, a *version* of free-will theism; see William Hasker, "A Philosophical Perspective," in Clark Pinnock et al., *The Openness of God: A Biblical Challenge to the Traditional Understanding of God* (Downer's Grove, Ill.: InterVarsity Press, 1994), 134–35, 150; cf. David Basinger, *The Case for Freewill Theism: A Philosophical Assessment* (Downers Grove, Ill.: InterVarsity Press, 1996).

[91]Hasker, "A Philosophical Perspective," 150.

god under fire

edge of how we will respond."[92] And this is a consequence of God's having created us with libertarian freedom. A further consequence is that God is a "risk-taking" God, for "insofar as [God] chooses to permit [persons] the freedom to choose their own paths through the world, God runs a very real risk that they will reject his will and adopt a course of action that is seriously destructive."[93]

Hasker acknowledges that it would be most desirable for the theist to be able to maintain both of the following propositions:

(12) God fully controls everything that takes place in the world,
and
(13) Certain matters are within the control and responsibility of free creatures (e.g., human beings).[94]

Dissatisfied with all attempts to harmonize these two propositions, however, he is prepared to deny proposition (12). In this respect, Hasker's position resembles David Ray Griffin's process perspective. This is initially surprising, since Hasker desires to be recognized as a traditional theist. But Hasker is unwilling to abandon the doctrine of divine omnipotence, which is where he differs from Griffin.[95] Hasker allows that divine omnipotence is essential to traditional theism. How then can he deny that proposition (12) is essential to traditional theism? By holding that all attributes traditionally ascribed to God, including omnipotence and omniscience, are compatible with denying proposition (12).

For Hasker, proposition (12) is true just in case proposition (13) is false. If proposition (13) is true, it is because God has created free creatures. But it is precisely in virtue of creating free creatures that God has "willingly chosen to become self-limited."[96] In particular, God limits the scope of his knowledge by creating free persons, whose future free acts remain indeterminate as long as they are yet future.

This self-limitation of divine knowledge is compatible with omniscience, according to Hasker, if counterfactuals of creaturely freedom do not have truth values and hence cannot be known, even by an omniscient being. For relative to future free acts, there simply would not be any fact of the matter for God to know.[97] Creaturely freedom would thus impose "*logical* limitations on God's

---

[92]Ibid., 151.

[93]William Hasker, "The Antinomies of Divine Providence," unpublished paper presented at the Wheaton College Philosophy Conference (October 2000), 4; this paper is to be published in the spring 2002 issue of *Philosophia Christi*, the journal of the Evangelical Philosophical Society, with a reply by R. Douglas Geivett. See also Hasker, "A Philosophical Perspective," 135.

[94]Hasker, "The Antinomies of Divine Providence," 2. Proposition (12) is a direct quote of Hasker; proposition (13) is a modification of a direct quote.

[95]For an engaging discussion of the similarities and differences between process theology and openness theology, by representatives of these perspectives, see John B. Cobb Jr. and Clark H. Pinnock, eds., *Searching for an Adequate God: A Dialogue Between Process and Free Will Theists* (Grand Rapids: Eerdmans, 2000).

[96]Hasker, "The Antinomies of Divine Providence," 4.

[97]This is called the "grounding objection" to the doctrine of middle knowledge.

knowledge of the future."[98] On this suggestion, it is a property of such counterfactuals that they have no truth value.[99]

Lest one conclude that this endorsement of open theism exacerbates the problem of evil, Hasker maintains that open theism is in the best position, compared with the other traditional alternatives, to deal with this problem.[100] The alleged advantage of open theism has two dimensions. One concerns the problem of evil as such; the other relates to the phenomenon of "divine pathos."

## 5.2. Open Theism and Divine Pathos

*Divine pathos* refers to God's ability to undergo genuine emotive responses to events that happen—to be moved, for example, to genuine grief and compassion in response to instances of intense human suffering, or to anger in response to human sin.[101] How does this consideration support open theism? Hasker believes that the following two propositions stand in tension with one another.[102]

(14) God has a detailed plan for everything that occurs in the world.
(15) God exhibits powerful affective responses to the various things that take place.

While he acknowledges that the conjunction of these two propositions "does not even have the appearance of formal contradiction," he suggests that there is "at the very least a strong incongruity: if everything that happens is in accord with God's plan, then why is God so powerfully affected by these events when they occur?"[103]

Let us initially suppose, just for the sake of argument, that the conjunction of these two propositions does generate some sort of tension, as Hasker claims. One could resolve this tension by denying either the first or the second proposition. That is indeed what Hasker does; he denies (14), that God has a detailed plan for everything that occurs in the world, in order to safeguard the possibility of God's powerful and spontaneous response to events. So he apparently thinks that if the denial of one of these propositions is required, it is better to deny the first than the second. On what basis does he think this?

Hasker's main argument in support of proposition (15) is based on biblical data. He refers, for example, to the way God is represented by the Old Testament

---

[98]Hasker, "A Philosophical Perspective," 135; italics added. "God, who potentially has absolute, meticulous control [over the universe] ... has willingly chosen to become self-limited by creating free persons on whom he bestows limited but nevertheless quite significant powers to affect both their own lives and the world around them" (Hasker, "The Antinomies of Divine Providence," 4).

[99]For a discussion of this, see William Lane Craig's chapter in this volume, "What does God Know?" (ch. 6).

[100]Hasker, "A Philosophical Perspective," 152.

[101]For a more thorough discussion of God's emotions, see Patrick Lee's chapter in this volume, "Does God Have Emotions?" (ch. 9).

[102]See Hasker, "The Antinomies of Divine Providence," 14–20.

[103]Ibid., 14.

prophets as intensely emotionally involved with his people, singling out Hosea 2:2–3 and 2:14–15 for quotation. He summarizes by asserting that "similar dramatic portrayals of divine emotion are frequent in the pages of Scripture."[104]

The first thing to notice is that an argument in support of (15) is not, as such, an argument that (15) is preferable to (14), for there may be support for both (15) and (14), and the support for (14) may be even stronger than the support for (15). So having some justification for (15) will not be sufficient for denying (14). (Of course, this possibility cuts both ways.) This means that a rigorous argument for open theism from the reality of divine pathos should include an assessment of the comparative support for each of propositions (14) and (15).

One option available to the traditional theist is to deny (15) on the grounds that (14) is better supported than (15). But there may be other reasons for denying (15). One may feel, for example, that Hasker's exegesis of the biblical data cited in support of (15) involves a dubious form of literalism. Or, one may be committed to some version of divine impassibility, which precludes the specific sense of (15) required by Hasker's argument from divine pathos. What (15) says is that "God exhibits powerful affective responses to the various things that take place." What Hasker means by (15) is that God's affective response is spontaneous and more-or-less coterminous with the event that elicits this response.

This, it seems, requires some sort of change in the affective state in God. Moreover, it is a change that presupposes a change in God's cognitive state. God does not undergo the emotive response until God knows the occurrence of the event, which he knows only when the event occurs. So (15), as understood by Hasker, entails the denial of divine impassibility, one might think. Any good reason to affirm impassibility will therefore be a reason to deny (15) on Hasker's interpretation of (15)—call this interpretation (15*):

> (15*) God exhibits powerful affective responses to the various things that take place and God does not undergo the emotive response until God knows the occurrence of the event, which he knows only when the event occurs.

Of course, Hasker takes the evidence for (15*) to be evidence against impassibility.

So one type of response to Hasker would be to deny (15*). And there are at least two reasons one might have for denying (15*). One might not accept the degree of literalism that leads to ascribing emotional states to God, and/or one might argue for divine impassibility, which entails that (15*) is false.

Now let us suppose that one accepts both the literalism and the divine passibility required by Hasker's argument. Even then the argument from divine pathos faces several problems. First, it isn't at all clear why God's emotive response must be spontaneous and coterminous with the event to which he is responding. God's emotive response might have a kind of eternal quality—an ever-present feature of his being that becomes manifest, if God so desires, when the event occurs.

---

[104]Ibid., 16.

Nothing changes in God's emotional state at the moment of the occurrence of the event to which his emotional state is a "response." Here the word "response" may be misleading. It may be more apt to speak of an "attitude," an attitude that is as real in anticipation of the event as it is when the event occurs.

Second, it isn't clear how God's ability to respond emotively to an event depends on his knowing the event only at the moment of its occurrence. I guess we all should agree that God's emotive response would be misplaced if God did not know the occurrence of the event to which he is responding. But why shouldn't God know the event well in advance of its occurrence, but only respond with this or that particular emotion when the event actually occurs?

In support of this, one could plausibly argue, we have thoroughly mundane examples. As a parent, I know that my child will disobey a certain command that I issue. When my child disobeys, I'm not surprised, but I feel something, disappointment perhaps, that I didn't feel before, or that I didn't feel to the same degree before. A young woman knows that her boyfriend is going to propose to her, but she doesn't begin to feel certain emotions until the actual proposal. Or a groom, having set a date for his future wedding, knows when it will take place but begins to experience feelings he never experienced before as he stands next to his bride at the altar. The thrill in anticipation of a roller coaster ride is distinguishable from the thrill of the ride itself.[105] An adult child's knowledge that his mother will certainly die of cancer does not preclude fresh feelings of anguish and loss when she finally succumbs.[106] In all such cases of human emotion, the emotion occurs with no corresponding change in one's cognitive state. Perhaps the same possibility obtains in God's case (again, on the assumption, for the sake of argument, of divine passibility).

Third, the mundane examples just mentioned illustrate the point that knowledge does not entail emotional response or is not sufficient for emotional response. There must be the occurrence of the event (fore)known. This is the real trigger of the emotions in question. Hasker apparently disagrees, but he does not say enough about the connection between knowledge and emotion that is required by his argument from divine pathos.

Fourth, proposition (15) is ambiguous. It holds that God "exhibits" affective states in response to events. Does this mean (a) that God comes to have these states when the events occur, or (b) that God's emotive states are manifest or revealed (to us) when the events occur? It seems to me that (b) is sufficient for the requirements of divine pathos. But (b) is compatible with the proposition that God knows the events in advance of the events themselves. Indeed, a theist committed to divine impassibility might suggest that God always knows all events and always feels all emotions appropriate to the occurrence of those events but displays those emotions in a way accessible to us when the events occur.

We may distinguish between being in a particular emotional state and exhibiting that state. Of course, Hasker will claim that God's emotive response to our circumstances is somehow diminished and that there is something less than gen-

[105]An example suggested to me by Greg Ganssle.
[106]An example suggested to me by Michael Murray.

uine about the intimacy of relationship between God and us if God somehow knows in advance what will happen to us. But a close examination of Hasker's remarks reveals that the problem is not merely a matter of God's having the relevant sort of knowledge in advance of what happens. Rather, the problem is that God, in having such knowledge, in effect *plans* for all the events that happen. Hasker writes:

> Viewing the situation in a broader context, it remains true that, whatever wrongs and harms the world's history may contain, God has specifically chosen the enactment of *that particular history* in preference to any other history that is feasible, given the counterfactuals of freedom that are actually true. At most, God's bliss in contemplating this world might be tinged faintly with regret that, in certain respects, things are not even better.[107]

Hasker then suggests that on the open view of God, since *"things do not always go in accordance with God's plan,"* God may experience or undergo "a wide range of responses to ... worldly events."[108] The advantage gained by open theism turns on the fact that God plans for one thing and sometimes gets something very different in its place. And this proves to be such an irritant that it occasions more profound and relationally meaningful emotional responses from God. I fail to see the advantage of this. Rather, it strikes me as more plausible to suppose that God's affective response to events is a consequence of the violation of his moral will by the free acts of creatures and not the frustration of a plan for which God could not guarantee success. Such a violation of God's moral will is presumably sufficient for the full range of emotion that is attested in the pages of Scripture.

By way of review, the argument for open theism from divine pathos falls short, first because the way remains open for the traditional theist to deny proposition (15), and second because the literalism and the divine passibility assumed in Hasker's argument do nothing to strengthen his claim that God does not have infallible knowledge of future free actions.

## 5.3. Open Theism and the Problem of Evil

We come, finally, to Hasker's claim that "the *best* Christian theodicy ... will affirm forcefully that *God the Creator and Redeemer is a risk taker,"*[109] that "the advantage lies with a view which recognizes that a genuine though limited autonomy has been granted by God to created agents."[110]

---

[107]Hasker, "The Antinomies of Divine Providence," 19.

[108]Ibid., 19–20.

[109]William Hasker, *God, Time, and Knowledge* (CSPR; Ithaca, N.Y.: Cornell Univ. Press, 1989), 205. The risk-taking aspect of open theism is also emphasized and exploited for theodical purposes in the work of Gregory A. Boyd, which lacks the sophistication and plausibility of Hasker's exposition and defense of open theism. See Gregory A. Boyd, *Letters from a Skeptic* (Wheaton, Ill.: Victor, 1992), 29–31; idem, *God at War: The Bible and Spiritual Conflict* (Downers Grove, Ill.: InterVarsity Press, 1996); idem, *God of the Possible: A Biblical Introduction to the Open View of God* (Grand Rapids: Baker, 2000), 98–102; idem, *Satan and the Problem of Evil: Constructing a Warfare Theodicy* (Downers Grove, Ill.: InterVarsity Press, 2001).

[110]Hasker, "The Antinomies of Divine Providence," 22.

The alleged advantage of Hasker's open theism over other traditional positions hinges on his contention that "the more complete one asserts God's control over worldly events to be, the more difficult it is to find a viable solution to the problem of evil."[111] In the development of his argument for the superiority of open theism, Hasker makes three specific claims, each of which can be challenged.

First, Hasker suggests that in addressing the problem of evil, the key question is, "Which view of providence offers the best chance of reconciling the goodness and power of God with the evidence of evil in the world?"[112] This way of putting the question suggests that the goodness and power of God, perhaps even some definite conceptions of the goodness and power of God, are constraints on the search for a fitting view of providence when confronted with evil. But why should a particular conception of divine omniscience, if there is reason to believe that God has such knowledge, be excluded from the list of constraints on an adequate theory of providence? Perhaps the question should be, Which view of providence offers the best chance of reconciling the goodness, power, and omniscience of God with the evidence of evil in the world?

Thomas Flint argues that Hasker's risk-taking solution to the problem of evil would make the problem even more difficult for the Christian to handle. For if God knows only propensities, then he takes enormous risks in creating significantly free beings; he risks creating a world in which many, or most, or even all of his free creatures consistently reject him, a world in which they use their freedom to degrade others and themselves. It seems to me that one can reasonably argue that a good and loving God would not take such risks.[113]

It seems to me that Hasker's argument for open theism assumes that *if God knew that horrendous evils would result if God created this world, then God would not have created this world because God would not have been justified in creating it.* But I see no way for open theism to avoid an analogous difficulty. For on Hasker's own view, God must have known in advance that horrendous evils could result if he created this world. God's knowledge of the real possibility of such evils is no less a reason for God to abstain from creation than God's foreknowledge of such evils would be. In fact, if God could not be sure in advance of creating this world that its evils would not be too severe to justify his permission of them by his creation of this world, then Hasker's assumption is more telling against his open theism than it is against a classical view of omniscience, according to which God has infallible foreknowledge of all free acts. In any case, the assumption must be rejected. The more traditional theist is free to deny the assumption. The open theist needs the assumption to commend his position over more traditional theodicies. But the assumption he needs here has a scathing effect on his own view.[114]

---

[111]Ibid., 20.

[112]Ibid., 22.

[113]Flint, *Divine Providence*, 107; quoted in Hasker, "The Antinomies of Divine Providence," 20–21.

[114]Flint is right, I think, in pointing out that, on the openness view, God risked not only the occurrence of the horrendous evils of the actual world, but also even worse evils that could

Second, Hasker says there is "something obscene about supposing that there is some 'greater good' in terms of which [truly horrendous evils] can be justified."[115] More traditional theodicies are committed to this supposition, whereas open theism is not. But what is obscene about this supposition? Is it that we know that there is no greater good in terms of which horrendous evils are justified? Or is it that we can think of no good that is great enough to justify horrendous evils?

Furthermore, what about the supposition that God risks the possibility of unjustified horrendous evils? Is it any less obscene to suppose—as open theism does—that this risk is justified by some greater good that is achieved by God's self-imposed limitation of his knowledge via the creation of free agents? Is it not perhaps yet more offensive to our sensibilities that God knowingly created free creatures who might inflict horrendous evils on their fellows? Bear in mind that, on Hasker's own account, God created a world where horrendous evils are a reality and not a mere possibility. The fact that from God's perspective at creation such evils were a mere possibility does nothing to attenuate the severity of the evils in question.

Either God has the power to anticipate all specific horrendous evils in time to prevent their occurrence or he does not. If God has this power and he does not prevent their occurrence, then open theism is on a par with such traditional alternatives as Molinism, Calvinism, and Thomism.[116] Presumably God has some justifying reason for permitting them when he could have intervened in time to prevent them. If God is unable to prevent them, and no greater good justifies their occurrence, then what does it mean when Hasker claims that the eventual victory of God's cause is a sure thing? Hasker denies that God has complete control over the details of human history, but he is sure of the ultimate victory of God's cause. Strange that God's cause should be considered victorious even if there should be horrendous evils that cannot be justified in terms of some greater good. What "wise and good plan" does God have for the world—a plan that is destined to succeed, according to Hasker—if it does not include a justification for God's creation of the possibility of horrendous evils? And if it does include a justification for God's creation of the possibility of horrendous evils, why shouldn't that same justification be available to such other traditional theists as Molinists, Calvinists, and Thomists?

Third, on open theism, "the ultimate victory of God's cause is not in doubt. . . . Our God is a *fighting God*, one whose arm is strong and whose final triumph cannot be prevented."[117] Hasker does not suggest that other more traditional theodicies compromise the certainty of God's victory in achieving his purposes.

---

have occurred but did not. The actual world is better than any number of worlds that might have been. The traditional doctrine that God has exhaustive knowledge of the future avoids this problem, for on the traditional view God has always known how bad things would get. But here again we can go a tad further than Flint does in arguing against the open theist. For the traditional theist can maintain that God deliberately ensured that a world with worse evils than the actual world is not actualized.

[115]Hasker, "The Antinomies of Divine Providence," 23.

[116]See Flint, *Divine Providence*, for a comparison of these views and a detailed exposition and defense of Molinism.

[117]Hasker, "The Antinomies of Divine Providence," 23.

But he does claim that ultimate victory is not compromised by the openness view. But this is dubious. For what are the criteria in terms of which victory is to be measured, and what is it that guarantees the ultimate victory of God's cause? Hasker's answer is very sketchy. In fact, he says almost nothing about the criteria that determine whether God is ultimately victorious.

Of course, this will depend on God's purposes. But if we suppose that God's purposes include the meaningful provision of freedom for his creatures and the free cooperation of his creatures, then it is difficult to see how final triumph can be such a sure thing. The autonomy of God's creatures will, on the openness view, ensure that every plan of God that depends on their free cooperation may end in failure. Every version of traditional theism—from Molinism, to Calvinism, to Thomism—denies this.

I conclude that Hasker's preference for open theism, to the degree that it is based on a consideration of the facts of evil and its associated insistence on a greater degree of divine relationality, is ill-conceived.

## 6. Summary and Conclusion

It is logically possible that God has a morally sufficient reason for permitting every evil there is, including heinous inscrutable evils. This we may know even if we do not know that there actually are morally justifying reasons for God's permission of the evils that exist. Still less are we required to know what reasons actually do justify God's permission of each instance of evil, if indeed they are justified. So Mackie's logical argument from evil fails. Traditional theism need not repair to the theologies of liberation or process or divine openness to withstand the assault from the logical argument from evil.

What about the evidential argument from evil? Traditional theists believe that there are morally sufficient reasons for God's permission of all the evils there are. Does this not fly in the face of evidence to the contrary? Do not the most pernicious of inscrutable evils make it likely that they, at least, are not morally justified and hence that God does not exist? It is the existence of inscrutable evils that makes it seem to us that there are gratuitous evils. But inscrutable evils may or may not be actually gratuitous, just as evils that appear gratuitous may or may not be actually gratuitous. Again, traditional theism can reply without modulating its position in the direction of liberation theology, process theology, or open theism. Evidence for the existence of God is evidence that no inscrutable evils are genuinely gratuitous. The existence of inscrutable evil implies that if the God of classical theism exists, then such a God must have morally sufficient reasons for permitting inscrutable evil.

If anything, the existence of evil in the world places a greater burden on the traditional Christian theologian to justify belief in the existence of the God of classical theism. But the very possibility of recognizing evil for what it is, namely, a departure from the way things ought to be, suggests that some sort of theism may be implied by the existence of evil. For how can evil be a departure from the way things ought to be if there is no way things ought to be? But if there is a way things ought to be, then should there not be a design plan for such things? And if there is a design plan for things, should there not be some sort of designer as well?

god under fire

Chapter 8

# Does God take Risks?

*James S. Spiegel*

# 1. Introduction

When considering a particular interpretation of the new physics, Albert Einstein remarked that "God does not play dice." Both as a theoretical physicist and a theological layman, he was suspicious of the notion that the universe is, at bottom, a game of chance. In recent decades a similar issue has emerged as a matter of serious debate among Christian theologians. It has taken the form of disputes about the nature of divine providence. To what extent, if any, does God control the universe? Does he have a definite plan for human history?

The orthodox position of the church has been that God maintains ultimate control over creation and that his purpose for history cannot be thwarted. During the last century, however, this orthodox doctrine has been attacked by theologians from many quarters. For a variety of reasons these scholars have maintained that God's purposes can indeed be stymied and that human beings may even act so as to genuinely surprise him, change his thinking, and even alter divine plans for the world. Thus, God's control of the universe is not complete and the direction of human history is open-ended. So God does, in a sense, "play dice" with creation, insofar as he gambles on the choices of human beings. In short, God is a risk-taker.

Such "divine-risk" theists, as I will call them, emphasize God's loving care and personal engagement with human beings and the rest of creation. They do so with good reason. The Scriptures teach that God desires to commune with his people, relating to us intimately, person to person. God takes great joy in our worship, encourages us in our service, and is grieved when we sin. In the life of the believer God lovingly guides, comforts, chastises, and rewards. As the apostle John declares, God *is* love, which is demonstrated in the mercy and grace he shows to his people.

Such aspects of divine relationality are properly accented by divine-risk theists. Their perspective serves as a corrective to theologies in which divine predestination is overemphasized. But does their view suffer from its own excesses, particularly regarding the doctrine of providence? Does God really take *risks*? In this chapter, I will answer this latter question negatively and argue that the risk model of providence is unbiblical. In so doing, I will show precisely how recent theological scholarship departs from a classical view of divine providence, while recognizing where Christians can nonetheless profit from the contributions of those who believe in divine risk.

# 2. The Strong View of Divine Providence

Generally speaking, the doctrine of divine providence affirms that God "provides" for his creatures. His provisions flow from his nature as a caring, loving, and

GOD UNDER FIRE

purposeful almighty person who desires to bring about the greatest possible good. About this much Christian thinkers are agreed. Just what it means to say that God provides, however, is disputed among contemporary scholars. Before entering into this debate, it is essential that we situate ourselves historically. Therefore, I will first outline the development of the dominant position on this issue within church history, which I will call the "strong" view of providence. Then I will turn to an exposition of the competing model, or "weak" view of providence, which affirms divine risk.

The strong view of providence affirms that all things are subject to the sovereign control of God. His governance of the world involves more than just an initial creation, perfect knowledge, and loving concern for his creation, though it does involve these things. Rather, God actively and constantly directs history, according to his perfect redemptive plan, all the while maintaining real and vital personal relationships with his people. This view has been endorsed by the most renowned Christian theologians.

## 2.1 A History of the Strong View of Providence

The most influential early articulation of what I am calling the strong view of divine providence comes from St. Augustine. According to Augustine, God possesses infallible knowledge of all events throughout the course of history. God has complete foreknowledge, but he does not apprehend the future as we do, "for he does not pass from this to that by transition of thought, but beholds all things with absolute unchangeableness; so that . . . those things which emerge in time . . . are by him comprehended in his stable and eternal presence."[1] God, then, is not essentially a temporal being. He enters into time, but he is not bound by it.

God's exhaustive foreknowledge, Augustine maintained, implies the predetermination of all things, including human actions. Human wills "have just so much power as God willed and foreknew that they should have."[2] Furthermore, Augustine insisted that this divine foreknowledge and the determinism it implies are consistent with human freedom. God granted us a genuine power to will our actions, which is sufficient to secure our moral responsibility. Augustine affirms divine prescience and human freedom, saying "we faithfully and sincerely confess both. The former, that we may believe well; the latter, that we may live well."[3] So Augustine espoused an early version of "compatibilism," the view that determinism and human freedom (and therefore moral responsibility) are logically compatible.[4]

The Augustinian model of providence in particular, and the doctrine of God generally, was embraced and reiterated by the most preeminent Christian theologians and biblical scholars over the course of the next fifteen hundred years. For example, Thomas Aquinas argued that God is a sort of cosmic artist, directing the

---

[1]Augustine, *The City of God*, 1.11.21 (p. 460); page numbers in parentheses refer to Augustine, *The City of God*, trans. Marcus Dods (New York: Hafner, 1948).
[2]Ibid., 1.5.9 (p. 194).
[3]Ibid., 1.5.10 (p. 196).
[4]See ch. 6 in this volume by William Lane Craig for a fuller discussion of God's knowledge.

world down to every last detail, as "the causality of God ... extends to all being."[5] This includes human beings, who differ from "natural things" by their capacity to deliberate and freely choose courses of action. And "since the very act of free will is traced to God as a cause, it necessarily follows that everything happening from the exercise of free will must be subject to divine providence."[6] In this way, Aquinas, like Augustine before him, affirmed both human freedom and theological determinism. The two teachings are compatible, he maintained, "for human providence is included under the providence of God."[7]

With the Protestant Reformation came a renewed emphasis on divine providence. Martin Luther emphatically reiterated the Augustinian doctrine, saying "it is ... essentially necessary and wholesome for Christians to know that God foreknows nothing contingently, but that he foresees, purposes and does all things according to His immutable, eternal and infallible will."[8] Luther was aware that this strong view of providence invites criticism regarding the problem of evil: If God controls even human wills, then how can we be blamed for our vicious choices? And doesn't divine sovereignty over evil threaten God's goodness? Luther's approach to the matter was typical among classical theologians. He preferred simply to affirm divine sovereignty and goodness in the face of human evil rather than try to explain *how* they are compatible. God's actions are not to be measured or evaluated by us. On the contrary, his will "is itself the measure of all things." God's will is perfect, so "what takes place must be right, because He so wills it."[9]

Although theological determinism had been espoused by many theologians before John Calvin reiterated the doctrine, it is his name that is most commonly identified with it. Calvin asserted that "there is no erratic power, or action, or motion in creatures, but that they are governed by God's secret plan in such a way that nothing happens except what is knowingly and willingly decreed by him."[10] All divine decrees are for the purpose of bringing about God's own glory. But Calvin's emphasis on divine sovereignty was not so austere as to ignore the obvious human benefits of this doctrine, as he notes that "in times of adversity believers [may] comfort themselves with the solace that they suffer nothing except by God's ordinance and command, for they are under his hand."[11]

The Puritan theologian Jonathan Edwards revitalized the Augustinian tradition with his extraordinary philosophical rigor. He, too, affirmed divine atempo-

---

[5]Thomas Aquinas, *Summa Theologiae*, 1.Q22.A2 (1:122); page numbers in parentheses refer to Thomas Aquinas, *Summa Theologica*, trans. English Dominican Fathers, 3 vols. (New York: Benziger Brothers, 1947).

[6]Ibid. (1:123).

[7]Ibid.

[8]Martin Luther, *The Bondage of the Will* in *Erasmus-Luther: Discourse on Free Will*, trans. Ernst F. Winter (New York: Frederick Ungar, 1961), 106.

[9]Ibid., 130.

[10]John Calvin, *Institutes of the Christian Religion*, 1.16.3 (1:201); page numbers in parentheses refer to John Calvin, *Institutes of the Christian Religion*, trans. Ford Lewis Battles, 2 vols. (Philadelphia: Westminster, 1960).

[11]Ibid., 1.16.3 (1:200).

rality, impassibility, and exhaustive foreknowledge. Furthermore, he maintained that the predetermination of all things is directly implied by God's foreknowledge. For if the prior knowledge of the event is infallible, "then it is impossible it should ever be otherwise ... and this is the same thing as to say, it is impossible but that the event should come to pass: and this is the same as to say that its coming to pass is *necessary*."[12] Like other Augustinians, Edwards espoused compatibilism, defining freedom as the ability to act according to one's choice.[13]

## 2.2 The Strong View of Providence and Divine Risk

The strong view of divine providence, as we have seen, has been affirmed by some of the most important theologians in the history of the Christian church.[14] The doctrine may thus be summarized as affirming each of the following:

(1) *Divine omniscience and exhaustive foreknowledge*. God knows every true proposition, and he cannot be mistaken in any of his beliefs. Since God is not limited by time, events that will occur in our future are already known to him, even as certainly as he knows past events. So God cannot be taken by surprise by anything that happens.

---

[12]Jonathan Edwards, *Freedom of the Will*, in *The Works of Jonathan Edwards*, 2 vols. (Edinburgh: Banner of Truth, 1974), 1:38–39 (emphasis his).

[13]An alternative interpretation of the strong providence perspective, called "Molinism," has been much discussed in recent years and, therefore, deserves attention. The theory dates back to the sixteenth century when it was devised by Jesuit theologians, most prominently Luis de Molina, after whom the theory is named. Molinists note that God knows all possible worlds as well as the actual world. Moreover, he possesses knowledge of which worlds he could create that are consistent with creaturely freedom. For only some possible worlds contain genuinely free beings. And God has complete knowledge of what all free beings *would* do in those various possible worlds. Molinists refer to this as divine "middle knowledge." God chose to create the world he did based upon his middle knowledge of how free beings would freely act in various circumstances.

The Molinist perspective preserves a strong notion of divine providence. God's plan for the world is guaranteed to be realized because he knew prior to creation just what every person in that world would do in every circumstance that would arise. But the freedom of all human beings is also respected. For God's middle knowledge of how they would freely act forms the basis of his choice in creation, not vice versa. Typically, Molinists embrace a libertarian conception of freedom, where a free act is seen as one that is solely determined by the person's will. Molinism can be seen largely as an attempt to reconcile the strong view of providence with this view of freedom. The result is that Molinists are even able to affirm divine predestination. They do so by asserting the logical priority of God's foreknowledge to his predetermining of the elect.

See Luis de Molina, *On Divine Foreknowledge*, trans. Alfred Freddoso (Ithaca, N.Y.: Cornell Univ. Press, 1988). For recent expositions of Molinism, see Thomas Flint, *Divine Providence: The Molinist Account* (Ithaca, N.Y.: Cornell Univ. Press, 1998); William Lane Craig, *The Only Wise God: The Compatibility of Divine Foreknowledge and Human Freedom* (Grand Rapids: Baker, 1987).

[14]The representative survey of proponents of the Augustinian position that I offer here highlights only some of the more outstanding figures. Scores of others could have been cited, particularly since the eighteenth century, including Charles Hodge, B. B. Warfield, Charles Spurgeon, Louis Berkhof, and John Murray.

(2) *Divine control*. God sovereignly controls the world. Some affirming the strong view regard this as involving immediate, active control of all particular events, including human choices. Others understand such control to include divine permission of some events, though God created the world knowing precisely how and when those events would occur. So whether the details of history are directly or indirectly governed, divine control over the world is absolute.

(3) *Divine purpose*. God governs his creation intentionally, directing the details of the universe with the highest end in view, his own glory. He acts redemptively in history on behalf of his people, the church of Christ. God loves, forgives, protects, preserves, and will ultimately reward us. His ultimate plan for the world is guaranteed to succeed, because he is the cosmic sovereign.

(4) *Divine sovereignty over evil*. Human suffering and immorality are sovereignly governed by God. Although undesirable in themselves, God works to use these things for the betterment of his people and the advancement of his own glory. Defenders of strong providence disagree among themselves about the mode of divine control over evil, but all assert that God knowingly and intentionally created a world in which such evils were bound to occur.

Having now spelled out the strong view of providence, we are nearly positioned to answer the question whether, from this perspective, God takes risks. But first we must answer the question, What does it mean to say that one "takes a risk" in performing an action? I think there are at least three conditions required for an act to be properly considered risky: (a) The agent must not know (in advance) all of the effects of her act; (b) the agent must not completely control all of the effects of the act; and (c) there must be some real possibility of harm or loss resulting from performance of the act, whether that misfortune befalls the agent herself or persons for whom the agent cares. To summarize this definition, we might say that *a risky act is one that might result in unforeseeable and uncontrollable misfortune*. Given this understanding of risk, it is clear that the strong view of divine providence denies that God is a risk-taker.[15]

## 3. Modern Alternatives to the Strong View of Divine Providence

Thus, the strong view of providence denies that God takes risks. Historically, this has been the predominant position of Christians on the matter, but every era of church history has seen critics of this view. However, in the twentieth century the strong view of providence was subjected to especially fierce criticism by scholars from diverse theological camps, so much so that this view might now be a minority position in the church. In particular, challenges to the strong view of providence have come from process theology, liberation theology, feminist theology, and open theism.

---

[15]Augustinians reject divine risk because they believe neither conditions (a) nor (b) describe any of God's actions, most significantly his creation of the world. Others, such as Molinists and Arminians, who see God's foreknowledge as logically prior to his control of the world, deny only that condition (a) applies to God.

GOD UNDER fire

In what follows, I will discuss each of these views. Among these, open theism will be discussed most extensively, for two reasons. First, among proponents of divine risk the open theists' treatment of the doctrine of providence is the most explicit and thorough. Thus, it best illustrates the rejection of the strong view of providence. Second, the open theists are especially concerned to offer biblical textual support for their view. Thus, special attention to this view will make for greater efficiency in critical assessment of all the alternative theologies discussed here. To critically refute open theism is likewise to refute the other views, at least from the perspective of the strong view of providence that I defend.

## 3.1 Early Twentieth-Century Alternatives

The twentieth-century views that rejected the strong view of providence in most cases are also challenges to Christian orthodoxy itself.

### 3.1.1 Process Theology

The idea that God changes in diverse ways as a result of his relation to the world is the main distinctive of process theology. The founder of this movement, philosopher Alfred North Whitehead, distinguished between two aspects of the "dipolar" nature of God: a "primordial" nature and a "consequent" nature. According to Whitehead, the primordial nature of God is "free, complete . . . eternal, actually deficient, and unconscious," whereas the consequent side of God's nature "is determined, incomplete . . . 'everlasting,' fully actual, and conscious."[16] Although God is distinct from the world, he does not really transcend the world. He is *with* and *in* the world, changing and growing through his interaction with the world.

Charles Hartshorne further developed this idea of a dipolar, changing God, addressing the most common objection to process theology: How can God be perfect and yet change? In response Hartshorne redefines divine perfection to mean that God is "better than any individual other than himself."[17] So God is surpassable, but only by himself. As for God's knowledge, he anticipates the future as we do. He "know[s] future events only in their character as indefinite, or more or less problematic, nebulous, incomplete as to details."[18] In other words, God grows in understanding as he experiences the world with us. Hartshorne's explanation for so truncating divine knowledge: "This seems to be the only view of God's knowledge that does not make human freedom impossible."[19]

Thus, the God of process theism is a far cry from the God of historic Christian theism.[20] Whereas the latter is independent of the world, unchanged

---

[16]Alfred North Whitehead, *Process and Reality* (New York: Free Press, 1978), 345.

[17]Charles Hartshorne, *Reality As Social Process* (Glencoe, Ill.: Free Press, 1953), 157.

[18]Ibid., 158.

[19]Ibid., 162.

[20]For an excellent summary and critique of process theology, or, as it is sometimes called, "panentheism," see Norman Geisler, *Encyclopedia of Christian Apologetics* (Grand Rapids: Baker, 1999), 576–80. For a more thorough critical analysis, see David Basinger, *Divine Power in Process Theism* (Albany, N.Y.: SUNY Press, 1988).

by historical events, and essentially atemporal, the former is dependent on the world, conditioned by events, and essentially temporal. On this view, God is neither sovereign over nor creator of the world, but he influences the world, even as the world influences him.[21]

### 3.1.2 Political Liberation Theology

The liberation theology movement of the 1970s and 1980s represented a further departure from classical Christian thought as some influential Latin scholars used theology to work toward radical political change. In this movement, the focus and purpose of theological scholarship shifted from understanding the nature of God to the practical function of freeing the oppressed, particularly Latin Americans dependent on an exploitative capitalistic economic system. Many liberationists argued that this requires the defeat of capitalism and justified the use of violence to free the oppressed. In some cases, political revolution was explicitly called for. The more extreme liberation theologians even espoused wedding Marxism to their Christian theology.[22]

A leading figure in this movement, Gustavo Gutiérrez, strove to make a biblical case for his theology but rejected the traditional approach to divine providence. Gutiérrez endorsed "a historical vision in which mankind assumes control of its own destiny."[23] He envisioned "the creation of a new man and a qualitatively different society."[24] This vision for a new society is, for liberationists, defined in terms of freedom. As fellow liberationist Leonardo Boff proclaims, "total liberation and its attendant freedom is the essence of God's kingdom."[25] For liberationists this freedom is an emancipation from oppression and other forms of suffering that are constituted by unjust relations between human beings.[26]

As in Latin liberation theology, black liberation theologians focus heavily on relief of suffering, specifically the oppression of African Americans by the white American majority. This emphasis often impacts their doctrine of God. James Cone is an excellent example: "Providence ... is not a statement about the future. It does not mean that all things will work out for the best for those who love God.

---

[21]Process theist John B. Cobb Jr. sums it up this way: "The character of the world is influenced by God, but it is not determined by him, and the world in its turn contributes novelty and richness to the divine experience" (*God and the World* [Philadelphia: Westminster, 1969], 80).

[22]See Jose Porfirio, *Marx and the Bible: A Critique of the Philosophy of Oppression*, trans. John Eagleson (Maryknoll, N.Y.: Orbis, 1974); idem, *Communism in the Bible* (Maryknoll, N.Y.: Orbis, 1982).

[23]Gustavo Gutiérrez, *A Theology of Liberation*, trans. Caridad Inda and John Eagleson (Maryknoll, N.Y.: Orbis, 1973), 25.

[24]Ibid., 36–37.

[25]Leonardo Boff, *Jesus Christ Liberator: A Critical Christology for Our Time* (Maryknoll, N.Y.: Orbis, 1978), 281.

[26]For critical discussions of liberation theology from an evangelical perspective, see Humberto Belli and Ronald Nash, *Beyond Liberation Theology* (Grand Rapids: Baker, 1992); Raymond C. Hundley, *Radical Liberation Theology: An Evangelical Response* (Wilmore, Kent: Bristol, 1987).

GOD UNDER FIRE

Providence is a statement about present reality—the reality of the liberation of the oppressed."[27] He adds: "It is within this context that divine omnipotence should be interpreted. Omnipotence does not refer to God's absolute power to accomplish what he wants."[28] Thus, as is typical with liberation theologians, Cone rejects the strong view of divine providence in two respects: first, by limiting its scope to liberation of the oppressed; second, by denying that God has absolute power to achieve his ends.

### 3.1.3 Feminist Theology

Like political liberationists, feminist theologians focus on the problem of human oppression. But rather than simply rejecting the orthodox doctrine of God, they see this perspective itself as the *source* of much oppression. In particular, they critique the tendency to conceive of God as dominating rather than working with the world, as is manifest in such traditional metaphors for God as "king," "ruler," and "sovereign." Sallie McFague writes that this "monarchical model is dangerous in our time: it encourages a sense of distance from the world . . . and it supports attitudes of either domination of the world or passivity toward it."[29] Feminists underscore the mutuality and reciprocity in God's relations with his creatures. Their metaphors of choice, therefore, include God as "mother," "lover," "healer," and "friend."

The advantage of such terminology is that it portrays the intimacy of God's relationship to us. As Anne Carr explains, "feminist images of God as mother, sister, and friend suggest that God's self-limitation is such that in a relational and incarnational framework God's power is *in humans* as embodied human agents. God's liberating action occurs through human power and action that imitates the persuasive, nonviolent power of God."[30] McFague explores the more radical alternative conception of the world as "God's body" or, less fancifully, as "the self-expression of God."[31] Such a model, she notes, "emphasizes God's willingness to suffer for and with the world, even to the point of personal risk."[32]

Feminist theologians reject orthodox theism in favor of a doctrine of God that stresses the cooperative work of God (concerned primarily with ending oppression), the liberating power of God, the suffering love of God, and the compassionate, comforting presence of God with his creatures. All of these themes are aspects of the broader feminist emphasis on the relationality of God, a vital concern they share with process theists and political liberationists.[33]

---

[27]James Cone, "God Is Black," in *Lift Every Voice: Constructing Christian Theologies from the Underside*, ed. Susan B. Thistlethwaite and Mary P. Engel (San Francisco: HarperCollins, 1990), 93.

[28]Ibid.

[29]Sallie McFague, *Models of God* (Philadelphia: Fortress, 1987), 69.

[30]Anne Carr, *Transforming Grace* (New York: Continuum, 1988), 152.

[31]McFague, *Models of God*, 72.

[32]Ibid.

[33]For an excellent critical assessment of feminist theology, see Mary A. Kassian, *The Feminist Gospel: The Movement to Unite Feminism with the Church* (Wheaton, Ill.: Crossway, 1992).

## 3.2 The Open Theist View of Divine Providence

None of the process theists, liberation theologians, or feminist thinkers mentioned in the preceding brief survey can be categorized as theologically orthodox.[34] That open theists often regard themselves as orthodox is what is distinctive about these most recent proponents of divine risk.[35] Yet to summarize the open view of providence is to see just how closely akin it is to some of the unorthodox theologies just discussed. Open theists maintain the following: (1) God is bound by time and does not entirely know the future; (2) God's power is limited by human freedom; (3) God fundamentally opposes human suffering; (4) God himself suffers, as his involvement with the world leads to divine surprise, disappointment, sorrow, anger, and other real passions.

### 3.2.1 Divine Omniscience and Omnipotence

Open theists emphasize God's relational nature.[36] Accordingly, they eschew the strong view of providence because they deem it to be irreconcilable with the belief that God maintains real personal relationships with human beings. John Sanders, for instance, prefers to call his view "relational theism," meaning by this "any model of the divine-human relationship that includes genuine give-and-take relations between God and humans such that there is receptivity and a degree of contingency in God. In give-and-take relationships God receives and does not merely give."[37]

For open theists, divine relationality implies that God cannot be omniscient as traditionally understood. They reject the notion that God has exhaustive knowledge of all events, past, present, and future. Instead, with William Hasker

---

[34]By "orthodox" I intend a commitment to the fundamental doctrinal positions affirmed by all mainstream theological traditions of the church and articulated in the classic Christian creeds, including the Apostles' Creed, the Nicene Creed, and the Creed of Chalcedon.

[35]I have two terminological disclaimers to make here. First, the general tag "open theism" is not a precise label, nor are some other terms that I have used above, such as "process theology," "liberation theology," and "feminist theology." The diversity of opinion among scholars typically given these labels makes neat and uncontroversial grouping impossible. Nevertheless, there is enough uniformity of opinion to justify use of these terms to gather scholars together under single names for ease in discussion. Second, many open theists prefer the appellations "relational theism" or "free-will theism" for their view. I have decided against usage of these designations only because such terminology might suggest that those of a classical persuasion do not affirm the relationality of God or the free will of humans—which, on the contrary, most in fact do.

[36]Vincent Brummer's theological "model of love" has been very influential among some of the open theists and has helped to stimulate this emphasis on God's relational nature. See Vincent Brummer, *The Model of Love: A Study in Philosophical Theology* (New York: Cambridge Univ. Press, 1993); idem, *Speaking of a Personal God: An Essay in Philosophical Theology* (New York: Cambridge Univ. Press, 1992).

[37]John Sanders, *The God Who Risks: A Theology of Providence* (Downers Grove, Ill.: InterVarsity Press, 1998), 12. Like the process theists, open theists defend a dipolar theism, at least to the extent that God's nature may be conceived as both "actual" and "potential." God is not only absolute, necessary, eternal, and changeless, but *also* relative, contingent, temporal, and changing, insofar as he relates and responds to his creation. See Richard Rice's assertion of this essential common ground between process theism and open theism in *God's Foreknowledge and Man's Free Will* (Minneapolis: Bethany, 1980), 33.

they affirm that "God knows everything about the future which it is logically possible for him to know."[38] Future free human actions are not knowable in advance, so they cannot be included among the things God knows. Therefore, open theists affirm divine "present knowledge" whereby, as David Basinger puts it, "God's infallible knowledge extends over everything that is (or has been) actual and that which follows deterministically from it," excluding any future states of affairs that involve free human choices.[39]

Open theism also modifies the traditional understanding of divine omnipotence. God's power is restricted by the freedom of human beings, and the fulfillment of his plans for history is somewhat dependent on the choices we make. Such assurances do not guarantee that God will not fail in some of his projects. On the contrary, to the open theists, biblical history shows that God is sometimes disappointed and frustrated.[40]

Sanders sums up God's efforts to accomplish his goals: "God persuades, commands, gives comfort and sometimes brings judgment in order to get humans to sign on to his project. God genuinely wrestles with his human creatures. Sometimes God gets everything he wants, and sometimes he does not."[41] This is the essence of the "risk model" of providence endorsed by open theists. The outcome of some events is neither controlled nor known in advance by God. He awaits eagerly to see what will happen next, just as we do. And "sometimes God's plans do not bring about the desired result and must be judged a failure."[42]

### 3.2.2 Divine Temporality and the Problem of Evil

An implication of this notion of divine risk is that God is an essentially temporal being, dwelling entirely inside time with his creatures. The open theists base their case, in part, on biblical descriptions of divine action in the world. William Hasker asks: "If God is truly timeless, so that temporal determinations of 'before' and 'after' do not apply to him, then how can God *act* in time, as the Scriptures say that he does?"[43] Although insisting that God is time-bound, the open theists do not necessarily oppose usage of the term "eternal" to describe him. They simply understand it to mean that he always has and always will exist.[44]

---

[38]William Hasker, *God, Time, and Knowledge* (Ithaca, N.Y.: Cornell Univ. Press, 1989), 187.

[39]David Basinger, "Can an Evangelical Christian Justifiably Deny God's Exhaustive Knowledge of the Future?" *Christian Scholar's Review* 25.2 (1995): 134. Richard Swinburne defends a similarly temporally restricted account of divine omniscience in *The Coherence of Theism* (Oxford: Oxford Univ. Press, 1993), 167–83.

[40]See Richard Rice, "Biblical Support for a New Perspective" in *The Openness of God: A Biblical Challenge to the Traditional Understanding of God*, Clark H. Pinnock et al. (Downers Grove, Ill.: InterVarsity Press, 1994), 56.

[41]Sanders, *The God Who Risks*, 60.

[42]Ibid., 88.

[43]William Hasker, "A Philosophical Perspective," in *The Openness of God*, 128.

[44]See, e.g., Clark Pinnock's discussion of God's eternity in "Systematic Theology" in *The Openness of God*, 119–21. For a more philosophically rigorous defense of the temporality of God, see Nicholas Wolterstorff, "God Everlasting," in *God and the Good*, ed. Clifton Orlebeke and Lewis Smedes (Grand Rapids: Eerdmans, 1975), 181–203.

There is a further motive for the open theists' rejection of divine atemporalism. As Richard Rice observes, "there seems . . . to be no way to avoid making God responsible for evil if we accept the usual view of God's relation to time."[45] If God is outside time, then he knows the future as well as the past. This implies that before the creation of the world God knew all the evil that would occur and yet still permitted it. Thus, open theists affirm instead that God is within time and did not know in advance that human beings would sin.

The open theists hold that God is absolutely opposed not only to moral evil but to human suffering of all kinds. He works to relieve pain and suffering in all its forms, whether caused by human beings or not. We who are involved in the work of God contribute to that redemptive project. Because the people he loves often suffer terribly, God himself suffers, say the open theists. As Pinnock explains, "the suffering or pathos of God is a strong biblical theme. . . . God suffers when there is a broken relationship between humanity and himself. . . . God is not cool and collected but is deeply involved and can be wounded."[46] Herein lies another key element of "risk" in God's creation of a world of free beings. In creating this world God risked potential harm to his people and to himself.

To sum up the open theists' view of providence, they affirm divine sovereignty only in a weak sense. God created human beings free and allowed history to proceed on its own without controlling every detail. He neither perfectly knows nor directly controls all of history. Providence involves divine risk, which, as Basinger points out, may be understood in at least two senses: "God is a risk-taker in the sense that he commits himself to a course of action without full knowledge of the outcome; and God is a risk-taker in the sense that he adopts certain overall strategies—for example, the granting of significant freedom—which create the potential for the occurrence of events that he wishes would not occur."[47]

### 3.2.3 Philosophical and Theological Motivations for Open Theism

Recalling the four theses of the strong view of providence outlined earlier, it is clear that open theism denies all of them: (1) exhaustive divine foreknowledge, (2) complete divine control of the world, (3) divine purpose in all the details of human history, and (4) complete divine sovereignty over evil. The open theists do not purely and simply inherit their convictions from the alternative theological models preceding them. There are also philosophical and theological concerns that make the open view of God more palatable to some scholars. From the foregoing discussion it should be clear that two such concerns driving the open theist perspective are the issue of human freedom and moral responsibility and the problem of reconciling God's goodness with human suffering and immorality. We will return to these issues to see if they warrant the open theists' perspective. But before doing so, let us review the biblical evidence for this model.

---

[45]Rice, *God's Foreknowledge and Man's Free Will*, 51.

[46]Pinnock, "Systematic Theology," 118.

[47]David Basinger, *The Case for Free-Will Theism* (Downers Grove, Ill.: InterVarsity Press, 1996), 48.

## 3.3 Open Theist Biblical Arguments

Unlike process and liberation theologians, the open theists are especially concerned to make a strong scriptural case for their perspective. They offer the following observations.

(1) *Conditional statements.* Sometimes God's instructions to his people in the Old Testament are framed in the form of "if-then" statements, such as in Nehemiah 1:8–9, where the Lord says to the Israelites, "If you are unfaithful, I will scatter you among the nations, but if you return to me and obey my commands, then even if your exiled people are at the farthest horizon, I will gather them from there and bring them to the place I have chosen as a dwelling place for my Name" (see also Ex. 4:8–9; Lev. 26). Such language suggests an uncertainty as to how the Israelites will behave; that is, the future is open, and God himself is not sure about the outcome. God also speaks about the future with such terms as "perhaps" and "maybe" (Jer 26:3; Ezek. 12:3). These too are not expressions one would expect from a God who knows the future exhaustively.

(2) *Divine regretting and relenting.* The Scriptures sometimes speak of God as grieving over a turn of events and regretting some of his own actions, such as his creation of human beings (Gen. 6:6) and his making Saul king (1 Sam. 15:11). Divine regrets suggest that history was not determined in advance or perfectly foreknown. Still other passages indicate that God relents from plans he has made, such as his apparent intention to destroy the Israelites because of their idolatry. Moses pleaded with God to have mercy; "then the LORD relented and did not bring on his people the disaster he had threatened" (Ex. 32:14; see also Isa. 38:1–5; Jer. 18:7–8; Joel 2:13; Amos 7:1–6; Jonah 3:10). These narratives seem to describe a God who is genuinely responsive to human choices and who, therefore, is essentially temporal.

(3) *Petitionary prayer.* The Bible enjoins us to make requests of God: "Ask and it will be given to you; seek and you will find; knock and the door will be opened to you. For everyone who asks receives; he who seeks finds; and to him who knocks, the door will be opened" (Matt. 7:7–8). James writes, "You do not have, because you do not ask God" (James 4:2).[48] If such prayers are to be meaningful and effective, there must be a real possibility of a literal divine response. Therefore, in the words of Pinnock, "prayer proves that the future is open and not closed. It shows that future events are not predetermined and fixed."[49]

(4) *Divine ignorance and error.* Biblical narrative depicts God as learning new truths on various occasions, such as when he says to Abraham, "Now I know that you fear God, because you have not withheld from me your son, your only son" (Gen. 22:12). According to some open theists, God occasionally makes mistakes.[50]

---

[48]See also Phil. 4:6.

[49]Clark H. Pinnock, "God Limits His Knowledge" in *Predestination and Free Will: Four Views of Divine Sovereignty and Human Freedom*, ed. David Basinger et al. (Downers Grove, Ill.: InterVarsity Perss, 1986), 152.

[50]See, e.g., John Sanders, *The God Who Risks*, 129–37, 205–6. Sanders supplements this argument with the claim that some biblical prophecies are not fulfilled.

For example, when commenting on the wanton behavior of his people, God says, "I thought that after she had done all this she would return to me but she did not" (Jer. 3:7; see also 32:35). These passages suggest that even God is subject to false beliefs about the future. If so, then indeed the future is not predetermined, and the doctrine of divine omniscience does need reworking along the lines suggested by the open theists.

## 4. An Assessment of the Risk Model of Providence

Having reviewed several versions of the risk model of divine providence, we must now assess this approach both theologically and philosophically. Is the doctrine of divine risk an advance from the traditional strong view of providence in either respect? In what follows, I argue that this view has some biblical support but not nearly so much as does the strong view of providence. Philosophically, a revision of the doctrine of God is unnecessary and could have been avoided with some careful conceptual work. In this section I will present biblical evidence for strong divine providence and respond to the four major arguments used by open theists. In the next section I will identify the philosophical oversights made by the open theists.[51]

### 4.1 Biblical Evidence for the Strong View of Providence

Earlier we saw how some of the greatest thinkers in the history of Christian theology—for example, Augustine, Aquinas, Luther, Calvin, and Edwards— affirm the strong view of providence. Now let us see *why* there is such agreement on this issue among these formidable theological minds. The Scriptures do teach that God is sovereign in the strong sense. According to the biblical account, God controls the world at every level:

(1) *God is sovereign over the entire cosmos.* God's cosmic sovereignty consists, first, in the fact that he created the universe, which is continually sustained by him. As Paul writes in Colossians 1:16–17, "by him all things were created. . . . He is before all things, and in him all things hold together" (cf. also Job 38:41; Rev. 4:11). Second, God's cosmic sovereignty consists in his carrying out a plan for the cosmos that is subject to no one's will but his own. Note what God says in Isaiah 46:10: "I make known the end from the beginning, from ancient times, what is still to come. I say: My purpose will stand, and I will do all that I please." Similarly, the psalmist writes in Psalm 135:6: "The LORD does whatever pleases him, in the heavens and on the earth, in the seas and all their depths."

(2) *God is sovereign over human history and leaders of nations.* God directs the courses of whole nations (see Josh. 24; Jer. 18:6; Ezek. 26:1–6; Dan. 5:18–21). He governs those who rule nations (see Prov. 21:1). The case of Pharaoh is a vivid example. In the face of numerous plagues on his people, he did not let Moses' people go. Rather, as the writer of Exodus states on several occasions, God hard-

---

[51]Although I will specifically address the doctrines of open theism, most of my criticisms here readily apply to the alternative theologies previously reviewed.

ened Pharaoh's heart (Ex. 4:21; 9:12; 10:20; 11:10). In 9:16, God explains to Pharaoh, "I have raised you up for this very purpose, that I might show you my power and that my name might be proclaimed in all the earth."

(3) *God is sovereign over particular human choices and "chance" events.* While the Scriptures emphasize human moral responsibility and the importance of wise counsel and decision-making, it is also clear that God governs all aspects of human decision-making. Proverbs 16:9 says, "In his heart a man plans his course, but the LORD determines his steps." Even seemingly random events are divinely controlled: "The lot is cast into the lap, but its every decision is from the LORD" (16:33). Indeed, was not divine sovereignty over chance events assumed by the disciples when they drew lots to choose Judas's replacement (Acts 1:24–26)?

(4) *God is sovereign over the church and individual Christians' lives.* The Scriptures speak especially clearly to God's meticulous care for his people, as the psalmist declares: "All the days ordained for me were written in your book before one of them came to be" (Ps. 139:16).

In the New Testament Paul repeatedly applies this strong notion of providence to individual salvation, saying that God "chose us in [Christ] before the creation of the world to be holy and blameless in his sight. In love he predestined us to be adopted as his sons through Jesus Christ, in accordance with his pleasure and will" (Eph. 1:4–5). A few verses later he asserts that in Christ "we were also chosen, having been predestined according to the plan of him who works out everything in conformity with the purpose of his will" (1:11).[52] Note that this passage not only affirms strong providence but also offers a three-tiered causal explanation of divine election, moving backward from specific choice to electing decree to divine purpose: God *chooses*, whom he *predestines*, according to the *purpose of his will.*

A strong view of divine providence is also assumed in the narrative of Acts. In the believers' prayer in chapter 4, Peter and John acknowledge how the "Sovereign Lord" works out his plan through the free choices of human beings, including even the evil plotting of Herod and Pilate, who "did what [God's] power and will had decided beforehand should happen" (Acts 4:24–28). And in chapter 13 Luke reports that among the Gentiles who heard the gospel message at Antioch, "all who were appointed for eternal life believed" (13:48). Such language is inexplicable on the view that God takes risks.

(5) *God is sovereign over suffering and moral evil.* Traditionally, Christians have taken great solace in the biblical teaching that God's sovereignty is not limited, even by suffering and immorality. However counterintuitive this might appear to some, this fact is repeatedly underscored in the Scriptures. For example, in Exodus 4:11 God assures Moses that not only his speech impediment but all such physical handicaps are his doing. Through Isaiah he says, "I am the LORD and there is no other. I form the light and create darkness, I bring prosperity and create disaster;

---

[52]Also, God's foreknowledge and predestination include the fates of unbelievers as well, as passages such as Rom. 9:14–24; Rev. 13:8; 17:8 reveal.

I, the LORD, do all these things" (Isa. 45:6–7).[53] The author of Lamentations declares, "Though [the Lord] brings grief, he will show compassion, so great is his unfailing love. For he does not willingly bring affliction or grief to the children of men" (Lam. 3:32–33).[54] This is an especially significant passage, as it affirms both the active hand of God in human affliction *and* divine regret about it. This directly confutes those open theists who assume the two are incompatible.

The biblical writers do not flinch in subsuming even the evil actions of sinful human beings under the sovereign influence of God. As was noted above, Pharaoh's evil resistance follows upon the Lord's hardening of his heart. Similarly, Saul's murderous pursuit of David was prompted by "an evil spirit from the LORD" (1 Sam. 19:9). All of the sufferings of Job are attributed, in the end, to God himself (Job 42:11), showing that Satan is but a pawn on the world's stage.[55] Finally, the scourging, crucifixion, and death of Jesus, as well as his resurrection, were all in God's plan. On the day of Pentecost Peter says to his fellow Jews that Jesus "was handed over to you by God's set purpose and foreknowledge; and you, with the help of wicked men, put him to death by nailing him to the cross" (Acts 2:23).[56]

## 4.2 Predictive Prophecy and Divine Sovereignty

God's sovereignty over all aspects of creation is further established by predictive prophecy in the Bible. In hundreds of instances God foretells events, often in extraordinary detail, long before they occur. Scores of prophecies are made and fulfilled within the Old Testament period. Over two hundred Old Testament messianic prophecies are fulfilled by Jesus Christ. Others are made and fulfilled within the New Testament, such as Jesus' prediction of Peter's threefold denial. This is powerful evidence that either God has predetermined history or, at least, he has exhaustive knowledge of the future.

Open theists deny this implication. Their standard response to this argument is to regard all unconditional predictive prophecies as "either the announcement ahead of time of that which God intends to ensure will occur ... or predictions based on God's exhaustive knowledge of the past and present."[57] The former explanation admits divine *determination* of the foretold events, which is essentially

---

[53]See also Lam. 3:38 and Amos 3:6.

[54]Adding to the force of these biblical passages are the testimonies of some prominent persons of faith in the Old Testament, who frankly affirm God's sovereignty, including Hannah's prayer (1 Sam. 2:6–7), the song of Moses (Deut. 32:39), and Job's reflections on his own agony (Job 2:10).

[55]See also 1 Sam. 2:25.

[56]Divine governance over all things is communicated in a variety of ways in the Scriptures, as we have seen. But perhaps the most descriptive metaphor is that of the potter and the clay. It is an image used by the Old Testament prophets (Isa. 29:16; Jer. 18:6) and by Paul in the New Testament (Rom. 9:20–21).

[57]Basinger, "Can an Evangelical Christian Justifiably Deny God's Exhaustive Knowledge of the Future?" 141. See also Hasker, *God, Time, and Knowledge*, 194–96; Rice, *God's Foreknowledge and Man's Free Will*, 77–79; Pinnock, "God Limits His Knowledge," 157–58. The same account of predictive prophecy is given by each of these scholars.

the classical position. In order to preserve human freedom as they understand it, then, open theists must rely on the latter explanation of unconditional predictive prophecies. William Hasker describes such prophecies as "predictions based on foresight drawn from existing trends and tendencies."[58] Just as we humans make forecasts based on our knowledge of the past and present, God makes his forecasts but can "do it much better" than we can.

The obvious problem with this approach is that it implies God's predictive prophecies are fallible. While he is vastly more reliable in his predictions, on the open theist view, God still could be mistaken in some of his predictions. This conclusion is clearly inconsistent with the biblical portrait of God as absolutely trustworthy.

Moreover, this view is not even philosophically plausible, given the open theists' libertarian assumptions about human freedom. If God cannot certainly know in advance any particular free choice a person makes, then even perfect knowledge of the past and present would not enable him to predict reliably events in the distant future. Even a partially accurate prediction about an event a century from now presupposes the ability to accurately predict millions of other free choices (which themselves arise from millions of other preceding free choices). These include decisions leading to human procreation, a single mistake about which would ramify so significantly throughout a few generations—let alone thousands of years—that reliable long-term prediction would be impossible. It seems, therefore, that exhaustive divine foreknowledge is the only reasonable explanation of predictive prophecy about the distant future, particularly as regards the sorts of detailed events foretold in the Old Testament.

## 4.3 Divine Atemporalism and Sempiternalism

The belief that God is bound by time, sometimes called "sempiternalism," is a crucial tenet of the divine-risk model and must be critiqued specifically. For if God is not essentially temporal, then he cannot literally "respond" to historical events, as defenders of this view claim. There are several reasons for rejecting sempiternalism. First, as Paul Helm has argued, God is not essentially a spatial being, so he cannot be essentially temporal.[59] The arguments that prove God to be spaceless are from a logical standpoint strictly parallel to arguments that prove him timeless. Conversely, arguments for sempiternalism are analogous to arguments that God is essentially spatial. Regarding the question of God's relation to time and space, then, there is logical parity. Either God is spaceless and timeless, or he is essentially spatial and temporal. Thus, proponents of divine risk must choose between admitting divine atemporalism or admitting that God is an essentially spatial being. Since the latter is not a plausible option, they must surrender their sempiternalism.

Second, the Bible's descriptions of God's acting in time and in space should be interpreted analogously. Spatial metaphors are used in the Bible to describe

---

[58]Hasker, *God, Time, and Knowledge*, 194.
[59]Paul Helm, "God and Spacelessness," *Philosophy* 55 (1980): 211–21.

God, and certain of his activities take place in space. The "hands," "arm," "mouth," "feet," and "nostrils" of God are referred to, as are his actions in space, such as dwelling in temples and cities and performing miraculous acts of parting seas, healing bodies, and impregnating a virgin. But neither spatial metaphors nor accounts of God's spatial activities are taken to imply that God is bound by space. The former aim to communicate something about God's nature, and the latter show that he can and does enter into space and perform actions. So why suppose that analogous temporal descriptions of God and divine actions in time are sufficient to show that he is essentially temporal?[60] Rather, temporal descriptions of God should be interpreted as showing that he enters and acts in time, not that he is bound by it.[61]

## 4.4 Replies to the Open Theists' Arguments

Having set forth the positive biblical case for the strong view of providence, we are now in a position to evaluate the key biblical arguments employed by the open theists.

### 4.4.1 Conditional Statements

Let us consider, first, the "if-then" conditional statements and promises used by God. Note, for example, 2 Chronicles 7:14, where the Lord says: "If my people, who are called by my name, will humble themselves and pray and seek my face and turn from their wicked ways, then will I hear from heaven and will forgive their sin and will heal their land." Do such expressions really imply that the future is undetermined or even unknown by him? Not at all. Rather, they serve some valuable functions pertaining to moral theology.

First, conditional statements are means of instructing people about God's moral will and informing them as to the consequences of their actions, depending on what course of action they take. In turn, such conditionals serve to prompt human action of some kind, such as repentance when wrath is threatened. Second, "if-then" promises express general truths about the nature of God's dealings with us, whether or not the conditional antecedent "if" is ever fulfilled. For example, even if no one trusts and obeys God, it remains true that God *would* bless those who trust and obey him. In this sense, conditional statements are timelessly true, applying to God's relations to all people at all times.

In any case, it must be borne in mind that if God is an essentially atemporal being who enters into time to communicate with essentially temporal creatures, then we should expect him to use language that is appropriately condescending. "If-then" conditionals and temporally tensed language (e.g., "now," "then," "before," "after," "yesterday," "tomorrow," etc.) serve as vehicles to assist our understanding and help us relate to God. Thus, it is no surprise that such expres-

---

[60]On this point see Hugh J. McCann, "God Beyond Time," in *Philosophy of Religion*, 2d ed. (Belmont, Calif.: Wadsworth, 1994), 232.

[61]For an extended treatment of this issue, see Paul Helm's essay in this volume (ch. 5).

sions are used in biblical narrative. How else would a timelessly eternal being communicate with temporal creatures to whom the future is largely unknown?

### 4.4.2 Divine Relenting and Regretting

A similar approach may be taken for cases of divine relenting and regretting. That such passages are not to be interpreted as literal descriptions of the mind of God follows from the fact that God is not essentially temporal. Moreover, some biblical passages caution us against taking this interpretation, such as 1 Samuel 15:29: "The Glory of Israel does not lie or change his mind; for he is not a man, that he should change his mind." This is not to say that those passages describing God as relenting are misleading or false, for they do communicate something important, namely, that the course of God's actions in history *do* change, relative to our temporal experience of his work.

Furthermore, as in the case of conditional statements, the point of references to divine relenting is often moral. God makes threats and warns of coming wrath to prompt righteous behavior. Descriptions of divine relenting are simply a powerful way of communicating the usefulness of repentance to avoid that wrath which, without repentance, *would* have been visited on those God warns. Similarly, references to divine regret should be interpreted as describing God's disapproval of some human behavior, not as an indication that God literally wishes he had not performed some action.

### 4.4.3 Petitionary Prayer

What of the open theists' appeal to petitionary prayer as evidence for their perspective? What are we to make of the biblical injunction to make requests of God? Here the relationality of God is especially evident, and the open theists are correct in pointing this out and emphasizing it. The believer personally communes with God through prayer, and God is genuinely responsive. However, this does not imply that he lacks exhaustive foreknowledge, much less that God takes risks.

In what sense, then, do our prayers really make a difference? There are two points worth noting in response. First, God has ordained prayer as a secondary cause for the accomplishment of his will. Our petitions really do impact the world.[62] But God does not *need* our prayers to realize his plans in history and in human lives. To believe so would undermine his omnipotence. Nor is he ignorant of our needs such that he must be made aware of them before he can properly assist us. To believe so would undercut his omniscience. Second, prayer is not so much for God's sake but for ours, and the effect it has on the believer should not be underestimated.[63] To pray is to exercise faith, to remind oneself of one's

---

[62]As Aquinas notes, "Divine providence disposes not only what effects shall take place, but also from what causes and in what order these effects shall proceed. Now among other causes human acts are the causes of certain effects." And, of course, prayer is one such act. So, says Aquinas, "we pray, not that we may change the Divine disposition, but that we may impetrate that which God has disposed to be fulfilled by our prayers"; *Summa Theologiae*, 2–2.Q83.A2 (2:1539).

[63]On this point see Calvin, *Institutes of the Christian Religion*, 2.20.3 (1:851–53).

dependence on God, to grow in the virtue of humility, and to be directly comforted by God's Spirit in the process of prayer.[64]

### 4.4.4 Divine Ignorance and Error

The argument from divine ignorance and error is less frequently made by open theists, but it deserves to be addressed nonetheless, for it constitutes a direct attack on the doctrine of divine omniscience. As with the previous open theist arguments, this one can be dismissed once it is shown that God is not bound by time. Since God dwells outside of time, he cannot "come to know" anything. Rather, he knows all things from a timelessly eternal standpoint, the future as well as the past. Therefore, narratives in which God is depicted as apparently learning something new or being mistaken in his beliefs must be taken as nonliteral. They are included in the biblical accounts presumably to underscore God's real interaction with his people within time.

Other functions are served by such expressions as well. For example, when God asks Cain, "Where is your brother Abel?" (Gen. 4:9), it is for the purpose of confronting him with his sin rather than to express actual divine ignorance. And when he says to Abraham, "Now I know that you fear God" (Gen. 22:12), this communicates to Abraham (and the reader) that he has proven his faith in action. The point of the story concerns the way Abraham's behavior evidences his commitment to God, not to suggest that God has learned something new.

My responses to each of the open theists' arguments above interpret biblical data about God's relational nature in light of his sovereignty rather than vice versa.[65] But, one may ask, why reinterpret these expressions to make them fit with

---

[64]This perspective on petitionary prayer is also recommended by some philosophical arguments that aim to show that the belief that prayer may actually change the mind of God leads to absurdities. One argument, proposed by Eleonore Stump, goes as follows. It is God's will to bring about the best possible world, and every petitionary prayer enjoins God to perform some action that will change the world for better or worse overall. Now if taking such action will make the world worse overall, then obviously God will decline the request. But if it will make the world better overall, then God would have performed the action anyway, so the request was unnecessary. Therefore, petitionary prayer really does not change God's mind or alter his actions. See Eleonore Stump, "Petitionary Prayer," *American Philosophical Quarterly* 16.2 (1979): 81–91.

[65]It is useful here to distinguish between biblical teaching on the phenomenology and the metaphysics of the divine nature. The former regards the way God appears and relates to us, while the latter has to do with the way God actually works in the world and in our lives. Both are real and important aspects of the scriptural teaching about God, and we must affirm both fully without allowing our focus on the one to blind us to the other. The open theists have made this mistake, just as hyper-Calvinists have made the opposite mistake. The open theists' error is an understandable one, however, as there is much scriptural reflection on God that is done from a phenomenological standpoint. The open theists have mined these passages extensively and discussed them at length. Where they have gone wrong, however, is in their use of biblical phenomenological data as evidence for metaphysical claims about God. They have conflated the Bible's phenomenological and metaphysical reflection on God, to the peril of a complete scriptural portrait of God.

the biblical teaching about sovereignty rather than reinterpret God's sovereignty to fit these expressions? My answer relies on a basic hermeneutical guideline. When doing systematic theology, doctrine is more reliably built on didactic passages (those whose primary purpose is to instruct doctrinally) than on historical narrative. The didactic biblical passages heavily favor the strong view of providence, while the risk model rests predominantly on historical narrative. This is not to say that biblical narrative does not contain considerable evidence for strong providence, for it does, particularly in the area of predictive prophecy.

## 5. Further Flaws and a Few Benefits of the Risk Model

In spite of the serious problems with the risk model of providence, there are some valuable insights it has to offer. Orthodox Christians must admit that the concern to preserve and even heighten our recognition of God's relational nature is laudable. The biblical evidence for a strong view of providence ought not to blind us to this truth in their view. God is genuinely relational, personally engaged with human beings both individually and corporately. He is a caring, loving God, who is vitally concerned with every detail of his children's lives. It is crucial that all Christians affirm these essential truths.

The point of this critique of the risk model is that it is not a complete picture of the God of the Bible. In their zeal to emphasize God's relational nature, proponents of divine risk have abandoned other fundamental divine attributes. Let us look more closely at the philosophical and theological concerns motivating their disavowal of these elements of the doctrine of God. As we do so, it will become clear that while the risk model of providence is well-motivated, it is philosophically unnecessary.

### 5.1 Why the Departure from Classical Christian Theism Is Unnecessary

Earlier we noted the fundamental philosophical motivations for these departures from classical theism. They are: (1) the aim to preserve human freedom and moral responsibility in a world governed by God, and (2) the concern to reconcile God's goodness with human suffering and immorality. These are perhaps the two most challenging philosophical puzzles for any theist. So the efforts of open theists to resolve these tensions are admirable in principle. Unfortunately, as we have seen, the model they propose is unbiblical. It would be some consolation, however, if no adequate approaches to these problems were previously available to Christians. But there *are* other ways of reconciling the strong view of providence with human freedom and the presence of evil in the world. Helpful strategies for dealing with these problems already exist, which are philosophically coherent but do not compromise the biblical portrait of God.[66]

(1) Regarding the issue of human freedom and divine sovereignty, two different models have traditionally been used to reconcile the tension between doctrines:

---

[66]Due to spatial constraints, my remarks here will be merely schematic. But for an in-depth treatment of the problem of evil, see Doug Geivett's essay in this volume (ch. 7).

libertarianism and compatibilism. Numerous fruitful versions of each model have been articulated by proponents of strong providence. The open theists have not adequately considered, much less demonstrably falsified, these models. My own view is a version of compatibilism, and I have yet to see a compelling philosophical critique of this perspective.[67] Moreover, since the Bible implicitly affirms both human responsibility *and*, as we have seen, strong divine providence, this shows that the two must be compatible, even if the combination of the two doctrines is not fully comprehensible to us. So, arguably, even in the absence of a satisfactory model explaining human freedom and divine sovereignty, the Christian may justifiably affirm the two.[68]

(2) As with the issue of human freedom, there are various approaches to the problem of evil that do not require a rejection of the orthodox doctrine of God, including the free-will defense,[69] the "soul-making" theodicy,[70] the aesthetic theodicy,[71] and the view that suffering is God's will.[72] More to the point, however,

---

[67]Among defenses of the libertarian perspective, the best I have seen are to be found in William James, "The Dilemma of Determinism," in *The Will to Believe* (New York: Dover, 1956); C. A. Campbell, *In Defense of Free Will* (London: Allen & Unwin, 1967); Richard Taylor, *Metaphysics*, 2d ed. (Englewood Cliffs, N.J.: Prentice Hall, 1974). Although admirable efforts, each fails to adequately account for two crucial facts. First, there must be a sufficient condition for every choice a person makes (a fact unexplained by the common libertarian insistence that the will is "self-caused"). Second, ordinary, common-sense usage of the term *freedom* actually supports the compatibilist position. The former point is nowhere more rigorously defended than in Jonathan Edwards, *Freedom of the Will*. The latter point is clearly demonstrated by W. T. Stace in his classic discussion of the topic in *Religion and the Modern Mind* (Westport, Conn.: Greenwood, 1980).

[68]Some scholars, such as J. I. Packer and D. A. Carson, advocate seeing the issue as essentially mysterious, defying rational comprehension. See J. I. Packer, *Evangelism and the Sovereignty of God* (Leicester: Inter-Varsity Press, 1961); D. A. Carson, *Divine Sovereignty and Human Responsibility* (Atlanta: John Knox, 1981). See also Eric Johnson's discussion of such mysteries in ch. 3 of this volume.

[69]Alvin Plantinga's version of the free-will defense is among the most rigorous. See his *God, Freedom, and Evil* (Grand Rapids: Eerdmans, 1974).

[70]See John Hick, *Evil and the God of Love* (London: Macmillan, 1966); Richard Swinburne, "The Problem of Evil," in *Reason and Responsibility: Readings in Some Basic Problems of Philosophy*, ed. Joel Feinberg, 8th ed. (Belmont, Calif.: Wadsworth, 1993).

[71]An excellent recent version of this perspective has been elaborated in Marilyn McCord Adams, "Aesthetic Goodness As a Solution to the Problem of Evil," in *God, Truth and Reality: Essays in Honour of John Hick*, ed. Arvind Sharma (New York: St. Martin's, 1993).

[72]John T. Edelman ably defends this thesis, demonstrating that major objections to the notion that God wills suffering tend to beg the question. Furthermore, he shows the value of suffering for imparting wisdom. See his "Suffering and the Will of God," *Faith and Philosophy* 10.3 (1993): 380–88. While this notion is shocking to some, it ought not to be, given that the divine purposefulness of suffering is a plain biblical teaching. James writes, "Consider it pure joy, my brothers, whenever you face trials of many kinds, because you know that the testing of your faith develops perseverance. Perseverance must finish its work so that you may be mature and complete, not lacking anything" (James 1:2–4). Peter says that trials "come so that your faith—of greater worth than gold, which perishes even though refined by fire—may be proved genuine and may result in praise, glory and honor when Jesus Christ is revealed" (1 Peter 1:7). Such language indicates that suffering is not only consistent with God's will but intended by him to accomplish his most significant work in his children.

is the ironic fact that a weak view of providence does not itself shield God against culpability for evil (if he is culpable on the strong view). How is God any less guilty for allowing evil that he was able to prevent than he would be for ordaining such evil directly? In other words, since on the risk model God is at least the indirect cause of evil, how does the insertion of an intermediate causal step (human beings and their free wills) really exonerate God?[73]

## 5.2 Practical Problems with Divine-Risk Theism

The divine-risk theists maintain that their perspective provides practical benefits, such as making better sense of petitionary prayer from a psychological standpoint. But the negative practical fallout of their model is severe. For one thing, they cannot account for ultimate meaning in all human suffering. Since God does not control all things, there must be evil "that serves no higher end"[74] and "involves permanent loss."[75] This is a profoundly discouraging teaching and at odds with the Christians belief "that in all things God works for the good of those who love him" (Rom. 8:28).

Moreover, divine-risk theists cannot reasonably thank God for all the good things we receive from other people. If human wills possess libertarian freedom and God neither predestines nor foreknows all their good deeds, then he is not properly praised for them. In this sense the risk model dilutes the glory due to God and violates the spirit of the Scriptures, such as when James says that "every good and perfect gift is from above, coming down from the Father of the heavenly lights" (James 1:17). Surely James does not mean this in the trivial sense that everything comes from God merely in the sense that he is Creator. He must mean it in the more intimate (and compatibilist) sense that God works through human free will.

## 5.3 Lessons to Be Learned From Open Theism

What lessons may traditional theists learn from the open theist perspective? First, we need to take the problem of evil more seriously. We must further develop creative theodicies that are philosophically rigorous, theologically informed, and personally sensitive. Second, we need to do more work on our models of human freedom. Compatibilists and libertarians alike must continue to demonstrate the

---

[73]This leads to a further problem of coherence plaguing this view. If God can, as the open theists say, "predict what individuals will freely decide to do in the future in many cases" (Basinger, "Can an Evangelical Christian Justifiably Deny God's Exhaustive Knowledge of the Future?" 134) or even "anticipate perfectly the course of creaturely events" (Rice, *God's Foreknowledge and Man's Free Will*, 65), then why was God unable to predict that human beings would sin and that evil would enter the world? Here we discover a basic inconsistency in the open theists' model. They affirm that God has enough foresight to make reliable predictive prophecies, but they deny that God had the foresight to reliably anticipate the human fall into sin.

[74]Gregory A. Boyd, *God at War: The Bible and Spiritual Conflict* (Downers Grove, Ill.: InterVarsity Press, 1997), 20.

[75]Rice, *God's Foreknowledge and Man's Free Will*, 73.

consistency of freedom and divine sovereignty according to their models, but with a view to addressing some of the open theists' concerns more directly.

From a theological standpoint, orthodox theists must affirm the relationality of God. He genuinely loves and cares for his creation, and he is personally involved with our lives. He really hears and answers our prayers. He really does commune with us in our fellowship. He really is compassionate with us in our suffering. Defenders of the risk model of providence are correct in reemphasizing this crucial aspect of the biblical portrait of God, too often minimized within classical Christian theology.

Finally, we must reevaluate the doctrine of divine impassibility. Although this view might be strictly correct from the standpoint of cold logic, it is misleading. Perhaps instead of asserting that God is impassible, we should parallel our position to the doctrine of omnipresence, where although God is seen as nonspatial, his presence at every space is nonetheless affirmed. In this case, we would affirm that God is *omnipathic*. That is, God somehow is experientially acquainted with all creaturely feelings and passions without being limited by those feelings nor reduced to having any single overriding passion.

## 6. Conclusion

This chapter has posed and answered the question "Does God take risks?" We have seen that, from a biblical standpoint, this question must be answered in the negative. Einstein was right: God does not play dice. The risk model of providence is a theological innovation designed to solve some real philosophical problems. But these problems can be solved in a less costly fashion. Divine-risk theologians dismiss or ignore the best solutions available for dealing with the issues of human freedom and evil and resort to a truncated version of the biblical portrait of God. Theirs is a compromise that serves as a tragic example of curing a philosophical headache by theological decapitation.

Nevertheless, the divine-risk theists do properly emphasize divine relationality. Ours is indeed a loving and caring God, personally engaged in the lives of his people. But he is also a sovereign God, directing history according to his perfect will. The Scriptures might not show us *how*, but they plainly teach *that* both of these claims are true and, thus, fundamentally compatible. The biblically informed Christian, then, must affirm both divine relationality and divine sovereignty, without allowing either of these doctrines to undermine a commitment to the other.

Chapter 9

# Does God
# Have Emotions?

*Patrick Lee*

# 1. Introduction

In the last several decades process philosophers and theologians have vigorously criticized the traditional Christian beliefs that God is immutable and completely self-sufficient. The view of process philosophers and theologians is that God suffers along with his "creatures," that he does not create from nothing, that he depends in several ways on his "creatures," and that he is fulfilled or deprived by the success or failure of the world.[1] Recently, other thinkers, who reject the label of process philosophers or theologians and who prefer to be called "open theists," have also proposed such arguments.[2]

Process theologians and open theists argue that Scripture reveals that God is a person, that he knows and loves us, that he responds to our prayers, is pleased or displeased with us, and that he invites us to enter a personal relationship with him. These points, it is objected, imply that God changes and that what we do affects God. So, we must concede, contrary to classical theism (the argument continues), that God changes and is affected by our actions.[3]

Classical theism argues, however, that God is indeed immutable and is not dependent, for any perfection or fulfillment in himself, on his creatures. To hold otherwise, as Augustine, Anselm, Aquinas, and others like them have made abundantly clear, is to deny (in effect) that God is God; it is to fall away from theism itself. Classical theism, in fact, has much more to say in its defense than is usually admitted by its detractors. God is indeed personal and knows and loves us, but we simply cannot assume that what is true of *human* persons, knowledge, and love (which involve change and dependence) is true of *divine* persons, knowledge, and love. To make that assumption, as process and open theists blithely do, is to compromise God's transcendence.

---

[1]For example, Charles Hartshorne, *Divine Relativity* (New Haven, Conn.: Yale Univ. Press, 1948); Jürgen Moltmann, *The Crucified God* (London: SCM, 1991). Some theologians have argued for a *via media* between classical theism and process theism. They say that God is really spiritually affected or changed by his creation and so does literally have emotions, and yet God is not *radically* dependent on creatures and is indeed sovereign. Cf. Clark H. Pinnock et al., *The Openness of God: A Biblical Challenge to the Traditional Understanding of God* (Downers Grove, Ill: InterVarsity Press, 1994).

[2]See note 1. Also see Thomas V. Morris, *Our Idea of God: An Introduction to Philosophical Theology* (Downers Grove, Ill.: InterVarsity Press, 1991).

[3]Among other places, the case is presented clearly in: Richard Creel, *Divine Impassibility* (Cambridge: Cambridge Univ. Press, 1986). A useful survey and critical assessment of many of the arguments: Thomas Weinandy, *Does God Suffer?* (Notre Dame, Ind.: Univ. of Notre Dame Press, 2000), 1–26.

The following points will be examined: first, the fundamental truth that God is the Creator, and what that entails; second, two views on divine impassibility; and, finally, a more detailed look at a key claim of the second view on divine impassibility, namely, that even after revelation, what God is in himself remains unknown.

When we ask, "Does God have emotions?" the most straightforward answer is simply, "Yes, because he became man." Jesus Christ is both God and man, fully divine and fully human. Jesus indeed has human emotions: joys, desires, fears, sadnesses, and so on. The Christian faith holds that Jesus Christ is one divine person but with two natures, human and divine.[4]

I do not wish here to examine in detail this central dogma (since I will concentrate on the question of whether God has emotions *in his divine nature*), but briefly the following should be said. A *person* is an intelligent and free subject of actions, a morally responsible agent.[5] A *nature* is the intrinsic source of characteristic actions, that by which or with which one acts. In Christ, the one who acts is God himself, so he is a divine person. But Christ can act by his divine nature or by his human nature (or by both). Thus, after the Incarnation, literally, God *does* suffer as we suffer, he *does* have emotions as we have emotions, since it is the person of Christ who has the emotions, even though he has these emotions by his human nature.

Traditionally it was believed that at least one main reason why God became man was so that the God-man Jesus Christ could be a mediator. God's transcendence—that is, the infinite difference between his perfection and our humanness—made approaching him difficult in our sinful state, even somewhat frightening. God became man, however, and we humans can now be personally united to God, brought within the divine family (the Trinity), *in* Jesus Christ. So, if one complains that the classical theist's God seems too different from us and therefore difficult to approach, I believe it is fair to answer that God in his divine nature *is* difficult to approach, and it is partly for that reason that God became human.[6]

---

[4]This was defined at the Council of Chalcedon in A.D. 451. I will refer in the standard way to church councils by citing a work edited by Henricus Denzinger and Adolfus Schönmetzer, *Enchridion Symbolorum Definitionum et Declarationem de Rebus Fidei et Morum*, hereafter abbreviated as DS, with their enumeration. There will be two numbers; the lower one is found in an earlier edition of the handbook and in many publications using it. The reference here is to DS 148/301. Much of Denzinger-Schönmetzer is translated in *The Church Teaches, Documents of the Church in English Translation* (Rockford, Ill.: Tan Publications, 1973). The reference here can be found on p. 172.

[5]Even someone who is asleep, in a coma, or too young actually to reason and make free choices right now (such as a human fetus), is a person, since he or she is a subject who has the basic capacity to perform such actions, even though it may take him or her some time to actualize those capacities.

[6]I should add that the belief that God *became man* (i.e., that Jesus is God, a divine person with both divine and human natures) does not logically imply any change in God's divine nature. The human nature of Christ came to be personally united to the second person of the Trinity. The second person of the Trinity is the term of this personal union, and so no change is implied in the divine nature itself. See, for example, Thomas Aquinas, *Summa Theologiae*, 3.Q2.1; and 3.Q3.1–2. Also see Thomas Weinandy, *Does God Change?* (Still River, Mass.: St. Bede Publications, 1985), esp. 32–100; Herbert McCabe, *God Matters* (London: Geoffrey Chapman, 1987), 39–51.

Hereafter, when I discuss whether God does this or does that, I will mean God *in his divine nature*. If by *emotion* one means a sensate (psychosomatic) reaction to good or evil, then most would agree that God does not literally have emotions, since he does not have a body. But the question remains: Is God affected in some way by our actions? Does he literally suffer when we suffer or do wrong? Does he really become angry, repent of his actions, or rejoice at the repentance of a sinner? Does he feel joy over the way things are in himself and in his creation?

The classical view, as articulated by Augustine, Anselm, and Thomas Aquinas, said that God is immutable, impassible, and nontemporal. In other words, since God is perfect, he does not change. Since he is perfect, he does not undergo change from any other being (he is impassible). Since he does not change, there is in him no distinction between past, present, and future. On the classical view, to be sure, God does *delight* in his goodness and *loves* his creatures, but this cannot be interpreted as meaning that God is changed by, or different because of, his creatures.[7]

## 2. God the Creator of Heaven and Earth

Scripture and the teaching of the church reveal that God loves us and that he invites us to enter a personal relationship with him. This is indeed central to his revelation. But the very first part of that communication is an identification: It is *God* who speaks to us, who invites us to enter a personal relationship with him. What is meant by "God"? Prior to informing us that he invites us to a covenant with him, God must somehow indicate who it is that is speaking. It is just here that we find a tradition in Scripture as equally central as the theme of God's love or patience, namely, God's transcendence. The one who speaks to us is not to be confused with "other gods," but is the Creator, the Almighty.

The very first words of Genesis make this identification: "In the beginning *God* created the heavens and the earth." Moreover, God is so transcendent that no image should be made of him (Ex. 20:4). Ordinarily, mere humans cannot behold God directly and live (Ex. 33:20). He is the exalted One, who dwells in the high and lofty places (Isa. 33:5; 57:15).[8] Furthermore, this doctrine of God as Creator and transcendent is reaffirmed in the New Testament. For example, in writing to Timothy Paul says:

> In the sight of God, who gives life to everything, and of Christ Jesus, who while testifying before Pontius Pilate made the good confession, I charge you

---

[7]See, e.g., Aquinas, *Summa Theologiae*, 1.Q.20.

[8]The meaning of the name of God, *Yahweh*, revealed by God to Moses, is interpreted in different ways. However, it probably means either that God is transcendent, beyond what we can understand (on the interpretation that "He who is" was a way of refusing to tell Moses his name) or that God is the transcendent cause of all being. As McKenzie says in his *Dictionary of the Bible*, the name Yahweh is perhaps only the first word of the entire name *yāhweh ᵃ'šer yihyeh*, "He who brings into being whatever comes into being"; John L. McKenzie, *Dictionary of the Bible* (New York and London: Macmillan, 1965), 316. Cf. *The Interpreter's Dictionary of the Bible, An Illustrated Encyclopedia*, ed. G. A. Buttrick, 4 vols. (Nashville and New York: Abingdon, 1962), 2:408–17.

GOD UNDER FIRE

to keep this command without spot or blame until the appearing of our Lord Jesus Christ, which God will bring about in his own time—God, the blessed and only Ruler, the King of kings and Lord of lords, who alone is immortal and who lives in unapproachable light, whom no one has seen or can see. To him be honor and might forever. Amen. (1 Tim. 6:13–16)[9]

To say that God is the Creator is to refer to him as the ultimate explanation for the existence of the contingent beings in the material universe. Things in this world do not exist by reason of what they are but are caused to exist by others. Those causes may, in turn, be caused by still others. But such a causal series cannot go on indefinitely. There must be a cause of the existence of these contingent things that does not receive its existence but which exists by reason of what it is. That is, there must be a self-sufficient being, something that can explain the existence of the things in this world because it has existence of its own nature.

We find in ourselves various natural inclinations, basic tendencies toward activities or conditions such as life, health, knowledge, friendship, and artistic or skillful performance. These natural inclinations are toward activities or conditions that are objectively fulfilling or perfective of us as human persons. Such inclinations or tendencies must be from the Creator. It is reasonable, then, to conclude that the Creator is in some way intelligent (as directing) and benevolent (as responsible for directives toward our good).

Moreover, every aspect of the material universe, including its matter and energy, is contingent and thus needs causation. Hence, the uncaused cause of the existence of the material universe is the *Creator*.[10] Thus, whatever else is said about God must be consistent with the fundamental truth that he is the Creator and all that that legitimately implies. But can the Creator change, or can he be modified by creatures?

The proposition that God is the Creator implies at least three other points: (1) God creates freely; (2) God possesses his complete perfection within himself; and (3) God is immutable and is not in time (i.e., his existence is not measured by time). All three points are denied by process theism, but the last one is also denied by others, such as open theists.

(1) The basic Judeo-Christian belief that God is Creator implies that God did not have to create; it was only out of generosity that he did create. This point is taught by Scripture and the church. It is taught so frequently in Scripture, especially in the Psalms, that it is impossible to cite all the places that teach or imply it. The creation story of Genesis, while describing God's work of creation in a figurative rather than a literal sense, clearly teaches that God created out of generosity rather than need. Psalm 135 says that God wills events in heaven and earth:

---

[9]Cf. Rom. 1:20–23; 9:5; Rev. 4:8.

[10]In the strict sense, to create means to produce from nothing. That is, things other than the Creator always presuppose some preexisting material to work on and things are produced by forming preexisting material in a new way; the Creator, however, causes to exist the material as well as the new form or structure. Thus, every aspect of contingent things has its source in the Creator.

Praise the name of the LORD;
  Praise him you servants of the LORD,
you who minister in the house of the LORD. . . .
I know that the LORD is great,
  that our Lord is greater than all gods.
The LORD does whatever pleases him,
  in the heavens and on the earth,
  in the seas and all their depths.

(Ps. 135:1–6)

The book of Wisdom teaches:

Indeed, before you the whole universe is as a grain from a balance, or a drop of morning dew come down upon earth. But you have mercy on all, because you can do all things. . . . For you love all things that are and loathe nothing that you have made; for what you hated, you would not have fashioned. And how could a thing remain, unless you willed it; or be preserved, had it not been called forth by you.[11] (Wis. 11:22–25)

The book of Revelation teaches that God creates by his will: "You are worthy, our Lord and God, to receive glory and honor and power, for you created all things, and by your will they were created and have their being" (Rev. 4:11).[12]

As a Catholic, I believe that Scripture should be read in the context of the tradition of the church, which is articulated by the church's authoritative teachings. In the First Vatican Council, the Catholic Church defined that God created all things "by his will, free from all necessity."[13] The *Catechism of the Catholic Church* teaches: "We believe that God created the world according to his wisdom. . . . It is not the product of necessity whatever, nor of blind fate or chance. We believe that it proceeds from God's free will."[14]

That God creates freely rather than necessarily is implied also by the contingency of the things in this world. Each thing in this world might or might not be. But if God *had* to create, this would not be so; that is, these things would not be contingent.[15] Moreover, since the Creator may or may not cause these entities to be and may cause these or those to be, it is reasonable to conclude that the Creator causes them *freely*, somewhat as a free agent selects among possible courses of action which course of action to adopt.[16]

---

[11]The Book of Wisdom is in the Catholic Old Testament but not in Protestant versions, so I am using here the *New American Bible* (New York: Catholic Book Publishing, 1970, 1986).
[12]Cf. Ps. 33:6; 104:24; 145:9; Wis. 9:11; Eph. 1:11.
[13]Vatican Council I (DS, 1805/3025).
[14]*The Catechism of the Catholic Church* (New York: Doubleday, 1995), #295.
[15]If one says that the Creator had to create, then the self-sufficient, necessary being is the whole (Creator–creatures) rather than a being distinct from the world. One moves, then, to a worldview entirely different from theism. I believe one can show that this position is internally incoherent. See Germain Grisez, *Beyond the New Theism* (Notre Dame, Ind.: Univ. of Notre Dame Press, 1975), 181–204.
[16]Ibid., 266–72.

(2) The belief that God is Creator implies that he is perfect in himself. That is, God must have his complete perfection within himself. If God's perfection depended on others, then God would have to create at least something as a means toward his own fulfillment. In that case, again, the things in this world would not be contingent.

Moreover, every perfection and being in the universe is but a faint echo of the perfection in God. Whatever perfection is in the effect must preexist in the cause, though it may exist in the cause in a higher manner. This is because the cause *explains* the effect. If all of the perfection in the effect did not preexist in the cause (though perhaps in a higher manner), then the perfection in the effect that did not preexist in the cause would remain unexplained.[17] Since all being and all perfection in the universe finds its source in the Creator, the perfection and goodness in the universe is related to God somewhat as the rays of light are related to the unimaginable brightness of the sun.[18] So, God has his perfection within himself, and it is greater than the perfection of the created universe, which is but a reflection of it.

(3) That God is Creator entails a third truth: God does not change and is not in time (these are two aspects of one point). That which changes has its existence spread out over time, broken up, as it were. What is temporal must be composed of parts; part of it is now and part of it is not yet. But since God is perfect and self-existent, this cannot be true of God.

Some have argued that God's perfection entails his immutability, since to change would be to move away from perfection. My argument, however, does not presuppose that every change must be either for the better or for the worse. Rather, my argument is that temporality involves a continuous flow, a continuous transition from the present to the past, and so a temporal being cannot exist wholly in any moment.

What I am saying applies analogously both to spatial beings (bodies) and to things in time. No body in space, however small, can exist wholly at any one *point* (an unextended location) in space; if it could, the additions of those bodies could never add up to an extended space. But several bodies in space must constitute an extended (increasingly larger) space. Analogously, no temporal being can exist wholly at any one moment, for then the addition of new moments could not be added to equal an extended time.[19] Thus, every entity in time, every temporal being, must be spread out over time and must be composed of parts. But if a thing is composed of parts, then it cannot be actual of itself. It will depend on its parts;

---

[17]Sometimes this point is expressed in this way: The effect cannot be greater than the cause.

[18]However, the perfection that is in the world need not preexist in God in the same manner. Just as the degree of energy in the coil on an electric range preexists in a different manner in the electromagnetic generator in the city's electrical power plant (there it is not actually hot), so the perfection in a horse or a human can preexist in God without God being literally a horse or a human.

[19]See David Braine, *The Reality of Time and the Existence of God* (New York: Oxford Univ. Press, 1988), 23–63; Brian Leftow, *Time and Eternity* (Ithaca, N. Y.: Cornell Univ. Press, 1991), 31–49, and ch. 12.

and its parts, as being mere parts rather than wholes, will not be self-actual either (but dependent on something else). Thus, it seems to me that the traditional position that the temporal entails dependence in being—and thus cannot be predicated of God—is correct. Temporality must be denied of God.

Moreover, the church, in her creeds as well as in definitions by church councils, has taught definitively that God is eternal and immutable. These are prominent articles of the creeds. For example, the Fourth Lateran Council[20] proclaims:

> We firmly believe and confess without reservation that there is only one true God, eternal, infinite (*immensus*) and unchangeable, incomprehensible, almighty, and ineffable, the Father and the Son and the Holy Spirit; three persons indeed but one essence, substance or nature entirely simple.[21]

It is important to realize, however, that to say that God is the Creator does not describe God's essence. Rather, it refers to him, and says something about him, through the relationships that other things have to him (this will be discussed further below).

This negation of change and temporality, however, does not mean that God is in no way responsive. There is no contradiction in holding that a timeless God responds to our prayers. Suppose Joe prays for his wife to be healed and God heals her in answer to Joe's prayer. One need not suppose God has changed his mind. Rather, one can suppose that God eternally wills that if Joe prays, then his wife is cured. Joe's prayer brings it about that the world is different from what it would have been if he had not prayed, though God does not change.[22]

## 3. A First View on Divine Impassibility

Let us return to the question concerning God's emotions. Granted that God is not in time and that God has his perfection within himself—that he is not perfected or fulfilled by others—we need to examine two views. Both of these views are better than those offered by process and open theism, though I suggest the second view is preferable.

According to the first view, God does not change, nor is he perfected or fulfilled by others, since they receive all of their perfection from him. Still, God is

---

[20]I realize that not every Christian accepts the Fourth Lateran Council. However, in my judgment this council is a teaching of the community that Jesus founded to carry on his work, the body of Christ, a community to which Christ promised divine assistance and protection from doctrinal error. Hence, in my judgment this council is authoritative.

[21]DS, 428/800; *The Church Teaches*, 132. As I briefly explained above, after the Incarnation one can truthfully say that God changes *by his human nature*. Karl Rahner makes this point and does not deny that God is immutable in his divine nature when he says: "If we face squarely and uncompromisingly the fact of the Incarnation which our faith in the fundamental dogma of Christianity testifies to, then we have to say plainly: God can become something. He who is not subject to change in himself can *himself* be subject to change *in something else*" (Karl Rahner, *Foundations of Christian Faith* [New York: Seabury , 1978], 113–14 n. 3). On Rahner's position here, see Weinandy, *Does God Change?* 163–74.

[22]Cf. Leftow, *Time and Eternity*, ch. 13.

different in his being, in certain respects, from the way he could have been.[23] God freely and eternally wills that *these* creatures exist rather than *those* possible ones, though he also wills that they exist at particular times.[24] He could have willed other beings to exist rather than the ones he freely chooses to create. Furthermore, God's willing that *these* beings exist versus his willing that *those* beings exist is a real difference in God. God's will would be in some way different had he willed a different world to exist.

The same point applies to God's knowledge. God moves me to do a good deed. But suppose that, given my free choice,[25] I resist this movement, or I fall away from God's moving me to do the good deed (call it Y), and I do a bad deed (say, X) instead.[26] How does God know that I do the one deed rather than the other? According to the first view, the content of his knowledge is in some way different from what it would have been if I had done the other deed.

Suppose I freely do or will X rather than Y. To say that this choice is free is to say that in the very same circumstances it was possible for me to will Y or perhaps not to will at all. My willing X rather than Y somehow brings it about that the content of God's knowledge is in some way different from what it would have been if I had willed Y. However, it is important to note that my willing X rather than Y does not introduce into God some perfection he does not in some way already superabundantly possess. After all, I will X or Y only because these possibilities are already there for me because of God's inclining me toward fulfillment. It is also important to note that the badness of the bad choice is not a positive something, but the privation or falling away from what is proper and right.[27] So God's knowledge is different from what it would have been, had I chosen differently, but my action does not perfect or fulfill God.

According to this first view, one can literally say that God does have emotions, in the sense of spiritual affections. One can literally say that God is pleased with what I do or is displeased with it. He delights in it or is angry about it. He eternally delights in or is eternally displeased at this deed, just as he is eternally pleased or displeased by what I did yesterday or will do tomorrow. Since God is not in time (is not temporal), what is past or future with respect to us is not past

---

[23]On this view, there seems to be a type of potentiality in God so that one could not say that God is pure act, as, for example, Aquinas taught.

[24]So, from the fact that God eternally wills that you exist, it does not follow that you eternally exist—God also eternally wills that you begin to exist at a particular time.

[25]Both this first view and the second view (see below) hold that human beings make genuinely free choices. That is, both views presuppose a libertarian rather than a compatibilist notion of freedom. Not only does the choice spring from the character of the person (compatibilists admit this), but the person in the very same circumstances could have chosen otherwise (exclusive to libertarianism).

[26]Even this bad deed is done in virtue of God's moving me to desire fulfilling objects, such as life, pleasure, or even status. (Status is not in itself bad; only *disordered* or *undue* desire for status is bad.)

[27]Cf. Charles Journet, *The Meaning of Evil*, trans. Michael Barry (New York: P. J. Kennedy, 1962); Grisez, *Beyond the New Theism*, ch. 19; and my "The Goodness of Creation, Evil, and Christian Teaching," *The Thomist* 64 (2000): 239–69.

or future with respect to God, but is in some way "present."[28] So, although God is not in time, his will and knowledge are in some way different from the way they would have been if I had acted differently. Thus, God has spiritual responses or emotions.

But there are difficulties for this proposal. One difficulty is that it seems to involve thinking of God as composite. God is the uncaused cause and a necessary being. If one then says that in some respects God is caused, that some aspects of God are contingent (for example, in some way his willing and knowing creatures is in some way dependent on creatures), then it seems that one must distinguish the uncaused part of God from the caused part of God, since nothing, not even God, can be both uncaused and caused in the same respect.[29] But it does not seem possible for any composite being to exist necessarily. The whole will depend on the parts, but the parts could not be necessary beings—as parts, they must depend on their place within the whole. And so, just of itself, the composite being might or might not be.[30] As we saw above, the Creator cannot be a contingent being.

There also is theological warrant for the position that God is not composite but simple. The creed of the Fourth Lateran Council, as we already quoted above, taught that God is three persons, but "one, utterly simple essence, substance or nature" (*sed una essentia, substantia seu natura simplex omnino*).[31] Speaking of the three persons in God, the Council of Florence taught: "These three persons are one God, not three gods; for the three persons have one substance, one essence, one nature, one divinity, one immensity, one eternity. And everything is one where there is no distinction by opposition of relation."[32] And the First Vatican Council proclaimed that God is "one single, utterly simple and immutable spiritual substance."[33] Perhaps there is some way of interpreting this simplicity to be a special sort of simplicity. However, the Councils seem precisely to deny a substance-accident composition, like that in human persons, when they deny composition of God. It is just that sort of composition that the first view seems to suggest.

## 4. A Second View on Divine Impassibility

The first view seems to presuppose that when we say that God knows or wills, at least part of the meaning of the terms "knowing" and "willing" is the same as when we say that George or Mary knows or wills. But this, according to the second view, is to overreach the limits of our understanding and, what is more, to

---

[28]"Present" is in quotes to signify that it does not mean exactly what it means when we say that an event is present to us. The point is that God is *not* in time, not that he is perpetually in a "present" in our sense of this word.

[29]Cf. Thomas Aquinas, *Summa Contra Gentiles*, 1.23.3.

[30]A *composite* is a whole composed of parts. Parts of an actual being are less than the whole. Thus, the three persons of God do not constitute a composite, since each person is God, and none of the three is less than God.

[31]DS, 428/800l; *The Church Teaches*, 132.

[32]DS, 703/1330; *The Church Teaches*, 135.

[33]DS, 1782/3001; *The Church Teaches*, 152.

compromise God's transcendence. It wrongly supposes that we have apprehended some aspect of what God is in himself.

One can compare the existence of things in this world to the wetness of a patch of grass. The grass is wet, but not by reason of what it is, and so there must be an extrinsic explanation, a cause, for why it is wet. By contrast, one does not need an explanation of why grass is a plant, since that is what it is. Similarly, the existence of the things in this world requires explanation. The things in this world do not exist by reason of what they are, and so they need a cause of their existence. But the Creator of all things is quite different. To say that God is the Creator is to say that he is the uncaused cause of everything else, the ultimate explanation for the existence of the contingent beings in this world. So, unlike contingent beings, whatever God is in himself, he exists by reason of what he is. His existence must be related to him somewhat as being a plant is related to grass—that is, as self-explanatory. What-God-is is sufficient for his existing. And thus God exists necessarily.

Because contingent beings (i.e., the things in this world) do not exist simply by reason of what they are, it is possible for us to understand what any of them is without knowing whether it exists or not. Understanding what a contingent being is does not (by itself) tell us that it exists. For example, understanding what a human is or what a dinosaur is does not by itself tell us that there are any humans or dinosaurs. But the Creator exists by reason of what he is; what he is, is sufficient for his existing. Hence if we could understand what the Creator is, that understanding would just by itself tell us that he exists. (This is similar to grass's being a plant—since being a plant is what grass is, understanding what grass is just by itself tells us that it is a plant.)

Now, every essence or feature that we do understand is such that our understanding of it does *not* tell us by itself that something of that sort *exists*. That is, everything we understand is, if it exists, contingently existing, and we can understand it without thereby knowing that something of that sort exists. But whatever God is, God exists necessarily; hence if we knew what God is, we would know thereby that God exists. It follows that any essence, quality, or action that we truly understand or apprehend is *not* an intrinsic feature of God's essence.[34]

So, whatever we understand—which includes change, bodiliness, but also spiritual (nonphysical) actions such as knowing and loving—must be denied of God. That is, God does not change. God is not bodily. But also, God does not know in the sense of "know" that is true of us. He does not love in the same sense of loving that we understand. (This also means that God is not inert, is not ignorant, is not indifferent, and is not callous. God is not *sub*personal. Rather, God is *more than*, or *higher than*, what we can understand.)

With creatures, we often understand something intrinsic to a thing's nature even if we have not directly seen an individual of that kind. For example, if we have not seen a polar bear, we still might understand something of what a polar

---

[34]This argument is developed most clearly by Grisez, *Beyond the New Theism*, esp. 241–74.

bear is in itself. The polar bear shares the same nature (to a certain extent) with horses and dogs: Each is a mammal, each is of the class of mammals. So, directly understanding what a mammal is through observation of horses or dogs allows us to apprehend an aspect of the intrinsic nature of the unobserved polar bear (its being a mammal). However, God does not have the same nature or feature as any creature, since all the natures and features of a creature are such that they might or might not be, while what-God-is exists necessarily.

This means that one cannot know what God is through understanding some other thing of the same essence, the same specifically or generically. One cannot understand what God is as one might understand what a polar bear is—by first understanding what persons are, for example, then by inferring that God must have some of the same properties.[35]

Since creatures are effects of God, they are like God in some respect. But their likeness to God as creatures cannot consist in possessing the same nature or in being of the same genus. Thus, according to this second view, even our concepts that properly apply to ourselves—such as *understanding, willing* and *love*—cannot be directly applied to God in the sense that they apply to ourselves. Since our concepts of features found in ourselves present to our minds realities or natures that do not entail their existing, these realities or natures cannot be aspects of God's necessarily existing essence.[36]

Thus, to say that God understands or that God wills or loves should not be taken to mean that what is presented to our minds by those concepts are intrinsic aspects of God. Rather, such statements should be understood as being indirect or analogical. *God understands* should be understood somewhat as follows: Creatures are related to God in a way that is in some respects similar to the way what is understood is related to one who understands, and God is in himself what it takes to be the term of that relation. *God wills creatures to be* = contingent beings are related to God in a way that is in some respects similar to the way objects willed are related to a free agent, and God has in himself what is necessary to be the term of that relation.

But one might object that perhaps God could be uncaused and necessary in his existence but contingent in other aspects of his being. Then perhaps we might have concepts of features internal to his essence that do not entail existence.[37] In other words, granted that if we understood *fully* what God is we would thereby know that he exists, still, we can understand certain aspects of his being without knowing thereby his existence.

The difficulty with this position is that it seems to involve a compositeness in God. If God is not composed—and the arguments for this seem strong—then one cannot apprehend a contingent aspect of God while abstracting from the nec-

---

[35]We do indeed affirm that God is personal, but the meaning of "personal" must be understood analogically in the same way as I have indicated for the words "know" and "love." A person is a *subject* of actions such as knowing and loving.

[36]That is, the features we grasp are such that they do not entail their existence. Therefore, such features cannot be intrinsic to God's essence.

[37]William Hasker, "A Philosophical Perspective," in *The Openness of God*, 133.

essary aspect. The objection would succeed only if God's being could be divided into a substantial, necessary core, versus a contingent, accidental core. But we have already seen difficulties in that view.

How, then, is it possible to know and speak about God at all? The answer according to the second view is: through the relationships that other things have to him.[38] An analogy will clarify this position. In the late 1960s astronomers began to detect the reception of regular radio waves from outside our galaxy. The waves came with such regularity that some astronomers even suggested that perhaps their source was an extragalactic intelligence. Some time later it was correctly inferred that the source was actually neutron stars, whose rapid spinning caused the radio waves. Before this, however, astronomers coined the term "pulsar" to refer to the source of these radio waves. For some time, then, astronomers referred to pulsars, spoke about them, and theorized about them, but they did not know what they were in themselves. They referred to them only through the relations that other things had toward them.

This case is similar (in some respects) to our knowledge and language about God. We do not grasp what God is in himself; we do not know what God is. Still, we can refer to him through the relationship creatures have to him. He is the ultimate source of the existence, perfection, and moral order in the universe. He is the Creator of heaven and earth. This causal relation, the relation of creation, enables us to know and speak about him. He is the entity at the term of this relation. However, this causal relation does not enable us to apprehend what he is in himself. On the basis of this relation we can affirm the existence of the Creator and can know that the Creator is perfect (as the source of all perfections in this universe), is not bodily, is not limited by time or space, and is a personal being, creating the world with something like freedom and intelligence.[39] All of this we can know even through natural reason, before or without logical dependence upon, the aid of special revelation (e.g., Scripture).

However, there is an important sense in which our relationship to pulsars is *unlike* our causal dependence on the Creator. The pulsars are quite distant from us, outside our galaxy. That is, they are separated from us by quantities of space and time. God, however, is immediately present to every creature. God causes every creature directly and is causally present in every effect.[40] God is also present

---

[38]Cf. "Concerning God, we cannot grasp what he is, but only what he is not, and how other beings are related to him"; Aquinas, *Summa Contra Gentiles*, 1.30. This is quoted favorably by *The Catechism of the Catholic Church* (New York: Doubleday, 1995), at #43.

[39]We know that other entities are possible. So the Creator brings it about that these entities, and not the other possible ones, come to be, and the Creator cannot be determined by anything else to bring about these possibilities rather than those (otherwise, he would not be uncaused). Hence, contingent beings are related to the Creator similar to the way possible courses of action are related to a free agent. This similarity entitles us to conclude that there is something like free will in the Creator and thus also intelligence, even though we cannot know what these are like in the Creator in himself. Cf. Grisez, *Beyond the New Theism*, 268–72.

[40]The argument for this is that an adequate cause must be proportionate to its effect, since it explains the effect. But contingent beings do not have existence of themselves, which means

in another and deeper manner to persons who abide in his friendship. He is present in them as the lover is to the beloved, as a friend to another friend. That is, God is present to them because he is in personal communion with them.

However, although God is not separated from us by space or time, if by "distant" one means *greater than*, or *other than*, or *beyond what we can understand*, then in that sense one can truthfully say that God is "distant." Thus, with picturesque language of distance Isaiah can say of God, "He sits enthroned above the circle of the earth, and its people are like grasshoppers" (Isa. 40:22), and the letter to the Hebrews can say that Christ, "sat down at the right hand of the Majesty in heaven" (Heb. 1:3).

Scripture emphasizes that God is beyond what we can understand. He is like no other god. He so transcends our understanding that no images should be made of him (Ex. 20:4).[41] This, of course, has been taken up in the tradition in the church. One formulation of the church's faith recites as follows:

> We firmly believe and confess without reservation that there is only one true God, eternal, infinite (*immensus*), and unchangeable, incomprehensible, almighty and ineffable, the Father, and the Son, and the Holy Spirit.... [42]

God's being or nature is incomprehensible and ineffable. To think that we understand what God is in himself is to compromise his transcendence, to carve him down to something much less than he is.

The relation of creation allows us to speak about God through natural reason (i.e., without the aid of special revelation).[43] But with grace and revelation God initiates a new relation to created persons. With grace and revelation God is known not only as the first cause of all things and as the source of moral directives, but now as the initiator of the covenantal relationship, a personal communion. What God is, is still not apprehended. But now God is known on a new level, on the basis of a deeper relationship.

In this way, according to the second view, it is possible to understand something about God and speak about God without understanding what God is—that is, without apprehending any perfection intrinsic to God's essence. All of our understanding and language about God are through the relationships creatures have to him, the causal relationship (which all creatures have), the relationship of moral directives to their source, and the personal relationship (shared by persons who have not rejected his offer of grace).

---

they do not have existence as identical or part of what they are, their natures. So their natures cannot explain the existence of their effects. Hence they can cause new existence (which occurs with each new effect) only as cooperating with a being that does have existence as identical with its nature. And since only the Creator has existence as identical with its nature, it follows that the Creator is immediately operative in every effect.

[41]Cf. Lev. 10:1–3; Num. 1:48–53.

[42]Fourth Lateran Council (DS, 428/800; *The Church Teaches*, 132); cf. *The Catechism of the Catholic Church*, #202.

[43]What one knows through natural reasoning, inferring from the visible effects in the world, is sometimes called "natural revelation." *Special* revelation is a personal communication, through selected effects, such as words and deeds of prophets and of Jesus.

It is important also to note that, according to the second view, even these causal relationships are not understood as they are in themselves. That is, God's causality, as well as God himself, is known only through analogy. To say that God is the first cause is to say something like this: The way the warmth of the sidewalk is related to the sun (namely, as explained by it) is similar to the way the existences of the things in this world are related to God. To say that God is present by grace in a person is to say something like this: The way the bridegroom is present to the bride is similar to the way God is present to the person in grace.

Scripture and the teaching of the church reveal that God loves us, that he invites us to enter into personal communion with him, that he is three persons in one being, that the second person became man and died for our sins. However, according to the second view of divine impassibility—the view I think more likely correct—even revelation does not enable us in this life to know what God is in himself. Revelation tells us about God through this new personal relationship. That is, the personal relationship, which involves much more than a mere causal relationship, remains the vehicle by which we know about God.

But what, for example, does Scripture and the teaching of the church mean when they say that God is personal and that God loves us? According to the second view, Scripture reveals to us who God is primarily by shaping our covenantal relationship to God. How we are to relate to God, what this relationship involves, is not summed up entirely in any one statement. Moreover, the statements about this relationship modify each other. So, one must read Scripture as a whole and, in the context of the tradition and life of the church, understand the covenantal relationship God is setting up with us. Then, *through* that relationship, one understands much more about God than one could by natural reasoning unaided by revelation. We still do not understand God's intrinsic essence. But we understand that God has in himself what is necessary for this relationship to him to be possible and appropriate.

Scripture reveals that we should fear God (i.e., respect him), that we should trust him, that we should ask things of him. Scripture teaches that we should relate to God as to a king, as to a Lord. Most significantly, Scripture reveals that we should relate to God as to a *father*. To say that God is Father clearly does not mean that the nature (a relation) we apprehend in human beings is found also, though in a higher degree, in God. Rather, in his being God has what is necessary for this personal relationship in us toward him to be a fitting one. Scripture is not telling us that God is not really our Father but to act *as if* God were. Rather, God is bringing us into a relationship such that we fittingly call God Father. And God really is in his own being fittingly related to as to a father. But to try to abstract some aspect of fatherhood common to biological fathers and God is to miss the point and to evacuate the meaning that father really has, as said of God.

In one way, thinking that the language about God in Scripture is a straightforward description of God's essence overestimates our cognitive grasp of God. But, paradoxically, it also underestimates the depth of what Scripture and the teaching of the church reveal about God's personal being. If we want to learn about who God is, then we need to enter that rich, multifaceted, covenantal relationship. *In* that relationship we come to understand what God must be like. As the relationship develops, our indirect understanding of God becomes richer.

Consider the central affirmation that God is love (1 John 4:8). First, the form itself of the expression indicates that the way in which love is in God transcends our understanding. For the love we understand is never identical with the persons who love. The love we understand is an act that inheres in the person who loves. To say that God *is* love rather than just that God does love clearly suggests, in support of the second view, that God's actions are identical with his substance and being.[44] We do not apprehend a nature of love common to God and creatures, abstract from finitude, and then predicate this notion of God. This would assume that we directly grasp a feature intrinsic to God's essence. Rather, to say that God is love is to say that we are being treated by God as a beloved is treated by his true and faithful lover and that God is in himself what is necessary for this relationship to be real. The love that we can understand is only a faint echo of the divine love.

Scripture contains many descriptions of God that are clearly intended as metaphors. For example, God is a rock, a shepherd, a husband, one who repents of his actions, one who shows the strength of his arm, and so on. Should we think of God (in his divine nature) as really changing, as really feeling regret, as really having an arm? There clearly needs to be a criterion, or criteria, for determining how literally to take these comparisons. I suggest that the fundamental truths that God is Creator and that God transcends our understanding, which are basic and central truths affirmed in Scripture, do provide, in part, the needed criteria.

## 5. The Mystery of God

Arguments against classical theism sometimes assume that to deny one property of God—for example, suffering or grief in our senses of these terms—commits one to affirming the contrary of that property. For example, to deny that God suffers or grieves (in the normal senses of those terms) is taken to mean that God is aloof and indifferent. Thus, Clark Pinnock describes the disagreement between classical and open theism as follows:

> Two models of God in particular are the most influential that people commonly carry around in their minds. We may think of God primarily as an aloof monarch, removed from the contingencies of the world, unchangeable in every aspect of being, as all-determining and irresistible power, aware of everything that will ever happen and never taking risks. Or we may understand God as a caring parent with qualities of love and responsiveness, generosity and sensitivity, openness and vulnerability, a person (rather than a metaphysical principle) who experiences the world, responds to what happens, relates to us and interacts dynamically with humans.[45]

---

[44]Cf. "I am the way and the truth and the life" (John 14:6).
[45]Clark H. Pinnock, "Systematic Theology," in *The Openness of God*, 103.

Pinnock's argument here, however, is based on an incomplete disjunction. He mistakenly assumes that one or other of those descriptions must apply to God. He assumes that to deny one property is to affirm the contrary. Later in the chapter Pinnock returns to this contrast: "God is not cool and collected but is deeply involved and can be wounded."[46]

It must be admitted that classical theists themselves are partly responsible for this confusion. For they have not sufficiently emphasized, or have not consistently held to, the point that we do not know what God is in himself. Perhaps their doctrine has at times seemed to imply that God is aloof and indifferent. However, to deny one property of God is not the same as to affirm the contrary of that property. According to the second view, which I hold is probably correct, we should deny that God (in his divine nature) suffers, because we understand what suffering is, and whatever we can apprehend about other things cannot be a feature intrinsic to God's essence. God is greater than what we can understand. But we must also deny, with equal insistence, that God is indifferent or callous, for these also are properties we understand and are contingently existing. Similarly, to say that God is immutable is not the same as to say that God is static. To say that God is impassible is not to say that God is indifferent. Rather, in each case both contrary properties should be denied of the Creator.

One should not, then, think of God as *inert* or unresponsive. To do so is to make the very mistake that the negation was meant to exclude, namely, to compromise God's transcendence. God is greater than what we can understand, so we must deny of him those attributes that imply imperfection. But in doing so, we must not impute to him even worse imperfections.

Even if this mistake is not made (inferring a contrary affirmation from a negation), critics of classical theism almost always assume that we must have some concept of what God is like in himself. For example, the process theologian Schubert Ogden has argued as follows:

Because it [classical theism] rests on the premise that God can be in no sense really relative or temporal, it can say that he "knows" or "loves" only by contradicting the meaning of those words as we otherwise use them.[47]

Richard Rice argues that the biblical view of God entails that God does change, is affected by our actions, and suffers when we suffer. Summing up, he says:

So the statement *God is love* embodies an essential biblical truth. It indicates that love is central, not incidental, to the nature of God. Love is not something God happens to do, it is the one divine activity that most fully and vividly discloses God's inner reality. Love, therefore, is the very essence of the divine nature. Love is what it means to be God.[48]

---

[46]Ibid., 118.
[47]Schubert Ogden, *Process Theology: Basic Writings*, ed. Ewert Cousins (New York: Newman, 1971), 122–23.
[48]Richard Rice, "Biblical Support for a New Perspective," in *The Openness of God*, 19.

God certainly knows and loves. God certainly *is* love, but, according to the second view, we do not apprehend any nature of knowledge or love held in common by us and God. Thus, we cannot infer from the characteristics of human knowledge or love to divine knowledge or love. Both Rice and Ogden assume that many of the descriptions in the Bible—not all, for they admit that many are meant metaphorically—present to our mind features or aspects intrinsic to God's essence.

As another example, Thomas Morris actually criticizes what he calls "creation theology" for the fact that it cannot give us a clear idea of what God is:

> As a way of thinking about God, creation theology has much to recommend it. . . . But as a sole, independent method for articulating a conception of God, creation theology looks frustratingly incomplete. The idea of God arising exclusively out of this sort of explanatory reasoning inevitably has a rather minimal content which is both religiously and philosophically unsatisfying.[49]

But Morris assumes that for some reason we really must have, or are due, an idea of what God is, an idea of God that is not "frustratingly incomplete." Of course, revelation adds tremendously to our knowledge of God, as I explained above; but even with revelation, in this life our notion of God is indirect and must remain incomplete.

Process philosophers and theologians have correctly argued, I think, that classical theists have sometimes implied that God is indifferent or callous to our triumphs and sufferings. Process theism, by contrast, has overemphasized God's immanence to such an extent that what process theists call "God" cannot be identified with the one "creator of all that is visible and invisible," in whom Christians profess their belief. But the solution is not to compromise God's transcendence a little less in order to find a *via media*. Rather, the solution is to see that both extremes—viewing God as indifferent or viewing God as changing or suffering (in his divine nature)—result from a single mistake, namely, presuming that we must have a notion of what God is in himself. Once this presumption is *consistently* given up, we can see that denying that God changes, or that God is modified or altered by us, in no way implies that God is indifferent, cool, or callous.

Denying that God changes and that God is internally modified by our actions is not a result of undue influence on the part of Greek philosophy. Nor is it a purely philosophical conclusion imposed on the data of revelation. In an essay defending an "open theist" conception of God, William Hasker refers to "an a priori exegesis that knows in advance exactly what can and cannot be truly said of God."[50] Clark Pinnock says of traditional theology, which insisted on God's immutability and impassibility, the following:

> Traditional theology has been biased in the direction of transcendence as the result of undue philosophical influences. Greek thinking located the ultimate

---

[49]Morris, *Our Idea of God*, 32.
[50]Hasker, "A Philosophical Perspective," in *The Openness of God*, 126.

and perfect in the realm of the immutable and absolutely transcendent. This led early theologians (given that the biblical idea is also transcendent) to experiment with equating the God of revelation with the Greek ideal of deity.[51]

However, what led Jewish, Christian, and Islamic thinkers to conclude that God is immutable and independent was *the doctrine of creation*, the doctrine that God is the source of the total being or existence of the things in this world. This doctrine was not found in ancient Greek metaphysics.[52] When Jewish, Christian, and Islamic philosophers and theologians began to seek an adequate explanation of the existence of things, rather than simply of their motion (as in Aristotle) or of their structure and design (as in Plato), they began to develop a distinctive outlook on the relationship between God and the world. My job is not to recount that history here. But it is important to note that the truth at stake does not originate in ancient Greek metaphysics; rather, it is a fundamental truth of Scripture and the creeds that God is the creator of heaven and earth, of all things visible and invisible.

So, does God have emotions or spiritual affections? I have presented two views that I think have some plausibility. On both views the doctrines that God does not change and that God is not perfected by creatures are retained. According to the first view, God really is affected by what we do and suffer, although he is not changed and he is not perfected by his relations with creatures. He is in his being different from what he would have been had we acted or suffered differently—for his knowledge and will are different from what they would have been had we acted differently—though he does not change and is not perfected by the actions of creatures. On this first view there are emotions in God, though of a different sort than what we normally conceive.

However, the second view seems to me more probably correct. According to this view, one does not simply deny that there might be in God (in his divine nature) something like emotion. If the question "Are there emotions in God?" means: Do our concepts of various emotions present to our minds aspects of what God is? then the answer is, No. But we should remember that this is equally true of other concepts, such as our concepts of knowledge and willing. By contrast, if one means (when one asks whether God has emotions), "Can one truly and literally, not just in an improper or metaphorical sense, say that God is pleased with us or is angry with us?" the answer is, Yes, in the relational sense explained above.

In other words, it is true to say that we are related to God as one who pleases is related to the one who is pleased, and that God has what is necessary to be

---

[51]Pinnock, "Systematic Theology," 106.

[52]Many works of Etienne Gilson have painstakingly demonstrated how the metaphysical thinking of Jewish, Christian, and Islamic thinkers of the Middle Ages was in its central tenets more influenced by revelation, specifically the teachings on creation and that God is "He Who Is" (Ex. 3:14), than by ancient Greek philosophy. See, for example, Etienne Gilson, *The Spirit of Mediaeval Philosophy* (New York: Charles Scribner's Sons, 1940), chs. 2 and 3; idem, *God and Philosophy* (New Haven, Conn.: Yale Univ. Press, 1941).

related to in this way. We are related to God as one who elicits anger is related to the one who is angry, and God is in his own being what is necessary to be the term of this relation. Each of these predications indirectly tells us something about God. When we learn through Scripture, through the teaching and liturgy of the church, and through our own meditation and prayer how God is calling us to relate to him, then we learn ever more about the transcendent being to whom it is possible and appropriate to relate to in this way.

Chapter 10

# Does God Change?

*Charles E. Gutenson*

# 1. Introduction

Within the course of the history of Christianity, there have been many proposals to modify various aspects of the church's conception of God. This is as it should be, for faithfulness to love God with our whole minds leads us to search for fitting conceptualizations that more closely approximate the Reality we seek to honor. However, what constitutes adequate warrants for abandoning existing conceptions in favor of a new proposal? This is a difficult question, and reasonable people may certainly disagree. Nevertheless, I will argue that those who propose abandonment of the tradition's commitment to the divine immutability do not provide adequate grounds to warrant their proposal. There are two grounds for saying this: (1) Their philosophical assessment of the problems associated with the divine immutability is inadequate, and (2) they underestimate the richness of the tradition in providing resources for affirmation of relationality *and* the divine immutability.

> The LORD saw how great man's wickedness on the earth had become, and that every inclination of the thoughts of his heart was only evil all the time. The LORD was grieved that he had made man on the earth, and his heart was filled with pain. So the LORD said, "I will wipe mankind, whom I have created, from the face of the earth—men and animals, and creatures that move along the ground, and birds of the air—for I am grieved that I have made them." (Gen. 6:5–7)

✦

> He who is the Glory of Israel does not lie or change his mind; for he is not a man, that he should change his mind. (1 Sam. 15:29)

✦

> But Moses sought the favor of the LORD his God. "O LORD," he said, "why should your anger burn against your people, whom you brought out of Egypt with great power and a mighty hand? Why should the Egyptians say, 'It is with evil intent that he brought them out, to kill them in the mountains and to wipe them off the face of the earth'? Turn from your fierce anger; relent and do not bring disaster on your people. Remember your servants Abraham, Isaac and Israel, to whom you swore by your own self: 'I will make your descendants as numerous as the stars of the sky and I will give your descendants all this land I promised them, and it will be their inheritance forever.'" Then the LORD relented and did not bring on his people the disaster he had threatened. (Ex. 32:11–14)

✦

> Don't be deceived, my dear brothers. Every good and perfect gift is from above, coming down from the Father of the heavenly lights, who does not change like shifting shadows. (James 1:16–17)

The task of the theologian who seriously considers the biblical witness would be much easier if the text did not contain the sorts of tensions represented by these passages. Historically, the various strands of Christianity have handled these tensions in different ways. One approach viewed the tensions as tantamount to contradictions in search of resolution, relieving the strain by elevating one set of passages to a primary status and hermeneutically subjugating the others.[1] Others—many of the church fathers among them—allowed the tensions to stand, believing that the tensions were due not so much to inner contradiction as to our limited human understanding.

These observations can be applied broadly to a variety of issues; our focus, however, is the divine immutability. Does God change? As one might expect, however, a simple answer either in the affirmative or the negative quickly elevates a number of broader issues, often definitional in nature, begging to be investigated. For example, if we say that God changes, how is change to be taken so that it does not threaten the divine faithfulness? Conversely, if God does not change, how does one adequately account for God's relationality?

Central to many feminist critiques of the classical doctrine of God, for example, is the notion of relationality. Any doctrine of God that does not adequately account for relationality must be rejected. The classical doctrine of God is alleged to be inadequate in just this way. Thus, Elizabeth Johnson writes:

> The perfections of the theistic God are developed in contrast to the finitude of creatures, leading to speech about God the creator who is "infinite, self-existent, incorporeal, eternal, immutable, impassible, simple, perfect, omniscient, and omnipotent," in the descriptive list drawn up by H. P. Owen....
>
> In response to the insufficiencies of classical theism, a goodly number of theologians have been seeking other ways of speaking about God. These theological efforts are leading to discourse about, in Anne Carr's felicitous summary, the liberating of God, the incarnational God, the relational God, the suffering God, the God who is future, and the unknown, hidden God of mystery. So profound are these changes and deviations from the classical approach that it is not uncommon for theologians engaged in their development to proclaim that a "revolution" in the idea of God is occurring in our day.[2]

I will argue that the equation of relationality with mutability is by no means necessary and that the tradition, including the work of the early church fathers, has readily recognized this relational aspect as a constitutive characteristic of an orthodox perception of God.

---

[1]Cf. Eric L. Johnson's contribution to this volume in ch. 3.
[2]Elizabeth A. Johnson, *She Who Is* (New York: Crossroad, 1995), 19–21.

While not solely in defense of relationality, a number of contemporary writers seem inclined to agree that a "revolution" in the doctrine of God is necessary. The authors of *The Openness of God*, for example, have proposed a modified doctrine of God that they claim alleviates the undesirable implications of the divine immutability and provides a more adequate understanding of the biblical texts.[3] By contrast, the authors of the present work believe that classic Christianity's doctrine of God has the resources to account adequately for this. Several issues call out for discussion:

1. What sense of immutability can be plausibly defended?
2. What range of meanings has immutability had within the tradition? And, more explicitly, what senses of mutability or change are problematic and which are not?
3. Does the challenge to immutability, exemplified in the work of open theists and others, do justice to the richness of the term within the broader Christian tradition?

From the outset let me state that I accept as central the claim that any proposal must do justice to the tenor of Scripture as a whole. Moreover, while my discussion focuses attention on the divine immutability, it is necessary to consider both the concepts of impassibility and divine eternity.[4] While open theism represents one voice calling for revision to the classical doctrine of God, I will engage other alternative Christian theologies as appropriate.[5]

## 2. Divine Immutability and the Classic Tradition

The call for revision of the doctrine of immutability is often related to criticism of *the* "traditional" or "classical" conception of God. But is there truly *a* classical conception of God? Even a casual perusal of the historical development of the concept of God reveals a range of conceptions of God that could equally be considered orthodox. For example, at least three differing conceptions of the nature of the divine eternity have a firm place within the tradition. Similarly, the precise nature of the inner-Trinitarian relations as well as the manner in which an incorporeal God interacts with an embodied creation is the subject of a good deal of debate.

I am not suggesting that the phrase "the traditional/classical conception of God" be discarded. It is appropriate to deploy the phrase in a broad sense, implying the entire range of "classical" conceptions.[6] It is only usages that fail to recognize the full richness of the tradition's use of the phrase by shackling the

---

[3]Clark H. Pinnock et al., *The Openness of God: A Biblical Challenge to the Traditional Understanding of God* (Downers Grove, Ill.: InterVarsity Press, 1994).

[4]See ch. 9 in this volume by Patrick Lee on impassibility and ch. 5 by Paul Helm on eternity.

[5]For example, process theology, liberation theology, feminist theology, etc.

[6]Thus, it can be argued that more than one detailed conception of the divine immutability has had a firm place within the broader tradition.

GOD UNDER FIRE

"classical" conception of God to the most problematic articulations of the divine attributes that present the most difficulty—for example, as occurs in the work of Charles Hartshorne.[7] Millard Erickson's critique makes the point:

> It appears that the strong objection to immutability has been motivated by a reaction to the Greek philosophical conceptions of static immobility. That kind of God, in the Aristotelian fashion, does not really act, and because thinking about what changes would itself entail a change, does not really think about anything except himself.... It appears that what we are encountering is a confusion of stable with static.[8]

How many, besides Aristotle, have actually held the conception of God termed "traditional" by those who propose revision to the doctrine of the divine immutability? Further, a brief review of the Church Fathers demonstrates their keen awareness of the tensions involved in maintaining immutability without sacrificing the divine relationality.

Consider, for example, the debates between Athanasius and the Arians. While the focus of these debates was the status of the Son, there is material relevant for the present discussion. The Arians, arguing the Son belonged to the created order, adduced passages that seem to show characteristics that may be predicated of humans but not of God (e.g., Mark 14:34–35, which shows Jesus' mental anguish in the garden, or Mark 13:32, which affirms that only the Father, not the Son, knows the day of the Son's return). Viewed in isolation, such passages are a problem for one who affirms the full deity of the Son *if* deity *and* a narrow understanding of immutability are necessarily linked. In our first example, changing passions seem evident; in the second, changing knowledge—thus creating tension if Jesus is to be affirmed as fully divine by one who feels constrained to affirm a restricted view of God's immutability.

It is interesting to note that neither the Arians nor Athanasius solved the problem by abandoning the concept of divine immutability. Instead, the Arians tried to solve the problem by arguing that the Son was a creature (albeit a special creature) and therefore not fully divine, thus removing the issue concerning immutability. Athanasius, however, surrendered neither the divine immutability nor the deity of the Son. Instead, he argued, with regard to the anguish in the garden, that Christ suffered according to his humanity but not according to his divinity. In this way, he sought to retain the tensions implied by retaining certain

---

[7]See Charles Hartshorne, *A Natural Theology for Our Time* (LaSalle, Ill.: Open Court, 1967). The denial of the divine immutability in a more traditional sense is part of process theism's attempt to defend a more dynamic and relational concept of God. For further details, consult John B. Cobb Jr. and David Ray Griffin, *Process Theology* (Philadelphia: Westminster, 1976); Schubert Ogden, *The Reality of God and Other Essays* (New York: Harper & Row, 1977); Lewis Ford, *The Lure of God* (Philadelphia: Fortress, 1978). For critical interaction see Ronald H. Nash, ed., *Process Theology* (Grand Rapids: Baker, 1987).

[8]Millard J. Erickson, *God the Father Almighty: A Contemporary Exploration of the Divine Attributes* (Grand Rapids: Baker, 1998), 112.

types of apparent change as over against the divine immutability—specifically, by affirming the latter of Christ's divinity and the former of his humanity.

In his second letter to Nestorius, Cyril of Alexandria makes a similar point. Commenting on the words of the Council of Nicea regarding the nature of the Son, Cyril writes:

> We must follow these words and teachings, keeping in mind what having been made flesh means; and that it makes clear that the Logos from God became man. We do not say that the nature of the Word was altered when he became flesh. Neither do we say that the Word was changed into a complete man of soul and body. We say rather that the Word by having united to himself hypostatically flesh animated by a rational soul, inexplicably and incomprehensibly became man.[9]

Cyril clearly recognizes the tension when he says that the Word *became* flesh but in so doing did not change his essential nature. How is this possible? Cyril says it is both inexplicable and incomprehensible. Is this merely avoiding the underlying philosophical issue? Or is it that, as Timiadis has written, "the early Church was fully conscious of the difficulties inherent in using human terms to describe God's actual Being"[10] and therefore, they were more willing than we are to let such tensions be attributed to God's incomprehensibility?

A couple of paragraphs later, Cyril addresses the suffering of Christ:

> Thus we say that he also suffered and rose again, not that the Word of God suffered in his own nature, or received blows, or was pierced, or received the other wounds, for the divine cannot suffer since it is incorporeal. But since his own body, which had been born, suffered these things, he himself is said to have suffered them for our sake. For he was the one, incapable of suffering, in the body which suffered.[11]

Here Cyril defends immutability (or, more accurately, the related concept of impassibility) by arguing that Christ's sufferings were not actually the sufferings of the Word but rather of the body the Word had taken. However, since it was the body *of Christ*, we can say that Christ suffered on our behalf. This is reminiscent of Athanasius, who would have said Christ suffered according to his humanity but not according to his divinity. Once again we see one of the Fathers, rather than insisting that the tensions between mutability and immutability be resolved, attempting to be faithful to the biblical witness they saw as affirming both.[12]

---

[9]Cyril, *St. Cyril of Alexandria: Letters 1–50*, trans. J. I. McEnerney (The Fathers of the Church 76; Washington, D.C.: Catholic Univ. of America Press, 1987), 39.

[10]Thomas F. Torrance, *Theological Dialogue Between Orthodox and Reformed Churches* (Edinburgh: Scottish Academic Press, 1985), 25.

[11]Cyril, *St. Cyril*, 40.

[12]I would be remiss not to note that Irenaeus is cited as one strongly affirming the sufferings of God and, therefore, more opposed to the implications of the divine immutability. However, as Grant observes, this must be understood in its context. Irenaeus was engaged in

Without unduly multiplying examples, let us consider two other ways in which particular Fathers attempted to affirm immutability without sacrificing divine relationality. Gregory Thaumaturgus, for example, argued that the immutable Christ so overwhelmed the sufferings of his passion that those sufferings had no real impact on his essence. Gregory writes:

> For the impassible one became the suffering of the passions, inflicting suffering on them by the fact that impassibility manifested itself as his impassibility in his Passion. For what the passions do to those who are passable, that same thing he, the impassible one, did to the passions by his Passion. . . . For if a piece of adamant struck with iron does not suffer by the impact, but on the contrary remains impassible as it was, to such an extent that the force of the impact returns upon the smiter, since adamant shows itself impassible by nature and does not yield to the impact of the passions, why should we not say that the impassible one became a cause of suffering for the passions?[13]

The nature of the blacksmith's anvil, Gregory argues, is to be immutable so that even though it bears the blows of the blacksmith's hammer, it in no way is affected by them. In essence, Gregory argues that Christ suffers without suffering.

With Clement of Alexandria, we can be more brief. The primary point of the divine immutability for Clement is the fact that the Son could not be distracted from his love for humankind by any of the pleasures or distractions of the world. There is a sense in which Clement is simply affirming the faithfulness of the Son in carrying out the task of effecting human redemption. Here the soteriological focus of the Fathers' concern is perhaps most evident: immutability and impassibility are primarily about the stability of God's saving will.[14]

This brief consideration of representative passages shows us that the classical tradition contains a much more rich and varied treatment of the divine immutability than is presented by Developmentalist Christian theologies. The Fathers did not merely embrace the antecedent Platonic/Aristotelian philosophical tradition that allowed divine immutability to consume the divine relationality; instead, the Fathers affirmed the immutability of God primarily because they were steeped in the biblical witness that they saw as indicating there was no alternative. At the same time, they had to deal with those texts that seemed to indicate that God was involved with change of one sort or another.

Because the biblical texts led them to affirm both immutability and certain kinds of change, the Fathers tended to offer solutions that maintained rather than eliminated the tensions. As we noted earlier, the wisdom of the Fathers resided

---

debate with Docetism, which argued that Christ only appeared to become human. In this context, then, Irenaeus must be seen as more concerned with defending the actuality of the Incarnation than denying the divine immutability. See Robert M. Grant, *The Early Christian Doctrine of God* (Charlottesville: Univ. Press of Virginia, 1966), 111–14.

[13]Gregory Thaumaturgus, *Life and Works*, trans. M. Slusser (Washington, D.C.: Catholic Univ. of America Press, 1998), 157–58.

[14]Grant, *The Early Christian Doctrine of God*, 111–14.

primarily in the fact that they were more acutely aware than we are of the difficulties of containing the infinite God within the bounds of finite human language. While the Fathers pushed the limits of their understanding in trying to articulate an adequate concept of God, they were more willing to recognize the humble boundaries of human reason in the face God's infinite mystery. At that point, they were willing to admit they had reached their limits. Rather than dismissing the tensions, they pointed where language could not go.

## 3. The Implications of Various Senses of Change

The preceding section has shown (1) that the richness of the tradition does not allow reduction to a false dichotomy, (2) that within the broader Christian tradition there is little embrace of the strong Aristotelian conception of immutability as criticized by the open theists and others, and (3) that the Fathers tended to hold in healthy tension the doctrine of immutability, which for them was more about stability than about stasis, while affirming a relational concept of God, which was an integral part of their soteriology.

With this background in place, it becomes apparent that the argument can be narrowed to a discussion covering the differing concepts of immutability. To facilitate this conversation I will examine different ways in which "change" may be applied to a thing. Three types or categories of immutability readily present themselves: (1) types of change that do not preclude claiming God is immutable, (2) types of change most deny of God—even many who propose revision of the divine immutability, and (3) types of change seen as problematic and thus suggested by alternative theologies for modification. Since there is general agreement that no modification is warranted in light of changes of the first two types, the subsequent section will deal in more detail with the third category.[15]

### 3.1 Nonproblematic Types of Change

Erickson provides an enlightening analysis of various ways in which the terms *change* and *immutability* have been taken. Perhaps the most innocuous is characterized by the following example. Imagine Sam has attributes such that the following proposition is true.

(1) Sam is the tallest person in the room.

Now, imagine that some person, say Robert, enters the room and is taller than Sam. Proposition (1) is no longer true; in fact, some other proposition—namely, the denial of (1) is now true. But, of course, it is hard to see how Sam has changed.

In similar fashion, consider the following propositions regarding Robert's love for God.

(2) At time $t^1$, Robert does not love God.
(3) At time $t^2$, Robert loves God.

---

[15]In what follows, I will be using certain insights from ch. 5 of Erickson's *God the Father Almighty*.

GOD UNDER fire

Now, there is a sense in which one could say God "changed." Specifically, at time $t^1$ God does not have the property of being loved by Robert, while at time $t^2$ he does. But, again, it is hard to see how this constitutes any real change in God. Geach has called this meaning of change a "Cambridge change," and no one maintains that immutability implies that "changes" of this sort must be denied.

Another sort of "change" with which we can dispense quickly is that of a change of location. Either on the basis of God's nonspatiality or on the basis of the divine omnipresence, it is hard to see how the notion of a change in location makes any sense when applied to God.

## 3.2 Types of Change Denied of God, Even by Revisioners of the Divine Immutability

There are certain senses of change that virtually all theologians agree are to be denied of God. One of these relates to the divine being itself: that which makes God be God, does not change.[16] Thus, for example, if God is essentially omnipotent, he cannot cease to be omnipotent. If God is a necessarily existent entity—that is, one that cannot fail to exist—then it is impossible that he should cease to exist. If God is perfect and complete in his essence, then he can never become imperfect or incomplete. Drawing from the text of *The Openness of God*, it seems clear that this particular sense of divine immutability is affirmed by the authors.[17] As such, many, though not all, who propose to modify the concept of immutability tend to affirm the unchangeableness of the divine nature.

Another aspect of the term *change* deals primarily with either improvement or deterioration. Thus, one who is ill may change for the better by overcoming one's illness. Equally, one who is healthy may change for the worse/deteriorate by contracting some disease. This sense of change may be applied in a variety of other ways: One may improve/deteriorate with regard to one's skills, one's financial condition, one's ability to love, one's personality traits, and so on.

Can this aspect of change be consistent with an orthodox conception of God? The Christian tradition looks disparagingly on such a claim, insofar as it is generally accepted that God possesses all of his attributes to the maximal degree.[18] If this is the case, then clearly God could never improve; furthermore, it is unimaginable that he could deteriorate. In other words, improvement and deterioration are types of change that theologians generally agree must be denied of God. One possible area where there may be an exception to this claim is with regard to the divine knowledge; this issue I treat separately in the next section.

On immutability there is one domain in which an almost universal consensus does exist: the question of God and his salvific purpose towards his creation.

---

[16]Though the process theologians would deny even this since they conceive the divine essence itself as changed by God's interaction with humans.

[17]This is one reason why open theists distinguish themselves from process theists.

[18]Again recognizing the exception of the process theologians, who argue that God, as he interacts with the creation, improves. God, so they argue, is unsurpassable by another but may surpass himself as he learns/develops in the grand cosmic process.

While there may be some debate about what precisely it means to claim that God intends the salvation of his creatures, definitional matters aside, all seem to agree that God cannot be swayed in his ultimate aim for his creation. This position is often cast in terms of God's being faithful to the promises contained in Scripture or revealed in salvation history. In fact, some theologians make this sense of immutability primary; thus, the German systematic theologian Wolfhart Pannenberg writes:

> Whereas the predicate of immutability that derives from Greek philosophy implies timelessness, the thought of God's faithfulness expresses his constancy in the actual process of time and history, and especially his holding fast to his saving will.... We read already in Num. 23:19 that God is not a man that he should repent. The same is said with reference to a resolve upon judgment in I Sam. 15:29. Yet in the story of the Flood (Gen. 6:6–7), the story of Saul's rejection (I Sam. 15:10–11; cf. v. 35), and many prophetic texts we are told that God does change his mind. In the story of Israel, however, it becomes increasingly apparent that he does not change his mind about his will to save.[19]

In this instance, we see a particular sense of "change" that virtually all theologians, whether or not they propose other modifications to the divine immutability, agree must be denied of God. This illustration is obviously related to the divine will. We will later return to the topic, addressing both this case and others in which the divine will can be spoken of as immutable.

## 3.3 Types of Change Denied or Proposed for Modification

Within the broader Christian tradition, a divine attribute that has virtually universal acceptance is omniscience, the claim that God knows all true propositions. The argument relating immutability of the divine knowledge to God's omniscience is straightforward: If God infallibly knows all true propositions and since the truth of propositions that God infallibly knows cannot change, it follows that God's knowledge is immutable. Propositions that God infallibly knows come in a variety of forms.

(4) The sum of the angles in a triangle equals 180 degrees.
(5) A parent is older than his/her child.
(6) Sacramento is the current capital of California.
(7) Helium is the second element in the periodic table.

However, open theists and process theologians argue that certain types of propositions are such that they are neither true nor false, and therefore their truth is unknowable. Just as affirming God's omnipotence does not mean that God can do the logically impossible, open theists and process theologians argue that God's not knowing these unknowable propositions does not threaten the divine omni-

---

[19]Wolfhart Pannenberg, *Systematic Theology*, trans. Geoffrey W. Bromiley, 2 vols. (Grand Rapids: Eerdmans, 1991, 1994), 1:437.

science. Under these conditions they believe it can be said that God's knowledge is mutable (changes) and yet simultaneously affirm his omniscience. Unknowable propositions are those dealing with future contingent acts. For example:

(8) Henry will freely have a bacon and cheese omelet for breakfast tomorrow.

God, so the argument goes, knows everything that is logically knowable, but they propose to modify the concept of omniscience so it does not include God's knowing future contingent acts. If God cannot know these unknowable propositions, God's knowledge would be ever-expanding as future contingents are actualized. Thus, in the terms of this argument, God's knowledge is not immutable.

Many of these alternate theologies also propose modification to our concept of the immutability of God's will. Consider the following:

(9) At time $t^1$, God willed the preservation of the cities of Sodom and Gomorrah.
(10) At time $t^2$, God willed the destruction of the cities of Sodom and Gomorrah.

Those who propose either to modify or deny the divine immutability argue that the divine will changed between times $t^1$ and $t^2$; consequently, we must deny immutability of the divine will in such matters. Many individual texts appear to fit this model, demonstrating that God's intentions to bless or punish individuals, as well as groups, is contingent on their behavior. For example, 1 Samuel 15 shows God's rejection of Saul as king of Israel—the very same Saul whom God had earlier chosen. Does this indicate a change in God's will?

A third, closely related sense of God's immutability that is often called into question is his "disposition." Consider the following:

(11) At time $t^1$, God is favorably disposed toward Sam.
(12) At time $t^2$, God is not favorably disposed toward Sam.

Again, according to those who propose modification or denial of God's immutability as it relates to divine disposition, it seems clear that a change in the divine disposition toward Sam has occurred sometime between $t^1$ and $t^2$. Thus, on these grounds, they claim this sense of immutability must be denied.

Again, an exemplary case is Saul as presented in 1 Samuel 15. As in the previous case, our concern is not the potential reasons for this change of disposition; at this point, we merely need to recognize that such a modification in disposition, at least on the surface, appears to be a "change." In the same vein, examples suggesting change in God's love are apparent within Scripture, providing additional examples of potential shifts within the divine disposition. We must examine the arguments of those who consider the affirmation of God's love as inconsistent with divine immutability along with the others noted.

We have identified three possible senses of change that require detailed examination in the next sections: change of God's knowledge, change of the divine will, and change of God's disposition, both generally and as relates to God's love.

## 4. Assessment of Change in Divine Knowledge

As noted, many alternative theologies see the problem with the immutability of God's knowledge revolving around the concern with God's knowing future contingent propositions. At the heart of the concern with God's knowing exhaustively the future are two significant questions. First, is it possible for God to interact responsively with us if he knows in meticulous detail everything that will come to be? Second, does God's exhaustive foreknowledge of the future render human actions inevitable, thereby foreclosing the possibility of human freedom?[20]

As we noted above, to reject God's knowing future contingent acts is to reject or redefine the immutability of the divine knowledge since with every single event God comes to know something as actual which before he either did not know or knew only as potential. Open theists and process theologians argue that "omniscience" only means knowing all *knowable* propositions, and they argue that propositions about future free acts are unknowable. Such propositions, so they claim, do not have a truth value, and propositions that do not have a truth value are, by definition, unknowable.

This line of argumentation suggests three additional questions that we must examine in order to evaluate this proposal. First, do propositions about future contingent acts have a truth value? Second, if they do, is it knowable? Third (and directly related to our greater theme), hypothetically speaking, if God were to know future contingent acts, would it foreclose the possibility of human freedom and preclude true interaction between God and his creation?

The first two questions receive an informative assessment in an essay by Alvin Plantinga entitled "Divine Knowledge."[21] Regarding the first question, Plantinga writes, "it is at best monumentally difficult to see how a proposition could fail to have a truth value." On the second, he argues that we often mistakenly think that *our* inability to say *how* God knows something precludes his knowing it. As these issues are taken up by my colleague, I refer the reader to chapter 6 in this volume by William Lane Craig for further detail.

It is the third question—on God's knowledge of yet unrealized contingencies and the effect that this knowledge might have on both the possibility of freedom and the interaction between God and his creation—that I will explore. To consider whether God's foreknowledge of future propositions has the consequence of precluding human freedom, we must briefly develop a doctrine of the

---

[20]Some argue that human freedom can be preserved under a compatibilist definition of freedom. However, I do not find this conception of freedom adequate and agree that if future acts are inevitable, they cannot be free.

[21]Alvin Plantinga, "Divine Knowledge" in *Christian Perspectives on Religious Knowledge*, ed. C. Stephen Evans and Merold Westphal (Grand Rapids: Eerdmans, 1993), 40ff.

divine eternity.[22] The position I present here probably originated with Plotinus, was taken up by Boethius, and has been developed by Pannenberg. It argues, in short, that all times—those past to us, those present to us, and those future to us—are all present to God in complete and undivided wholeness. God knows things in their temporal sequence (i.e., he *knows* what events are experienced *by* us as before or after others), but the divine life is not such that it *experiences* them in this fashion.

More specifically, events do not fade from God's presence into the past as they do for humans, nor must God wait in anticipation of the future; rather, he holds all times in actual presence so that the divine life is not subject to the temporal fragmentedness experienced by humans. This is not Augustinian timelessness, wherein God "observes" time from outside. Rather, it might more accurately be represented as temporal omnipresence—that is, just as God is spatially omnipresent by virtue of his presence to all space at once, so God, as the Lord of time, is present to all times at once.

At the heart of this conception is the claim that, rather than time being the antithesis of eternity, eternity is the whole that is constitutive of time. In other words, time is to eternity as part is to whole. With the creation of the world of time and space, the whole is experienceable by the creatures as the temporal sequence of times within which the creatures live and develop. However, in creating this reality for creatures, God does not himself become subject to time, but rather maintains the undivided wholeness of eternity.

Pannenberg notes an important consequence: The eschatological future has priority as concerns God's knowledge of the world.[23] Since we think inevitably in temporal terms, let us consider a temporal example to help clarify this claim and its significance. Imagine that the march of temporal history is complete and that the eschatological future has arrived. Imagine also that a great supercomputer exists that is able to recapture all data concerning all events that occurred during the history of the universe. This computer would be able to reconstruct something like a view of the totality of universal history, thereby providing "simultaneous" access to history in its fullness.

---

[22]The view I present here, though having a long and storied history, is often absorbed into Augustinian timelessness (cf. Paul Helm's contribution to this volume in ch. 5). While the distinction is subtle for the immediate discussion, it is important for the overall discussions of this chapter. Augustinian timelessness conceives God as outside of time, in effect, separated from his creatures. While this creates no problem for God's "seeing" events in time, Nelson Pike (*God and Timelessness* [New York: Schocken, 1970]) has plausibly argued that placing God in a "timeless realm" raises significant problems for the issue of divine action, for if God is outside time, can he act in time? The position I argue for here does not place God outside time; it makes him present to time—though not just one time but rather the totality of times. This has the additional benefit of overcoming the objection of many alternative Christian theologies that timelessness conceives God as separated from, and therefore not intimately involved with, his creation. Pannenberg often deploys this concept of the divine eternity. Similarly, in response to process proposals, W. N. Clarke deploys a comparable notion in Nash, *Process Theology*, 239ff.
[23]Pannenberg, *Systematic Theology*, 1:401–10.

When Pannenberg writes that the future has ontological priority as regards God's knowledge of the universe, he means that God does not know the results of free choices "until" they happen. In this sense, one might be sympathetic to those theologians who are concerned about the consequences of divine "fore-knowledge." The difference in the proposal made here is that by virtue of divine eternity and God's actual presence to all times in undivided wholeness, he knows what is future to us just as readily as he knows what is present to us. Consequently, from our perspective, God knows what is future to us, but from the divine perspective God simply "knows."

Within the divine life, though God possesses the wholeness of time in actual presence, he still knows the chronological sequence in which they exist for us. So, while "before" and "after" do not carry *temporal* significance for the divine life, they do bear something of *logical* significance. Further, in its fullness the divine eternity contains the actual life and the cumulative result of the free choices instantiated within the lives of free creatures.

Consequently, the proposition

(13) Martha Dandridge married George Washington.

has always been true in the divine eternity precisely because Martha Dandridge chose to marry George Washington. If she had chosen to marry someone else, then the proposition describing that alternative state of affairs would have been true in God's eternity. Thus, by assigning priority to the eschatological future regarding the divine knowledge, we make explicit that God's knowing is not a "foreknowing" and the freedom of the creatures is clearly preserved. Thus, God knows what is future to us only by virtue of the nature of his eternity. In fact, according to this proposal, if one could somehow remove God from his eternity, constraining the divine mind to a temporal location alongside humans, he would not know what is future to us, for then it would be future to him as well.[24] In this way, then, the immutability of God's knowledge can be held together with the reality of human freedom since immutability so understood is a consequence of the divine eternity and is not related to foreknowledge.[25]

The second reason some alternative theologies reject the immutability of God's knowledge is that it seems to rule out true responsiveness on God's part, a responsiveness and free interaction that would seem to be a prerequisite for true relation with his creatures. Does the proposed concept of the divine eternity offer any relief? First, let us recall that within the broader Christian tradition it has been argued that God's interaction with the world consists of a single, eternal act. Second, let us couple this notion with the claim that the divine life is such that it

---

[24]Could this explain Jesus' claim that only the Father knew the day of the Son's glorious return, since the Son had at that point taken up a temporal location within the Incarnation?

[25]Some will no doubt challenge this proposal by suggesting that this makes time and change mere illusion, but surely this is mistaken in the same way that it would be to claim that the parts of a car are an illusion and only the assembled whole is real. Time is real *as time*, while eternity is real *as the wholeness of time*.

GOD UNDER FIRE

holds all temporal history in eternal, actual presence. So, from our perspective "now" is a point that resides between what has been and what has not yet come to be, but from the perspective of the divine eternity, "now" embraces all of our "nows" in actual, undivided, and eternal presence.

Thus, a single, eternal act, undertaken by God from the reality of his own divine life, becomes *for us* a series of acts—that is, God's acting "now" in the divine eternity easily involves *all* of the "nows" of linear temporal existence. This single eternal act involves for us and God real interaction and responsiveness, albeit from differing perspectives as to the experience of "time." In this manner the plausibility of real and intimate interaction can be preserved.

In summary, then, I have argued with Plantinga that there are no adequate reasons to deny that propositions about future contingent actions have truth values. Similarly, I do not find adequate the claim that we may reject God's knowing these propositions just because we cannot say *how* God knows them. Finally, I suggest that the conception of the divine eternity presented here provides a means of holding together the immutability of God's knowledge with both human freedom and real responsiveness on God's part. Consequently, while I am sympathetic to the concerns raised by those proposing modification or rejection of immutability in this sense, I do not concur that the immutability of God's knowledge has the consequences they suggest.

## 5. Assessment of Change in the Divine Will

Perhaps the strongest arguments advanced in favor of the mutability of the divine will are biblical passages such as Genesis 6:5–7 and Exodus 32:11–14 (cited at the beginning of the chapter). In the first case, one might conclude that God's will changed with regard to the preservation of the creatures. A similar claim may be made with regard to God's will to preserve or destroy the Israelites at the base of Sinai. Thus, how do we assess the nature of God in light of those particular passages? Must we deny the immutability of his will?

First of all, we must recall our earlier discussion regarding the common belief that God's will is immutable with regard to his saving intentions. As the passages in question appear to be an expression of the divine will, it seems clear that in some sense we must affirm that will's immutability without thereby deserting the biblical text.

Let us note that, given the concept of the divine eternity deployed above, one could simply argue that God's "single, eternal act" must be conceived as the expression of a single, eternal divine willing. However, for the sake of argument, let us consider another solution.[26] Let us use as our paradigm case the first passage cited, which concerns God's "repenting" that he had created life. One might reasonably abstract the following two propositions:

(14) At $t^1$, God wills that the creatures that he has created will live.

---

[26]For the following, I am indebted to some insights in Thomas V. Morris's essay "Properties, Modalities, and God," *The Philosophical Review* 93.1 (1984): 33–55.

(15) At $t^2$, God wills that the creatures that he has created be destroyed (with certain exceptions).

From this isolated passage, individuals on both sides of the immutability argument might conclude that there has been a radical change in God's will between $t^1$ and $t^2$. But in the light of the greater narrative, is this really the case? Consider the following proposition:

(16) God wills that if conditions C1 are satisfied, then the creatures should be preserved, but if conditions C2 come to be, then the creatures should be destroyed.

I will not presume to give a precise definition of conditions C1 and C2, but one might imagine that conditions C2 are like those mentioned by Paul in Romans 1:20–25. Let us say that at $t^2$, conditions C2 come into existence. In this scenario, has the divine will changed from $t^1$ to $t^2$? I do not think so. Consider the following quote from Thomas V. Morris:

> The position I am presenting is perfectly consistent with the divine intentions being indexed to, or conditional upon, contingencies arising in the created universe.... Why can't it always and immemorially have been the case that God intends to do A if B arises, or C if D comes about?[27]

Further, Richard E. Creel cites Aquinas similarly:

> The will of God is altogether immutable. But notice in this connection that changing one's will is different from willing a change in things. For a person whose will remains unalterable can will that something should happen now and its contrary afterwards.[28]

Interestingly, Ben Witherington examines a number of prophecies from the Old Testament and concludes that there are often clear markers in the text suggesting that many are, in fact, conditional in nature[29]—that is, God's will is tied to creaturely contingencies.

This line of argumentation suggests that our distillation of the divine will into propositions such as (14) and (15) is too simple. Even proposition (16) is too simple, partially because we have not clarified the content of conditions C1 and C2, but also because it deals with only a pair of specific moments. An accurate expression of the divine will is far too complex to be recorded, but it might, as regards human salvation, have a form something like the following:

(17) God immutably wills the salvation of all creatures and will save all those receiving his offer of salvation. Consistent with this statement of the overarching divine will, W1 will come to be under conditions C1, W2 will come to be under conditions C2, etc., etc., etc.

---

[27]Morris, "Properties, Modalities, and God," 47–48.

[28]Richard E. Creel, *Divine Impassability: An Essay in Philosophical Theology* (New York: Cambridge Univ. Press, 1986), 18.

[29]Ben Witherington III, *Jesus the Seer* (Peabody, Mass.: Hendrickson, 1999).

In the actual proposition expressing the divine will, all creaturely contingencies and all states of affairs throughout the world's history would be incorporated. I see no reason to deny the existence of such a detailed proposition that expresses in exhaustive detail the divine will. Given that God, minimally, eternally knows all possibilities and, maximally, eternally knows all actualities, it seems clear that such an expression would never need to be modified or altered by God in any way.

Therefore, I see no reason to deny the immutability of the divine will. Charles Hartshorne and others have argued that God's love is not consistent with an immutable divine will, for an unchanging will suggests a nonresponsive lack of intimacy and, therefore, a loss of relationality. However, it seems clear that the necessary responsiveness is built into the possible expressions of the divine will, manifestation of which is contingent on human action. In summary, I believe there is more than adequate reason to affirm the immutability of the divine will.

## 6. Assessment of Change in the Divine Disposition

To speak of God's disposition toward some person, Pat, is to comment on whether God is pleased with Pat. If so, then God is favorably disposed toward Pat; if not, then God is not favorably disposed toward Pat. The question, then, becomes whether God's being pleased with someone changes. If we consider the case of Saul, it seems that one could clearly argue that God's disposition changed over time. We might propositionally capture this as follows:

(18) At time $t^1$, God is favorably disposed toward Saul. (1 Sam. 10:1)
(19) At time $t^2$, God is not favorably disposed toward Saul. (1 Sam. 15:26)

To determine whether there is anything more than a prima facie appearance of change here, let us utilize the conceptual framework developed in the last section. Just as we argued that the outworking of the divine will could be understood as the expression of an eternal, immutable willing by God, here we can argue that God's disposition toward humans is similarly conditioned upon creaturely contingencies. In the case of God's disposition toward humanity, we must make God's will to save primary. Consequently, we might make dispositions of being pleased/being displeased one of the expressions of the divine will (W1 and W2) in proposition (18), so that God would be, say, pleased with Pat under conditions C1 but displeased under conditions C2.

Would we, then, have to admit that God's dispositions are mutable? No, for as we have already seen, God's being disposed can be conceived as an eternal, single act. Consequently, we might describe God's overarching disposition as:

(20) God is immutably disposed toward Pat in the manner most consistent with Pat's being saved.

Therefore, we may argue that God's disposition is immutable even if expressed differently as a consequence of a person's actions. We must now turn our attention to our last major issue regarding God's unchangeableness: Is God's perfect love compatible with conceiving him as immutable?

## 7. Assessment of God's Love in Light of the Divine Immutability

It is hard to see how one can meaningfully speak of God's being loving apart from his engaging in acts that express that love. Thus, it seems immediately obvious that one could deploy an argument similar to that deployed in the last sections—specifically, we could first affirm that God unchangeably loves all of his creatures. I am sure that those who object to more traditional senses of the divine immutability would not object to this affirmation; in fact, in many cases the concern with immutability is precisely whether or not it precludes truly loving relationships. Second, we can construct a suitable proposition expressing God's loving responses conditioned upon the circumstances and decisions his creatures make. Thus,

> (21) God unchangeably loves Sam and thus desires Sam's best. Under circumstances C1, God's loving response to Sam will be R1; under circumstances C2, God's loving response to Sam will be R2, etc., etc.

As we have seen previously, in light of the conception of God's eternity developed earlier and considering God's expression of love to his creatures as a single, eternal act, we need not concede that God's love for his creatures requires that he change even if the expression of that love is expressed differently under differing creaturely contingencies. I argue that this provides an adequate response to the challenge raised that conceiving God as perfectly loving requires denial of the divine immutability. However, given the attention focused on this issue by those denying or radically reformulating the divine immutability, it is appropriate to consider additional lines of defense.[30]

Michael J. Dodds, in a fine work examining the doctrine of God's immutability in the theology of Thomas Aquinas, notes that human love generally involves movement of some type: "Human love is often associated with motion—the restlessness of desire, the impulse of passion, the steady unfolding of affection and commitment."[31] Dodds characterizes both human love and divine love as containing elements both of motion and immutability; as a result, he uses the phrase "dynamic stillness." The precise nature of the dynamic stillness that characterizes divine love, however, is different from that of human love.

In both cases, love is characterized as a "motion" in the broad sense of the word as it is comprised of an "immanent activity of the will."[32] Human love, however, contains other elements of change/motion. First, human love implies a change in will as the subject changes from indifference or ignorance concerning the object of love to a state of loving that object. Second, a certain desirability or goodness recognized in the object of love gives rise to or causes this change in the human will. Third, whenever the object of love is absent, the subject may engage in a variety of different acts aimed at regaining closeness.

---

[30]See also ch. 12 in this volume by D. A. Carson.

[31]Michael J. Dodds, *The Unchanging God of Love* (Fribourg: Editions Universitaires, 1986), 277.

[32]Ibid., 280, here writing specifically of the divine will.

Additionally, Dodds points out that all forms of human love are to some extent colored by self-centeredness. Nonetheless, coupled with these elements of change and impurity in human love, there is also an element of immutability in human love. Once the subject has gained union with the object, "it is pleased with it and adheres to it as though fixed ... in it, and then is said to love it."[33] Thus, human love gives rise not only to change but also to stability when the subject and object are united. Further, as the lover remains faithful to its object, the immutability of love is evidenced. Let us see how the divine love differs and how it is similar.

In the first place, in light of the immutability of the divine will to save, there is no change from indifference toward or ignorance of those whom the divine will may embrace. Further, since love is precisely the willing of some good to another and since willing the salvation of the creatures is to will their most excellent good, God's will to save must be seen as the epitome of love. Additionally—and this is a critical point—the divine love is always fully engaged, as it is purely actualized without any element of potentiality. Therefore, God's love can neither increase nor decrease. Consequently, it seems clear that the divine love is immutable in this sense.

Second, any goodness that the creatures may have originates in God, so that there is nothing separate from God that can serve to *cause* God to love his creatures. In other words, the divine love toward creation is entirely and absolutely gratuitous,[34] being totally uncaused.

Third, God, by virtue of the divine omnipresence, can never be separated from his creatures—one only need consider Psalm 139.

Finally, since the self-centeredness of human love is a consequence of some lack or defect in the subject that he or she hopes to make up by union with the object of love, and since there is absolutely no lack in God, the divine love can never be colored by self-centeredness that is rooted in deficiency. Consequently, the elements of change and impurity that comprise human love are completely absent in the divine love. Therefore, God's love is pure and unchangeable.

There is, however, one other challenge relating to the divine love. Since compassion is a perfection of love, the divine love must have compassion as a central element. Yet, it has often been argued that compassion necessarily involves compassionate suffering. If this applies to the divine compassion, it seems clearly to imply change—unless one wishes to claim that the divine suffering is always maximized, which certainly seems problematic, making God into something of a divine codependent person. The question, then, is whether the divine compassion necessarily involves suffering.

It must be readily admitted that intuitions on this matter are deeply divided; nevertheless, I find Dodds's analysis and his appropriation of certain insights from Aquinas instructive. In the first place, compassionate suffering is comprised of two elements: compassionate love and the suffering that attends it. While suffering in and of itself is an evil, it "may be reckoned as good insofar as it is a response

---

[33]Ibid., 278, citing Aquinas.
[34]Dodds explores this notion in some detail on pp. 282ff.

to the suffering of another."[35] Now while it is true that the elements of compassionate love and suffering go together in the closest manner, they are distinguishable. In fact, "in human compassion, the evil which the suffering of compassion implies in itself and the good which the suffering of compassion represents as a response to another's misfortune are inseparable."[36]

But must these be inseparable in God's love as well? Initially, one is inclined to answer that they are. Since this compassionate suffering is a perfection in humans and since God is the source and most excellent instantiation of whatever perfection appears in humans, it seems the good of compassionate suffering in humans must exist superlatively in the divine love. However, Thomas writes, "it is not necessary that whatever is of the excellence of the creature must be of the excellence of the creator . . . as something is of the excellence of a dog such as to be ferocious which may be to the discredit . . . of a man."[37]

In other words, while the general rule is that the perfections of the creature may be predicated par excellence of the Creator, there are exceptions since there are perfections predicated of humans, owing to finitude and sin, which are not predicated of God. Dodds uses the example of shame, which is a human good under the appropriate conditions, but shame would never be appropriately predicated of God. Thus, Dodds's summary of Thomas:

> In a similar way, the suffering of compassion, though recognized as good in a human being insofar as it is a response to the misfortune of another, is nonetheless seen as an evil insofar as it is in itself a sort of unhappiness. It is therefore not predicated of God. Similarly, the absence of the suffering of compassion, though indicative of some evil or lack of love in the human being, is indicative of the perfection of love and goodness in God.[38]

Thus, Thomas argues, compassion is expressed differently in God than in humans.

Now, it does not follow from this that compassion is not to be predicated of God; in fact, Thomas holds that compassion must be predicated of God. At this point, we must draw out the implications of distinguishing between the suffering of compassion and the love of compassion. "Is it . . . suffering as such that we admire in the compassionate person, or is it not rather the magnitude of the love that is manifested in that suffering?"[39] Again, in the case of humans these may not be separable, but this only means that the best humans can do is the limited good evident in the combination of suffering and love.

However, we need not conceive the divine love as so limited. Rather, the divine compassion may be composed only of the most praiseworthy elements of human compassion—specifically, the love that is manifested in compassion, a love

---

[35]Ibid., 295.
[36]Ibid., 296.
[37]Ibid., 297, citing Aquinas.
[38]Ibid., 297.
[39]Ibid., 298–99.

that involves suffering in the human case but not in the divine case. Therefore, the immutability of the divine love need in no way detract from the reality of the divine compassion; thus, the divine immutability need not be surrendered.

## 8. Summary and Conclusions

With the analysis of the divine immutability complete, it is time now to summarize our findings. In the first place, I have argued that the criticisms of those rejecting or radically redefining God's unchangeableness lack appropriate subtlety at a number of points. Throughout their critique, they consistently refer to *the* classical doctrine of God and of *the* classical conception of immutability without recognizing the full spectrum of concepts actually deployed within the classical tradition. The result is the false dichotomy discussed early in this chapter. By narrowing the field, they have been able to establish something of a "straw man" that focused on the more extreme visions of the divine immutability, a position that I have argued may well have been held by few other than Aristotle. Further, we have considered numerous citations from the early church fathers that demonstrate that they understood the tensions inherent in affirming that God is immutable and yet profoundly relational. Their solutions varied somewhat, but they generally tried to hold together both aspects of the doctrine of God.

Additionally, we have considered a number of ways in which the concept of change can be understood. Initially, we showed that several of those conceptions are not really contested, as they constituted no "real change" in God; subsequently, we focused our attention on those that have been the subject of some debate. These were immutability as regards God's knowledge, his will, and his disposition, especially as it impacts the claim that God is perfectly loving. In each case, we have found there to be no necessity in denying the divine immutability in order to preserve either the divine relationality or God's love—that is, in each case we identified plausible means of affirming both immutability and relationality/love.

In conclusion, we must admit a certain sympathy for the project undertaken by those seeking to reformulate the doctrine of God. Surely we must agree that preservation of the personhood of God, his intimate relationality, and the profundity of his love are essential to the Christian doctrine of God. Where we tend to part company is in the extent to which modification of the tradition is necessary to accomplish this. I hope we have shown that the modifications they propose are not entirely necessary, and more notably, that contained within the broader classical Christian tradition are resources capable of addressing these potential problems. These resources are a good deal more varied and useful than many suggest, requiring only arduous philosophical and theological groundwork to appropriate them adequately.

Finally, at the outset I suggested that the Fathers' treatment of immutability tends to be superior in two ways. First, they tended to recognize the limits of language and were more willing to admit that certain aspects of the doctrine of God might be beyond those limits. I share the concern of many philosophers that the "mystery button" ought not be deployed too quickly; nevertheless at some point, the reality of God extends beyond our best attempts at conceptualization. Second, the Fathers were less concerned to have the doctrine of God neatly tied off in all aspects. They recognized and accepted tensions within their thought, largely because they thought this was most consistent with the biblical witness. We would do well to profit from their example.[40]

---

[40]I would like to express my appreciation to Randy Shrauner for his input and recommendations on the final form of this essay.

Chapter 11

# How Shall
We think about
the trinity?

*Bruce A. Ware*

# 1. Introduction

To someone not conversant with contemporary theological writings, it may come as something of a surprise to learn that the historic doctrine of the Trinity is undergoing considerable scrutiny, reassessment, reformulation, and/or defense.[1] For many, this doctrine seems so abstract and unrelated to real life that they wonder: What *here* warrants and elicits such concentrated attention? What is at stake in *this doctrine* that provokes such interest and concern?

To others, however, what is at stake is nothing less than the integrity and reality of the Christian faith itself. The church's historic Trinitarian understanding is being assaulted in ways unimaginable in previous periods, and tremendous harm is being done both to the church's doctrine and to its faith expression by ideologically driven revisions of the doctrine of the Trinity. God is under fire as the church's long-standing affirmation of the one true God as Father, Son, and Holy Spirit is despised and rejected.

Donald Bloesch surprised many in the theological world with the publication in 1985 of his book entitled, *The Battle for the Trinity*.[2] He charged the feminist rejection of the Bible's own and traditional theology's predominantly masculine language for God as a rejection of the Trinity itself and, as such, the imposition of a different faith (i.e., not the *Christian* faith) onto those quarters of the church inclined to accept the feminist critique. Such charges and concerns have continued unabated. Consider, for example, the sobering words of Duke University's professor of systematic theology, Geoffrey Wainwright:

> The signs of our times are that, as in the fourth century, the doctrine of the trinity occupies a pivotal position. While usually still considering themselves within the church, and in any case wanting to be loyal to their perception of truth, various thinkers and activists are seeking such revisions of the inherited doctrine of the trinity that their success might in fact mean its aban-

---

[1] Consider a sampling of recently published works; notice the variety of theological perspectives and interests represented among their authors: Colin E. Gunton, *The Promise of Trinitarian Theology* (Edinburgh: T. & T. Clark, 1991; 2d ed., 1997); Ted Peters, *God As Trinity: Relationality and Temporality in Divine Life* (Louisville: Westminster John Knox, 1993); Thomas F. Torrance, *Trinitarian Perspectives: Toward Doctrinal Agreement* (Edinburgh: T. & T. Clark, 1994); Duncan Reid, *Energies of the Spirit: Trinitarian Models in Eastern Orthodox and Western Theology* (Atlanta: Scholars Press, 1997); Kevin J. Vanhoozer, ed., *The Trinity in a Pluralistic Age: Theological Essays on Culture and Religion* (Grand Rapids: Eerdmans, 1997).

[2] Donald Bloesch, *The Battle for the Trinity: The Debate over Inclusive God Language* (Ann Arbor: Servant, 1985).

god under fire

donment, or at least such an alteration of its content, status, and function that the whole face of Christianity would be drastically changed. Once more the understanding, and perhaps the attainment, of salvation is at stake, or certainly the message of the church and the church's visible composition.[3]

What are some of these proposed contemporary revisions of the doctrine of the Trinity that provoke such strong reaction? This chapter proposes to focus on four dimensions of Trinitarian reconstruction, all of which are prominent, even influential, in various quarters within the church, and represent a significant departure from Trinitarian doctrine inherited from the classical tradition, particularly by the Western church. (1) The first dimension will focus on the conceptual relation between the immanent and economic Trinities. Whereas once the immanent Trinity took priority conceptually, the shift today is to give pride of place to the economic Trinity. Just what this means and what difference it makes will be explored in section 2.

(2) A movement is underway to employ the largely Eastern understanding of the Spirit's procession from the Father (and *not* also from the Son) so as to envision a salvific presence of God, by his universal Spirit, in which no Christological content of the Spirit's revelation must be present. Rejection of the Western church's affirmation of the *filioque* ("and the Son") is used, then, for purposes of grounding an inclusivist soteriology.

(3) The mainline church rejection of masculine Trinitarian language (or any masculine God-language, more generally) has been occurring for nearly three decades. Whether such changes leave us with the God named in the Bible will be explored here, with argumentation offered to support traditional and biblical masculine language for the triune God.

(4) Finally, many contemporary evangelical egalitarians are urging the church to retain masculine language for God while denying that this masculine language indicates any kind of inner-Trinitarian distinction of authority.

These arguments will be weighed, and support will be offered for the church's long-standing commitment to the Trinitarian persons' full equality of essence and differentiation of persons, the latter of which includes and entails the eternal functional subordination of the Son to the Father, and of the Spirit to both Father and Son.

## 2. Priority and Relation of the Immanent and Economic Trinities

### 2.1 Immanent and Economic Trinities

In orthodox theology, God is, in himself, eternal, self-existent, and fully self-sufficient. Yet he has freely chosen to create a world with which he is intimately and fully involved. In accounting for both sides of this wondrous reality, church theologians from the beginning have distinguished senses in which we talk about God.

---

[3]Geoffrey Wainwright, "The Doctrine of the Trinity: Where the Church Stands or Falls," *Interpretation* 45 (1991): 117.

God *ad intra* (or God *in himself*) must be distinguished carefully from God *ad extra* (or God *in relation to the world*). Although it is marvelously true and glorious that God has created and is related to this world, it is a mistake to so identify God with the world such that somehow God's independence from the world is lost.

To understand God correctly we must see that the God who chooses to create and relate is also (antecedently, as Barth would say) the God who exists eternally apart from this or any world, in need of no world at all, complete in the splendor of his own infinitely glorious being. Thus, his relation to creation is not necessary to his existence, nor does it somehow add fullness to the divine life. Rather, the biblical portrait of God affirms, as Paul articulates to the Athenian philosophers, that "the God who made the world and everything in it is the Lord of heaven and earth and does not live in temples built by hands. And he is not served by human hands, as if he needed anything, because he himself gives all men life and breath and everything else" (Acts 17:24–25).

God *ad intra*, then, is fully God, independent of the world, infinitely rich and full in the splendor of his own majesty and intrinsic glory. He needs no world, and nothing exists that can add to his fullness. To the contrary, all that comes into existence does so because God originates "life and breath and all things." Only understood in this way can we go on to marvel that *this* God, the God of self-existence and infinite self-sufficiency, would choose to create and to relate, to take on the freely chosen role of God *ad extra*. He creates, then, to give, not to get; to overflow of his bounty, not to fill up his supposed emptiness.

Yet, having insisted that God *ad extra* is logically and conceptually dependent on God *ad intra*, the theologians of the church have also insisted that this does not leave us with two gods. That is, because God reveals *who he is* when he makes himself known to his finite creatures, we can have confidence that we come to know God *in himself* through his revelation to us. Karl Barth, perhaps more than any other theologian of the twentieth century, stressed this point. God is not different in himself from what he is in his revelation to us. If this were the case, then the God we *know* would be a different god from the God *who is*.[4]

This understanding of the relation of God *ad intra* and God *ad extra* forms the backdrop for the distinction between the Trinitarian relations of God understood immanently (i.e., the three persons relating *ad intra* within the eternal Godhead, apart from the world) and economically (i.e., the three persons relating *ad extra* in intimate involvement in every facet of creaturely life and history). Furthermore, just as the notion of God *ad intra* has priority over God *ad extra*, so the immanent Trinity is logically prior to and explains the nature of the economic Trinity. As Paul Molnar writes, "The immanent trinity is the indispensable premise of the economic Trinitarian action *ad extra* but cannot simply be identified with these historical events."[5]

---

[4]Karl Barth, *Church Dogmatics*, 4 vols. in 13 parts (Edinburgh: T. & T. Clark, 1936–1969); see esp. vol. 1, part 1; vol. 2, part 1.

[5]Paul D. Molnar, "The Function of the Immanent Trinity in the Theology of Karl Barth: Implications for Today," *SJT* 42.3 (1989): 373.

The three persons of the Godhead exist, apart from the world, in an eternal relation that stands independent of, and apart from, their freely chosen relation to a world they freely and jointly bring into existence. Yet, as the three divine persons act in freedom to create and to relate, they likewise manifest in their economic dealings with the world what is true of their logically prior and intrinsic immanent relations.

## 2.2 Reducing the Immanent to the Economic Trinity

In the face of this traditional Trinitarian understanding, a prominent modern reformulation has occurred. Whereas traditionally priority has been given to the immanent Trinity, this revision seeks to give primacy to the economic Trinity. Karl Rahner began what has become a groundswell of theological revisionism when he proposed his "axiomatic unity of the 'economic' and 'immanent' trinity," defending his view that "the 'economic' trinity is the 'immanent' trinity and the 'immanent' trinity is the 'economic' trinity."[6] One might take this claim to mean, with Barth, that we do not have *two* triune beings when we speak of the immanent and economic Trinities. If this were all Rahner meant, there would be no real reformulation. But clearly Rahner means more. Since we know God only in his self-revelation (i.e., economically), and more particularly only as he is savingly revealed through the incarnation of the Son, we must use as our starting point on Trinitarian understanding the historic and redemptive revelation of the triune God who, as Father, Son, and Spirit, bring to us salvation. Rahner affirms, then, "that no adequate distinction can be made between the doctrine of the Trinity and the doctrine of the economy of salvation."[7]

This reductionism of the immanent Trinity to the economic Trinity has become commonplace in current Trinitarian writings. Discussions by such notable writers as Eberhard Jüngel,[8] Jürgen Moltmann,[9] Wolfhart Pannenberg,[10] and

---

[6]Karl Rahner, *The Trinity*, trans. Joseph Donceel (New York: Herder & Herder, 1970), 21–22.

[7]Ibid., 24. For a helpful discussion and critique of Rahner's view in light of religious pluralism, see Gary Badcock, "Karl Rahner, the Trinity, and Religious Pluralism," in Vanhoozer, ed., *Trinity in a Pluralistic Age*, 143–54.

[8]See Eberhard Jüngel, *God As the Mystery of the World*, trans. Darrell L. Guder (Edinburgh: T. & T. Clark, 1983), where Jüngel asserts that "Karl Rahner's thesis should be given unqualified agreement" (369).

[9]See esp. Jürgen Moltmann, *The Crucified God*, trans. R. A. Wilson and John Bowden (New York: Harper & Row, 1974); idem, *The Trinity and the Kingdom of God*, trans. Margaret Kohl (San Francisco: Harper & Row, 1981). Richard Bauckham, "Jürgen Moltmann," in *One God in Trinity*, ed. Peter Toon and James D. Spiceland (Westchester, Ill.: Cornerstone, 1980), cautions that whereas Moltmann roots the being of God in his historical (even eschatological) unfolding, he nonetheless acknowledges a kind of immanent Trinity that he prefers to call the "Trinity in the origin," yet "the Trinitarian history of God is grounded in the missions of the Son and the Spirit" (126).

[10]Wolfhart Pannenberg, *Systematic Theology*, vol. 1, trans. Geoffrey W. Bromiley (Grand Rapids: Eerdmans, 1991). See, e.g., Pannenberg's claim that "a systematic grounding and development of the doctrine of the Trinity must begin with the revelation of God in Jesus Christ,

Catherine Mowry LaCugna[11] urge their distinctive variations of this basic maxim. The result is that we are limited to God's historical manifestation of his triune being for understanding the nature of that divine Trinity. But, if all we see and therefore know of God is God in historical manifestation, then at least two problems arise.

First, if God's immanent being is identical to his economic manifestation, then God's own independence from creation is called into question. Concerning Rahner's own reduction of immanent to economic Trinities, John Thompson observes that Rahner has "failed to distinguish between the mystery of grace in the economy and the *necessary* mystery of the Trinity per se. This risks making God's actions *ad extra* a necessity of being rather than a freely willed decision."[12] Process theologians have argued for the necessity of the world from the very existence of God.[13]

Orthodoxy, by contrast, has long held to God's eternality, self-existence, and self-sufficiency, in which God, as triune, exists apart from the world in the splendor of his own excellencies, with no need whatsoever of an external world. That he chooses to create a world expresses his freedom to do what he need not do but does not imply a lack in the divine nature or a need for some world or other. These contemporary understandings of the Trinity run the risk of compromising this essential understanding of God's full independence from this or any world. If the immanent Trinity collapses into the economic, then some world or other becomes the necessary medium of God's self-expression. This is a tragic implication of much of contemporary Trinitarian reformulation.

Second, if our knowledge of God is limited to his economic and historical self-disclosure, this denies an important category of divine revelation by which we know about God, namely, propositional revelation. Surely if God utilizes the medium of divine discourse[14] to tell us about aspects of his divine reality that tran-

---

just as the historical path to the construction of the doctrine in Christian theology started with the message and life of Jesus and the apostolic preaching of Christ" (300). As with Moltmann, while Pannenberg acknowledges implicitly a place for the immanent Trinity, the rule and revelation of God in history so constitutes the being of God that the priority of the immanent Trinity is jeopardized.

[11] See Catherine Mowry LaCugna, *God for Us: The Trinity and Christian Life* (San Francisco: HarperCollins, 1991), 209–41 (ch. 7, "The Self-Communication of God in Christ and the Spirit"). Concerning Rahner's thesis, LaCugna writes, "Rahner's principle is invoked and endorsed by virtually every theologian now writing on the topic of the Trinity, even if sometimes in a slightly modified form. Rahner's axiom is a sound starting point for rethinking the Christian theology of God" (13).

[12] John Thompson, *Modern Trinitarian Perspectives* (New York: Oxford Univ. Press, 1994), 27.

[13] That is, in process thought one world or other, though not necessarily this exact world, is necessary to God's very being. See John B. Cobb Jr. and David Ray Griffin, *Process Theology: An Introductory Exposition* (Philadelphia: Westminster, 1976), 41–68; Charles Hartshorne, *Omnipotence and Other Theological Mistakes* (Albany, N.Y.: SUNY Press, 1984), 73–95.

[14] See discussions and defenses of divine discourse in Nicholas Wolterstorff, *Divine Discourse: Philosophical Reflections on the Claim That God Speaks* (New York: Cambridge Univ. Press, 1995); Kevin J. Vanhoozer, *Is There a Meaning in This Text? The Bible, the Reader, and the Morality of Literary Knowledge* (Grand Rapids: Zondervan, 1998). While Wolterstorff, in

scend our own limitations and historical conditioning, we should not reject such knowledge of God simply because we have not somehow experienced those aspects historically.

An example here might help. If someone describes to a friend his experience eating dinner in a Japanese sushi bar, the friend should not reject this knowledge on the basis that he, having never eaten at a sushi bar, cannot identify with this reality. Rather, it is possible that knowledge might be conveyed of a reality that transcends one's own current experience and frame of reference. Surely, divine revelation *about* who God is in himself apart from creation falls into this category. How foolish and presumptuous to reject such revelation, should it be graciously given by God, simply because we must live in the historically, culturally conditioned context of our finite lives.[15]

The glory of the doctrine of divine revelation is precisely that God has *made himself known* such that without this free self-disclosure, we would be left fully in the dark. Certainly, while this revelation comes partly through the vehicle of historical manifestation (e.g., when he delivers Israel from the Egyptians through the parted waters of the Red Sea, or when Jesus steps forth as the Lamb of God who takes away the sin of the world), it comes also when God *tells* us what we cannot observe or experience of his transcendent life and work (e.g., that he exists apart from this or any other created order, or that he brought into existence *ex nihilo* all that is via his creative Word, or that he needs nothing that might be provided by this or any other finite and feeble creation, or that his glory fills and surpasses all that he has made). In light of this revelation of God, it seems only right to ask, if God has defined his immanent life as a Trinitarian unity, then is it right for us to reduce his reality to his economic manifestation?

With the orthodox heritage, we should affirm, then, that God's economic revelation of himself as a triunity indicates his life antecedently and apart from creation in the immanent fullness of his eternal tripersonal unity. Even though the "order of knowing" gives priority to the revelation of God over his immanent and eternal reality, even this order of knowing and revelation itself indicates, from what we learn about God apart from creation, that priority in the "order of being" clearly belongs to the immanent Trinity. It is the God who eternally and immanently *is* the one triune God as Father, Son, and Holy Spirit, who chooses to create and relate economically and to make known who he is, both in propositional and historical self-unfolding.[16]

---

particular, wishes to distinguish "revelation" from "divine discourse," it is clear that his discussion of the latter demonstrates that divine discourse must be understood in its broadest sense as comprising a revelatory expression of God's mind and thoughts to his created beings.

[15]Perhaps here even Barth, who otherwise upholds God's immanent Trinity as antecedent to the economic Trinity, is guilty of a dangerous reduction when he recognizes only actual acts of divine revelation in historical events as fully authoritative revelation.

[16]As an example of a recent theological development moving in quite a different direction from what is here argued, see John Sanders, *The God Who Risks: A Theology of Providence* (Downer's Grove, Ill.: InterVarsity Press, 1998), 26–34, who suggests that we may actually sin against the Lord when we imagine God in ways that transcend our experience of him.

## 3. A Movement to Divorce Pneumatology from Christology

### 3.1 Eastern Pneumatology Employed to Support Inclusivism

One of the sharpest divisions between the Western (Latin) and the Eastern (Greek) church traditions is over whether we should rightly understand the procession of the Holy Spirit as from the Father *and the Son* (*filioque*) or from the Father alone. The original Nicene Creed revision at Constantinople (A.D. 381), won largely by the relentless efforts of the Cappadocian fathers of the Greek church (Basil, Gregory of Nyssa, and Gregory of Nazianzus), worded the third article to say that the Holy Spirit proceeds "from the Father." Centuries later, a regional synod in the West (A.D. 589, at Toledo) inserted the now-famous *filioque* into the creed's third article and, by this, simply followed the clear language of Augustine's earlier Trinitarian discussion.[17] By the eleventh century, this insertion and revision had been accepted fully in the West and rejected fully in the East. These differences on the *filioque* clause have persisted so that even contemporary efforts to resolve these differences have failed.

While the differences over the *filioque* debate are too complex to elucidate in this brief discussion, one contemporary development arising out of this debate warrants our attention. Soteriological *inclusivism* is a movement that has grown in recent years.[18] It places itself between an all-out pluralism (by insisting on the uniqueness of Christ for salvation) and exclusivism (by denying that knowledge of and faith *in Christ* is necessary to be saved). That is, inclusivism holds that while Jesus and his atoning death and resurrection are the only basis for anyone's salvation (*contra* pluralism), it is nonetheless not necessary, strictly speaking, to know of and believe in Jesus to be saved (*contra* exclusivism).

In other words, according to inclusivists, one may trust in God as known through his revelation in the created order or known, perhaps, as he has revealed himself to some limited though sufficient degree in one of the world's non-Christian religions. The "wideness of God's mercy" is such that God will accept and save those honest, humble, and heartfelt God-seekers when, through no fault of their own, they lack knowledge of Jesus the Christ and yet turn humbly to God as he *is* revealed in creation and in their cultural setting. Thus, there is salvific

---

[17]St. Augustine, *The Trinity*, 4.29; 15.47–48; see the edition trans. by Edmund Hill in vol. 5 of *The Works of St. Augustine* (Brooklyn, N.Y.: New City Press, 1991).

[18]See, e.g., John Sanders, *No Other Name: An Investigation into the Destiny of the Unevangelized* (Grand Rapids: Eerdmans, 1992); Clark H. Pinnock, *A Wideness in God's Mercy: The Finality of Jesus Christ in a World of Religions* (Grand Rapids: Zondervan, 1992); as well as briefer treatments in William J. Crockett and James G. Sigountos, eds., *Through No Fault of Their Own? The Fate of Those Who Have Never Heard* (Grand Rapids: Baker, 1991); John Sanders, ed., *What About Those Who Have Never Heard? Three Views on the Destiny of the Unevangelized* (Downer's Grove, Ill.: InterVarsity Press, 1995); Dennis L. Okholm and Timothy R. Phillips, *More Than One Way? Four Views on Salvation in a Pluralistic World* (Grand Rapids: Zondervan, 1996). For substantive criticism of inclusivism, see, e.g., Ronald H. Nash, *Is Jesus the Only Savior?* (Grand Rapids: Zondervan, 1994); Millard J. Erickson, *How Shall They Be Saved? The Destiny of Those Who Do Not Hear of Jesus* (Grand Rapids: Baker, 1996).

hope, according to inclusivists, for all who sincerely come to God even when they are without any specific understanding of Christ and his atoning death.

One of the vexing questions faced by inclusivists is how the Spirit of God might work to bring people to salvation when these people have no access to truth about the Savior, Jesus Christ the Messiah of God. That is, how is God's saving presence manifest in the non-Christian world so that hope of people's salvation is grounded where no Christian gospel witness exists? Clark Pinnock has recently turned to the *filioque* controversy afresh for theological and conceptual assistance in answering this question. For too long, says Pinnock, the Spirit, in both creation and redemption, has been subordinated to Christ. The effect of this has been "to exalt Christ above the Spirit"[19] and so minimize the distinctive contribution of the Spirit. As a corrective, Pinnock suggests, "Let us see what results from viewing Christ as an aspect of the Spirit's mission, instead of (as is more usual) viewing Spirit as a function of Christ's. It lies within the freedom of theology to experiment with ideas."[20]

One distinguishing aspect of the Spirit's work upon which Christ's own work is dependent is simply that the Spirit is the Spirit of grace, who brings to lost people everywhere the reality of the salvation Christ won. The universal presence of the Spirit, then, is a theme Pinnock embraces but does so in a manner that must, of necessity, be separated from knowledge of the historically and geographically rooted work of Christ. Herein lies the problem with the Western church's adoption of *filioque*. Pinnock writes:

> The idea of adding *filioque* was not perverse theologically. The risen Lord did and does pour out the Spirit on the church. But the phrase in the creed can lead to a possible misunderstanding. It can threaten our understanding of the Spirit's universality. It might suggest to the worshiper that Spirit is not the gift of the Father to creation universally but a gift confined to the sphere of the Son and even the sphere of the church. It could give the impression that the Spirit is not present in the whole world but limited to Christian territories. Though it need not, the *filioque* might threaten the principle of universality—the truth that the Spirit is universally present, implementing the universal salvific will of the Father and Son. One could say that the *filioque* promotes Christomonism. . . . It does not encourage us to view the divine mission as being prior to and geographically larger than the Son's. It could seem to limit Spirit to having a noetic function in relation to Christ, as if the Spirit fostered faith in him and nothing more. It undercuts the idea that Spirit can be active where the Son is not named and supports the restrictive reading of the axiom "Outside the church, no salvation."[21]

One clear implication of the Spirit's universal yet non-Christocentric salvific presence is that saving truth and grace is as universally present as is the Spirit

---

[19]Clark H. Pinnock, *Flame of Love: A Theology of the Holy Spirit* (Downer's Grove, Ill.: InterVarsity Press, 1996), 80.

[20]Ibid.

[21]Ibid., 196.

himself. How, in non-Christian lands where no knowledge of Christ exists, can saving truth be present? Pinnock is ready with his answer. Consider these representative claims:

> Spirit is present everywhere, and God's truth may have penetrated any given religion and culture at some point.
>
> ✦
>
> Though Jesus is not named in other faiths, Spirit is present and may be experienced. God can speak to people's hearts through the Spirit.
>
> ✦
>
> Regardless of time and place, it is possible for anyone to receive God's offer of grace because of the Spirit, who is active everywhere.
>
> ✦
>
> One can avoid the one-sided Christic view by referring to the Holy Spirit, who renders effective the mission of Christ and makes God's reign present everywhere. There are elements of grace found in other religious traditions, and one hopes they may mediate God's presence for people.[22]

## 3.2 On Uniting What Is Wrongly Divided:
## The Spirit As the Spirit *of Christ*

A deeply troubling aspect of Pinnock's "experiment" is its clear avoidance of Scripture's own testimony to the necessary linkage of the Spirit's saving work in the world with that of Christ's. As Pinnock and other inclusivists would surely initially agree, it is clear that God the Father and Christ want, and have commanded, that God's saving presence be made known throughout the world. Jesus' Great Commission, as recorded at the ends of the Synoptic Gospels and the beginning of Acts, requires for its fulfillment that the whole world know of the saving grace of God in Christ and his saving death on the cross.

But notice clearly how this is to occur. Jesus never anywhere suggests that somehow, apart from the proclamation of the gospel, people will know about God's free offer of salvation as the Spirit brings God's saving truth and grace into the cultures and religions of the peoples of the world *independent of the knowledge of Christ and the need to believe in Christ to be saved*. Never! Instead, Jesus' only instruction and mandate is to take the gospel to the world in the power of the Spirit. Spirit and gospel truth are inextricably linked by Jesus, as they are likewise inextricably linked in the apostolic mission of the early church. Apart from the gospel of Christ, people are without hope.

As this relates to the question of the *filioque*, I suggest that biblical fidelity requires that we retain the notion that the Holy Spirit's procession into this world of fallen human beings occurs as the Father *and the Son* send him to carry out the Spirit's clearly Christocentric work. In John 16:12–15, Jesus made clear that when the Spirit comes, he will both honor the Son and speak the truth of the Son:

---

[22]Ibid., 202–6.

GOD UNDER FIRE

I have much more to say to you, more than you can now bear. But when he, the Spirit of truth, comes, he will guide you into all truth. He will not speak on his own; he will speak only what he hears, and he will tell you what is yet to come. He will bring glory to me by taking from what is mine and making it known to you. All that belongs to the Father is mine. That is why I said the Spirit will take from what is mine and make it known to you.

Contrary to Pinnock, the Spirit "will not speak on his own" but will take what is Christ's and bring glory to the Son. The coming of the Spirit, as first manifested in Acts 2, is a coming in which the name of Christ is elevated and made known. The Spirit's empowerment is not generic, salvific in some general sense; it is rather empowerment to witness *of Jesus*, as the book of Acts indicates over and over again.[23]

What of the notion that the Spirit is present in the non-Christian cultures of the world, already having brought them saving grace apart from knowledge of Christ? Jesus' own commission and the record of the book of Acts present exactly contrary evidence. Consider Jesus' own final commission as recorded in Luke 24:46–49:

He told them, "This is what is written: The Christ will suffer and rise from the dead on the third day, and repentance and forgiveness of sins will be preached in his name to all nations, beginning at Jerusalem. You are witnesses of these things. I am going to send you what my Father has promised; but stay in the city until you have been clothed with power from on high."

Notice four items. (1) Those to whom he sends his disciples are "all nations." This leaves no one out! Every country, culture, language group, and religion is included in the scope of those to whom Jesus commissions his disciples to go.

(2) The current salvific status of these "nations" (i.e., all people everywhere) is indicated when Jesus implies that they require "repentance and forgiveness of sins." That is, all nations inclusively are currently in sin and in need of forgiveness of their sin. There is no indication that somehow, apart from the witness the disciples are to bring, these nations already have access to saving grace. All are in sin; all need to repent; all must be reached.

(3) This repentance and forgiveness of the sins of the nations will occur as their message is "preached *in his name* to all nations." The name of Christ is central to the gospel of the saving grace of God. Yes, salvation is to be broadcast

---

[23]Appeals by inclusivists to salvation in the Old Testament where, presumably, knowledge of the Christ to come is minimal at best, miss the radical redemptive, historical significance of the coming of the long-awaited Messiah. Now that the Savior has come, *all* New Testament evidence points to the fact that the gospel *is* the gospel of Christ died and risen; by faith *in Christ* one may be saved. As one clear evidence of this, consider the logic of Gal. 3:23–26, where Paul actually speaks of the period of the law as a time "before faith" had come (3:23). It is clear, as one continues reading, that he means specifically "before faith *in Christ*" had come, since the law was our tutor to lead us to Christ (3:24), and that by "faith *in Christ Jesus*" we might be made sons of God (3:25–26).

universally, but only as the name of Christ is proclaimed universally. There is no universal Spirit presence of saving grace devoid of the gospel of God's grace in Christ.

(4) The implied reference to Spirit-empowerment energizes this gospel proclamation. Jesus tells the disciples they are witnesses, but they are not alone! They are to "stay in the city" and wait to receive "what my Father has promised," by which they will be "clothed with power from on high." As we know from Acts 1 and 2, Luke unmistakably intends his readers to connect this with the outpouring of the Spirit by which the disciples were empowered to bear witness of Jesus, "in Jerusalem, and in all Judea and Samaria, and to the ends of the earth" (Acts 1:8).[24]

With Pinnock, then, I affirm that the Spirit's mission is to spread the universal saving grace of God. But contrary to Pinnock, this saving grace comes only as the Spirit empowers the proclamation of Christ and his gospel. The Spirit comes to glorify Christ! How dishonoring to Christ, and how disregarding of Scripture's clear instruction of the Spirit's own mission, to suggest a universal saving work of the Spirit that is devoid of the very One whose name he seeks to exalt and whose saving work he seeks to spread. We do not honor the Spirit when we imagine him separated from Christ's person, work, and gospel. We do not understand the Spirit if we fail to see him, above all, as the Spirit *of Christ*.[25]

## 4. Mainline Feminist Rejection of Masculine Language for the Triune God
### 4.1 Central Feminist Arguments for Rejecting Masculine Trinitarian Language

A radical representative of the feminist movement, Mary Daly, has captured the heart of the feminist criticism of the church's biblical and historic adherence to masculine God-language in her claim, "If God is male, the male is god."[26] While *no* respected theologian of the church has claimed that God *is male*, the force of Daly's objection is simply that to refer to God with masculine language gives the impression that masculinity is more godlike. By this impression, then, women are held in subservient positions and granted less than their rightful dignity, so it is asserted. The only corrective can be to remove the predominance of masculine God-language from our Scripture, liturgy, and preaching.[27]

---

[24]One clear evidence of this fact is the connection Luke draws with the Spirit's coming as the fulfillment of "the promise of the Father," first declared by Jesus in Luke 24:49, reaffirmed and reinforced in Acts 1:4–5, and finally ratified in the Pentecost outpouring of the Spirit in Acts 2:33.

[25]See Acts 16:6–7, where "the Holy Spirit" is named specifically "the Spirit of Jesus," and Rom. 8:9–11, where "the Spirit," "the Spirit of God," is also named more specifically "the Spirit of Christ," and even "Christ."

[26]Mary Daly, *Beyond God the Father: Toward a Philosophy of Women's Liberation* (Boston: Beacon, 1973), 19.

[27]See, e.g., Carol Christ and Judith Plaskow, eds., *Womanspirit Rising: A Feminist Reader in Religion* (San Francisco: Harper & Row, 1979); Virginia Mollenkott, *The Divine Feminine: The*

Only brief attention can be given here to the several lines of argument put forth for inclusive God-language,[28] and our focus will be particularly on the concern over the traditional masculine Trinitarian formulation. (1) Appeal is made to the metaphorical nature of the Bible's own masculine language for God. All agree that when Scripture calls God "Father" or "King," we are not to understand by these that God is literally male. They operate metaphorically to speak of fatherly and kingly functions, such as provision, protection, and rulership. So, while God literally is provider, protector, and ruler, he is metaphorically father and king.

This being so, feminists argue that we ought also to describe God with feminine metaphors that express some other functions of God more characteristically feminine, such as comforter, healer, and sympathizer. Thus, while God is (literally) neither father nor mother, the metaphors "father" and "mother" are equally appropriate in describing of God qualities and functions literally true of him. We ought, then, to balance feminine names of God with traditional masculine names to give a more complete view of God, or else we ought to avoid such gender-specific terms altogether since the risk is just too great that people might take these as implying that God *is* a sexual being.

As applied to language for the Trinity, feminist advocates have suggested revised language in both directions. Either we should speak of the first person of the Trinity as "Father/Mother" and the second as "the Child of God,"[29] or we should move to a strictly gender-neutral Trinitarian language, such as "Creator, Redeemer, and Sustainer," to replace "Father, Son, and Holy Spirit." Both approaches are advocated within mainline feminism; what both have in common is the avoidance of any dominant masculine language for the triune God.

(2) When one inquires why both biblical and traditional ecclesial language for God has been predominantly masculine, one immediately realizes the intrinsically culturally conditioned nature of the Bible's and the church's God-talk. Patriarchal culture in biblical days and throughout the history of the church has given rise to this predominantly masculine language for God. For feminism, upon

---

*Biblical Imagery of God As Female* (New York: Crossroad, 1983); Rosemary Radford Ruether, *Sexism and God-Talk: Toward a Feminist Theology* (Boston: Beacon, 1983); Ruth Duck, *Gender and the Name of God: The Trinitarian Baptismal Formula* (New York: Pilgrim, 1991); Elizabeth A. Johnson, *She Who Is: The Mystery of God in Feminist Theological Discourse* (New York: Crossroad, 1992); Gail Ramshaw, *God Beyond Gender: Feminist Christian God-Language* (Minneapolis: Fortress, 1995); Aída Besançon Spencer et al., *The Goddess Revival* (Grand Rapids: Baker, 1995).

[28]For careful and thorough study and critique of this argumentation, see Alvin F. Kimel Jr., ed., *Speaking the Christian God: The Holy Trinity and the Challenge of Feminism* (Grand Rapids: Eerdmans, 1992); John W. Cooper, *Our Father in Heaven: Christian Faith and Inclusive Language for God* (Grand Rapids: Baker, 1998).

[29]Note that the early creeds speak of the second person as "begotten" not made, which, as such, contains no gender connotation. So, for these advocates, to speak of the Child begotten of the Father/Mother is consistent with the language of the early church and preserves continuity while making a desirable correction.

realizing this reality, it seems both obvious and necessary that we work to revamp our God-talk. We can maintain this predominantly masculine language for God only at the expense of perpetuating the illicit patriarchy that gave rise to it. While most mainline feminists would not agree wholly with Mary Daly, they would adjust her claim to say that if God is seen and spoken of as masculine, what is masculine will be viewed, naturally and unavoidably, as of higher value and authority. Again, then, one of two lines of response is needed: Either we must balance traditional masculine usage with appropriate and meaningful feminine language of God, or we should leave behind all gender-specific God-referencing altogether.

(3) Following from the above two items, feminist political and ideological advancement requires that we reject the biblical and traditional dominance of the masculine in regard to God. The true liberation of women generally, and the cause of women's rights to serve in all levels of church and denominational leadership in particular, can never happen when God, our highest authority and only rightful object of worship, is spoken of in masculine terms. Affirming the language of God as masculine perpetuates the servile nature of the feminine. Since God is above gender and since he created both genders in his image, then we dare not continue to focus our discussion of God in terms that favor one gender, thus subordinating the other as inferior and subservient.

## 4.2 Responding to the Feminist Case Against Masculine Trinitarian Language

Interestingly, many from within mainline churches as well as the majority of evangelical feminists (i.e., egalitarians) from within and without mainline denominations are opposed to this revisionist feminist agenda. For most in this group, while embracing the values and aspirations of Christian feminism, these opponents join evangelical complementarians in claiming boldly that to change the language of the Bible and church tradition in which God is revealed as Father, Son, and Holy Spirit is to jeopardize the integrity of Christianity itself and to promote what is, in fact, another deity and another faith.[30] Their argumentation is complex and involved, but we will sketch some of their main concerns.

(1) While it is true that the Bible uses masculine metaphorical language for naming God (while never teaching that God is literally male), it is also true that the Bible never employs feminine metaphorical language *to name* God. True, God is sometimes said to be or to act in ways *like* a mother (or some other feminine image),[31] but never is God called "Mother" as he is often called "Father." Respect for God's self-portrayal in Scripture requires that we respect this distinction. While we have every right (and responsibility) to employ feminine images of God,

---

[30]Note the telling title of an article opposed to feminist God-language revisionism: Elizabeth Achtemeier, "Exchanging God for 'No Gods': A Discussion of Female Language for God," in Kimel, ed., *Speaking the Christian God*, 1–16.

[31]For an exhaustive discussion of biblical references to God employing feminine imagery, see Cooper, *Our Father in Heaven*, ch. 3: "The Bible's Feminine and Maternal References to God," 65–90.

GOD UNDER fire

as is done often in Scripture itself, no biblical example or precedence would lead us to go further and to name God in ways he has not named himself. He has named himself "Father" but not "Mother." This stubborn fact of scriptural revelation must itself restrain our talk of God.

(2) One might be tempted to dismiss the above factual point by appealing to the inherently patriarchal culture in which our biblical language of God was framed. But appeal to culture shows just how odd and even unique it is that Israel chose to use only masculine (and *not* feminine) language when naming God. The fact is that it would have been most natural for Israel to follow the lead of the nations surrounding her that spoke with regularity and frequency of their deities as feminine.[32] That Israel chose *not* to do this shows her resistance to follow natural and strong cultural pressures, and it indicates that she contemplated the true God, the God of Israel, as distinct from these false deities.

In defending her assertion that "the Bible's language for God is masculine, a unique revelation of God in the world," Elizabeth Achtemeier continues:

> The basic reason for that designation of God is that the God of the Bible will not let himself be identified with his creation, and therefore human beings are to worship not the creation but the Creator.... It is precisely the introduction of female language for God that opens the door to such identification of God with the world, however.[33]

Whether one follows Achtemeier here fully or not,[34] it is clear that Scripture never names God as "Mother" or with any other feminine ascription, and this stands against the prevailing practice of the cultures surrounding Israel and the early church.

(3) While Scripture surely does reflect the various cultural and historical settings in which it was written, the God of the Bible is presented, ultimately, by self-revelation or self-disclosure. The Bible's language of God, then, must be received with respect and gratitude as the divinely ordained conveyer of the truth God himself intended his people to know about him. To alter biblical language of God is to deny and reject God's self-disclosure in the terms he chose and used in making himself known.

Clearly, at the pinnacle of this self-disclosure of God stands the revelation of Jesus the Christ, who became flesh that we might know in visible, physical form what the invisible, nonphysical God is like (John 1:14–18). Here, with shocking regularity, Jesus refers to God in a manner scandalous to his Jewish listeners, as

---

[32]Elaine Pagels, "What Became of God the Mother? Conflicting Images of God in Early Christianity," in Christ and Plaskow, eds., *Womanspirit Rising*, comments that "the absence of feminine symbolism of God marks Judaism, Christianity, and Islam in striking contrast to the world's other religious traditions, whether in Egypt, Babylonia, Greece and Rome, or Africa, Polynesia, India, and North America" (107).

[33]Achtemeier, "Exchanging God for 'No Gods'," 8–9.

[34]Achtemeier acknowledges that many feminists deny that naming God as feminine links God with creation, but she asserts and then supports with numerous citations her claim, "But feminist writings themselves demonstrate that it does" (ibid., 12).

none other than "Father." That Jesus is the *Son* sent by the *Father* is so deeply and widely reflective of God's self-revelation in and through the Incarnation that to alter this language is to suggest, even if only implicitly, that one speak instead of a different deity. Divine self-revelation, then, requires the glad retention of God as Father, Son, and Holy Spirit.

(4) One last caution will be mentioned. Revisionist feminists could still grant that biblical language speaks of the triune God as Father, Son, and Holy Spirit. But, they argue, since those same Scriptures also employ the language of God as Creator, Redeemer, and Sustainer, may we not use this other biblical language of God and, by so doing, both honor God's self-revelation and avoid the illicit equation of God with masculinity that the traditional masculine language risks? However, while the terms "Creator," "Redeemer," and "Sustainer" are biblical terms for God, they cannot function as substitutes for the persons of the Godhead named with "Father," "Son," and "Holy Spirit"—for at least three reasons.

(a) One risks a modalistic understanding of God who is first Creator, and then changes to the next historical phase of Redeemer, and likewise then to sustainer. The phases and aspects of activity can then be seen as historical modes of the manifestation of the one God, as has been advocated by Sabellius and other modalists.

(b) This substitution implies that the world is eternal, not temporally finite, and that God's redemptive work is necessary, not free. The church's affirmation of God as "Father, Son, and Spirit" is a claim not merely of his economic manifestation as the Father of the incarnate Son in the power of the Spirit (though this is true, in part), but also of the immanent Trinity who is *eternally* Father, Son, and Spirit. The Father, then, is the *eternal* Father of the Son; the Son is the *eternal* Son of the Father. Now, if we substitute "Creator, Redeemer, and Sustainer" as names for these *eternal* realities, it requires that we see God as eternal Creator, implying an eternal creation, and eternal Redeemer, implying necessary redemption.

It is clear, in other words, that while "Father, Son, and Spirit" work well as names of the immanent and economic Trinitarian persons, "Creator, Redeemer, and Sustainer" are merely economic and functional designations. As such, they simply cannot substitute for the language of Scripture and church tradition of the eternal God who is in himself (i.e., immanently and eternally) and in relation to creation (i.e., economically) Father, Son, and Spirit.

(c) The personal names of "Father," "Son," and "Holy Spirit" simply do not reduce to the supposed functional substitutes of "Creator," "Redeemer," and "Sustainer."[35] Is the Father, and the Father alone, the Creator? Is the Son alone the Redeemer? Is the Spirit alone the Sustainer? Biblical teaching instructs us that each of these activities is accomplished by all three divine persons working together. Yes, the Father creates, but he does so through the power of his Word

---

[35]Karl Barth, *Church Dogmatics*, 1/2, writes: "The content of the doctrine of the Trinity ... is not that God in His relation to man is Creator, Mediator and Redeemer, but that God in Himself is eternally God the Father, Son and Holy Spirit.... [God] cannot be dissolved into His work and activity" (878–79).

GOD UNDER FIRE

(John 1:3), who acts as implementer of his creative design (Col. 1:16; Heb. 1:2). The Spirit, likewise, energizes the formation of the creative work of the Father through the Son (Gen. 1:2).

Redemption, likewise, is destroyed altogether if the work of redemption is reduced to that of the second person of the Trinity. Biblically, redemption only occurs as the Father sends the Son into the world to receive the wrath of the Father against him for our sin (Rom. 3:25–26; 2 Cor. 5:21). And, of course, the Son accomplishes this work only by the power of the Spirit, who rests on him, empowers him to go to the cross (Heb. 9:14), and raises him from the dead (Rom. 8:11).

Likewise with sustaining and sanctifying, it is the work of the Father (1 Thess. 5:23–24), the Son (Eph. 5:25–27; Col. 1:17; Heb. 1:3), and the Holy Spirit (2 Cor. 3:18) to preserve believers and move them toward the holiness of life and character designed for them from all eternity (Eph. 1:4).

One realizes, then, that the substitution of "Creator, Redeemer, and Sustainer" for "Father, Son, and Holy Spirit" not only fails as a functional equivalent of the traditional and biblical Trinitarian formula, but worse, if followed, the resulting faith would contain such major theological distortions that it would bear only a superficial resemblance to the faith of true biblical and Christian religion. In the words of Geoffrey Wainwright, "Consideration of creation, redemption, and sanctification shows that an account of them that is true to the biblical narrative will also imply and depend on the Trinitarian communion and cooperation of Father, Son, and Holy Spirit."[36]

## 5. Evangelical Feminism's Rejection of Eternal Functional Subordinationism Within the Trinity

### 5.1 Embrace of Masculine Language and Rejection of Functional Subordination

Evangelical feminists, otherwise known as egalitarians, have generally favored retaining traditional masculine Trinitarian language. For reasons given above, particularly because egalitarians view Scripture as God's inspired Word and self-revelation, the vast majority of egalitarians have sought to defend masculine God-language against the criticism of many of their feminist colleagues. In the process, however, they deny that such masculine God-language implies either that what is masculine is superior over what is feminine or that the eternal relations of Father, Son, and Holy Spirit indicate any kind of eternal functional hierarchy within the Trinity.

Let it be said clearly that nonegalitarian, complementarian[37] evangelicals agree wholly with the first of these denials. Because God created the man and the

---

[36]Wainwright, "Doctrine of the Trinity," 123.

[37]The term "complementarian" is the self-designation of the evangelical constituency that would see God's created design for men and women as comprising male headship in the created order, reflecting itself in the requirement of a qualified male eldership in the church and the husband's overarching responsibility in the leadership of the home. The single best volume describing and defending a complementarian vision is John Piper and Wayne Grudem, eds., *Recovering Biblical Manhood and Womanhood* (Wheaton, Ill.: Crossway, 1991).

woman fully as his image (Gen. 1:26–27), no use of masculine language for God is ever meant to signal some supposed greater value, dignity, or worth of men over women. Furthermore, that women and men alike are redeemed by the Savior who bestows on believing males and females the full riches of Christ (Gal. 3:28–29), and that the believing husband is to grant his believing wife honor as a fellow heir of the grace of life (1 Peter 3:7), also clearly indicate the full equality of personhood and worth vested in women and men, through both creation and redemption, by our gracious God. Egalitarian and complementarian evangelicals agree, therefore, that both men and women are, in creation and redemption, prized, sought, and loved by God equally; women with men stand before God fully equal in their essential humanness, dignity, worth, and personhood.

Concerning the second denial, however, there is significant reason to challenge the egalitarian position. What *does* it mean that the Father is the eternal *Father* of the Son and that the Son is the eternal *Son* of the Father? Is not the eternal and inner-Trinitarian Father-Son relationship indicative of some eternal relationship of authority *within* the Trinity itself? Furthermore, if, as most egalitarians agree, the masculine language about God in Scripture is not a concession to a patriarchal culture but rather represents God's own chosen means of self-disclosure, what *is* conveyed by this masculine terminology? As just noted, while egalitarians and complementarians agree that masculine God-language never indicates the superiority of the male or inferiority of the female, one must ask: Does this masculine language not intentionally link God's *position and authority as God* with the concept of *masculinity* over femininity?

Egalitarians reject these implications.[38] They see clearly that if an eternal relationship of authority and obedience is grounded in the eternal immanent inner-Trinitarian relations of Father, Son, and Holy Spirit, then this gives at least *prima facie* justification to the notion of creational human relations in which authority and submission inhere.[39] Yet both features of the orthodox view mentioned above—the eternal nature of the Father-Son relationship within the Godhead and the predominant biblical masculine language for God—might be seen to suggest just such correspondence. That is, both features could lead one to think that authority and obedience is *rooted in the Trinity* and that authority in some special way *corresponds to masculinity*.

To counter these lines of thought, egalitarians argue fundamentally along three lines. (1) They assert that the predominant masculine references to God in

---

[38]See, e.g., Gilbert Bilezikian, "Hermeneutical Bungee-Jumping: Subordination in the Godhead," *JETS* 40.1 (1997): 57–68; Stanley J. Grenz, "Theological Foundations for Male-Female Relationships," *JETS* 41.4 (1998): 615–30; Royce G. Gruenler, *The Trinity in the Gospel of John: A Thematic Commentary on the Fourth Gospel* (Grand Rapids: Baker, 1986); Millard J. Erickson, *God in Three Persons: A Contemporary Interpretation of the Trinity* (Grand Rapids: Baker, 1995).

[39]Some egalitarians acknowledge the eternal inner-Trinitarian Father-Son relation, yet do not understand this as implying or entailing relations of authority and submission in the created order. See Craig Keener, "Is Subordination Within the Trinity Really Heresy? A Study of John 5:18 in Context," *TrinJ* 20 NS (1999): 39–51.

no way convey some corresponding authority attaching to the male. As already seen in the previous section, the appeal to woman and man being created fully in the image of God indicates no such subordination of the female to the male. Equality (only) characterizes their relation as human persons. As Paul Jewett has put it, to affirm the functional subordination of women to men in any respect cannot avoid the charge that women are thereby inferior to men.[40] But the creation of woman and man in the image of God renders this impossible. Masculinity is never inherently superior, though it is, admittedly, the gender in which God has chosen to name himself most commonly.

(2) They assert that any suggestion of subordination within the Godhead, even the claim of a functional subordination of the Son to the Father, cannot avoid at least an implicit Arianism.[41] The early church theologians, it is argued, rejected all talk of subordination regarding any member of the Trinity to any other. Full equality of Father, Son, and Holy Spirit precludes any and all types of subordinationism. Since the Son is *homoousios* with the Father, we are wrong ever to speak of the Son's subordinate status to the Father and by so doing undermine the orthodoxy won by Athanasius at Nicea and affirmed ever since by the church.

(3) All of Scripture's language of the authority of the Father and submission of the Son is rightly accounted for within the incarnational mission of the Son. Precisely because Christ was the second Adam and fully human, it was necessary for him to subject himself to the will of the Father. Thus, as Gilbert Bilezikian states, "Christ did not take upon himself the task of world redemption because he was number two in the Trinity and his boss told him to do so or because he was demoted to a subordinate rank so that he could accomplish a job that no one else wanted to touch."[42]

Furthermore, when the mission of redemption was completed, the Son resumed his former stature and full equality within the Trinity, leaving forever behind the role in which he had to submit himself in obedience to the Father. As Bilezikian again comments, "Because there was no subordination within the Trinity prior to the second person's incarnation, there will remain no such thing after its completion. If we must talk of subordination it is only a functional or economic subordination that pertains exclusively to Christ's role in relation to human history."[43] So, while masculine language predominates in the biblical depiction

---

[40]See, e.g., Paul K. Jewett, *Man As Male and Female: A Study of Relationships from a Theological Point of View* (Grand Rapids: Eerdmans, 1975), where he asks, "How can one defend a sexual hierarchy whereby men are over women . . . without supposing that the half of the human race which exercises authority is superior in some way to the half which submits?" (71). He continues by asking further whether anyone can "establish the mooted point—woman's *subordination to* the man—by underscoring the obvious point—woman's *difference from* the man—without the help of the traditional point—woman's *inferiority to* the man? The answer, it appears to us, is no" (84).

[41]Bilezikian, "Hermeneutical Bungee-Jumping," says, e.g., that any talk about subordination "smacks of the Arian heresy" (67).

[42]Ibid., 59.

[43]Ibid., 60.

god under fire

for God, and while the divine Father-Son relationship is eternal, none of this indicates a relationship of authority and obedience within the Godhead or a corresponding relationship of authority and submission in human relationships.

## 5.2 Response to the Egalitarian Rejection of Inner-Trinitarian Functional Subordination

Egalitarianism appears to be in a difficult position. It affirms the predominance of masculine biblical references for God and yet seems incapable, logically, to explain this divinely chosen use of masculine language. Granted, one can argue, as we have seen earlier with Achtemeier, that referring to God in feminine language would result in a confusion between Creator and creation. But must this be so? Even Achtemeier admits it need not, while she is convinced it likely will. But if God himself thought and believed as egalitarians do, could he not overcome this supposed faulty Creator-creature confusion that might be drawn if he so chose, deliberately, to employ masculine and feminine metaphors in equal proportion? Certainly he could make clear, as he has, that he is Spirit and so not a sexual or gendered being. Furthermore, he could make clear that when he refers to himself as Mother, he is not by this conveying an ontological connection with the world. Therefore, I find it difficult to accept this as a full or adequate answer to the question of why God chose to name himself in masculine, but never feminine, terms.

(1) Another obvious answer exists, one that egalitarians seem to bump up against regularly without acknowledging it for what it is. For example, in Wainwright's musing over God as "Father," he notes that "'Father' was the name that the second person in his human existence considered most appropriate as an address to the first person." But why is this? To this question, Wainwright can only say that *there must be . . . something* about human fatherhood that makes Father a suitable way for Jesus to designate the one who sent him. In Trinitarian terms, the crucial point is that Father was the address Jesus characteristically used in this connection."[44]

Just what the "something" is, Wainwright does not tell us. But is it not obvious? Jesus said often throughout his ministry that he came to do the *will* of his *Father*. Clearly, a central part of the notion of "Father" is that of fatherly authority. Certainly this is not all there is to being a father, but while there is more, there certainly is not less or other. The masculine terminology used of God throughout Scripture conveyed, within the patriarchal cultures of Israel and the early church, the obvious point that God, portrayed in masculine ways, had authority over his people. Father, King, and Lord communicate, by their masculine gender-referencing, a rightful authority that was to be respected and followed. Malachi 1:6, for example, indicates just this connection between "father" and authority: "'A son honors his father, and a servant his master. If I am a father, where is the honor due me? If I am a master, where is the respect due me?' says the LORD Almighty." God as Father is rightfully deserving of his children's honor, respect,

---

[44]Wainwright, "Doctrine of the Trinity," 120 (italics added).

and obedience. To fail to see this is to miss one of the primary reasons God chose such masculine terminology to name himself.

(2) While the early church clearly embraced the full essential equality of the three Trinitarian persons (because each of the three divine persons possesses fully and simultaneously the identically same infinite divine nature), nonetheless the church has always affirmed the priority of the Father over the Son and Spirit. Since this priority cannot rightly be understood in terms of essence or nature (lest one fall into Arian subordinationism), it must exist in terms of relationship.[45]

As Augustine affirmed, the distinction of persons is constituted precisely by the differing relations among them, in part manifest by the inherent authority of the Father and inherent submission of the Son. This is most clearly seen in the eternal Father-Son relationship, in which the Father is eternally the Father of the Son, and the Son is eternally the Son of the Father. But, some might wonder, does this convey an eternal authority of the Father and eternal submission of the Son? Hear how Augustine discusses both the essential equality of the Father and Son and the mission of the Son who was sent, in eternity past, to obey and carry out the will of the Father:

> If however the reason why the Son is said to have been sent by the Father is simply that the one is the Father and the other the Son then there is nothing at all to stop us believing that the *Son is equal to the Father* and consubstantial and co-eternal, and yet that the Son is sent by the Father. Not because one is greater and the other less, but because one is the Father and the other the Son; one is the begetter, the other begotten; the first is the one from whom the sent one is; the other is the one who is from the sender. For the Son is from the Father, not the Father from the Son. In the light of this we can now perceive that *the Son is not just said to have been sent because the Word became flesh, but that he was sent in order for the Word to become flesh*, and by his bodily presence to do all that was written. That is, we should understand that *it was not just the man who the Word became that was sent, but that the Word was sent to become man*. For he was *not sent in virtue of some disparity of power or substance or anything in him that was not equal to the Father*, but in virtue of the Son being from the Father, not the Father being from the Son.[46]

---

[45]For a discussion of evidence that early church theology upheld the simultaneous eternal equality of essence yet functional relationship of authority and obedience among the persons of the triune Godhead, see Robert Letham, "The Man-Woman Debate: Theological Comment," *WTJ* 52 (1990): 65–78; Stephen D. Kovach and Peter R. Schemm Jr., "A Defense of the Doctrine of the Eternal Subordination of the Son," *JETS* 42.3 (1999): 461–76. In limited space, Kovach and Schemm cite examples from Hilary of Poitiers, Athanasius, the Cappadocian fathers, and Augustine, with supporting commentary from John Calvin, Philip Schaff, Jaroslav Pelikan, J. N. D. Kelly, Charles Hodge, W. G. T. Shedd, and they cite (p. 471) the conclusion of Paul Rainbow, "Orthodox Trinitarianism and Evangelical Feminism," 4 (unpublished paper, based on his dissertation, "Monotheism and Christology in 1 Corinthians 8:4–6" [D.Phil. diss., Oxford University, 1987]), in which Rainbow concludes, "From the earliest form of the creed we can see that the Father and the Son are united in being, but ranked in function."

[46]Augustine, *The Trinity*, 4.27 (italics added).

god under fire

Notice two observations from Augustine's statement. First, Augustine sees no disparity between affirming, on the one hand, the full *equality* of the Son to the Father, and on the other hand, the Son's eternal position as *from* the Father, whose responsibility it is to carry out the will of the Father as the one *sent* from all eternity from the Father. Jewett's claim that functional subordination entails essential inferiority is here denied by Augustine. Second, notice that Augustine denies Bilezikian's claim that all subordination of the Son to the Father rests fully in the Son's incarnate state. To the contrary, Augustine affirms that "the Son is not just said to have been sent because the Word became flesh, but that he was sent in order for the Word to become flesh." In other words, the sending of the Son occurred in eternity past in order that the eternal Word, sent from on high from the Father, might take on human flesh and then continue his role of carrying out the will of his Father.

As P. T. Forsyth writes, the beauty of the Son's simultaneous equality with and obedience to the Father expresses the willing service God intends his people to render. "Subordination is *not* inferiority, and it *is* God-like. The principle is imbedded in the very cohesion of the eternal Trinity and it is inseparable from the unity, fraternity and true equality of men. It is not a mark of inferiority to be subordinate, to have an authority, to obey. It is divine."[47] Elsewhere Forsyth makes clear that the Son's obedience to the Father was indeed an eternal obedience, rendered by an eternal equal, constituting an eternal subordination of the Son to do the will of the Father. He writes:

> Father and Son co-exist, co-equal in the Spirit of holiness, i.e., of perfection. But Father and Son is a relation inconceivable except the Son be obedient to the Father. The perfection of the Son and the perfecting of his holy work lay, not in his suffering but in his obedience. And, as he was eternal Son, it meant an eternal obedience.... But obedience is not conceivable without some form of subordination. Yet in his very obedience the Son was co-equal with the Father; the Son's yielding will was no less divine than the Father's exigent will. Therefore, in the very nature of God, subordination implies no inferiority.[48]

(3) Another intransigent fact faces all who wish to account rightly for the nature of God's self-revelation in Christ: As God condescended to take on our human nature in Christ, he chose to come as a *male*, not female, human. One must not conclude from this that as Christ is male, so God *is* male. As noted earlier, this deeply erroneous misconception stands against the uniform orthodox tradition that has denied of God literal genderedness. But is it not significant that Jesus of Nazareth was conceived by the Spirit as male, not female? Surely it is, and surely the reason for this is that Christ came to be *Savior and Lord*.

---

[47]P. T. Forsyth, *God the Holy Father* (1897; reprint, London: Independent Press, 1957), 42.
[48]P. T. Forsyth, *Marriage: Its Ethic and Religion* (London: Hodder & Stoughton, 1912), 70–71.

Clearly, the male gender of Christ relates to his becoming the second Adam (recall that Adam, the male human, brought sin upon the human race) to be offered as the spotless male Lamb of God to take away the sin of the world. Furthermore, Christ's male gender was involved in conveying his rightful lordship, rulership, and authority, which is reflective of the very supreme authority of God, who chooses to reveal himself not only with masculine language but through masculine human form.

(4) The egalitarian denial of any eternal submission of the Son to the Father makes it impossible to answer the question why it was the "Son" and not the "Father" or "Spirit" who was sent to become incarnate. Even more basic is the question why the eternal names for "Father" and "Son" would be exactly *these* names. John Thompson has indicated a trend in much modern Trinitarian discussion to separate Christology from Trinitarian formulations. He writes: "Christology and the Trinity were virtually divorced. It was both stated and assumed that any one of the three persons could become incarnate. . . . There was thus only an accidental relation between the economy of revelation and redemption and the eternal triune being of God."[49]

It appears that contemporary egalitarianism is vulnerable also to this criticism. Since, in their understanding, nothing *in God* grounds the Son being the Son of the Father, and since every aspect of the Son's earthly submission to the Father is divorced altogether from any *eternal relation* that exists between the Father and Son, there simply is no reason why the *Father* should send the *Son*. In Thompson's words, it appears that the egalitarian view would permit "any one of the three persons" to become incarnate. Yet we have scriptural revelation that clearly says that the Son came down out of heaven to do the will of his Father. This sending is not ad hoc. In eternity the Father commissioned the Son, who then willingly laid aside the glory he had with the Father to come and purchase our pardon and renewal. Such glory is diminished if there is no eternal Father-Son relation on the basis of which the Father sends, the Son willingly comes, and the Spirit willingly empowers.

(5) Finally, what biblical evidence exists for the eternal functional subordination of the Son to the Father? A running theme in the history of this doctrine (as seen above in Augustine and Forsyth) is that the Son was commissioned by the Father in *eternity past* to come as the incarnate Son. As Jesus declares in well over thirty occasions in John's Gospel, he was *sent to the earth* by the Father to do the Father's will. Could this be reduced merely to the sending of the *incarnate* Son to fulfill the Father's mission for him, now that he has already come into the world? Or should we think of this sending, this commissioning, as having taken place in *eternity past*, a commissioning then fulfilled in time? Scripture, it seems clear, demands the latter view.

Consider, for example, Peter's statement in his Pentecost sermon recorded in Acts 2. Concerning Christ, he says, "This man was handed over to you by God's

---

[49]Thompson, *Modern Trinitarian Perspectives*, 22.

god under fire

set purpose and foreknowledge; and you, with the help of wicked men, put him to death by nailing him to the cross" (2:23). The crucifixion of Christ fulfilled God's "set purpose," which he established far in advance of the actual Incarnation. Though this verse alone does not tell us exactly how far back God's plan was set, we know from numerous biblical prophecies (e.g., Ps. 22; Isa. 9:6–7; 53; Mic. 5:2, to name a few) that God had planned and predicted, long before the Incarnation, precisely the birth, life, ministry, death, and ultimate triumph of the Son. If Christ's coming fulfilled God's "set purpose" and if this purpose was established long in advance of the Incarnation, then clearly the commissioning of the Son occurred in Christ's relation with the Father in the immanent Trinity and not after he had come as the incarnate Son.

Consider another of Peter's claims. In regard to Christ's redemptive work, Peter writes "He [Christ] was chosen before the creation of the world, but was revealed in these last times for your sake" (1 Peter 1:20). If we wonder how far back this commissioning of the Son took place, this verse settles the question. Before the world was made, the Father chose (lit., "foreknew") the Son to come as the Redeemer. The Son's coming in time to shed his blood reflects not an ad hoc decision or a toss of the Trinitarian coin, but the eternal purpose of the *Father* to send and offer his *Son*.

Two other passages confirm this understanding. In Ephesians 1:3–5, Paul gives praise to God the *Father* for choosing his own *in Christ* before the foundation of the world and for predestining them to adoption as sons *through Jesus Christ* to himself. Since Paul specifically (1) gives praise to the *Father* for this election and predestination, (2) designates *Christ* as the one toward whom our election and predestination is directed, and (3) states that the Father's elective purpose and plan occurred before the creation of the world, it follows that the Father's commissioning of the Son is based in eternity past and that the Son's submission to the Father is rooted in their eternal relationship within the Godhead.

Revelation 13:8 likewise indicates that "the book of life," in which believers' names have been recorded, (1) is from the *foundation of the world*, and (2) is of the *Lamb who was slain*. Again, here is clear evidence that the Father's purpose from eternity past was to send his Son, the Lamb of God, by which his own would be saved. The authority-obedience relation of Father and Son in the immanent Trinity is mandatory if we are to account for God the Father's eternal purpose to elect and save his people through his beloved Son.

But will Christ one day, as Bilezikian argues, be elevated to the same status or equality of role as that of the Father? Consider Paul's discussion of the consummation of Christ's reconciling work in a day yet future:

> For he [the Father] "has put everything under his [Christ's] feet." Now when it says that "everything" has been put under him, it is clear that this does not include God himself, who put everything under Christ. When he has done this, then the Son himself will be made subject to him who put everything under him, so that God may be all in all. (1 Cor. 15:27–28)

Because Christ was commissioned in eternity past to come to carry out the will of his Father in time and in history, when this work is completed, Christ will place himself in the very position he had with the Father previously. While possessing again the full glory of the Father (John 17:5), he will put himself in subjection to the Father (1 Cor. 15:28). The relation of the Father and Son in eternity past, in Christ's historic and incarnate life, and in eternity future, then, is the same. Christ is fully equal in essence with the Father yet subordinate in role. Scripture clearly upholds these truths, and we in the church should likewise do the same.

## 6. Conclusion

We have examined four areas where significant and widespread revisionism is currently taking place in the doctrine of the Trinity: the reduction of the immanent to the economic Trinity, the separation of the work of the Spirit from the specific saving gospel of Jesus Christ, revisionist feminism's rejection of Scripture's predominantly masculine Trinitarian language, and evangelical feminism's rejection of the eternal inner Trinitarian relations of authority and obedience. Each of these areas calls for great care by thoughtful and prayerful Christian people. Because we have God's inspired Word and because God has made known his own triune life in this Word, we must with renewed commitment seek to study, believe, and embrace the truth of God as made known here.

Where we have been misled by the history of this doctrine, may Scripture lead to correction. But where contemporary revision departs from Scripture's clear teaching, may we have courage to stand with the truth and for the truth. For the sake of the glory of the only true and living God, who is Father, Son, and Holy Spirit, may we pledge to him alone our fidelity, obedience, and love.

Chapter 12

# How Can We Reconcile the Love and the transcendent Sovereignty of God?

*D. A. Carson*

✦

# 1. Introduction

Toward the beginning of his influential book *God at War*,[1] Gregory Boyd introduces us to Zosia. Zosia was a young Jewess in the Warsaw ghetto. With gory cruelty, the Nazis blinded her. Boyd spares us none of the ghastly details and keeps pressing the question of God's morality—assuming, of course, that God knew in advance that this was going to happen. The narration becomes a powerful reason to want to believe that God did *not* know what was going to happen, *could* not know what was going to happen. The book ends by returning to Zosia and arguing in effect that our confidence in God is restored if we fully see that God was *not* morally delinquent, because he did *not* know what those Nazis would choose to do in advance. Because of his ignorance of what would take place, God must not be held accountable for preventing it from happening. This, Boyd argues, is pastorally superior to the moral anguish that wonders where God is or concludes that God himself must be a devil, if he knows in advance about the torture of a Zosia and chooses to do nothing about it.

Thus Boyd's concern is partly pastoral and partly theological—but his pastoral objectives will be attained, he believes, if he can revise the theology of classical theism. To phrase the challenge in this way means that Boyd is inviting us to think not only about the fairly narrow (though clearly important) subject of the nature and extent of God's (fore)knowledge but also about the relation of that knowledge to God's goodness. In fact, Boyd's attention is not on God's goodness in some general and comprehensive sense but in particular on God's love. How can the God of classical Christian theism be considered to be a God of love if he knows in advance what the Nazis will do to Zosia's eyes and does not intervene to prevent it, when preventing it is clearly within his power?

Before we think through some elements of the relationship between God's love and God's transcendent sovereignty, it may be helpful to offer four preliminary reflections.

First, the emotive appeal to an individual story is both a help and a hindrance. It is a help in that it will not allow us to escape by appealing to vague generalities; it will not allow us to retreat to cold philosophical abstractions without clearly perceiving what this means on the street. It has the same appeal as an image on television that attempts to convey, say, the horrors of a particularly severe drought by focusing on one child who is starving to death, one child out of hundreds of thousands.

---

[1]Gregory A. Boyd, *God at War: The Bible and Spiritual Conflict* (Downers Grove, Ill.: InterVarsity, 1997), 33–34.

But the same individual image may become manipulative. Because we identify with the one starving child or with Zosia, we may be driven by tender emotions rather than by clear thought, by images rather than by even-handed and thoughtful evaluation. In the same way, a television image of the plight of, say, one hard-pressed and unfairly treated family in an urban slum may distort what is the best fiscal policy for the most people in the most slums. In fact, the one emotive image may even blind us to the scale of the problem. Why focus on Zosia? Why not on the rape of Nanking, or on the Holocaust, or on the slaughter of the Armenians, or on the butchery of Genghis Khan, or on the Death March of Bataan, or on the fire-bombing of Tokyo, or on Stalin's slaughter of millions in the Ukraine?

Not for a moment am I suggesting that Boyd has not thought about such matters. But the focus on Zosia's eyes, as emotive as it is, actually obscures the countless instances of barbaric violence in the twentieth century, and in every preceding century. Boyd's scale is too small, and too big. I doubt that we will be able to think clearly about what the Bible would have us think of Zosia's eyes unless we can also think clearly about Job, about Habakkuk, about the rape of Nanking, about the Holocaust.

Second, even at the most superficial level, I am not persuaded that this theodicy is an adequate defense of God. After all, the "openness of God" theists deny that God has knowledge of *future* contingent events; they do not deny that God has exhaustive knowledge of all events in the present and the past, in our present and our past. So when God saw that the Nazis were about to take out Zosia's eyes, why did he not intervene? Or if he still wasn't sure what they were going to do, why didn't he intervene after they took out the first eye? If God's goodness and love can only be preserved in the first instance by ascribing ignorance to God, what will protect his goodness and love now? Slow reaction times?

But that is also why the large-scale examples that I mentioned a few lines ago are so important. Doubtless many Allies were a bit slow coming to terms with the evidence for the Holocaust, but what about God? Why didn't he intervene when the first deaths occurred at Dachau, Auschwitz, Birkenau, Therienstadt, and the rest? Even if he did not know the outcome of future free contingent decisions, once the Nazis had been burning corpses in their smaller ovens at Auschwitz, wasn't it pretty obvious what the new and bigger ovens at Birkenau were for? Why did he not intervene? Perhaps the first plane to crash into the World Trade Center caught God by surprise, but why didn't he stop the second? In fact, did he not listen into all the plans constructed in secret that brought about this devastation? So why didn't he stop it, since this was clearly in his power?

In short, the ugly reality is that the worst atrocities take time, and after the first few seconds—let alone the first few years—God cannot claim ignorance. So it is difficult to see how an appeal to his alleged ignorance of future outcomes constitutes a substantial theodicy. And if at that point Boyd or some other openness theologian were to appeal (as they do not, so far as I have been able to observe) to other factors—compatibilism, free will, the inscrutable mystery of providence, whatever—

then, of course, they are appealing to the sorts of arguments that many Christians have appealed to for two millennia, arguments that the openness theologians claim are both inadequate and now surpassed by their own revisionist views of God.[2]

Third, even at the level of pastoral comfort, although Boyd's approach to theodicy may comfort some, it clearly does not comfort others. Openness theologians tell us of people they have known who are helped by coming to the conclusion that God did *not* know in advance of the rape of their daughter. They were thereby enabled to stop thinking troubling, negative thoughts about God. Nevertheless, pastors in the classical tradition are currently finding more and more people who, influenced by the openness theologians, are even more troubled. The rape of their daughter was not only an instance of evil in an evil and fallen world, but an instance where God was not in control in any significant sense—and there are countless numbers of such instances. So precisely how can such a God be trusted? In the varied approaches of classical theism, the rape is a horrible evil, but God can still be trusted. Moreover, many people want to know if there was *any* element of providential care even in the midst of this barbarity— or was it simply an instance where Satan won one, and God was absent?

Fourth, although I have begun this discussion with reference to the work of Gregory Boyd, that was merely for convenience. There is, of course, a larger body of work that embraces openness theology (whether or not it always chooses that particular label).[3] That body of work is in certain respects largely congruent with some broader currents of philosophical theology,[4] and especially with process theology,[5] even if there are differences between openness theologians and process theologians.[6] On the scale of history, these developments, with rare exceptions, are

---

[2]Some of the more technical dimensions of this problem I briefly deal with below, under section 3.7.

[3]See, among others, Clark H. Pinnock et al., *The Openness of God: A Biblical Challenge to the Traditional Understanding of God* (Downers Grove, Ill.: InterVarsity Press, 1994); Richard Rice, *God's Foreknowledge and Man's Free Will* (Minneapolis: Bethany, 1980); John Sanders, *The God Who Risks: A Theology of Providence* (Downers Grove, Ill.: InterVarsity Press, 1998); Gregory A. Boyd, *God of the Possible: A Biblical Introduction to the Open View of God* (Grand Rapids: Baker, 2000).

[4]See, e.g., J. R. Lucas, *The Future* (Oxford: Blackwell, 1989); Richard Swinburne, *The Coherence of Theism* (Oxford: Clarendon, 1977), passim (e.g., see p. 176); see discussion in William Hasker, *God, Time and Knowledge* (CSPR; Ithaca, N.Y.: Cornell Univ. Press, 1989). See further, among others, Vincent Brümmer, *Speaking of a Personal God: An Essay in Philosophical Theology* (Cambridge: Cambridge Univ. Press, 1992); Keith Ward, *Relational Theology and the Creativity of God* (Oxford: Blackwell, 1982); Terence Fretheim, *The Suffering of God: An Old Testament Perspective* (Philadelphia: Fortress, 1984).

[5]For instance, Gregory A. Boyd acknowledges his indebtedness to process thought in the published form of his dissertation, *Trinity and Process: A Critical Evaluation and Reconstruction of Hartshorne's Di-Polar Theism Towards a Trinitarian Metaphysics* (New York: Peter Lang, 1992). See, e.g., the preface of this book: "It is our conviction that the fundamental vision of the process world view, especially as espoused by Charles Hartshorne, is correct." Similarly, Richard Rice acknowledges his fundamental indebtedness to Hartshorne in "Process Theism and the Open View of God: The Crucial Difference," in *Searching for an Adequate God: A Dialogue Between Process and Free Will Theists*, ed. John B. Cobb Jr. and Clark H. Pinnock (Grand Rapids:

fairly recent: that is, although Christian thinkers have adopted a wide diversity of positions on the nature of the human will and on how the human will comports with God's transcendence (that he is above the created order and thus above space and time) and God's sovereignty, the overwhelming majority of them have held that God does enjoy exhaustive (fore)knowledge.[7]

The previous chapters of this book have addressed many of the theological and philosophical issues that such an account of God's relative ignorance entails. The issues are sufficiently complex that no one imagines that this book will be the last word.[8] Certain exegetical matters stand in particularly urgent need of further discussion.[9] But in this paper my aim is modest. Because among the relatively recent alternative Christian theologies openness theologians have presented their views as, in part, a more believable account of the goodness of God, and in particular of the love of God, I propose to offer some reflections on biblical presentations of the love of God and their bearing on openness theology.

A further reason for approaching the subject from this angle turns on the fact that many scholars in the openness tradition insist that love is the supreme divine attribute, trumping holiness or any of the traditional "omni-" attributes.[10] In other words, a certain conceptual and methodological priority is given to God's relational attributes as opposed to his transcendent attributes—and love is said to be the supreme relational attribute of God.

---

Eerdmans, 2000), 166. In the same essay, Rice affirms, "It is clear, then, that process and open theists hold views of God that are similar in a number of important ways. For both, love is the supreme divine attribute, the essential nature of God. For both, God's experience exhibits relationality, temporality, and contingency. And for both, the world has significance for the inner life of God" (184). Clark Pinnock prefers to think of his approach as a "via media" between classical theism and process theism ("Between Classical and Process Theism," in *Process Theology*, ed. Ronald Nash [Grand Rapids: Baker, 1987], 321).

[6]These differences are articulated in slightly different (though not mutually incompatible) ways. In line with classical theism, Richard Rice affirms "God's ontological independence of the world," insisting that the relationship between God and the world is "asymmetrical," since the latter is dependent on him while the reverse is not true (*God's Foreknowledge*, 32–33). Not dissimilarly, Clark Pinnock affirms that God created the world *ex nihilo*, which brings with it the assumption of God's ontological independence from his creation ("Between Classical and Process Theism," 317–20). Pinnock ultimately ties this stance to the doctrine of the Trinity (which, of course, he shares with classical theism). William Hasker asserts that process theism goes too far when it insists that God's power is always persuasive and never coercive; that may be the regular way of things, but it leaves God with too little control ("A Philosophical Perspective," in *The Openness of God*, 139).

[7]There is a useful historical summary of the question in the unpublished doctoral dissertation of Steven C. Roy, "How Much Does God Foreknow? An Evangelical Assessment of the Doctrine of the Extent of the Foreknowledge of God in Light of the Teaching of Open Theism" (Ph.D. diss., Trinity Evangelical Divinity School, 2001), esp. 19–128.

[8]For other useful treatments from the perspective of historic confessionalism, see especially Paul Helm, *The Providence of God* (Downers Grove, Ill.: InterVarsity Press, 1994); Bruce A. Ware, *God's Lesser Glory: The Diminished God of Open Theism* (Wheaton, Ill.: Crossway, 2000).

[9]Some of these are nicely treated in Stephen C. Roy, "How Much Does God Foreknow?" I hope to address some others in a forthcoming publication.

[10]The statement of Richard Rice in n. 5, above, is typical.

## 2. A Summary of Biblical Ways of Thinking About the Love of God

Before thinking through some of the issues that bear on the relations between God's love and God's transcendent sovereignty, I must beg the indulgence of summarizing an argument I have made before.[11] The Bible talks about God's love in at least five distinguishable ways.

### 2.1 The Peculiar Love of the Father for the Son, and of the Son for the Father

The theme is most explicit in the Gospel of John. Twice we are told that the Father loves the Son (John 3:35; 5:20); once we are told that the Son loves the Father (14:31). This sort of language marks Christian monotheism off from all other monotheisms and lies, finally, at the heart of Trinitarianism. Clearly this is not the love of redemption, for neither the Son nor the Father needs redeeming. Moreover, the ways in which the respective loves of Father for Son and Son for Father are manifested differ slightly: The Son displays his love by perfectly obeying his Father (e.g., 8:29; 14:31); the Father displays his love for the Son by placing everything in his hands, by "showing" him all things—such that whatever the Father does the Son also does, to the end that all should honor the Son even as they honor the Father (3:35; 5:16–30).

### 2.2 God's Providential Love over All That He Has Made

The creation account includes God's pronouncement that what he has made is "good" (Gen. 1–2); this is the conclusion of a loving, provident Creator. Jesus teaches that God clothes the grass with the glorious color of wild flowers, even where no human eye can see them; he says that the birds of the air find food because of God's oversight, and not a sparrow falls from the heaven apart from his sanction. When Jesus says these things, he is teaching that God's providence is *loving*, for otherwise the moral lesson that Jesus is driving home, namely, that such a God can be trusted to provide for his own people, would be incoherent (Matt. 6:26; 10:29).

### 2.3 God's Salvific Stance Toward the Fallen World

To rebels under the old covenant, the sovereign Lord calls out, "As surely as I live ... I take no pleasure in the death of the wicked, but rather that they turn from their ways and live. Turn! Turn from your evil ways! Why will you die, O house of Israel?" (Ezek. 33:11). Under the new covenant, the Lord Jesus commands that the gospel be preached to all human beings; the good news is to be issued to everyone, and all are commanded to repent. God so loved "the world" that he gave his Son (John 3:16); even if the primary focus of "world" in John's Gospel is on the badness of the fallen moral order rather than on its bigness, this is still a sweeping statement, for "the world" cannot be identified with the elect, for the disciples themselves were drawn out of the world (e.g., 15:19).

---

[11]D. A. Carson, *The Difficult Doctrine of the Love of God* (Wheaton, Ill.: Crossway, 2000).

## 2.4 God's Particular, Effective, Selecting Love Toward His Elect

The referent of "elect" may be the entire nation of Israel, or the church, or particular individuals, depending on the passage; the purpose of the election also varies. Nevertheless, in some passages God unambiguously sets his love on some and not on others. The people of Israel are told:

> The LORD did not set his affection on you and choose you because you were more numerous than other peoples, for you were the fewest of all peoples. But it was because the LORD loved you and kept the oath he swore to your forefathers that he brought you out with a mighty hand and redeemed you from the land of slavery, from the power of Pharaoh king of Egypt. (Deut. 7:7–8; cf. 4:37)

✦

> To the LORD your God belong the heavens, even the highest heavens, the earth and everything in it. Yet the LORD set his affection on your forefathers and loved them, and he chose you, their descendants, above all the nations, as it is today. (Deut. 10:14–15)

In other words, what distinguishes Israel from the entire universe ("the heavens, even the highest heavens, the earth and everything in it") is not merit, Israel's wise choice, greatness, or anything else intrinsic to Israel. What distinguishes her is the choosing love of God. God directs his love toward Israel; he sets his affection on Israel in a way in which he does *not* set it on others. The prophet Malachi rightly summarizes God's election of Israel by reporting God as saying: "I have loved Jacob, but Esau I have hated" (Mal. 1:2–3). Similarly in the New Testament: "Christ loved the church and gave himself up for her" (Eph. 5:25).

## 2.5 God's Provisional or Conditional Love Toward His Own People

God's love is sometimes said to be directed toward his own people in a provisional or conditional way—conditional, that is, on their obedience. Already in the Decalogue, God declares himself to be the one who shows his love "to a thousand generations of *those who love me and keep my commandments*" (Ex. 20:6). "For as high as the heavens are above the earth, so great is his love *for those who fear him*.... As a father has compassion on his children, so the LORD has compassion *on those who fear him*.... But from everlasting to everlasting the LORD's love is *with those who fear him ... with those who keep his covenant and remember to obey his precepts*" (Ps. 103:11, 13, 17–18, italics added). In the New Testament, Jesus declares, "If you obey my commands, you will remain in my love, just as I have obeyed my Father's commands and remain in his love" (John 15:10). Similarly, Jude exhorts his readers, "Keep yourselves in God's love" (Jude 21), making it clear that it is possible *not* to remain in God's love.

These sorts of passages presuppose that there is already a relationship between God and his people. Such passages do not depict how we become Christians or the like; they insist, rather, that the believer's relationship with God must be maintained by obedience, and there is threat of falling out of God's love and into his judgment if we disobey—in exactly the same way that my children may fall out of my love (in one sense) and under my discipline if without good cause they do not return with the car when they have promised to do so. Of course, that is not the only way in which I will speak of loving my children. In some contexts, I am able to speak of loving my children regardless of what they do. Nevertheless, there is this familial structure of obligation, this covenantal structure, that makes it possible to speak of my love for them being conditioned on their obedience. Similarly for God's love.

## 3. Reflections on the Relations Between God's Love and God's Transcendent Sovereignty

The following points are not meant to be an exhaustive probe into the nexus between God's love and God's transcendent sovereignty. They are nothing more than a few preliminary reflections aimed at clarifying some of the issues.

### 3.1 On God As a Person

Biblical depictions of God's love constitute abundant evidence that the God of the Bible is not an impersonal force. It is wrong to think of the God of the Bible as nothing more than raw power, whether that power is totally sovereign or not. The God of the Bible is a person who interacts with other persons.[12] He is not the God of deists—very powerful, perhaps, but so far removed from the microscopic organisms that we call human beings that he cannot be thought to enter into personal relationships with them. Nor is he the God of pantheists—the life force of the universe, the one into whom or into whose essence we should be absorbed, but not an "Other" who can address us from outside the order that he himself has created and choose to love us, to enter into personal relationships with us who have been created in his image.

In fact, the diversity of these depictions of the love of God—at least five, according to the last section—argue for the importance of thinking of God as a person. For finite human persons enter into numerous kinds of love relationships. "I love playing the tenor sax"; "I love solitude"; "I love my wife"; "They made love"; "She loved her children regardless of their conduct"; "The brothers loved each other with bonds that would never be broken"; "The Lord gave him a love for the whole world, which became his parish"—these and countless more expressions hint at the diversity of subtle shadings that "love" as a noun and as a verb can have in the English language, depending on the context. This diversity of usage is not merely a linguistic matter;[13] more importantly, it reflects the diverse relationships into which persons may enter.

---

[12]The literature on what it means to be a "person" is substantial and complex, but most of it is irrelevant to this essay, since on most fronts the meaning of "person" is not disputed between classical and "openness" theists. The only place where there is substantive dispute between them over the meaning of "person" lies in the implicit attempt of "openness" theologians to make "person" a category that *cannot* be applied to a sovereign God with exhaustive foreknowledge.

[13]I have dealt with this in several places, in particular in *Exegetical Fallacies*, 2d ed. (Grand Rapids: Baker, 1996).

Somewhat analogously, God as Person enters into a diversity of love relationships as well. Of course, God's diversity of love relationships cannot be mapped *exactly* onto the diversity of love relationships into which his image-bearers may enter. For instance, the love of the Father for the Son, and the love of the Son for the Father, is the love of one perfect Person for another perfect Person. This side of the consummation, human beings cannot experience exactly that, even though this intra-Trinitarian love can be used, in certain respects, as the archetypal love, the archetypal oneness, that Christians must display (John 15:9–17).

Similarly, God's providential love over the entire creation, at least in its scope, cannot be duplicated by creatures as small as we are. Nevertheless it is precisely this aspect of God's love that Christ can use as a normative model for followers of Christ; their love must embrace enemies as well as friends, just as God's (providential) love embraces all without distinction (Matt. 5:45). But although God's diversity of love relationships cannot be mapped exactly onto the diversity of love relationships into which his image-bearers may enter, the diversity of the patterns nicely attests God's personhood. His love is not the impersonal beneficence of the good side of "the Force," but a panoply of loving relationships that reflect the diversity of relationships he has with the created order, and not least with his image-bearers.

Perhaps it should be made clear that nothing I have said warrants talking about discrete "*loves*" of God, as if God, as it were, selects one of the possible "loves" that he might display. That would be altogether too mechanical. By analogy, I might speak of loving my children regardless of what they do and thereby speak of love that is unconditioned, or, in another context, I might tell my children to finish a certain task or face sanctions, thus implicitly telling them to remain in my love by obedience (or face my wrath!). But it would be altogether too mechanical to think that in this distinction I have opted for one "kind" of love over against another "kind" of love. In a complex world, personal beings with a capacity to love enter into a diversity of love relationships.

As a result, there are different ways of talking about love, different dimensions to love. It does not follow that there are several hermetically sealed kinds of love, mutually exclusive "loves." By the same token, for analytical reasons it is helpful to recognize the different ways in which the Bible can talk about the love of God; it is not particularly helpful to think of these as mutually exclusive "loves" of God.

All of this is to say nothing more than that the ways in which the Bible depicts the love of God fully support the view that God is a Person, a relational Being.

## 3.2 On Classical Theism's View of God As a Person

It is vitally important to acknowledge that *all* sides of this debate insist on this first point. No classical theist, any more than an openness theologian, disputes the truth that God is a Person or that God enters into a variety of loving relationships. When I was still a young man, I recall reading passages from Francis Schaeffer that insisted that God is, on the one hand, transcendent and sovereign, and, on the other, personal.[14] I was impressed by the way in which he insisted that both truths are crucial for the maintenance of Christian orthodoxy, for I was discovering how the Christian understanding of "God" differs from alternatives in the marketplace of ideas. Later on, of course, I discovered that what Schaeffer was emphasizing was a mere truism of the Christian faith; none of the great Christian theologians of the past two millennia would have disputed the point. Some, doubtless, laid more emphasis on God's transcendence and sovereignty than on his personal attributes. But Christian theology, with but rare exceptions, did not, until the twentieth century, follow the option of the process theologians and the open theists.

The reason why it is important to reiterate this point now, however, is that in reading most of the literature produced by openness theologians, one would not likely guess it to be the case. Openness theologians regularly depict theologians who hold to a sweeping view of God's sovereignty, or to exhaustive divine foreknowledge, as if they did *not* equally insist on human accountability or on God's goodness and love. Because openness theologians judge inadequate the way classical theologians put together God's unconditioned sovereignty and exhaustive foreknowledge with his love and personal interaction, they tend to depict their opponents in terms that those opponents would not recognize. The result is that, intentionally or otherwise, their depiction of the stance of their opponents often has the flavor of ugly caricature.

I quote some examples of just one author, though it must be said that these are all too typical of the literature.

> Such distorted images of omnipotence end up with a *loveless power*. God is the powerful, domineering Lord who always gets precisely what he wants.[15]
> +
> One simply cannot have it both ways: either God controls everything and the divine-human relationship is impersonal, or God does not control everything and so it is possible for the divine-human relationship to be personal. I have argued that God is wise, competent and resourceful in dealing with us instead of manipulating all that happens. This may seem to diminish sovereignty, but "the sovereignty that reigns unchallenged is not as absolute as the sovereignty that accepts risks." It requires tremendous wisdom, patience, love, faithfulness and resourcefulness to work with a world of independent beings. A God of sheer omnipotence can run a world of exhaustively controlled beings. But what is magnificent about that?[16]

According to this writer, when the compatibilist's God saves people, he engages in

---

[14]E.g., *The God Who Is There* (Chicago: InterVarsity Press, 1968), 87–91.
[15]Sanders, *The God Who Risks*, 190.
[16]Ibid., 215.

divine rape because it involves nonconsensual control; the will of one is forced on the will of the other. Of course, the desire God forces on the elect is a beneficent one—for their own good—but it is rape nonetheless.[17]

Nor will this writer permit distinctions between proximate causes and remote causes:

> If a child is raped and dismembered, there is a human agent who is the proximate cause, but God is the remote cause. The rapist is doing specifically what God ordained him to do. Hence the human agent is the immediate rapist and God is the mediate rapist.[18]

Certainly it is easy enough to find passages in Augustine or Calvin or (to cite contemporaries) J. I. Packer or R. C. Sproul where God's exhaustive foreknowledge and utter sovereignty are both affirmed. But that is not all that these authors say on these subjects. If one refers exclusively to such affirmations, it is possible to develop a dismissive caricature of this "providential blueprint"[19] model that charges God with evil, that destroys human responsibility, and that makes God appear to be a power and not a person. But the truth is that all of these writers include passages that show they draw no such inferences. Far from it; rather, they persistently and emphatically disown them.

For instance, a Calvin may affirm in strong language God's utter sovereignty, but he can also write the following:

> Moreover, though their perdition depends on the predestination of God, the cause and matter of it is [sic] in themselves. . . . Whence then the depravity of man, which made him revolt from God? Lest it should be supposed that it was from his creation, God expressly approved what proceeded from himself. Therefore, man's own wickedness corrupted the pure nature which he had received from God, and his ruin brought with it the destruction of all his posterity. . . . I think I have said enough, not only to remove the ground, but also the pretext of throwing blame on God. The reprobate would excuse their sins by alleging that they are unable to escape the necessity of sinning, especially because a necessity of this nature is laid upon them by the ordination of God. We deny they can thus be validly excused.[20]

Or again, speaking of Satan in various biblical texts:

> This much, therefore, he has of himself, and his own iniquity, that he eagerly, and of set purpose, opposed God, aiming at those things which he deems most contrary to the will of God. But as God holds him bound and fettered

---

[17]Ibid., 240.

[18]Ibid., 255–56.

[19]This and related expressions are found as the depiction of classical theism by many of the "openness" theologians.

[20]John Calvin, *Institutes of the Christian Religion*, 2 vols., ed. John T. McNeill, trans. Ford Lewis Battles (LCC; Philadelphia: Westminster, 1960), 3.23.8–9.

by the curb of his power, he executes those things only for which permission has been given him, and thus, however unwilling, obeys his Creator, being forced, whenever he is required, to do Him service.[21]

Again, Calvin can say such things as the following about the love of God:

Hence he both calls himself our Father, and is pleased to be so called by us, by this delightful name relieving us of all distrust, since nowhere can a stronger affection be found than in a father. Hence, too, he could not have given us a stronger testimony of his boundless love than in calling us his sons. But his love towards us is so much the greater and more excellent than that of earthly parents, the farther he surpasses all men in goodness and mercy (Isaiah lxiii.18). Earthly parents, laying aside all paternal affection, might abandon their offspring; he will never abandon us (Ps. xxvii.10), seeing he cannot deny himself. For we have his promise, "If ye then, being evil, know how to give good gifts unto your children, how much more shall your Father which is in heaven give good things to them that ask him?" (Matth. vii.111.) [sic] In like manner in the prophet, "Can a woman forget her sucking child, that she should not have compassion on the son of her womb? Yea, they may forget, yet will I not forget thee" (Isaiah xlix.15). But if we are his sons, then as a son cannot betake himself to the protection of a stranger and a foreigner without at the same time complaining of his father's cruelty or poverty, so we cannot ask assistance from any other quarter than from him, unless we would upbraid him with poverty, or want of means, or cruelty and excessive austerity.[22]

The open theists may, if they like, argue that this position is inconsistent. In that case, they must engage it on its own terms. It will not do, for instance, to assume a libertarian definition of the will and thereby prove that the Calvinist synthesis is self-contradictory. Of course it is, on the assumption of a libertarian view of freedom—but Calvinists do not think that the Bible embraces a libertarian definition of the will. It is simply unfair, not to say uncharitable, to charge Calvinism, or virtually any form of classical theism, with an impersonal fatalism.

### 3.3 On Synthesizing God's Love and God's Transcendent Sovereignty

All who wrestle with what Scripture says about God's transcendent sovereignty, on the one hand, and about God's personal interaction with his morally accountable image-bearers, on the other, find themselves in the position where they must adopt one of several possible syntheses. Putting to one side the skepticism of those who say that any synthesis is impossible (the sort of stance made popular by David Hume), classical theism has resorted to several approaches. In one of his books, Paul Helm, for example, lists three:[23]

---

[21]Ibid., 1.14.17.
[22]Ibid., 3.20.36.
[23]Helm, *The Providence of God*, 55–68. Although I differ from Helm at one or two points (as will become clear), I am indebted to him for the brief discussion that follows.

GOD UNDER FIRE

(1) An appeal to middle knowledge. Developed by the Jesuit Luís de Molina (1535–1600), it has recently been given new life and vigor by Alvin Plantinga[24] and William Lane Craig.[25] There are several ways of getting at middle knowledge. One way is to distinguish between "necessary truths" and "free knowledge." God knows all "necessary truths," for example, the truths of logic, or the fact that in base 10 arithmetic two plus two equals four. God does not have to will these things for them to be true; they simply are true, and he knows all such truths because he is omniscient. But he also knows that the President of the United States, as I write these lines, is George W. Bush, and that the capital city of Canada is Ottawa.

But such truths are not true by virtue of some intrinsic necessity. Ask Al Gore, for instance, or recall that the capital of Canada has not always been Ottawa. These truths are true because God has willed them; God knows them to be true, but his knowledge of them is in function of his will having brought them about. In addition, however, apart from these two kinds of knowledge is "middle knowledge," that is, a knowledge of all the possibilities that God in fact did not will. He might have willed that Al Gore become president; he might have willed that Toronto be the capital of Canada. Thus, lying somewhere between God's knowledge of necessary truths and his knowledge of things he has willed to bring about (sometimes called his "free knowledge") lies his middle knowledge—that is, his exhaustive knowledge of all the things that might have been true had he willed them, but are not because he did not will them.

But Molina and his followers develop middle knowledge in a distinctive way. They think that among the conditional propositions that God knows (i.e., among the propositions belonging to middle knowledge) are those that state what would happen if under certain conditions a person freely (i.e., in a nondetermined way) performed an action. Because God knows all the results of all the possible choices that an individual would freely make if such-and-such conditions prevailed, he is able so to rule through the establishment of precisely the right conditions to bring about the free decision that he himself wants and determines should take place. In this way, the Molinist argues, God's sovereignty and human freedom are simultaneously preserved.

(2) An appeal to antinomy. J. I. Packer is perhaps the best-known exponent of the view that the relationship between God's sovereignty and human responsibility is, for human beings in our current state, fundamentally incomprehensible. Packer applies the word "antinomy" to the pairing of divine sovereignty and human responsibility:

---

[24]His first and most important foray into this discussion is his *The Nature of Necessity* (Oxford: Clarendon, 1974), esp. ch. 9.

[25]Craig has written extensively on this subject, but for easiest access see his *The Only Wise God* (Grand Rapids: Baker, 1987). From his most recent work, see his unpublished paper, "Middle Knowledge, Truth-Makers, and the 'Grounding Objection,'" from the 47th Annual Wheaton Philosophy Conference. See also his article in this volume, "What Does God Know?" (ch. 6).

The whole point of an antinomy—in theology, at any rate—is that it is not a real contradiction, though it looks like one. It is an *apparent* incompatibility between two apparent truths. An antinomy exists when a pair of principles stand side by side, seemingly irreconcilable, yet both undeniable. There are cogent reasons for believing each of them; each rests on clear and solid evidence; but it is a mystery to you how they can be squared with each other. You see that each must be true on its own, but you do not see how they can both be true together.[26]

Packer is not saying that divine sovereignty and human responsibility are mutually contradictory. Nor is he saying that God cannot reconcile them. He is claiming, rather, that human beings, at least in our current existence (Who knows what will prevail in the new heaven and the new earth?) simply do not have access to enough information to sort things out. For instance, we do not know exactly how the eternal God interacts with human beings in (our) time. Packer's stance usually brings with it a view of will that is not libertarian, for a libertarian understanding of the will is harder to align with divine sovereignty (unless one adopts a Molinist position). The great advantage of Packer's approach to antinomy, however, is that it enables the Christian to read the Bible straightforwardly without trimming either side of the biblical evidence: God is sovereign, and God is exhaustively omniscient; human beings are morally responsible creatures, and the decisions they make are significant.

(3) An appeal to compatibilism. This is the stance that Helm himself adopts.[27] Compatibilism is the view that God's positive, providential control is compatible with human freedom (though not with libertarian human freedom). Usually this position is tied not to a libertarian understanding of human freedom but to some other understanding—commonly a "voluntaristic" understanding of human freedom: Human beings are morally responsible for what they do, because they do what they want to do. In other words, regardless of necessity, we are morally accountable because we do what we want to do.

(4) One might usefully add another stance often adopted by classical theists: an appeal to God's timelessness. This argument has many forms. A common one is the view that the Bible's talk of *fore*ordination and *pre*destination and *fore*knowledge is simply the language of accommodation. God himself is timeless; he sees all things timelessly. In some accounts of timelessness, it is argued that all of God's perception of everything that to us occurs in chronological sequence is to him eternally present. When such matters are taken into account, it is argued, it is possible to preserve divine sovereignty and some version or other of human freedom.[28]

---

[26]J. I. Packer, *Evangelism and the Sovereignty of God* (Leicester: Inter-Varsity Press, 1961), 18–19.

[27]See especially his book *Eternal God: A Study of God Without Time* (Oxford: Clarendon, 1988), esp. ch. 9. His views are nicely and more simply set forth in his unpublished paper, "Providence and Compatibilism," from the 47th Annual Wheaton College Philosophy Conference. See also Robert Young, *Freedom, Responsibility and God* (London: Macmillan, 1975).

[28]See ch. 5 in this volume, "Is God Bound by Time?" by Paul Helm.

These four views are not mutually exclusive, as we will see. What all of them have in common, however, is the acknowledgment that God's foreknowledge is exhaustive (a confession that is a "given" in classical theism). The openness theologians, however, not to mention process theologians and some contemporary philosophers of religion, reject all of these syntheses. It may be simplest at this juncture to cull some representative statements:

> It is evident that the view of God's governance of the world here proposed differs from others that are commonly held. But wherein precisely does the difference lie? I believe it can be formulated in a simple, yet crucial question: *Does God take risks?* Or, to put the matter more precisely, we may ask: *Does God make decisions that depend for their outcomes on the responses of free creatures in which the decisions themselves are not informed by knowledge of the outcomes?* If he does, then creating and governing a world is for God a risky business. That this is so is evidently an implication of the views here adopted, and it is equally evident that it would be rejected by some Christian thinkers—those, for example, who hold to a theory of predestination according to which everything that occurs is determined solely by God's sovereign decree.[29]

> God must take real risks if He makes free creatures (thousands, millions, or trillions of risks, if each creature makes thousands of morally signficiant free choices). No matter how shrewdly God acted in running so many risks, His winning on *every* risk would not be antecedently probable.[30]

> God does not have a specific divine purpose for each and every occurrence of evil. . . . When a two-month-old child contracts a painful, incurable bone cancer that means suffering and death, it is pointless evil. The Holocaust is pointless evil. The rape and dismemberment of a young girl is pointless evil. The accident that caused the death of my brother was a tragedy. God does not have a specific purpose in mind for these occurrences.[31]

With respect to what takes place in Gethsemane:

> Jesus wrestles with God's will because he does not believe that everything must happen according to a predetermined plan. . . . Together they determine what the will of God is for this historical situation. Although Scripture attests that the incarnation was planned from the creation of the world, this is not so with the cross. The path of the cross comes about only through God's interaction with humans in history. Until this moment in history other routes were, perhaps, open. . . . Jesus is in the canoe heading for the falls. There is

---

[29]Hasker, *God, Time and Knowledge*, 197.

[30]Robert Merrihew Adams, "Middle Knowledge and the Problem of Evil," in *The Problem of Evil*, ed. Robert Merrihew Adams and Marilyn McCord Adams (Oxford: Oxford Univ. Press, 1990), 125.

[31]Sanders, *The God Who Risks*, 262.

yet time to get over to shore and portage around the falls. Jesus seeks to determine if that option meets with his Father's favor. But the canyon narrows even for God.[32]

As for Acts 2:23 ("This man was handed over to you by God's set purpose and foreknowledge"), one author writes:

> It was God's definite purpose . . . to deliver the Son into the hands of those who had a long track record of resisting God's work. Their rejection did not catch God off guard, however, for he anticipated their response and so walked onto the scene with an excellent prognosis (foreknowledge, *prognōsei*) of what would happen.[33]

In some ways, open theism aligns itself well with the some strands of the classical theism that espouse libertarian freedom. There are two crucial differences: (a) Open theists insist that God is everlasting through time, that is, that he is not timeless, above time, transcendent in that sense. This reflects, of course, indebtedness to *process* theology. (b) Open theists affirm that God has exhaustive knowledge of all necessary truths, but they deny that God has exhaustive definite knowledge of future contingent events. God must await (in time) the outcome of free human decisions before he can know it himself. He may make shrewd guesses, but he cannot *know*, and sometimes his guesses are mistaken.[34]

Out of this matrix, then, openness theologians preserve the integrity and significance of human free decisions, but in the process (no pun intended) they deny God's exhaustive foreknowledge and lose his sovereign control. Although they like to think of their position as a modification of traditional free-will theism,[35] this assessment is misleading. Openness theologians share with Arminians and Molinists a commitment to libertarian freedom, but Arminians and Molinists properly align themselves with classical theism in that they insist God enjoys exhaustive knowledge of all future events (indeed, the Molinists insist he enjoys middle knowledge as well), and they insist that God finally (if somewhat mysteriously) remains in control. It is not clear how many Arminians and Molinists would be happy with an approach to time and eternity that posits a God who lives everlastingly through time. Indeed, it is not uncommon for Arminians of various stripes to dissociate themselves from the openness movement.[36]

The point to be drawn from this discussion is modest. Christian theologians have long been aware of the challenges raised by the openness theologians and

---

[32]Ibid., 100–101.

[33]Ibid., 103.

[34]These distinguishing points of openness theology are nicely acknowledged by John Sanders in his unpublished paper, "Mapping the Terrain of Divine Providence," 47th Annual Wheaton College Philosophy Conference.

[35]It is merely a "family squabble," Sanders says; ibid., 5.

[36]E.g., Robert E. Picirilli, "Foreknowledge, Freedom, and the Future," *JETS* 43 (2000): 259–71; esp. idem, "An Arminian Response to John Sanders's *The God Who Risks: A Theology of Providence*," *JETS* 44 (2001): 467–91.

have created a variety of syntheses to address them. At root, these syntheses depend on finding ways to link the biblical evidence that God is, on the one hand, sovereign and transcendent, and, on the other, that he is personal and interacts with his image-bearers in personal ways—not least in love. So it does not help the discussion if those who hold these diverse syntheses are portrayed as fixating on the control side of the equation and teaching that God is a divine rapist. That may be a fair analysis *given the premises and structures of open theism,* but it is a caricature of the positions as they are in themselves. It is demeaning and manipulative rhetoric, not fair debate.

## 3.4 On Choosing a Synthesis Model

How, then, shall we choose among these five syntheses, the four that I have outlined from classic theism and the fifth as put forth by the open theists? There are two primary avenues. One may probe, and probe hard, for internal weakness; put positively, one looks for coherence and consistency. That is one of the reasons why I began this chapter with some brief reflections on whether open theism provides a superior theodicy. I offered only one of several reasons why I don't think it does; I am not aware of any open theist who has attempted to rebut this particular point. The previous chapters of this book have raised substantial questions about many aspects of open theism (as well as other theisms), and those arguments need not be repeated here. At the risk of traversing well-trodden ground and offering comments that are simplifications of complex debates, I might venture some comments about the consistency and coherence of the other syntheses.

(1) Although the Bible supports the view that God enjoys middle knowledge (e.g., 1 Sam. 23:7–13; Matt. 20:20–24, both of which passages assert that God has knowledge of contra-factuals and that this knowledge is significant for divine/human intercourse), I remain unpersuaded that the Molinist use of this datum is justified. For if God knows that under certain conditions (which he has the sovereignty to bring about), drawn from a vast array of possible conditions, a human being will freely choose a certain course of action, and if God chooses to bring about those conditions, such that the human being makes the perfectly predicted choice, it is difficult to see how appeal to middle knowledge assigns genuinely libertarian freedom to the human individual.[37]

(2) The antinomic approach of J. I. Packer has one minor problem and is commonly charged with a much greater problem. The minor problem is the terminology.[38] According to the *Oxford English Dictionary,* an antinomy is: (a) "a contradiction in a law, or between two equally binding laws"; (b) "a contradictory law, statute, or principle; an authoritative contradiction"—and here an illustration is drawn from Jeremy Taylor, who in 1649 wrote that certain signs of grace "are

---

[37]This criticism of Molinism is deployed, with various degrees of sophistication, by both compatibilists (e.g., Helm, *The Providence of God,* 58–61) and open theists (e.g., Hasker, *God, Time and Knowledge,* 52).

[38]I discussed these matters briefly in *How Long, O Lord? Reflections on Suffering and Evil* (Grand Rapids: Baker, 1990), 268 n. 13.

direct antinomies to the lusts of the flesh"; (c) "a contradiction between conclusions which seem equally logical, reasonable, or necessary; a paradox; intellectual contrariness"—and this last meaning *OED* attributes to Kant.

Packer, however, means none of these things. He does not think these paired truths embrace genuine contradiction (meanings a and c), nor is the opposition between them like the opposition between signs of grace and the lusts of the flesh. He means something like "an apparent contradiction that is not in fact real." But Packer is borrowing the term, as he uses it, from certain philosophical traditions. In *The Critique of Pure Reason*, Kant was occupied with exposing the fallacies that arise when one applies space and time and some other categories to things that are not experienced. He argued that if these categories are *not* appealed to, we necessarily find four antinomies (which we need not detail here). Thus, superficially Kant uses the term in the *OED* sense of real contradictions: that is, the antinomies arise only when the categories of space and time are adopted. But precisely because he says these categories should *not* be adopted, the antinomies turn out *not* to be real contradictions but only apparent ones—which of course is in line with the usage Packer adopts. Because of this ambiguity between the normal use of "antinomy" and its use in a restricted philosophical tradition, however, some of Packer's critics think he is saying something that he is not.

Assuming we let the term *antinomy* stand, however (in the sense carefully defined by Packer), we find that the position is commonly assaulted on another ground. This assault assumes that what Packer is saying is that this antinomy appears to us to be a logical contradiction but that we simply accept, on faith, that in the mind of God there is some sort of reconciliation to which we do not have access.[39] If that were the case, it is argued, the appeal to "mystery" does not and cannot absolve a contradiction: "If logical contradiction does not constitute a sufficient reason for rejecting a position, then I will turn in my philosopher's union card; I no longer know any way of practicing my trade."[40] Surely we would be better (it is argued) seeking out alternative syntheses than those that embrace contradictions and label them antinomies or mysteries.

I can understand how someone might read Packer that way. It seems to me, however, that there is a more charitable interpretation. To cite Packer's own words:

> The whole point of an antinomy—in theology, at any rate—is that it is not a real contradiction, though it looks like one. It is an *apparent* incompatibility between two apparent truths. An antinomy exists when a pair of principles stand side by side, seemingly irreconcilable, yet both undeniable. There are cogent reasons for believing each of them; each rests on clear and solid evidence; but it is a mystery to you how they can be squared with each other.

---

[39]So, e.g., William Hasker, "The Antinomies of Divine Providence," unpublished paper from the 47th Annual Wheaton College Philosophy Conference.
[40]Ibid., 2.

You see that each must be true on its own, but you do not see how they can both be true together.[41]

✦

Man is a responsible moral agent, though he is *also* divinely controlled; man is divinely controlled, though he is *also* a responsible moral agent. God's sovereignty is a reality, and man's responsibility is a reality too.[42]

✦

The antinomy we face now is only one of a number that the Bible contains. We may be sure that they all find their reconciliation in the mind and counsel of God, and we may hope that in heaven we shall understand them ourselves. But meanwhile, our wisdom is to maintain with equal emphasis both the apparently conflicting truths in each case, to hold them together in the relation in which the Bible itself sets them, and to recognize that here is a mystery which we cannot expect to solve in this world.[43]

The point to observe is that Packer does not say that this pair of realities constitutes a strict, logical contradiction but that we trust God to overcome it anyway. The pair of principles are "*seemingly* irreconcilable"; there is "an *apparent* incomparability" between the two. Nevertheless "it is not a real contradiction"; our duty is to maintain "the apparently conflicting truths." Moreover, Packer insists these truths are not in conflict in the mind of God, and certainly he is not suggesting that God mysteriously reconciles truths that are in fact logically contradictory. He even hopes that in heaven we ourselves will understand them.

In short, Packer's understanding of antinomy turns on human ignorance—ignorance that may be necessary at the moment but is not to be confused with belief in logical contradiction.[44] Hasker, of course, may think that Packer's "antinomy" is an "antinomy" in the dictionary sense, that is, a real contradiction. He may think this because he espouses a libertarian definition of freedom. But if Packer avoids that trap, it is difficult to see that he is advocating logical contradiction, even if he does not see exactly how ultimate reconciliation can be effected.[45]

(3) In my view and against Helm, it is not helpful to list Packer's antinomic approach and traditional compatibilism as separate categories. If Packer's antinomy is not a logical contradiction, then Packer holds that the two truths are mutually compatible. On that score, he is a compatibilist. And the compatibilist usually does not attempt to show exactly how the two truths *must* be compatible; rather,

---

[41] Packer, *Evangelism and the Sovereignty of God*, 18–19.

[42] Ibid., 23.

[43] Ibid., 24. Helm, *The Providence of God*, 62–63, cites these same three passages from Packer.

[44] R. Douglas Geivett makes an analogous argument regarding the problem of evil in ch. 7 of this volume, "How Do We Reconcile the Existence of God and Suffering?"

[45] For more on the concepts of contradictions, antinomies, and paradoxes, see Eric L. Johnson's remarks in ch. 3, "Can God Be Grasped by Our Reason?"

the compatibilist argues that we have enough evidence to show there is insufficient reason for thinking them *in*compatible and indicates the kinds of things that must prevail for them to be compatible. Although the respective foci of Packer's antinomy and traditional compatibilism are slightly different, it is difficult not to see in them two sides of the same coin.

(4) The appeal to God's timelessness may be part of the defense of compatibilism (as it is in the work of Helm). The best exponents are alert to abandon any view of timelessness that makes everything "eternally present" to God or the like. That is surreptitiously to slip a time-based category through the back door, as it were. Careful appeal to God's timelessness[46] means that one of the dimensions of unknownness is explored, with the result that although we may not have enough pieces to put the polarities of the antinomy together, we can see enough to recognize that there is no necessary logical contradiction. In other words, on some readings of timelessness and on the most obvious reading of Packer's antinomy, the three distinct approaches—antinomy, compatibilism, appeal to God's timelessness—become part of the same synthesis.

The second (and more important) avenue to help us choose among the five syntheses described earlier (four belonging to classical theism, and the fifth open theism) is to examine how closely the various syntheses correspond to Scripture. Clearly, that exploration could take a book or two on its own, not merely a subpoint of a single chapter. Mercifully, more resources are becoming available.[47] Here I must restrict myself to a few observations.

(1) There is a tendency among the openness theologians, when talking of the love of God, to focus on a short list of biblical texts thought to support the third way the Bible speaks of God's love (above), namely, God's yearning, salvific love. These texts are then absolutized and read into every discussion about the love of God.[48] This, I think, actually has the slight effect of *de*personalizing God. As we have already seen, it is precisely because of the different personal relationships into which God enters that the Bible can speak of the love of God in a variety of ways, with a variety of emphases.

---

[46]See especially Helm, *Eternal God*. The issues, inevitably, are complicated. I suspect that some of them will be clarified, for the general reader, in Gregory E. Gaannsle, ed., *God and Time: Four Views* (Downers Grove, Ill.: InterVarsity Press, 2001). See also Helm's article in this volume, "Is God Bound by Time?" (ch. 5).

[47]In addition to the book by Bruce A. Ware and the dissertation by Steven C. Roy, to which references have already been made, see the important book by John M. Frame, *No Other God: A Response to Open Theism* (Phillipsburg: Presbyterian & Reformed, 2001). I hope shortly to finish my own book on the subject, devoting a substantial part of it to questions of exegesis and hermeneutics.

[48]E.g., Boyd, *God of the Possible*, repeatedly lists passages that, he says, teach a universal saving will of God and uses them to dismiss or domesticate passages that teach individual predestination (e.g., pp. 11, 40, 46–47, 58, 71, 100, 138, 140, 171). He never wonders whether these themes might be mutually complementary or what it does for the doctrine of God to have an astronomical number of instances where human intransigence means that God's will, in the only sense in which Boyd is willing to talk about the will of God, is necessarily defeated.

(2) There are many texts that deal with the theme of God's knowledge or control, texts that cannot easily be skirted. For example, twelve times between chapters 40 and 49, Isaiah emphasizes God's knowledge of the future (Isa. 41:4, 22–23, 26; 42:9; 43:9; 44:7–8, 25–28; 45:19–21; 46:9–11; 48:4–5, 14). In his book *God of the Possible*, Boyd mentions only two of them and understands them to mean no more than that God declares his own intentions, not that he foreknows or declares the future.[49] But this will not do. Taken as a whole, the theme that Isaiah develops is that pagan idols are ignorant of the future while God declares it in advance; God himself insists that this is the test of true deity (41:23). In fact, God goes so far as to name Cyrus in advance (45:1–7), and something similar can be said for the naming of Josiah (1 Kings 13:2), forcing Boyd to concede that in these cases God "set strict parameters around the freedom of the parents in naming these individuals."[50]

But if the parents "freely" chose the name Cyrus, yet God determined that that would be the name, even in advance, then somehow God not only foreknew but arranged to bring to pass what he predicted. The expression "set strict parameters around the freedom of the parents in naming these individuals" is a spectacular circumlocution. If the strict parameters that constrained the parents meant that at the end of the day they could choose only the name that God had predicted, then it is difficult to see how this differs from compatibilist theory.[51]

It is easy to mount similar evidence from the New Testament.[52] It is hard not to see that Christian suffering in 1 Peter 3:17; 4:19 is providentially ordered, even though not in itself good. Paul's imaginary interlocutor asks how anyone can be held responsible when no one can resist God's will, and the context shows that Paul does not question the premise, even though he vehemently denies the conclusion (Rom. 9:19). Second Corinthians 12:7–10 assumes that Paul's thorn in the flesh, though a messenger from Satan, was given (almost certainly a divine passive) for a good purpose that Satan himself never had in mind; behind the first agent, with all his malign intent, is God himself, with only good intent. Neither the blindness of the man born blind nor the death of Lazarus were to be considered defeats for God or instances where Satan won while God was blindsided (John 9:3; 11:4).

(3) Apart from such themes, which surface in scores of passages, there are texts where some of these themes come together in very tight array. One of these is Genesis 50:19–20, where Joseph says to his brothers, "Don't be afraid. Am I in the place of God? You intended to harm me, but God intended it for good to accomplish what is now being done, the saving of many lives." Sanders interprets

---

[49]Boyd, *God of the Possible*, 29–31.

[50]Ibid., 34.

[51]Cf. the review article by Roger Nicole, in *Reformation and Revival* 10.1 (2001): 167–94, esp. 172, who reaches much the same conclusion.

[52]See the useful essay by Simon Gathercole, "The New Testament and Openness Theism," in *Reconstructing Theology: A Critical Assessment of the Theology of Clark Pinnock*, ed. Tony Gray and Christopher Sinkinson (Carlisle, Eng.: Paternoster, 2000), 49–80.

this to mean, "It is the glory of God to be able to bring good out of evil human actions. But nothing in the text demands the interpretation that God actually desired the sinful acts."[53] Sanders's view is curiously right and wrong. Certainly he is right to say that there is nothing in the text to suggest that God desired the sinful acts, if by that is meant that somehow God stands symmetrically behind good and evil, righteousness and sin, and brings both about in some amoral fashion. But no classic Christian thinks that. Sanders is constructing a straw man in order to leave his own interpretation in place.

But that interpretation is certainly wrong. This text does not provide an instance where God brings good out of evil. There are, of course, some biblical narratives where that is what takes place, but in this case both God and Joseph's brothers have intentions when Joseph is sold into slavery—the one good, the other bad. The text does not conjure up a scene in which the brothers plan the nasty deed and then God brings good out of it anyway. (Incidentally, if God did not know in advance what the brothers were going to do, then the good he eventually did to counteract their evil would also have to be unknown, which would mean that the entire sojourn in Egypt, the rescue, and the Exodus were unforeseen.) Still less does the text picture God planning to bring Joseph down to Egypt in comfort and honor, but unfortunately the brothers made a mess of this plan by getting in there first and, in a quick action God had not foreseen, sold Joseph into slavery. Let the text speak: In the one action the brothers' intentions were evil, and God's intentions were good. That may not be neat, but it is what the text says, and it preserves both God's goodness and God's knowledge and sovereignty.[54]

Or consider Isaiah 10:5–23. God pronounces his woe on the Assyrian invader. Why? Because although God himself is the one who sent the Assyrian against a godless nation (i.e., Judah) with the express purpose of seizing loot and trampling them down like mud in the streets, that is not what the Assyrians themselves intend. Their intention is to destroy many nations out of the sheer arrogance of their strength. That is why God says that when he has finished "all his work against Mount Zion and Jerusalem" (10:12)—that is, the work of punishing them with the savage weaponry of war—he will turn around and punish the king of Assyria "for the willful pride of his heart and the haughty look in his eyes" (10:12).

The following verses flesh out the charge: The Assyrians think they have managed all their victories by themselves. But God's charge against them is that they do not recognize his sovereignty, his use of them as a carpenter uses tools; therefore, their arrogance must be punished. "Does the ax raise itself above him who swings it, or the saw boast against him who uses it?" (10:15). Therefore the Lord God will cut them down (10:16–17).

The passage is remarkable. God uses the Assyrians, known for their ferocious violence in war, against his covenant people, and then he holds the Assyrians responsible, in turn, for their vaunted self-autonomy in these attacks and pun-

---

[53]Sanders, *The God Who Risks*, 55.
[54]Similarly, cf. Ware, *God's Lesser Glory*, 199–200.

god under fire

ishes them. This is *not* the language of God *permitting* something awful, which he has foreseen as likely, in order to punish his people. Scores of Old Testament passages make it clear that God himself is the one punishing them, and this passage goes so far as to picture God using the Assyrian the way an axeman brandishes his tool. Even so, the Assyrians are held accountable and are punished in turn. This sort of passage is precisely in line with classic theism; it is difficult to see how it can be reconciled with any form of open theism, if we remain faithful to the actual exegesis. I have not yet seen this passage treated by the openness theologians (nor, e.g., Deut. 32:23–27; 2 Kings 19:25–28; Jer. 51).

The treatment of Acts 4:27–28 by John Sanders is (I don't know how I can use a weaker expression) frankly shocking. This text says: "Indeed Herod and Pontius Pilate met together with the Gentiles and the people of Israel in this city to conspire against your holy servant Jesus, whom you anointed. They did what your power and will had decided beforehand should happen." On the face of it, the political leaders were involved in a wicked conspiracy, but in some sense God himself was behind it all (without weakening their responsibility)—for otherwise the inevitable conclusion is that the cross was not foreseen and planned by God. But Sanders, as we have seen, after arguing that in Gethsemane the Father and the Son worked out together what should be done under these circumstances, holds that in this text we are told that it was God's purpose (*boulē*, as he points out, i.e., "a boundary-setting will") "to deliver the Son into the hands of those who had a long track record of resisting God's work. Their rejection did not catch God off guard, however, for he anticipated their response and so walked onto the scene with an excellent prognosis (foreknowledge, *prognōsei*) of what would happen."[55]

This is, as I say, shocking. First, it betrays an abysmal grasp of Greek. Whatever the Greek word *prognōsei* means when God is the subject, it does not mean something as weak as "prognosis," a kind of statistically likely foretelling. Second, Sanders goes on to argue that the Jewish leaders could have rejected God's plan here, since elsewhere Luke says that certain leaders "rejected God's purpose [*boulēn*] for themselves" (Luke 7:30). But that argument presupposes, without warrant, that *boulē* always means the same thing, regardless of context, whereas on the face of it the fuller construction here, God's *tē hōrismenē boulē*, his determinate will or his definite will (cf. Acts 2:23), leaves little room for such maneuvering. But third, this sort of analysis means that for Sanders, the cross itself is nothing more than something that enjoyed an excellent prognosis. If Pilate, say, had released Jesus, then God's plan would have been thwarted, but doubtless he would have thought up something else.[56]

(4) Although it might be profitable to examine many more such passages, no less telling are certain biblical books in which how we are to think of God becomes the central issue. We may begin with Job. Surprisingly, Job receives only one brief

---

[55]Sanders, *The God Who Risks*, 103.

[56]See the treatments in A. B. Caneday, "Putting God at Risk: A Critique of John Sanders's View of Providence," *TrinJ* 20 (1999): 131–63; and in Roy, "How Much Does God Foreknow?" 250–57.

reference in Sanders.[57] I assume that Greg Boyd will deal with Job in a more substantive way in his forthcoming book on theodicy, which has not yet reached me.[58] Judging by his website, however, he is moving toward some creative exegesis. The book of Job, Boyd says,

> shows that Job's view of God was essentially *unbiblical*. One of the central points of this incredible book, I believe, is to *refute* just this theology. (The other is to refute the theology of Job's friends). [*sic*] How interesting, and sad, that this slogan "the Lord gives and the Lord takes away" is so often quoted as the stance Christians are *supposed to take*. I read in the paper last week the man whose wife killed his five kids quote this verse. *As though God was working through his insane wife to kill his five kids.* [emphasis Boyd's][59]

The book of Job offers its own comment on Job's words, "Naked I came from my mother's womb, and naked I will depart. The LORD gave and the LORD has taken away; may the name of the LORD be praised" (Job 1:21–22). The very next words are, "In all this, Job did not sin by charging God with wrongdoing." This does not sound like pagan superstition.

Above all, however, it is the flow of the drama in Job that is so convincing. Chapter 1 makes it clear that Satan can go after Job only by God's sanction. Since God knows that Satan wants to go down a certain path, he knows that by giving his sanction, Job will suffer unjustly. In that sense, Job's suffering is determined by God. Job knows nothing of this "behind-the-scenes" exchange between God and Satan. Although he begins with extraordinary patience and trust, precisely because he knows he is suffering unjustly, he cannot follow the advice of his friends and repent of some imaginary evil he has committed in order to get on God's good side again. That would be to deny his own faithfulness and integrity and demean God. But the more desperate he becomes, the more he comes within a whisker of charging God with injustice. The very least he demands of God is an opportunity to plead his case.

When God does speak, he does not reply directly to Job's questions. He responds with several chapters of rhetoric designed to prove to Job how small his understanding really is. In other words, God is teaching Job to appeal to mystery, to admit what he does not know. At the end, Job does not say, "Now I understand," but "I repent" (Job 42:6)—not, of course, of ostensible sins that have brought on this suffering but of his drift toward accusing God. In the fundamental issues, however, Job has it right, and the three miserable comforters have it wrong (42:7).[60] Job's final vindication and restored blessings are a way of saying that at the end, justice will be done, and will be seen to be done.

---

[57]Sanders, *The God Who Risks*, 103.

[58]Gregory A. Boyd, *Satan and the Problem of Evil* (Downers Grove, Ill.: InterVarsity Press, 2001).

[59]This quote comes from an informal conversation as reported on Boyd's website: www.gregboyd.org/gbfront/forum/topic.asp?TOPIC_ID=331

[60]I have laid out this drama and its theology, in much greater detail, in *How Long, O Lord? Reflections on Suffering and Evil*, 153–78.

If the God of the book of Job had been an openness theologian, surely he would have had to say something rather different from what he did say—something like this, perhaps: "Come on, Job, stop blaming me. I've done the best I can. I can't foresee everything. Satan got by me on this one. Otherwise there is no way I would have permitted him to kill your ten kids. You can't believe that I would ever sanction anything like that!" But that is not what God says, nor does this square with chapter 1. What God does is appeal to mystery, to the vastness of his own understanding and purpose; what he teaches is humility.[61]

Or consider Habakkuk. The prophet is terribly exercised because he cannot fathom why God would use a more wicked nation to chasten his own covenant people, who on any reading constitute the less wicked nation. Although God promises ultimate justice—there is an eschatological dimension to the answers that will come—Habakkuk ends, not by unambiguous responses to all his questions, but by expressions of trust (e.g., "I will wait patiently for the day of calamity to come on the nation invading us," Hab. 3:16) and by expressions of enduring confidence in God even in the midst of crushing suffering (e.g., "Though the fig tree does not bud and there are no grapes on the vines, though the olive crop fails and the fields produce no food, though there are no sheep in the pen and no cattle in the stalls, yet I will rejoice in the LORD, I will be joyful in God my Savior," 3:17–18).

Certainly Habakkuk does not end with a meditation along these lines: "Well, I have to face the fact that this suffering isn't fair and is nothing more than the result of the fact that God didn't foresee this one in time. But it's all right, because God's justice will guarantee that the invaders will get theirs in due course." The last part—assurance that justice will ultimately be served—is part of Habakkuk's confidence. But the book repeatedly insists that the punishment God's people face at the hands of the invaders is also his work and is merited. In short, this book is entirely in line with passages such as Isaiah 10:5–23 (see above).

These observations must be placed in a broad framework. The reason why a Job or a Habakkuk can agonize over these matters, the reason why there are various complementary theodicies in the Bible, is precisely because God is known to be all powerful and all good. He is sovereign, but he is the God of love and grace. That is what engenders the need for theodicy. Under openness theology, there is no need for theodicy, because there is nothing to be explained.[62]

---

[61]Perhaps I should mention that in recent years there have been numerous innovative readings of Job. See, for example, the essay by D. J. A. Clines, "Why Is There a Book of Job, and What Does It Do to You If You Read It?" in *The Book of Job*, ed. W. A. M. Beuten (Leuven: Leuven Univ. Press, 1994), 1–20, and the same author's more recent commentary.

[62]Compare, for instance, the literature of ancient Egypt: Theodicy is not a preoccupation, because the "gods are not held responsible for human suffering in Egypt; therefore there is no need to defend divine justice. All human suffering, whether innocent or deserved, is seen as a result of the failure on the part of humans to observe *ma'at*, the standard of fairness or veracity" (Daniel P. Bricker, "Innocent Suffering in Egypt," *TynBul* 52 (2001): 83–100, esp. 100. See D. Geivett's critique of open theism's handling of theodicy in ch. 7 of this volume.

## 3.5 On the "Obvious" Reading of a Text

The openness theologians reply, of course, that in many passages their reading is the straightforward reading, the obvious reading. If texts say that God "repents" or "relents" or "changes his mind," that should be taken at face value. When God says he does not know something, why not simply accept this confession of ignorance? Surely, they say, the future is partly settled in God's mind and partly unsettled. Pinnock gives the example of the Lord's interaction with Hezekiah (2 Kings 20:1–7): The Lord announces that the king will soon die, but in response to Hezekiah's prayer the Lord gives him fifteen more years.[63]

These matters have been extensively discussed in earlier chapters in this volume (e.g., Mark R. Talbot's article on God's revelation and James S. Spiegel's article on God's providence—chs. 2 and 8) and elsewhere.[64] Some aspects of this question I hope to pursue in a later volume. It would be tedious to survey again here the evidence that virtually all God-talk embraces an element of analogy. That is, for all sides of this debate, it is insufficient to say what is "obvious" about a text, for the much harder question is how certain texts are to be reconciled with others that, equally "obviously," appear to say something contradictory (e.g., that God does not repent, Num. 23:19; 1 Sam. 15:29; Ps. 110:4; Hos. 11:8–9). Close exegesis requires us to look at text after text and to make, within the context of specific corpora, many kinds of qualifications. For the immediate purposes of this chapter, one observation will suffice.

All sides recognize that in certain passages, what may superficially *appear* to betray ignorance in God does not in fact do so. In the account of the Fall, for instance, God calls out to Adam, "Where are you?" (Gen. 3:9). If this figure called "God" were merely a human being, it would be hard to resist the conclusion that he is here asking the question because he does not know the answer. He wants Adam to disclose himself. But no openness theologian draws that inference. The reason, of course, is that openness theologians confess (or insist) that God knows everything about the past and the present; his ignorance concerns the future, where contingent decisions are at stake. In this case, Adam is hiding, so God cannot possibly be thought to be ignorant of his whereabouts. Therefore his question "Where are you?" must be understood in some sort of rhetorical way. In other words, openness theologians are prepared to shunt aside what might be judged the obvious reading if there are larger textual issues that call such a reading into question.

Classic theologians claim they are merely doing the same thing in passages where open theists insist that the "obvious" reading of the text supports the postulate that God is ignorant of future contingent decisions. Classic theists find rhetorical, contextual, logical, and other reasons for what God says apparently betraying ignorance of future events; the works already mentioned discuss many of the texts in great detail. Let me observe here that, quite apart from factors that

---

[63]Clark Pinnock, "Response to Part 1," in *Reconstructing Theology*, 85.
[64]See in particular the works of Steven C. Roy, Bruce A. Ware, and John M. Frame.

stem from God's uniqueness (e.g., that human-sounding questions must not necessarily be thought to reflect human limitations) and the accommodating nature of revelation, there are instances *even in human relationships* where ostensible admissions of ignorance really should not be "read" that way. One recently sent me by a young medical doctor in Scotland is too good to pass up:[65]

> As a very newly qualified doctor (aged 23) in my first months in a job in a Glasgow teaching hospital, I stood at the side of a patient during the process known then as the Grand Round. This involved the Senior Consultant, known as The Chief, and a retinue of three other Consultants, two trainee consultants, the Ward Sister, a nurse, and often students and paramedicals of various kinds. This parade went from bed to bed in an eighteen-bed Ward, each morning, especially reviewing new admissions, for whom I was responsible, and whom I alone had so far examined.
>
> The Chief stood on the opposite side of the bed, and I gave a short account of the case. "Is the spleen palpable?" he asked. "Yes," I answered. He bent down and examined the area of the patient's spleen. "I can't feel it," he said. I paused for a second or two, took a deep breath, and then spoke quietly. "Sir, you taught me to examine a patient's spleen from *this* side of the bed." (The technique enabled an enlarged spleen to be more easily detected.)
>
> Dr X was a "character" and had a range of facial expressions that are etched on my memory. He turned to the assembled multitude with a pseudo-startled expression, as if to say, "The insolence of the boy!"—but with a twinkle in his eye. The crowd parted to allow him to come round to my side of the bed, and he bent over and examined the patient again. As he stood up, he exclaimed, "The boy is right!" and another of his expressions appeared. It was one of a kind of triumph, and pleasure.
>
> He might have been angry with me for appealing to him in this way to think again, but in fact he was pleased with me that I had learned well, and pleased to have his own technique vindicated through me in this public way. This was not simply a meaningless joust, since the welfare of the patient hung on whether the spleen could be felt, for a palpable spleen was considered to be an abnormal spleen, and an abnormal spleen could be a serious sign and an aid to diagnosis.
>
> As an illustration of prayer the incident has major flaws, but as I recalled it, I felt it helped me understand Moses' action and God's response. In fact, although God might have been angry with Moses for a presumptuous intervention, we read that in fact he was pleased with Moses. "I will do the very thing you have asked, because I am pleased with you, and I know you by name" [Ex. 33:17]. He was pleased with Moses, I think, because what Moses was putting to him was what God had already put in Moses' heart—a concern for his people, but more than that, a concern for God's reputation in the world.

---

[65]This is in private correspondence dated June 20, 2001. The doctor in question prefers not to be identified. I have very lightly edited his letter, primarily to preserve anonymity.

In fact there was already a senior–junior, old man–young man relationship between Dr X and myself. I had been a student in his Unit for nearly three years before qualifying. I had learned a great deal from him, and I think he was quite fond of me. I also had the highest respect for him, and in intervening as I did there was not the slightest intention of criticising or disputing with him. I did it to establish a fact I was sure of, in defence of something that he had taught me, and for the welfare of the patient. He was pleased that something which he had put in me was working with him for his purpose—the cure of his patient.

## 3.6 On "Literal" Descriptions of God

We are ready, then, to reflect a little further on God's love, not least in connection with other things the Bible says about God. Consider Hosea 11:1, 3, 4, 8 (NRSV):[66]

> When Israel was a child, I loved him,
>    and out of Egypt I called my son. . . .
> It was I who taught Ephraim to walk,
>    I took them up in my arms. . . .
> I led them with cords of human kindness,
>    with bands of love. . . .
> I bent down to them and fed them. . . .
> How can I give you up, Ephraim?
> How can I hand you over, O Israel? . . .
> My heart recoils within me;
>    my compassion grows warm and tender.

The first thing to observe is not the metaphorical language used of God, but the metaphorical language used of Israel. Israel is a child; Israel is God's son; Israel was taken up in God's arms. If metaphorical language is used of Israel, why should we be reluctant to think it is used of God? Does God have arms? When God says, "I led them with cords of human kindness," were the cords literal cords? Is there any reason to think, then, that the kindness was merely or narrowly "human"? Does God have to bend down to feed his people? Does God have a heart, recoiling or otherwise? Do God's emotions exist at various temperatures, growing "warm" on occasion?

On the face of it, then, the Bible is prepared to use anthropomorphic language to talk about God, not least in the domain of his emotions (technically, we are dealing with anthropopathisms).[67] Eventually, however, such reflections force

---

[66]Here I am following part of the argument of Patrick Richmond, "A Traditional Response to Pinnock's Understanding of God," in *Reconstructing Theology*, esp. 102–7.

[67]The discussion of Richard Rice, "Biblical Support and Free-Will Theism," in *The Openness of God*, 11–58, esp. 34–36, mounts a case to argue that biblical descriptions of God's deciding, acting, and feeling should be taken at face value. Unfortunately, he really does not

one to ask further, "If God does not have a literal heart, why must we conclude that he has literal emotions?" Or, to approach the same problem from another angle, "If God has literal emotions, why should we not infer that he has a literal heart?" After all, human emotions are inseparable from our bodily existence, and

> we have little idea of what feelings and sensations would be like without an apparent bodily aspect. Emotions activate the involuntary, autonomic nervous system. For example, anger unconsciously raises the heart rate and blood pressure, reduces blood flow to the gut, increases it to the brain and muscles, affects glandular secretions and releases hormones such as adrenaline.[68]

So why should we think that God has "literal" emotions? What would "literal" emotions look like in an incorporeal God?

Moreover, in human beings a substantial part of our emotional life is involuntary, almost reflexive. That is why we speak of "losing" our temper or "falling" in love; it is why we think of fits of jealousy and crimes of passion. Our emotions, in other words, not infrequently interfere with our reason, control our will, and distort our rational judgment. Is this also true for God? If not, can what he experiences rightly be called "emotion"?[69]

For much of the history of the church, theologians have spoken of the "impassibility" of God. Exactly what they have meant has varied somewhat. If this expression is interpreted to mean that God is without "passions," such that he is indistinguishable from Aristotle's "unmoved mover," or that all of the biblical expressions of, say, God's love and God's wrath are merely anthropopathisms that express his strong, willed preferences or the like, the term is inadmissible. At this juncture, the criticisms offered by the openness theologians of some parts of the Western theological heritage are very much to the point. Unfortunately, however, they swing too far and fail to recognize the elements of metaphor in almost all language of God, the elements of anthropopathism where God's emotions are concerned.

If we do justice to the biblical language, we will simultaneously insist that God is love (and has other "passions" too, though they do not so directly concern us here), while recognizing that God's love is not exactly like ours. All of God's perfections operate all the time; he is never less than all he is. So the perfection of his love operates along with the perfection of his wisdom, the perfection of his knowledge, the perfection of his holiness, the perfection of his omnipotence, and so forth. If that is true, then God cannot "fall" in love in the way that we do, nor is his "love" suddenly elicited by something he had not foreseen. *In that sense*, we may usefully affirm God's impassibility even while we affirm, with the greatest

---

probe very deeply into the nature of metaphor in the texts he discusses. For a preliminary response, cf. Richmond, "A Traditional Response to Pinnock's Understanding of God," in *Reconstructing Theology*.

[68]Richmond, "A Traditional Response to Pinnock's Understanding of God," 103.

[69]For further discussion, see ch. 9 in this volume, "Does God Have Emotions?" by Patrick Lee.

delight, God's passionate love—indeed, so great a love that, while we were yet sinners, Christ died for us (Rom. 5:8).[70]

What must be avoided is a certain nasty swing of the pendulum. Having observed, rightly, that some parts of the Western tradition adopt a form of impassibility that makes the biblical picture of God incoherent, openness theologians swing too far the other way. They treat biblical descriptions of God's love not only with a flatness that fails to distinguish different ways the Bible has of speaking of God's love (discussed above), but also with an insensitivity to the metaphors that lie on the surface of the text. Consequently, other things the Bible says about God are either implicitly or explicitly denied.[71] The result, of course, is a new incoherence.

### 3.7 On the Reductionism of Openness Theology

Let me put this another way: It is becoming apparent that openness theologians are mired in several reductionisms. They have sometimes done some useful work by exposing other reductionisms (e.g., formulations of impassibility that leave God emotionless and with little more that raw will). But their treatment of God's love is singularly lacking in nuance. Similarly, it has repeatedly been shown

---

[70]In brief compass, see the chapter "Does God Suffer?" in Frame, *No Other God*, 179–90. See also ch. 10 in this volume, "Does God Change?" by Chuck Gutenson. One might fairly suggest, too, that the insistence by many open theists that God's relational attributes, and love in particular, must occupy the supreme place in our understanding of God, is difficult to justify and becomes dangerous when the texts that deal with God's love are handled with such a lack of sophistication.

[71]The problems implicit in theological terminology are endemic to these discussions and sometimes pass unnoticed. In a spirited response (*Modern Reformation* 10.5 [Sept./Oct. 2001]: 4), John Sanders, Clark Pinnock, Gregory Boyd, William Hasker, and Richard Rice object that an earlier essay by Michael Horton treated them unfairly in two respects. First, Horton charged them with attributing change to God's essence. This they never do: "God can change in his will, thoughts, and emotions," they write, but not his essence. This response to Horton is entirely fair. Second, they write:

> Horton begins by stating that proponents of openness theology reject the 'biblical' doctrines of divine omnipotence, omniscience, aseity, and simplicity. It is true that some (not all) open theists reject simplicity. However, we certainly do not reject omnipotence, omniscience, and aseity. The only way Horton can get away with this spurious charge is to claim that everyone has to accept his own peculiarly Calvinistic categories. As such, God never takes risks, is unaffected by creatures in all respects, and does not allow for human autonomy. But if this is the case, then huge numbers of Christians in various traditions (including Eastern Orthodox, Roman Catholics, Wesleyans, and others) are guilty of rejecting these terms as well.

This is at best disingenuous. Certainly the openness theologians do not deny, say, God's omniscience; indeed, they repeatedly affirm it. But their redefinition is most emphatically *not* in line with Eastern Orthodox, Roman Catholic, or Wesleyan traditions. It is in line with some process and Socinian traditions. Horton's understanding of what divine omniscience refers to is indistinguishable from that of, say, Wesleyanism; how he configures divine omniscience within larger constructions of theology will, of course, distinguish him from Wesleyans. But as to omniscience itself, it is the openness theologians who are cut off from the "great tradition," as it is now often called, and they should be brave enough and candid enough to admit it instead of trying to marginalize Calvinists.

that one cannot make sense of biblical texts without recognizing that the Bible speaks of the "will" of God in more than one way.[72]

A recent article by Paul K. Helseth argues, convincingly, that there is another element in openness theology that approaches incoherence.[73] The openness approach requires two classes of future events—"a future that is partly open (because God cannot know the future free decisions of his creatures) and partly closed (because God in fact knows what he is going to do in the future"[74]—and this distinction cannot be consistently maintained. Openness theologians think that (libertarian) freedom can be preserved only on the assumption that God cannot know in advance the results of free, contingent decisions. But this leads to massive ignorance on God's part. In the words of Ronald Nash:

> How can God know what he is going to do in the future, when God's own future acts are a response to future human free actions that he cannot know? In all of the open theist rhetoric, the fact that there is nothing about the future for God to know has been lost or obscured. The fact that propositions about future contingents have no truth value has been forgotten. The open theist closes the door to divine foreknowledge but then proceeds to act as though God can know things about the future after all....
>
> The facts are these: According to open theists, God can have no knowledge about future human contingents. Why? Because any alleged proposition about such human choices possesses no truth value; it can be neither true nor false. God cannot know these things because there is nothing to know. There is something seriously wrong, then, when an open theist begins to suggest that his constraints upon divine knowledge are not as severe as one might think. Either God knows future contingents or he doesn't. If he doesn't, then any part of the future resulting from human free choices is also closed to God.... If he knows as few as one future contingent, then the door is open for him to know more; perhaps it is open wide enough for God to know all future contingents. My advice to open theists is please don't cheat and talk in ways that suggest God can know some future contingents.[75]

It is not an adequate response to appeal to middle knowledge, namely, to say that God does know all possible responses and therefore has planned out what he would do under every conceivable circumstance. For that still leaves the shape of the future undetermined. It means God knows only the range of possibilities. That is why various openness theologians insist that God intervenes from time to time to ensure that his own plan for the future does not go too far astray.

---

[72]See, e.g., John Piper, *The Pleasures of God: Meditations on God's Delight in Being God*, rev. and exp. ed. (Sisters, Ore.: Multnomah, 2000), esp. the Appendix, 313–40. On the distinction that John Sanders does make, see especially Frame, *No Other God*, 105–18.

[73]Paul Kjoss Helseth, "On Divine Ambivalence: Open Theism and the Problem of Particular Evils," *JETS* 44 (2001): 493–511.

[74]Ibid., 499.

[75]Ronald Nash, *Life's Ultimate Questions: An Introduction to Philosophy* (Grand Rapids: Zondervan, 1999), 320–21; quoted in Helseth, "On Divine Ambivalence," 499.

Boyd, for instance, in the matter of Jesus' prediction of Peter's denial,[76] admits that God not only arranged parameters that "squeezed" Peter, but he also reckons with God's exhaustive knowledge of Peter's moral character. When a particular individual is "squeezed" by external parameters and his or her character is thoroughly known, that individual's future behavior may well be "certain."[77] Yet how is this so very different from what a compatibilist would say? Boyd gives no hint that Peter could have done anything else, so where is the (libertarian) freedom? More importantly yet, how do even these constraints explain the fact that Jesus predicted that Peter would betray him *three times*? How does knowledge of a person's character guarantee that the particular perversity in question will show up three times, as opposed to two or four? And if the answer is in terms of the number of times that Peter was challenged by someone in the courtyard, were not those individuals "free" to challenge or not? How could Jesus have known, in advance, that there would be *three* challenges to Peter, at a time when the challengers had not yet decided to act?

Helseth's conclusion about the openness theologians is not too strong:

> If nothing else, their willingness to allow for God to work in a coercive fashion jettisons the coherence of the openness program, for it establishes that God cannot accomplish his ultimate purpose without violating a significant component of that purpose. Since God can accomplish his goals only by revoking the autonomy of the will, it follows that not only is Open Theism's distinction between two classes of future events hopelessly conflicted, but at an even more foundational level the God of Open Theism is as well.[78]

## 3.8 On Theology's Outside Influences

Finally, it is a commonplace among openness theologians to argue that classic theology is on these matters so compromised by Greek thought that it has taken two millennia to overturn the darkness. They are right, of course, to point out that all theological reflection—indeed, all reflection of any kind—is necessarily dependent on some antecedent thought. They are also right, as I have already noted, to point out that some strands of the Western tradition have been so influenced by the line of thought from Aristotle through Plato and neo-Platonic thought to the Stoics, that God became less personal, less "emotional" (that tricky word again), than the Bible seems to demand. One particular understanding of impassibility is one of the results.

But I remain unpersuaded that the best of the classic tradition was unaware of the dangers and often raised some powerful grids to screen out the worst influ-

---

[76]Cf. Boyd, *God of the Possible*, 35–37.

[77]Ibid.

[78]Helseth, "On Divine Ambivalence," 503. I should add that this criticism is particularly germane to Greg Boyd. It appears that John Sanders's God is somewhat less conflicted. But the price is high: It will be recalled that for him, even statements alleging God's control over events that led to the cross turn out to have not more than an excellent prognosis.

ences.[79] Moreover, some of the charges betray a considerable ignorance of Greek thought. In a typical disjunction, Pinnock writes:

> We may think of God primarily as an aloof monarch, removed from the contingencies of the world, unchangeable in every aspect of being, as an all-determining and irresistible power, aware of everything that will ever happen and never taking risks. Or we may understand God as a caring parent with qualities of love and responsiveness, generosity and sensitivity, openness and vulnerability, a person (rather than a metaphysical principle) who experiences the world, responds to what happens, relates to us and interacts dynamically with humans.[80]

Frame astutely replies:

> Here Pinnock contrasts what he considers to be the Greek philosophical view of God with his open view. He seems to think that classical theology is closer to the Greek view. But I wonder which Greek philosophers he has in mind here. No Greek philosopher, to my knowledge, thought of God as a monarch. In most Greek philosophical systems, God was impersonal, and monarchs are, of course, personal. Greek religion included personal gods, one of which, Zeus, was monarchical in a sense, but these gods were certainly not "aloof," "unchangeable," "irresistible," etc. Plato's Demiurge was not "all-determining," and his divine Good caused only good things, not evil. Aristotle's impersonal Prime Mover was not aware of anything that took place in the finite world—not "aware of everything." The Stoic deity approached Pinnock's characterization, but was pantheistic or panentheistic.[81]

In short, one begins to sense another straw man.

Further, most contemporary critics are better at pointing out the ostensible antecedents of the thought they wish to criticize than the antecedents of their own thought. In the case of openness theology, there are, it appears, at least three principal streams: process theology (Hartshorne's influence, at least, is admitted by Boyd); a deep commitment to a libertarian understanding of freedom, such that it can control the exegesis of text after text without ever being scrutinized by biblical texts to see if it is a presupposition that should be jettisoned; and Socinianism.[82]

There are, of course, some distinctions between openness theology and process thought, and between openness theology and Socinianism. Moreover, not a few scholars adopt libertarianism without espousing openness theology. But it is worth pointing out links and antecedents in order to insist, on all sides, that

---

[79]On this, see ch. 4 in this volume, "Has the Christian Doctrine of God Been Corrupted by Greek Philosophy?" by Gerald L. Bray.
[80]Clark H. Pinnock, "Systematic Theology," in *The Openness of God*, 103.
[81]Frame, *No Other God*, 32.
[82]See especially the detailed work of Roy, "How Much Does God Foreknow?" and, on this last point, Frame, *No Other God*, 25–40.

one does not have the right to "paradigm out" another's views on the grounds of alleged historical antecedents.

## 4. Concluding Reflections

What we need, then, are theologians who listen well to biblical texts in their context, eschew reductionism, and are willing not only to perceive the biases they bring to the text but to test them, as much as possible, by the text.

In this instance, the result will be an understanding of God who is, on the one hand, sovereign and transcendent and, on the other, personal and loving. One set of attributes or characteristics will not be used to domesticate another set. The biblical writers can speak of God's will and of God's love in quite different ways; local context is determinative. If the resulting portrait drives us to recognize God's uniqueness as well as his connections with his image-bearers, so be it; if we listen carefully and confess there are some things we simply do not understand, we will be content. For this is far better than a picture of God who has been tamed by doctrinaire presuppositions that cannot themselves be tested or corrected by Scripture.

# Scripture Index

# Author Index

# Subject Index

323

# JESUS UNDER FIRE
## Modern Scholarship Reinvents the Historical Jesus

MICHAEL J. WILKINS, J. P. MORELAND, GENERAL EDITORS

## Who is Jesus?
## What did he do?
## What did he say?

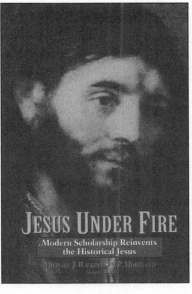

- Are the traditional answer to these questions still to be trusted?
- Did the early church and tradition "Christianize" Jesus?
- Was Christianity built on clever conceptions of the church, or on the character and actions of an actual person?

These and similar questions have come under scrutiny by a forum of biblical scholars called the Jesus Seminar. Their conclusions have been widely publicized in magazines such as *Time* and *Newsweek*. *Jesus Under Fire* challenges the methodology and findings of the Jesus Seminar, which generally clash with the biblical records. It examines the authenticity of the words, actions, miracles, and resurrection of Jesus, and presents compelling evidence for the traditional biblical teachings. Combining accessibility with scholarly depth, *Jesus Under Fire* helps readers judge for themselves whether the Jesus of the Bible is the Jesus of history, and whether the gospels' claim is valid that he is the only way to God.

Softcover ISBN: 0-310-21139-5

## Pick up a copy at your favorite bookstore today!

GRAND RAPIDS, MICHIGAN 49530 USA

WWW.ZONDERVAN.COM

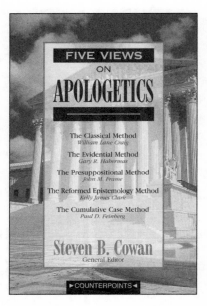